Data Analytics Made Easy

Analyze and present data to make informed decisions without writing any code

Andrea De Mauro

Pack‹t›

BIRMINGHAM - MUMBAI

Data Analytics Made Easy

Producer: Tushar Gupta
Acquisition Editor – Peer Reviews: Saby Dsilva
Content Development Editor: Bhavesh Amin
Technical Editor: Gaurav Gavas
Project Editor: Namrata Katare
Copy Editor: Safis Editing
Proofreader: Safis Editing
Indexer: Tejal Daruwale Soni
Presentation Designer: Ganesh Bhadwalkar

First published: August 2021

Production reference: 2200921

Published by Packt Publishing Ltd.
Livery Place
35 Livery Street
Birmingham B3 2PB, UK.

ISBN 978-1-80107-415-5

www.packt.com

Acknowledgments

Writing a book that tries to combine theory and practice of such a vast field has been possible only thanks to the eye-opening inputs, the rigorous feedback, and the heartfelt encouragement of so many wonderful people. Towards all those colleagues and friends, I am now left with a sense of profound gratitude. Although writing the names of some of them does not do them full justice, let me thank: Dimitrios Skoufakis, Maria Navrotskaya, Francesco Pisanò, Salvatore Gatto, Leonardo and Alessandro De Mauro, Lenka Dzurendova, Michele Pacifico (how could I do without his brilliant advice?), Adam Graham, Kate Daley, Angelo Spedicati, Francesco Lefons, Marcin Czajkowski, Alessio Villardita, Antonio Faraldi, Giorgio Binenti, Giuseppe Papaianni, Jacek Ludwig Scarso, Jon Thomson, Piril Paker Yagli, Paolo Palazzo, Gilda Notaro (whom I dearly miss), Felice Di Tanno, Giorgio Demetrio, Roberto Bellotti, Marcello Lando, my dear parents Gianfranco and Maria Teresa, Dyi Huijg, Cristina Trapani-Scott and all the other hosts at the Shut Up & Write!® events that accompanied so much of my evenings and weekend writing, Katia Cocca, Davide D'Emiliano, Simona Palomba, Luisa Fabro, Antonio Gatto, Daniela Meo, Rachel Breslin, Laurent Eyers, Antonella Rossi, Kasia Bojanowska, Fabio Pistilli, Jerryn Cherian, Saurabh Dichwalkar, Michael Leonhardt, Kacper Hankiewicz, Nori Reis, Tutku Oztekin, Carolina Martinez, Miguel Estrella (the picture of me on the front cover is his, although I recognize that—given the poor subject—it doesn't give full justice to his outstanding skills as a photographer), Mario Galietti, Nicola Lopez, Antonio Fazzari, Paola Lucetti, Vinay Ahuja, Giuliana Farbo, Taide Guajardo, Luca Merlo, Paolo Grue, Francesca Sagramora, Nicolas Kerling, Guy Peri, and all the other amazing friends, colleagues, and leaders at P&G who have passionately worked alongside me to elevate the role of data analytics in the way business is done. It would have been impossible for me to address this subject without having the opportunity to investigate it systematically alongside my many precious partners in academic research and university teaching: Valentina Poggioni, Mohamed Almgerbi, Adham Kahlawi, Andrea Sestino, Paola Demartini, Cristiano Ciappei, Gianluca Cubadda, Luca Petruzzellis, Pasquale Del Vecchio, Giusy Secundo, Andrea Bacconi, Gaetano Cascini, Francesca Montagna, Nikos Tsourakis, Dogan Duven and the amazing staff at the IUG, Alberto Pezzi, Simone Malacaria, Marco Greco, and Michele Grimaldi. I am in debt to the authors of the two thought-provoking forewords, Andy Walter and Francesco Marzoni: the best pages of the entire book are certainly theirs.

I am also very grateful to Tushar Gupta, Ravit Jain, Namrata Katare, Bhavesh Amin, Gaurav Gavas, and the rest of the amazing team at Packt for their high-quality professional support (they made a real book out of a shaky manuscript) and the vast patience they had with me throughout the last few months, and with Scott Fincher for making the book way better thanks to his careful content review and precious feedback. A special thank you goes to my dear Sławka G. Scarso: her true writing talent has always been my primary source of inspiration. Without her patience, support, and writing coaching, I wouldn't have gone far.

If it weren't for all these people, this book wouldn't be in your hands. So, if you find it helpful, the full appreciation should solely go to them.

Andrea De Mauro

Forewords

A common misconception undermines the effectiveness of most digital transformations across industries. It's about the belief that hiring a pool of data and digital experts is enough to become a data-enabled, cognitive organization.

The continuum of data, analytics, and artificial intelligence is pervasive in nature. Creating sustainable value with data requires multifunctional teams of data experts, digital experience designers, business strategists, business process experts, and many more roles to partner up and work together with a common denominator of knowledge about both data and business. It's a team sport, as Andrea will say.

Hence, at least two types of capability development efforts are needed to shape a future-ready organization. They are the ones that develop:

- business literacy of the *few* digital experts, so that they can proactively identify data-driven business opportunities and influence, with inclusive collaboration and credibility, different functions and processes;
- data literacy of the *many* professionals in the organization and beyond, so that they can be key actors in co-developing digital and cognitive capabilities as well as leaders of process transformation and systemic adoption of those capabilities.

Several efforts of Andrea over the past years and the pages in this book are an important contribution to the industry and an essential tool for anybody who has stakes in the development of *Data Literacy for The Many* in their professional (or personal!) ecosystem. In fact, it's not just about the professional arena. It's about enabling every individual to play an active role in the quest to improve the state of the world. It's about making better collective decisions for our society. All with the power of data.

By democratizing data literacy and understanding analytics, we drive positive progress on at least three levels.

1. **The single organization**. Analytics is ultimately about creating actionable knowledge from data and then combining that knowledge with newly available data to create further actionable knowledge. And so on so forth in a systemic series of iterations. Attempting to drive analytics with the sole effort of analytics experts is equivalent to starting that loop of knowledge and data from scratch, as if an organization had no history and as if its people had no domain expertise. With data literacy democratization, multifunctional teams can build value with a common dictionary together.

2. **An entire industry**. It's linked to AI Ethics and Trustworthiness, which means a responsible use of data and algorithms, without which data is not an asset, it's a liability. Having leaders that are fluent in data analytics across the value chain of a specific industry is a pre-condition for responsible AI. Why? Because building value with AI requires at least two steps: defining an objective function (what you want to optimize, like costs, sales, customer convenience, and so on) and codifying a set of constraints (within which to find an optimal solution) into mathematical equations. These constraints are ultimately the business decisions of non-analytics practitioners. Limiting the amount of sugar in food products despite a negative impact on sales growth potential or limiting the screen time of users of a digital platform despite a negative impact on advertising revenue, are just two examples of business decisions that leaders need to take to provide relevant inputs to a good data-enabled business strategy.

3. **Society at large**. A higher penetration of data literacy across society means a higher number of decisions and actions that individuals will make based on facts and not on opinions. As the good Hans Rosling taught us over the years, data is the best tool we have to understand the world and think with clarity about its evolution. Being it facing a pandemic, reducing our carbon footprint, redesigning a justice system, increasing access to education, managing a healthcare system…the more we learn to do it based on data, instead of following guts and opinions, the more resilient our society becomes.

Shaping digital transformation with the *many*, and not only with the *few*, creates sustainable shared value. Join us in driving the *good data* revolution to build a better society. Enjoy the learning!

Francesco Marzoni

Chief Data & Analytics Officer of IKEA Retail (Ingka Group)

In January 2010, I was presented with a unique opportunity from our P&G CEO and CIO to lead the analytics transformation of the company. They believed that "analytics" was going to transform P&G, our industry, and business in general. They wanted me to lead a *complete transformation* of analytics, data, talent, technology, and how we approach and drive value for individual business units, functional areas, and the company overall.

Driving a holistic/business-impacting analytics program is not easy. One of the many challenges is helping the leadership across the company: executives, functional leaders, analytics practitioners, and even the "frozen middle" – individuals happy with the status quo, understand the analytics journey they are embarking on; call it the basics of analytics, or call it **Data Analytics Made Easy!**

Andrea does a great job of providing the analytic fundamentals that professionals of all levels need on this journey. Whether you are a junior professional breaking into data science, a business leader across marketing, supply chain, HR, etc., or the executive tasked with starting/fixing/transforming your company's analytics journey, you are starting in the right place. Dig in!

As Andrea unfolds the key steps of data analytics, keep the following in mind:

Start with the business need and strategy – Sounds simple but is done incredibly poorly by most. All analytics start with the business problem you are trying to solve! It is not about fancy technology, interesting datasets, or impassioned leaders preaching to the crowds. It is about the business need. *Chapter 1* provides insights into the types of analytics and how to tie them to business needs.

Invest in talent – Special Operation Forces, Rule #1: Humans are more important than hardware. Talent is critical! But like any asset, how you leverage it makes all the difference. The best analysts have three skills: 1) Analytics expertise, 2) Deep business knowledge in the domain or business unit they are working in, and 3) Effective communications skills. Focus on developing all three aspects of great analysts. Great analytics expertise without context is useless. Great business knowledge and analytics without the ability to communicate/influence makes it slow and tedious. Great communication without substance is smoke and mirrors – you know, the PowerPoint warriors. *Chapters 7* and *8* are critical to the journey.

Don't wait for the data to be perfect – In talking with numerous Fortune 500 companies, one of the insights I always share is do not wait to get the data perfect. I remember the CIO during this discussion who turned as white as a ghost! They had been spending money for two years trying to get the data right before trying to do any analytics with the business. This is a waste! First, you do not know what data will be most critical without driving true business analytics. Second, nothing gets data cleaner faster than presenting it to the senior leadership of the company! *Chapter 3* jumps in here, but as stated, move fast to create value for the business.

Select tools that allow your analysts and data scientists to adapt/harmonize on the fly – It is key to select the tools that allow your analysts and business teams to adjust quickly, add new data sources, and so on. Do not create a model dependent on a central team to "code" for every new business problem or adaptation. Andrea does a nice job of laying out the tools, and *Chapter 9* provides key learnings as you extend the toolbox.

Network beyond your company and industry – I immediately realized there were extremely smart people working in other companies, industry bodies, academia, and non-profit institutes that could be incredibly valuable to the journey. Seek them out and learn with the best together.

Congrats on making the personal investment with this book and on your journey. Make *Data Analytics Made Easy* the start of your journey, and never stop learning!

Andrew J. Walter

Board and Strategic Advisor, former SVP at Proctor & Gamble

Contributors

About the author

Andrea De Mauro is director of business analytics at Procter & Gamble, looking after the continuous elevation of the role of data and algorithms in the business and the development of digital fluency across the global organization. He has more than 15 years of international experience in leading data analytics initiatives across multiple business domains, including sales, marketing, finance, and product supply. He is also a professor of marketing analytics and applied machine learning at the Universities of Bari and Florence, Italy, and the International University in Geneva, Switzerland. His research investigates the essential components of big data as a phenomenon and the impact of AI and data analytics on companies and people. He is the author of popular science books on data analytics and various research papers in international journals.

About the reviewer

Scott Fincher is a data scientist with KNIME based in Austin, TX. He routinely teaches, presents, and leads group workshops covering topics such as KNIME Analytics Platform, machine learning, and the broad data science umbrella. He enjoys assisting other data scientists with general best practices and model optimization. For Scott, this is not just an academic exercise. Prior to his work at KNIME, he worked for almost 20 years as an environmental consultant, with a focus on numerical modeling of atmospheric pollutants. Scott holds an MS in statistics and a BS in meteorology, both from Texas A&M University.

Table of Contents

Preface

Data analytics is a sexy topic these days. Skills such as machine learning, data visualization, and storytelling are becoming essential in virtually any professional field. The necessity to acquire data fluency is not a thing for data scientists and analysts only: it is becoming a development objective for pretty much everyone, irrespectively of their education, experience, business function, and seniority level. It is a universal need.

For the majority of people interested in using analytics, learning how to code in a programming language is an intimidating barrier to break and — sadly — the first reason for abandoning their intent. For this reason, this book leverages low-code analytical tools. This way, we decouple the objective of learning how to leverage data analytics effectively in our jobs (which is the primary focus of this book) from the requirement of learning how to program (which is, instead, an ancillary *nice-to-have* for scaling and expanding the role of analytics even further).

This guide offers an accessible journey through the most valuable techniques of data analytics, enabling you to move quickly from theory to practice using low-code environments. Although a large part of the content is application-agnostic and can be leveraged on any software you or your company decide to use, the book's tutorials are based on KNIME and Power BI.

KNIME and Power BI were selected because they make the best travel buddies for your journey through data analytics. KNIME is the "Swiss Army knife" among the analytical platforms according to Gartner. Its graphical interface enables everyone—managers, analysts, and students—to automate data pipelines and employ machine learning algorithms without writing any line of code. One positive aspect to keep in mind is that visual analytics tools like KNIME are not simplistic and "depowered" versions of the "real thing." With KNIME, you can do full-on data science, including sophisticated data crunching and serious AI applications, such as creating deep neural networks. Microsoft Power BI requires no introduction: it is among the most popular data visualization and dashboarding tools. It provides a comprehensive environment to build self-service business intelligence interfaces that are omnipresent in supporting decision-making. Both Power BI and KNIME offer full access to their main functionalities without any capital investment. You can download them for free, enabling you to put into practice what you learn immediately. The combination of KNIME as back-end and Power BI (or Tableau, which is also introduced) as front-end is versatile and robust, empowering organizations to cover the full range of data capabilities, from descriptive to predictive and prescriptive analytics. This book's step-by-step tutorials—based on real business cases and data—will provide you with confidence through practice and make you an independent user of such a powerful software combo. The hands-on journey that waits for you in the following pages has a high ambition: making data analytics a trusted companion for your *everyday* work.

Who this book is for

The learning path offered by this book has been designed with three types of readers in mind:

1. **Knowledge workers** of any background, level, and functional expertise who use data to facilitate data-based decisions or inform others about the state of the business with reports, visuals, and ad-hoc analyses. They want to modernize and expand their data fluency to both *simplify* their regular data-related chores and *augment* their business impact. Today, they mainly use Excel to manage data and reports: they understand the need to upgrade to more powerful tools but do not know where to start and have zero programming experience. Even if proficient with Excel, they feel the need to automate their workflows to gain personal productivity. They would also like to build professional-looking, self-serve dashboards and automate as much as possible the process for updating them, so they can focus on interpreting the data and go beyond the plain figures. This book will give them the tools and techniques for reaching these objectives.

2. **Business managers of any functional background** — including marketing, sales, finance, IT, and HR — who want to gain first-hand experience in data analytics to understand and unlock the true potential of data in their area of responsibility. They don't have the technical expertise and do not plan to become specialists but would like to understand what's possible and guide their teams through the required transformation. They want to be a source of help instead of a burden and are ready to roll up their sleeves and study. Today, many senior leaders appreciate the potential value of analytics but don't know how to make it happen in their organizations. This book will help them touch *with their own hands* the value creation opportunities and finetune their expectations with their teams appropriately. How many of us dream of having bosses who know what they are asking for? This book makes managers aware, reasonable, and confident when setting expectations on business data analytics.

3. **Business and data science students and junior professionals** who already have theoretical and academic knowledge but have little to zero business experience. They would like to see how their knowledge is used in companies in practice to have a *vertical start-up* in their first jobs. After so much theory, compartmentalized across different disciplines (computer science, data science, statistics, and business), they crave experiencing the end-to-end process which leads from raw data to actionable business decisions. They are looking for a book full of real-world examples: this is exactly what they are going to get here.

No prior knowledge is required for any of these types of readers. The little math you will find around the chapters is always introduced very gently and stays to the level needed to put analytics "at work," leaving it to the readers to dive deeper as they please. I wrote this book to make data analytics accessible to *everyone* who wants to invest some time to self-develop. I am thrilled that you are one of them.

What this book covers

The path I have prepared for you alternates two types of content. Some chapters equip you with the **unmissable foundations of data analytics** — things like the basics of statistical learning, model validation, and data visualization principles. Other chapters provide **practical guides on how to get things done** on your computer — like step-by-step tutorials on building a dashboard in Power BI or automating data crunching with KNIME. The two types of content are complementary and organized according to the following structure:

Chapter 1, What is Data Analytics?, paves the way for our journey together. This chapter equips you with the proper terminology and provides a few frameworks (such as the three types of analytics, the data technology stack, the matrix of data job roles and skills, and the data-to-value paths), offering you some broader perspective on the true business potential of data and algorithms.

Chapter 2, Getting Started with KNIME, initiates you to KNIME and shows you how visual programming works by going through a few hands-on examples. The chapter includes the first tutorial of the book, in which you will create a routine for automating the clean-up of some consumer-generated data.

Chapter 3, Transforming Data, introduces the concept of the data model and shows you how to apply systematic transformations to datasets and make them fully usable for analytics. You will learn how to combine tables, aggregate values, apply loops, and use variables. In the tutorial, you will build a workflow for creating some simple automated financial reports starting from raw transactional data.

Chapter 4, What is Machine Learning?, separates the myth from the reality of intelligent machines able to autonomously learn from data. This chapter gives you the foundations of machine learning (like the taxonomy of available algorithms, how to validate models, and how to assess their accuracy) and lets you start identifying ways for AI to impact your actual work.

Chapter 5, Applying Machine Learning at Work, puts in practice what you will have learned in the former chapter. Its three practical tutorials will let you experience what real-world machine learning is all about. You will feel the excitement of predicting real estate rental prices in Rome, anticipating the reaction of consumers in front of a bank marketing campaign, and segment customers of an online retailer. By following the tutorials, you will build your own "templates" of predictive machines that you can then adapt as needed to your specific business needs.

Chapter 6, Getting Started with Power BI, prepares you to face an ever-present, primary need: building effective dashboards that "democratize" access to data and insights. In the tutorial, you will build a fully operating management dashboard in Power BI, including preparing the underlying data model and creating links across charts to drive interactivity.

Chapter 7, Visualizing Data Effectively, explains how to build professional-looking data visualizations that transfer business insights. The chapter will give you a framework for selecting the correct type of chart according to your business need and a set of visual design guidelines ensuring that your business messages come across crisp, loud, and clear.

Chapter 8, Telling Stories with Data, trains you to systematically prepare and deliver data stories that drive business action. Starting from the basic principles of persuasion, this chapter will teach you several techniques for making your data-based points as compelling as possible. The chapter will leave you with a structured template (the Data Storytelling Canvas) that you can keep on your desk and use when needed.

Chapter 9, Extending Your Toolbox, lets you catch a glimpse of what's beyond the tools and techniques included in the previous chapters so that you can plan ahead for your next development steps. The chapter contains hands-on, guided demonstrations of Tableau, Python (including its integration with KNIME), and H2O.ai for automated machine learning. Reading this concluding chapter will prove the general value of the broad set of skills you will have acquired by completing this journey.

To get the most out of this book

Let me share a few tips that will help along the path you are about to begin:

- The book comes with multiple step-by-step, hands-on tutorials that are integral to the development path I have designed for you. Some of the most subtle — and fascinating — aspects of data analytics (like the need to interact with business partners and go back-and-forth during the setup process) can only be understood through real examples: tutorials do a great job explaining them. I strongly suggest you set some quality time for completing each tutorial. The entire execution of a tutorial will take up to two hours: make sure you have access to a computer on which you can install all the required software.

- At the end of the book, you will find a short series of useful resources organized by chapter. They offer an opportunity to complement your learning experience with selected additional readings. So don't forget to skim through them after you complete a chapter and see if any of them intrigues you.

- Depending on your background, some parts of the book might feel less "natural" to you. This is normal. Don't get discouraged if any portion of the book is less clear: the chapters are all closely interconnected to each other, and you might find the answers to your doubts in some subsequent pages, so just keep going until the end.

- Use the book's GitHub and KNIME Hub pages to download all the data you need to complete the tutorials. In there, you will also find the final result of each tutorial (like the complete KNIME workflow or the resulting Power BI dashboard). If you feel lost, you can refer to them to find your way forward.

- Software improves and updates continuously. This book relies on the latest versions of KNIME and Power BI available at the time of its launch (precisely: KNIME 4.4 and Power BI 2.93). Although the bulk of the content will stay valid for a while, it might be that some of the steps in a tutorial change slightly, making the windows a bit different versus what you find in the figures. This is unavoidable and will not jeopardize your learning. Keep an eye on the book's web page for any *errata* or addenda I post in case of any significant divergences due to a new version of the software. You can also get in touch with me using the contact details you find in the *And Now?* section.

- This book is targeted toward the "business application" of data analytics. For this reason, whenever I had to choose between a rigorous mathematical dissertation and a pragmatic and intuitive explanation of an analytical method, I went for the latter. The rationale is that you will always have the time to learn how to make statistical learning more accurate and dive deeper into the math behind the algorithms you will learn. Thus, the focus will stay on empowering you to use analytics in your work more than giving you the formal description behind each mathematical concept.

Download the data files

All the data and the supporting files related to the tutorials presented in the book are also hosted on GitHub at https://github.com/PacktPublishing/Data-Analytics-Made-Easy. The data and the completed KNIME workflows are also available on KNIME Hub, at the address http://tiny.cc/knimehub.

We also have other code bundles from our rich catalog of books and videos available at https://github.com/PacktPublishing/. Check them out!

Download the color images

We also provide a PDF file that has color images of the screenshots/diagrams used in this book. You can download it here: https://static.packt-cdn.com/downloads/9781801074155_ColorImages.pdf.

Conventions used

There are a number of text conventions used throughout this book.

`CodeInText`: Indicates user input, code words in text, highlighted keywords in code, paths, and file names. For example: "In the configuration window, type the expression `$Quantity$*$Price$`, to calculate revenues." In this book, you will find only a handful of blocks of example code in *Chapter 9, Extending Your Toolbox*. They will look like this:

```
predictions = model.predict(test_set)
print('R2 score is',r2_score(test_set.Rent,predictions))
print('Root Mean Squared Error is', \
      np.sqrt(mean_squared_error(test_set.Rent,predictions)))
```

Bold: Indicates a new term, an important word, a KNIME node, or words that you see on the screen, like in menus or dialog boxes. For example: "Click **OK** to close the window and execute the **CSV Reader** node."

Italic: Is used to emphasize specific words in the context of a sentence and when referring to columns in a dataset, like in: "*Neighborhood* is the single most useful column when predicting the rent, followed by the *Surface* of the property."

> Warnings, important notes, or interesting facts appear like this.

> Tips and tricks appear like this.

Get in touch

Feedback from our readers is always welcome.

General feedback: Email `feedback@packtpub.com`, and mention the book's title in the subject of your message. If you have questions about any aspect of this book, please email us at `questions@packtpub.com`.

Errata: Although we have taken every care to ensure the accuracy of our content, mistakes do happen. If you have found a mistake in this book, we would be grateful if you would report this to us. Please visit, `http://www.packtpub.com/submit-errata`, selecting your book, clicking on the Errata Submission Form link, and entering the details.

Piracy: If you come across any illegal copies of our works in any form on the Internet, we would be grateful if you would provide us with the location address or website name. Please contact us at `copyright@packtpub.com` with a link to the material.

If you are interested in becoming an author: If there is a topic that you have expertise in and you are interested in either writing or contributing to a book, please visit `http://authors.packtpub.com`.

Share your thoughts

Once you've read *Data Analytics Made Easy*, we'd love to hear your thoughts! Scan the QR code below to go straight to the Amazon review page for this book and share your feedback.

`https://packt.link/r/1-801-07415-1`

Your review is important to us and the tech community and will help us make sure we're delivering excellent quality content.

1

What is Data Analytics?

Before we start our journey across the vast and exciting land of **data analytics**, it is wise to get equipped with an up-to-date map that can show us the way. In this chapter, you will cover all those fundamental concepts you need to visualize, with clarity, the role of data analytics in companies. This will let you spot opportunities for leveraging data and decide how to distill business value out of it. You also want to feel confident about the naming conventions adopted in this domain to avoid any confusion and speak decisively with those around you. Given the hectic development of data analytics these days, it is a wise choice to build a robust foundation of the key concepts before getting our hands dirty with tables and algorithms.

Specifically, within this chapter, you will find answers to the following questions:

- What types of analytics can we find in companies?
- Who should be designing, maintaining, and using them?
- What technology is required for data analytics to work?
- What is the data analytics toolbox and what does it contain?
- How can data be transformed into business value?

Although this initial part of this book is more theoretical than the rest of it, let me make a promise: all the concepts you'll encounter are there to enable a better understanding of what you'll find ahead in your journey as a data analytics practitioner. We are now fully ready to go; let's get started!

Three types of data analytics

The term data analytics normally denotes those processes and techniques used to extract some sort of value from data. Sometimes, the same term indicates the actual tools used to make this transformation happen. In any case, data analytics represents *how* we can transform crude data into something more actionable and valuable. We can recognize three different types of data analytics, each one carrying its own set of peculiarities and possible applications: **descriptive**, **predictive**, and **prescriptive analytics**.

Descriptive analytics

Descriptive analytics is the unmissable "bread and butter" of any analytical effort. These methodologies focus on describing past data to make it digestible and useable as required by the business need. They answer the generic question "what happened?" by leveraging summary statistics (like average, median, and variance) and simple transformations and aggregations (like indices, counts, and sums), ultimately displaying the results through tables and visuals. The iconic (and most basic) deliverable within the camp of descriptive analytics is the *standalone report*: this can be a file in a portable format (PDF documents and Excel worksheets are the most popular ones) that is distributed on a regular basis via email or posted in a shared repository. Most managers love reports as they can find all the **Key Performance Indicators (KPIs)** of interest at hand, with minimal effort from their side. In fact, they don't need to "go and look" for anything: it's data by itself coming their way, right in the format they need. A more sophisticated deliverable within descriptive analytics is the *interactive dashboard*: in this case, users access a web-based interface from which they are guided through their data of interest. Visuals and tables will display the most relevant aspects of the business, while filters, selectors, and buttons offer users the possibility to customize their journey through data, drilling down into the aspects they are mostly intrigued by. Sometimes, dashboards are specifically designed to please senior executives, focusing on top KPIs only: in this case, they are known by the more picturesque name of *management cockpits*. If the standalone report gives you a preset guided tour, interactive dashboards will let you drive yourself through your data, giving you the possibility to take unusual paths. Although the latter have clearly more potential in relation to their ability to unveil useful insights, some less adventurous managers will still prefer the comfort of receiving standalone reports directly in their inbox. To please both cases at once, dashboards can be set to offer subscriptions: in this case, users can sign up to receive a selection of visuals or tables from the dashboard via email regularly, or as soon as the data changes. Subscriptions are a promising feature as they avoid the duplication of efforts in updating dashboards and disseminating reports.

Predictive analytics

Predictive analytics focuses on answering the natural follow-up questions that you have after learning what happened in the past, such as: "why did it happen?" and "what will happen now?". These methodologies leverage more sophisticated techniques, including AI, to go beyond the mere description of historical facts. By using them, we can make sense of the causal relationships that lie under our data and extrapolate them, to show what the future is most likely going to look like. The simplest examples of predictive analytics are **diagnostic tools**: they enrich the more traditional descriptive reports with a model-based inference of possible causes behind what we see in data. By using basic methods like correlation analysis, control charting, and tests of statistical significance, these tools can highlight interesting patterns, shedding light on the reasons why the business is going in a certain way. The next level of sophistication is brought by **business alerts**: in this case, diagnostic checks are carried out automatically and users get notified when some situation of business interest (like the market share for a brand going below a certain threshold) arises. Similarly, in the case of **anomaly detection**, algorithms continuously inspect data to find any inconsistency in patterns and flag it as such, so it can be managed accordingly: for instance, the data generated by sensors in a production line can be used to spot malfunctions early on and trigger the required maintenance. Predictive analytics also includes methods that anticipate the future by generating *forecasts* of measures, such as sales, price, market size, and level of risk, all of which can certainly help managers make better decisions and prepare for what's about to come. Also, the behavior of individual entities like consumers and competitors can be forecasted, producing a competitive advantage and an improved **Return on Investment** (**ROI**) of forthcoming activities. In the case of **propensity models**, AI is leveraged to predict how much a customer is going to like a commercial offer, or how likely are they to leave our store or service (churn), enabling us to finetune our retention activities. One last example of predictive analytics is when we use data and algorithms to create smart *segmentations* of our business, like when we're grouping together similar customers, stores, or products. By tailoring the way we manage them, we can make our operations more efficient and the experience of our customers more personalized and engaging.

Prescriptive analytics

Prescriptive analytics transforms data into a recommended course of action, by answering the ultimate question every business manager has: "what should be done?". If descriptive and predictive analytics produces insights and informs us about our business, prescriptive analytics is certainly more assertive and direct: it tells us what to do. For example, it can simulate a large set of alternative scenarios and implement a **systematic optimization** across them: the output would be the "best recipe" to follow to maximize profit or minimize cost, given the current conditions. Other examples of prescriptive analytics are the so-called **recommendation systems**: essentially, they provide users with recommendations on products. These algorithms are virtually omnipresent in our everyday digital experience. When we shop around on Amazon or struggle to pick which TV series to binge watch next on Netflix, we are going to be presented with the output of some recommendation systems, offering us a limited number of options we are likely going to like. The ultimate level of sophistication comes when prescriptive analytics is not only recommending what to do but is in charge of doing it! In fact, when they are run in real time, no human being might be able to fully control and explicitly approve every decision or recommendation that the machine has come up with. In some cases, algorithms are designed to behave like **autonomous agents**: these are in charge of learning through an iterative **trial and error** process. They will continuously test their strategy in the real world and correct it as necessary, with the ultimate objective of maximizing returns in the long term. This is what happens, for instance, with automated trading (a rising trend in FinTech) and programmatic advertising (which is the real-time buying of digital media through automatic bids).

> You will find in your readings that, as a naming convention, the descriptive layer is mostly associated with the term **Business Intelligence**, while predictive and prescriptive analytics are known by **Advanced Analytics**. Since there are no clear cuts across these domains, sometimes, it can get confusing – don't worry, it's normal.

Over the course of this book, you will encounter all types of data analytics, and you will learn how to make them come true in your business. *Figure 1.1* shows the trade-off between the potential value and complexity of these different types of analytics:

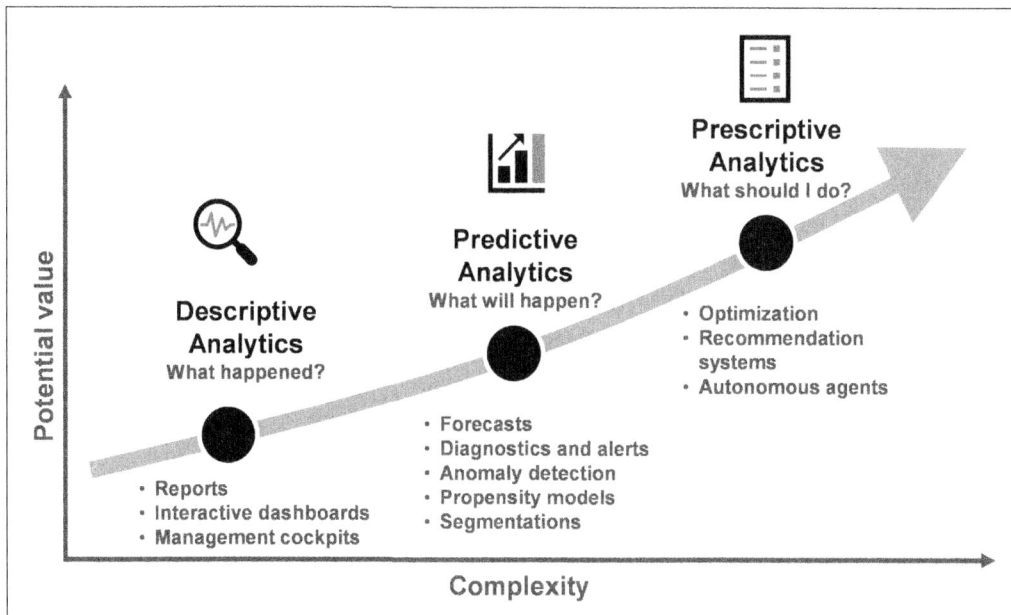

Figure 1.1: Types of data analytics – how much value would you like to unlock?

Data analytics in action

Now that we have grasped the fundamentals behind descriptive, predictive, and prescriptive analytics, it's time to see them in action. Katia is the proud **Chief Data Officer (CDO)** of a multinational hotel chain. Let's see how she summarizes a list of data analytics capabilities they have put together in the last few years:

- Board members receive a 5-page report every month via email. It includes a short executive summary prepared by analysts with key highlights and a set of standard tables and charts with KPI trends by country, banner, and hotel type.

- All managers have access to an online dashboard that's refreshed every week with top measures of interest and the possibility to drill down to very granular views, such as the latest occupancy levels of individual hotels or current room rates.

- Area managers are subscribed to an alerting tool that notifies them when some facilities are off course to meeting their monthly goals. An automated email is sent when the forecast for the month is below a certain threshold versus targets.

- Room rates are dynamically managed by a central system, which they've called **AutoPrice**. The system simulates different occupancy levels by facility, taking into account seasonality, trends, and interest displayed by web users. **AutoPrice** can adjust room rates daily so as to maximize profit, given the expected sales and costs.

- Customers who are part of the reward program occasionally receive special offers for room upgrades or weekend escapes in luxury hotels. A propensity model tailors the offer (controlling the level of discount) to maximize redemption and expected profit.

- Newsletter subscribers are grouped into four homogeneous segments (Business, Families, Deal-hunters, and Premium) according to their sociodemographic traits and interests. The content of each monthly newsletter is diversified by segment. Every new subscriber is automatically associated with a segment when they sign up.

- When the COVID-19 pandemic broke out, analysts built a statistical model to anticipate the upcoming impact on sales by country and built alternative scenarios of evolution. Based on this work, the company put together a successful response plan, which included temporary closures and down-staffing, conversions of restaurants into takeaway services, and conversions of rooms for low-care infected patients in partnership with local authorities.

- Following the launch of a competitive chain in France, the digital marketing team partnered with data scientists to build a data-enabled reaction plan to boost communication activities in the areas with the biggest risk of losing customers. Additionally, they built a churn model to send individual retention offers to those members who were most inclined to move to a new competitor.

We have to stop Katia right now; otherwise, she would go on and on for a few more pages! All these examples show how pervasive and versatile data analytics can be for a business. They also give us the opportunity to notice some general patterns whose value goes beyond the hotel chain's case:

- The three types of data analytics are not necessarily alternative to each other. In truth, they tend to co-exist in companies – you don't have to "pick" one. For example, you will always have a need for ongoing descriptive analytics, such as reports for management or dashboards, even if you have some forward-looking, advanced analytics tricks up your sleeve. You can't just "ignore" the basics; otherwise, you'll receive less traction for everything else.

- The same aspect of a business might get value from each of the three types of analytics. Take pricing in the example of the hotel: you can report average room rates (descriptive), you can forecast scenarios based on different prices (predictive), or you can automatically set the best room rates (prescriptive). For each aspect of the business, there is an opportunity for each type of analytics.

- The different types of analytics can partially overlap and cross-enrich. For example, in the management dashboard (descriptive), we might add some different color coding, depending on the likelihood that a hotel is going to meet its target for the year (predictive).

- Some opportunities to create value through data analytics are ad hoc, contingent on specific one-off circumstances: this was the case for the COVID-19 model and the response to a competitive move. Others are ongoing and systematic, like the regular reports and updates to the dashboard or real-time price optimization. Data analytics can bring value to both ad hoc and ongoing cases.

Thanks to this example, we now have a clearer picture of what the three different levels of analytics look like. Before moving on to the next topic, it's worth thinking about what differentiates business intelligence (descriptive) from advanced analytics (predictive and prescriptive) in terms of business impact, like *Table 1.1* summarizes:

Aspect	Descriptive (Business Intelligence)	Predictive/Prescriptive (Advanced Analytics)
User base	Broad	Limited
Implementation complexity	Low	High
Trust required by management	Low	High
Potential value	Low	High

Table 1.1: Business impact of different analytics

Descriptive analytics tends to have a broad set of potential users in the company. The same dashboards and reports can be of use for many colleagues across different levels of seniority, business units, and functions. Indeed, one of the widespread feelings in companies is that "data is there, but not sure where": the more data can be democratized with a solid business intelligence offering, the more its value is unlocked. Considering the potential breadth of the user base these capabilities have, it's worth planning well for "mass" deployment activities so that everyone has the opportunity to become a user and the business impact of the capability is maximized. Often, dashboards are underutilized in the long run – or simply forgotten – because people don't know how to use them: an even bigger reason to plan for regular training sessions is to keep them accessible to everyone, including newcomers.

Needless to say, the complexity of designing and implementing predictive and prescriptive analytics is higher than for descriptive. You will require skilled business analysts and data scientists (we'll talk more about roles in the next few pages), and the time needed for prototyping, and then deploying and scaling, is normally more. Hence, it's worth proceeding with an agile and iterative mode, so as to unlock incremental value progressively and avoid losing the momentum and the enthusiasm from stakeholders.

Advanced analytics has a tougher job to get accepted within a company and requires a more decisive sponsorship from senior managers to go through. Think about that: descriptive analytics enables better decisions by informing people about what's going on. On the other end, prescriptive analytics will bluntly tell you what the best decision you can make is, potentially restricting the ability of managers' gut feelings to guide the business. Algorithms who are "in charge" of decisions require higher trust to be accepted than just plain reports. The more you progress to advanced analytics, the more you need to involve top management and have them sponsor the transformation. This will counterbalance the natural tendency of people to "protect" their role and power against all threats, including those algorithms that assertively prescribe decisions.

Like most things in life, you get what you pay for. Advanced analytics is more complex to build and requires more management attention, but the potential value it can unlock is higher than what descriptive analytics can do. My advice is to look for opportunities to progressively elevate the role of analytics, moving the footprint of your capabilities toward the advanced end of the ladder. At the same time, you don't want to "forget" about the power of enabling a broad set of colleagues to manage their business in a smarter way, through democratized access to data via descriptive analytics.

Who is involved in data analytics?

The short answer to the heading of this section is also the most obvious: everyone has a role to play in data analytics – nobody is excluded! In fact, all knowledge workers will undoubtedly have to deal with data as part of their job: they will interact with analytics in one way or another, either solely as a passive user or all the way to the other end of engagement, as the main creator and owner of data capabilities. We can recognize four families of roles with regard to data analytics in companies: **business users**, **business analysts**, **data scientists**, and **data engineers**. Let's deep dive to understand what each role means and what competencies it requires:

Role	Vertical Business Knowledge	Data Analysis and Storytelling	Machine Learning Algorithms	Coding	Data Architecture
Business User	★ ★ ★	★	★		
Business Analyst	★ ★	★ ★ ★	★ ★	★	
Data Scientist		★	★ ★ ★	★ ★ ★	★
Data Engineer			★ ★	★ ★	★ ★ ★

Table 1.2: Competencies of different users

- **Business users** of any function and level, including senior managers, surely interact with data analytics to some extent. Although their main role is being a user, they will highly benefit from having a basic understanding of data analysis and storytelling techniques. These will enable business users to make the most out of the data as they integrate it with their business knowledge, interpret it properly, and communicate insights through effective visualizations and stories. Also, their personal productivity will be positively affected by knowing how to automate their routine "data crunching" work, using macros in Excel or, as we will learn later, workflows in KNIME. Lastly, they should have a basic understanding of what advanced analytics could do for them and acquire the fundamental concepts behind machine learning and its algorithms. They clearly don't need to become experts in this. However, until they see "what's possible," they will miss anticipating opportunities to impact their business with data.

- **Business analysts** (or data analysts) play the fundamental role of uniting the two – apparently detached – worlds of business and data. They have a very solid understanding of the business dynamics (market, customer, and competitor landscape) as they are constantly in touch with partners from all functions (sales, marketing, finance, and so on). Thanks to their strong business background, they can proactively intercept opportunities for analytics to make the difference and "translate" business needs into technical requirements for the next data capability to meet. Business analysts are proficient with data analysis (as they need to constantly "peel the onion" and extract business-relevant insights from large quantities of data) and storytelling (since they want their data findings to make strong impacts and drive action). At the same time, they are familiar with machine learning concepts: they will use them directly to solve their business needs, but also to prototype advanced analytics capabilities before leaving them in the capable hands of data scientists for scaling. Although not strictly required and not a focus for their job, they can benefit from having basic coding abilities to build queries for data extraction and untangle the more tedious data transformation steps.

- **Data scientists** focus on designing and scaling advanced analytics capabilities. They are the recognized experts of machine learning algorithms and can implement predictive and prescriptive analytics from scratch or build upon existing prototypes. They collaborate closely with business analysts, through whom they stay in touch with the "latest" business necessities, and data engineers, their primary partners for ensuring sustainability and scale to data capabilities. Data scientists are proficient at coding, especially when it comes to applying advanced transformations to data and leveraging state-of-the-art machine learning libraries.

> Data science is the multidisciplinary field at the intersection of maths, statistics, and computer science that studies the systematic extraction of value from data. Everyone – not only data scientists – can benefit from using some aspects of data science.

- **Data engineers** (and related roles, like systems engineers and data architects) ensure the systemic functioning of analytics by dealing with the technological complexity of the underlying data infrastructure. The work of data engineers is essential to building stable data pipelines and maintaining them to make sure they are consistently available. They interact with both data scientists – to adequately size storage and computational resources and to design a fitting data architecture – and with the rest of the **Information Technology (IT)** functions – to guarantee compatibility across corporate systems and ensure acceptable standards of information security.

These four actors, each with its specific part to perform, will jointly cover for the vast majority of interactions with data analytics in a company. Whichever character you feel closer with, you certainly have a role to play in extracting value from data. In the next section, you'll meet the tools that will let you perform at your best.

Technology for data analytics

The technology that empowers data analytics in a company does not look like a monolithic body. In fact, there are several hardware and software systems involved. For simplicity, you can think of them as being organized into three layers: these are piled upon each other and form the so-called **Technology Stack**. Every layer relies on the one below to function properly. Let's take a bottom-up "helicopter" view of the fundamental features that you need to know about for each layer of the stack:

- The underlying layer is the **Physical Infrastructure**. This is stuff you can touch. It is made up of servers or mainframe computers that store and process data. Companies can decide to either build and maintain a physical infrastructure of their own (normally kept in corporate *data centers*) or rely on *cloud providers* from whom they rent only the required resources.

- The middle layer is the **Data Platform**. The technology at this level implements a logical organization of the data stored in the infrastructure (*data architecture*) and the available computing power. Even if data resides in different databases, at the platform level, it gets virtually unified on a simpler, more harmonious view.

- The top layer is made of **Applications**. Here is where data analytics methods get implemented into user-facing apps. Applications leverage both the organized data and the horsepower provided by the underpinning platform to serve users in different ways. Some applications will provide interfaces for users to explore data, to make sense of it and to identify insights (*Business Intelligence*); others will enable expert users to take it to the next level and to build predictions or prescriptions (*Advanced Analytics*).

This three-layer stack model is certainly a simplification versus the multifaceted reality underneath real-world data infrastructures. However, it gives us the benefit of envisioning, at once, the different levels of abstraction that data can have and introduces several challenges that come with it:

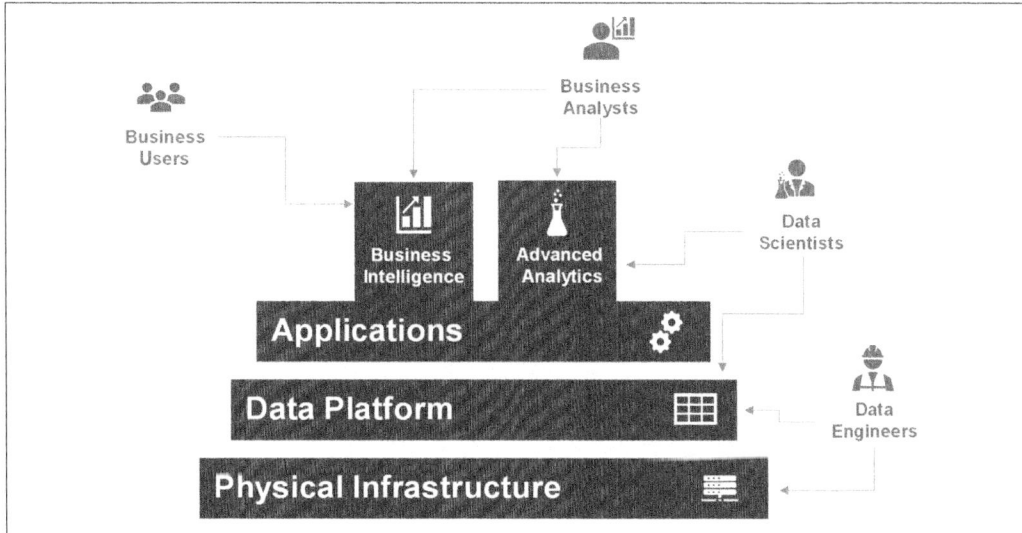

Figure 1.2: Technology Stack supporting data analytics.
The arrows clarify which roles interact with which layers of the stack

The four roles we have seen earlier will "operate" at different levels of the technology stack. Data engineers will deal with the complexity of the data infrastructure and its organization in a platform. Data scientists will normally leverage applications of advanced analytics to build models and will sometimes access data directly at the platform level to enjoy maximum versatility. Business analysts will feel at ease with both advanced analytics tools and business intelligence apps, which they can also use to design actionable data exploration routes for others. Business users will solely interact with easy-to-use business intelligence interfaces: all the complexities related to storing data and its organization in the platform will be conveniently far from their sight.

The data analytics toolbox

Out of all the technologies related to data analytics, this book is going to focus on the application layer. This is where the "magic" happens: analytics applications can transform data into actual business value and in the next chapters, you will learn how to do this.

There are many data analytics applications out there available for use. Each of them has its strengths and peculiarities. Although some can be very versatile, no single application will satisfy the full range of analytical needs we could encounter on our way. Hence, we should pick a selection of tools that will jointly cover an acceptable range of needs: they form our **data analytics toolbox**. By learning how to use and how to effectively combine the few tools we have put in the toolbox, we can become autonomous data analytics practitioners. Like a plumber would have his or her preferences on the instruments to use, you will also have your own predilections and can customize your toolbox to your personal tastes. You just want to ensure you pick the right mix of tool types, so that you have a broad range of functionalities readily available to you.

Let's go through the different types of tools that qualify for being added to our toolbox:

- **Spreadsheets**: Although their analytics ability is quite limited, spreadsheet applications are virtually omnipresent because of their ease of use and extended portability that facilitates sharing data with colleagues. Nearly everyone is able to open a *Microsoft Excel* file (or its open source alternative, *OpenOffice Calc*, or a cloud-based service such as *Google Sheets*) and add simple formula calculations to it. They can also be very helpful when creating simple, one-off data visualizations: their level of graphic customization is good enough for many day-to-day data presentation needs. On the other side, spreadsheet software is inadequate for creating robust and automated data workflows: refreshing even a simple report created in Excel requires manual steps and is prone to human error.

- **Business Intelligence**: These are the most-suited tools for creating advanced data visualizations and interactive dashboards. Tools like *Microsoft Power BI*, *QlikView/Qlik Sense*, *Tableau*, and *TIBCO Spotfire* let you implement user-friendly data apps with the objective of democratizing data and making it accessible to the masses. They have a vast choice of visuals to render and the possibility to link charts so as to enable a guided data exploration experience. Although some have algorithms implemented, advanced analytics is not their natural strength: they are, instead, best suited for enabling descriptive analytics at scale:

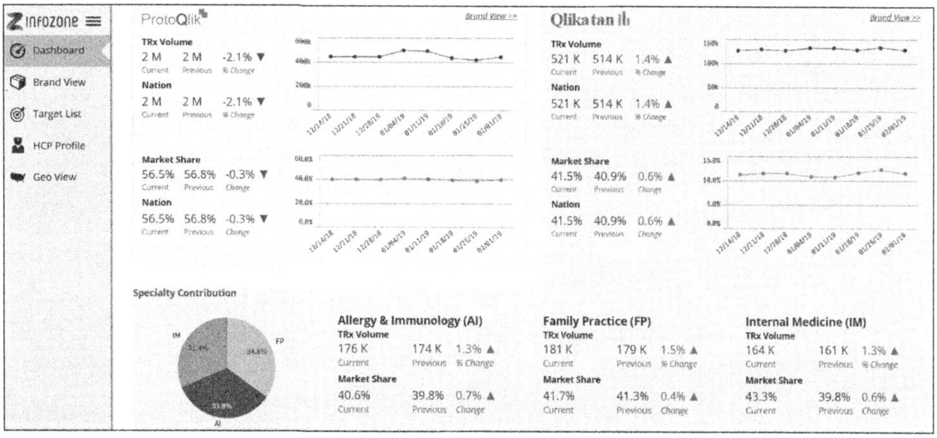

Figure 1.3: A dashboard built with Qlik Sense – the navigation pane on the left guides you through the different aspects to visualize

- **Low-code analytics**: These tools enable you to rapidly build advanced analytics workflows without having to write code. Their "secret" is the workflow-based user interface: by composing a flow chart made of incremental data transformation steps and customizable modeling modules, you can build a fully operating analytics application in record time. Because of their intuitive interface and lack of coding requirements, tools like *KNIME*, *RapidMiner*, and *Alteryx Designer* can be used by expert data professionals (like data scientists and business analysts, to quickly prototype advanced capabilities), as well as non-data-focused knowledge workers (who are looking for ways to automate their time-consuming, regular data reporting activities):

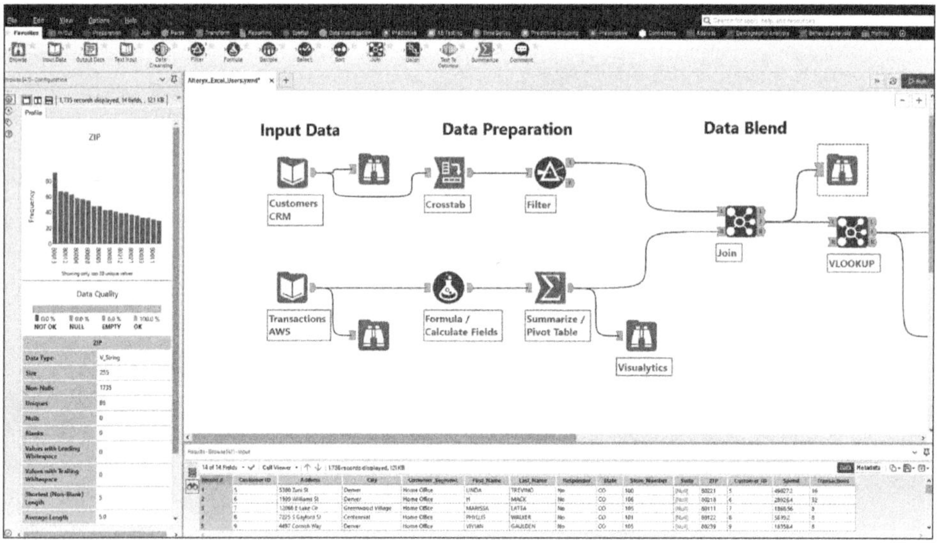

Figure 1.4: User interface of Alteryx Designer –
each icon is a transformation step through the data flow

- **Code-based analytics**: The most traditional approach to advanced analytics is to write code using data science-friendly languages such as Python, R, and Scala. Considering the vast availability of machine learning libraries written in these languages, a data scientist can use them to build highly customized and efficient analytics solutions. These can then be embedded in real-time applications and scaled across the company as needed. To do so, data professionals will use **Integrated Development Environments (IDEs)** such as RStudio for R and Jupyter Notebook, Visual Studio, or PyCharm for Python:

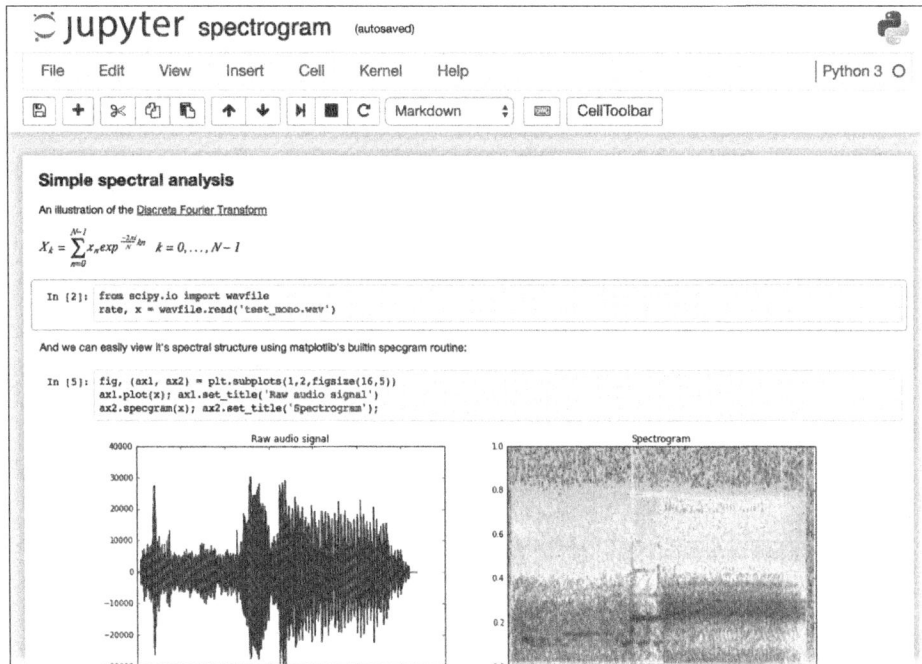

Figure 1.5: A screenshot of a Jupyter Notebook –
you can run your Python code through a web interface

You should not consider these four types of analytics as alternatives to choose from. Actually, it's quite the opposite – they have complementary strengths and weaknesses, and gracefully integrate into one another. Let's consider an example: Laura is a supply chain data analyst working for a car manufacturer. She needs to quickly put together a capability that's able to forecast the future demand for parts at the production line level, and then make results available to a number of purchasing analysts and plant managers across the globe. Laura decides to build a workflow in KNIME that pulls historical demand levels from a few corporate databases and combines it with inventory actuals. After an initial exploration phase, Laura builds a predictive model of demand using KNIME's native functionalities and – later – optimizes it by adding some custom line of Python code directly into KNIME. After that, Laura completes her workflow with the last clean-up steps and exports the forecast results directly into a Power BI dataset. Lastly, Laura builds a simple dashboard made of a few tables and simple line charts in Power BI that enable end users to explore the data, filter it to their area of interest, and export it into a handy Excel file for further analysis and sharing.

Laura was able to rapidly put together this great piece of work because she used her whole analytics toolbox made of KNIME, Power BI, and a little bit of Python. She skillfully picked which tool to use by leveraging their strengths and fitting them to her specific needs. Without a versatile toolbox at hand, Laura would have struggled to meet the stringent timing requirement that her business case required.

The story of Laura proves vividly the need to build a versatile data analytics toolbox: whatever your role is, having a selection of complementary tools for transforming, enriching, modeling, and visualizing data is going to give you an advantage in your everyday data needs.

In the rest of this book, I'll get you started with a pre-built "kit" made of a selection of tools that work very well together: KNIME and Power BI. These tools are quite powerful for multiple reasons. First of all, they can be downloaded and installed on your computer for free. Although both also offer a paid version, you will often find that the freely available versions provide plenty of functionality for the vast majority of your regular needs. The other advantage is that neither of them strictly requires any coding. This means that you can fully benefit from this toolkit without necessarily having to become a proficient Python or R programmer, making it a suitable kit for every professional who uses data, not just expert data scientists. For those who, instead, know how to program, this kit can be expanded further by integrating snippets of code, like Laura did in her project. Lastly, KNIME and Power BI are particularly well-suited to each other. If you look at *Figure 1.6*, they jointly cover most of the needs you might encounter, from data automation and advanced machine learning to professional-looking data visualization and dashboarding:

Tool type (and examples)	Best suited for	Data transformation	Advanced Analytics	Data visualization	User friendliness
Spreadsheets (Excel/OpenOffice Calc)	Basic visualizations, Portability	★		★★	★★★
Business Intelligence (PowerBI/Tableau)	Interactive dashboards, Advanced visualizations	★		★★★	★★
Low-code analytics (KNIME/RapidMiner)	Ad-hoc analytics, Data automation, Fast prototyping of advanced analytics	★★★	★★	★	★★
Code-based analytics (Python Jupyter/Rstudio)	Advanced machine learning, capability scaling, real-time analytics	★★	★★★	★★	

Figure 1.6: A comparison across multiple tools for data analytics – one size does not fit all

Before we start building our data analytics toolbox, let's understand the various ways we can create real value out of it.

From data to business value

Data is nothing without its chance to be transformed into value. However sophisticated and accurate our model is, whatever profound insights we manage to unveil, data will make a difference only when it finally drives some action that positively impacts the business. The bad news is that driving actions might be quite complex and often more difficult than building a powerful data capability. The good news is that we have not just one but multiple ways to impact the business with analytics: we call them **data-to-value paths**. It's important to have them clear in our mind before we start working on data, so that we can maximize the business relevance of what we build right from the start. The three most frequent data-to-value paths you can encounter in business are:

- **Ad hoc analytics**: In this case, you use data to influence a specific decision or to shed light on a unique opportunity or threat. This is the most time-consuming path to follow, as it certainly requires a lot of human interaction, but can also be extremely rewarding. By means of data exploration and, if necessary, leveraging some predictive algorithms, you start your path by identifying an insight hidden in the data. To maximize its chance of impact, you then build an engaging story that is able to bring decision makers onboard with you and willing to make the right decision. Only when (and if) this decision comes to life and gets transformed into action will you be in the position of claiming economic value thanks to data analytics. Many insightful data discoveries were never implemented because some steps along this path failed. Sometimes, the story is not well-prepared and delivered, making a good recommendation unheard. In other cases, the data-based plans are not followed through because they were not well-explained or tracked. In the rest of this book, you will learn how to maximize the chances for your ad hoc analytics to make it to actual value.

- **Ongoing Business Intelligence**: When you follow this path, your aim is to systematically enlighten managers with relevant information. This will make them better at what they do and ultimately maximize the value coming from their work. By means of descriptive analytics and, when necessary, using some diagnostics algorithms, you make the data "speak loud and clear" through visuals and alerts. By enriching others through data analytics, you generate better actions and, so, add incremental value to the business. This data-to-value path might be less sophisticated than the others, but it carries a large potential for value creation as it can impact the work of many people and in a continuous manner. Later in this book, you will learn how to make the most out of data capabilities enabling ongoing business intelligence.

- **Automatic optimization**: As you take this path, you use prescriptive analytics to obtain a plan of action to be taken and automatically follow through with it. In this case, the data and algorithm are not informing others or recommending a course of action: they are put in the driving seat and can steer the execution of business processes. The potential benefit is vast since algorithms can continuously optimize the performance of the company's operations without any human intervention or, at most, with some moderate supervision:

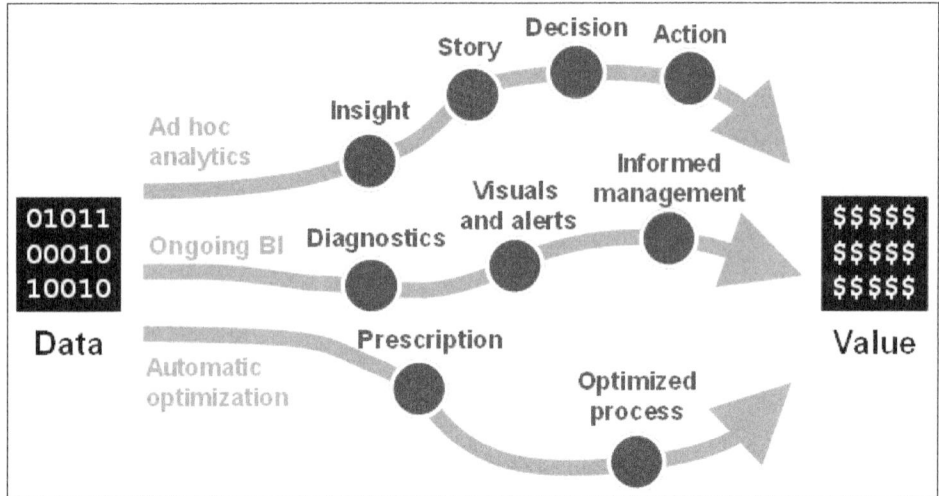

Figure 1.7: The three most frequent data-to-value paths – which one will you follow first?

It will be important to identify which data-to-value path we want to pursue on a case-by-case basis. Depending on the route we take, we might need to implement a certain type of data analytics and pick specific tools from our toolbox. In any case, having clarity on how we want to create value for a business will maximize our chance of success.

Summary

This chapter gave you all the background you needed to begin your journey through the practice of data analytics. We saw the differences between the three types of analytics (descriptive, predictive, and prescriptive) and recognized the underlying potential value of each. We realized how virtually everyone in a company can benefit from using data analytics and familiarized ourselves with the different roles and skills required across business users, analysts, data scientists, and engineers. We glimpsed at the complexity of the full technology stack required for analytics to work: specifically, we went through the tools that data analytics practitioners should keep handy in their toolbox, spotting the value of the KNIME/Power BI couple. At last, we distinguished between the several paths that data can take to be transformed into actual business value.

I hope that the last few pages convinced you even further of the massive business potential hidden in data. It's now time to get our hands dirty and, in the next chapter, meet one of our precious travel companions through the land of analytics: KNIME.

2
Getting Started with KNIME

It's time to get our hands finally dirty with data as we unveil KNIME, the first instrument we find in our data analytics toolkit. This chapter will introduce you to the foundational features of any low-code analytics platform and will allow you to get started with the universal need you face at the beginning of every analytics project: loading and cleaning data.

Let's have a look at the questions this chapter aims to answer:

- What is KNIME and where can I get it?
- What are nodes and how do they work?
- What does a data workflow look like?
- How can I load some data in KNIME and clean it up?

This is going to be a rather hands-on initiation to the everyday practice of data analytics. Since we will spend some time with KNIME, it's worth first getting some basic background on it.

> KNIME (/naɪm/) is pronounced like the word *knife* but with an *m* at the end instead of an f.

KNIME in a nutshell

KNIME is a low-code data analytics platform known for its ease of use and versatility. Let's go through its most prominent features:

- KNIME allows the **visual design** of data analytics: this means that you can build your sequence of transformation and modeling steps by just drawing it. In the same way as you would sketch a flowchart to describe a process using pencil and paper, with KNIME you will use a mouse and keyboard to depict what you want to do with your data. This is the fundamental difference versus the approach implemented in code-based analytics environments: using tools like KNIME means you don't need to write a line of code unless you want to. The visual approach will also let you have a clear line of sight of what's happening with your data at each step of the process. This makes even complex procedures intuitive to understand and easier to build. For advanced data practitioners like data scientists, this means saving a lot of time for debugging a prototype, as they can easily spot issues along the way. For business users in need of some data analytics, KNIME offers a very hospitable environment, accessible to everyone who wants to learn from scratch.

- It is **open source** and free to use: you can download its full version and install it on your computer at no cost. Different from what happens with the trial version of other products, it offers the complete set of functionalities for data analytics without limitations or time constraints. For the sake of completeness: KNIME also offers a commercial product (called **KNIME Server**) that enables the full operationalization of workflows as real-time applications and services, but we will not need to use any of this on our journey.

- It offers a rich library of **additional packages** for extending its base functionalities. These are available—in most cases—for free. Some of these extensions will let you connect KNIME with cloud platforms (like Amazon Web Services or Microsoft Azure), access other applications (Twitter or Google Analytics, to mention a few), or run specific types of advanced analytics (such as text mining or deep learning). Some packages will even let you add some Python or R code into KNIME so that you can implement even the most specific and sophisticated functionalities offered within their extensive set of libraries. This means that if you know how to program, you can leverage that as well in KNIME. The good news is that—in the vast majority of cases—you simply don't need to!

- Lastly, there is a broad and **growing community** of KNIME practitioners around the world. This makes it easier to find blogs and forums filled with examples (like the KNIME official one, `forum.knime.com`), tutorials, and answers to the most frequent questions you will encounter. Generous KNIME users can also share some ready-to-use modules with the rest of the community to enable others to replicate them: this further enriches the functionalities available out there at the time of need.

All these features make KNIME an all-inclusive tool, to the point that some have called it the **Swiss Army knife** of data analytics. Whatever nickname we prefer to give it, KNIME is well suited for learning and practicing everyday analytics and is certainly a tool worth adding to our kit.

It's time to get KNIME up and running on your computer: you can download it from the official website `www.knime.com`. Just go to the **Download** page and get the installation started for your operating system (KNIME is available for Windows, Unix, and Mac). When you are done with the installation, open the app. At the first run, you might be asked to confirm the location of the **Workspace**; this will be the folder where all your projects will be saved. After confirming the workspace folder (you can select any location you like), you are ready to go: the KNIME interface will be there to welcome you.

Moving around in KNIME

As we enter the world of KNIME, it makes sense to familiarize ourselves with the two keywords we are going to use most often: **nodes** and **workflows**:

- A **node** is the essential building block of any data operation that happens in KNIME. Every action you apply on data — like loading a file, filtering out rows, applying some formula, or building a machine learning model — is represented by a square icon in KNIME, called a **node**.

- A **workflow** is the full sequence of nodes that describe what you want to do with your data, from the beginning to the end. To build a data process in KNIME you will have to select the nodes you need and connect them in the desired order, designing the workflow that is right for you:

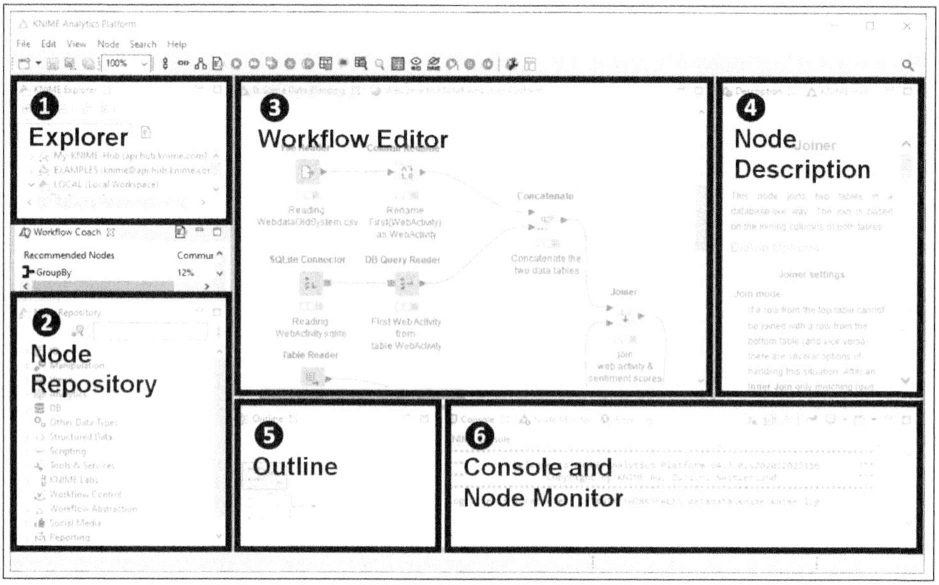

Figure 2.1: KNIME user interface: your workbench for crafting analytics

KNIME's user interface has got all you need to pick and mix nodes to construct the workflow that you need. Let's go through the six fundamental elements of the interface that will welcome you as soon as you start the application:

1. **Explorer**. This is where your workflows will be kept handy and tidy. In here you will find: the **LOCAL** workspace, which contains the folders stored on your local machine; the KNIME public server, storing many **EXAMPLES** organized by topic that you can use for inspiration and replication; the **My-KNIME-Hub** space, linked to your user on the KNIME Hub cloud, where you can share private and public workflows and reusable modules—called **Components** in KNIME—with others (you can create your space for free by registering at hub.knime.com).

2. **Node Repository**. In this space, you can find all the nodes available to you, ready to be dragged and dropped into your workflow. Nodes are arranged in hierarchical categories: if you click on the chevron sign **>** on the left of each header, you will go to the level below. For instance, the first category is **IO** (**input/output**) which includes multiple subcategories, such as **Read**, **Write**, and **Connectors**. You can search for the node you need by entering some keywords in the textbox at the top right. Try entering the word Excel in the search box: you will obtain all nodes that let you import and export data in the Microsoft spreadsheet format. As a painter would find all available colors in the palette, the repository will give you access to all available nodes for your workflow:

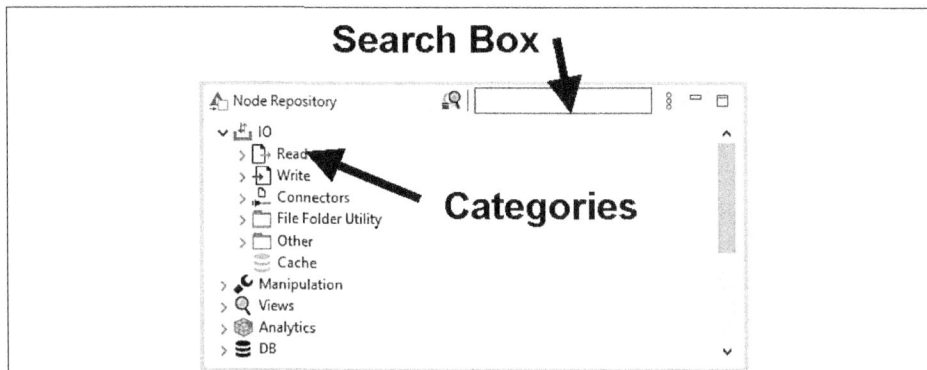

Figure 2.2: The Node Repository lists all the nodes available for you to pick

3. **Workflow Editor**. This is where the magic happens: in here you will combine the nodes you need, connect them as required, and see your workflow come to life. Following the analogy we started above with the color palette, the Workflow Editor will be the white canvas on which you will paint your data masterpiece.

4. **Node Description**. This is an always-on reference guide for each node. When you click on any node—lying either in the repository or in the Workflow Editor—this window gets updated with all you need to know about the node. The typical description of a node includes three parts: a summary of what it does and how it works, a list of the various steps of configuration we can apply (**Dialog Options**), and finally, a description of the input and output ports of the node (**Ports**).

5. **Outline**. Your workflow can get quite big and you might not be able to see it fully within your Workflow Editor: the Outline gives you a full view of the workflow and shows which part you are currently visualizing in the Workflow Editor. If you drag the blue rectangle around, you can easily jump to the part of the workflow you are interested in.

6. **Console** and **Node Monitor**. In this section, you will find a couple of helpful diagnostics and debugging gadgets. The **Console** will show the full description of the latest warnings and errors while the **Node Monitor** shows a summary of the data available at the output port of the currently selected node.

> You can personalize the look and feel of the user interface by adding and removing elements from the **View** menu. Should you want to go back to the original setup, as displayed in the figure above, just click on **View | Reset Perspective....**

Although these six sections cover all the essential needs, the KNIME user interface offers more sections that you might be curious enough to explore. For instance, on the left, you have the Workflow Coach, which suggests the next most likely node you are going to add to the workflow, based on what other users do. Lastly, in the same window of the Node Description, you will find an additional panel (look for its header at the top) called KNIME Hub: in here, you can search for examples, additional packages, and modules that you can directly drag and drop into your workflow, as you would do from the Node Repository.

Nodes

Nodes are the backbone of KNIME and we need to feel totally confident with them: let's discover how they work and what types of nodes are available:

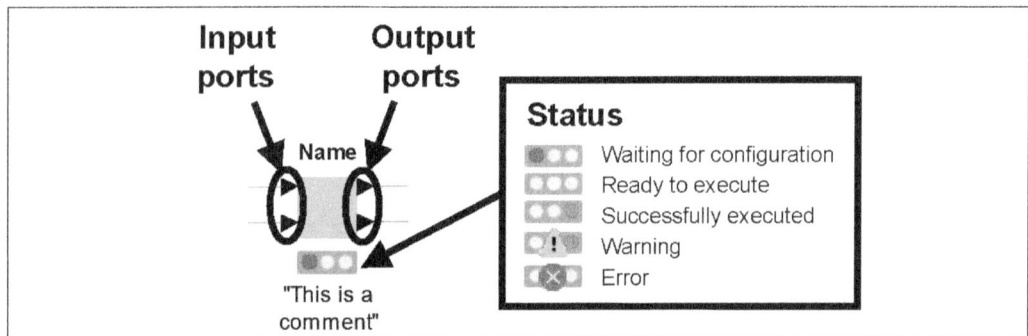

Figure 2.3: Anatomy of a node in KNIME: the traffic light tells us the current status

As you can see from the figure above, nodes look like square icons with some text and shapes around them. More precisely:

- On top of a node, you will find its **Name** in bold. The name tells you, in a nutshell, what that type of node does. For example, to rename some columns in a table, we use the node called **Column Rename**.

- At the bottom of the square, you find a **Comment**. This is a label that should explain the specific role of that node in your workflow. By default, KNIME applies a counter to every new node as it gets added to the workflow, like Node 1, Node 2, and so on. You can modify the comment by just double-clicking on it.

> I strongly encourage you to comment on every single node in your workflow with a short description that explains what it does. When workflows get complex you will quickly forget what each node was meant to do there. Trust me: it's a worthy investment of your time!

- Nodes are connected through **Ports**, lying at the left and at the right of the square. By convention, the ports on the left are input ports, as they bring data into the node, while ports on the right are output ports, carrying the results of the node execution. Ports can have different shapes and colors, depending on what they carry: most of them are triangles, as they convey data tables, but they could be squares (models, connections, images, and more) or circles (variables).

- At the bottom of every node, you have a traffic light that signals the current **Status** of the node. If the red light is on, the node is not ready yet to do its job: it could be that some required data has not been given as an input or some configuration step is needed. When the light is amber, the node has all it needs and is ready to be executed on your command. The green light is good news: it means that the node was successfully executed and the results are available at the output ports. Some icons can appear on the traffic light if something is not right: a yellow triangle with an exclamation mark indicates a warning while a red circle with a cross announces an error. In these cases, you can learn more about what went wrong by keeping your mouse on them for a second (a label will appear) or by reading the Console.

As we have already started to see in the Node Repository, there are several families of nodes available in KNIME, each responding to a different class of data analytics needs. Here are the most popular ones:

- **Input & Output**: these nodes will bring data in and out of KNIME. Normally, input nodes are at the beginning of workflows: they can open files in different formats (CSV, Excel, images, webpages, to mention some) or connect to remote databases and pull the data they need. As you can see from *Figure 2.4*, the input nodes have only output ports on the right and do not have any input ports on the left (unless they require a connection with a database). This makes sense as they have the role of initiating a workflow by pulling data into it after reading it from somewhere. Conversely, output nodes tend to be used at the end of a workflow as they can save data to files or cloud locations. They rarely have output ports as they close our chain of operations.

- **Manipulation**: These nodes are capable of handling data tables and transforming them according to our needs. They can apply steps for aggregating, combining, sorting, filtering, and reshaping tables, but also managing missing values, normalizing data points, and converting data types. These nodes, together with those in the previous family, are virtually unmissable in any data analytics workflow: they can jointly clean the data and prepare it in the format required by any subsequent step, like creating a model, a report, or a chart. These nodes can have one or more input ports and one or more output ports, as they are capable of merging and splitting tables.

- **Analytics**: These are the smartest nodes of the pack, able to build statistical models and support the implementation of artificial intelligence algorithms. We will learn how to use these nodes in the chapters dedicated to machine learning. For now, it will be sufficient to keep with us the reassuring thought that even complex AI procedures (like creating a deep neural network) can be obtained by wisely combining the right modeling nodes, available in our Node Repository. As you will notice in *Figure 2.4*, some of the ports are squares as they stand for statistical models instead of data tables.

- **Flow Control**: Sometimes, our workflows will need to go beyond the simple one-branch structure where data flows only once and follows a single chain of nodes. These nodes can create loops across branches so we can repeat several steps through cycles, like a programmer would do with flow control statements (for those of you who can program, think of `while` or `for` constructs). We can also dynamically change the behavior of nodes by controlling their configuration through variables. These nodes are more advanced and, although we don't need them most of the time, they are a useful resource when the going gets tough.

- **All others**: On top of the ones above, KNIME offers many other types of nodes, which can help us with more specific needs. Some nodes let us interact systematically with third-party applications through interfaces called **Application Programming Interfaces** (**APIs**): for example, an extension called KNIME Twitter Connectors lets you search for tweets or download public user information in mass to run some analytics on it. Other extensions will let you blend KNIME with programming languages like Python and R so you can run snippets of code in KNIME or execute KNIME workflows from other environments. You will also have nodes for running statistical tests and for building visualizations or full reports.

> When you are looking for advanced functionality in KNIME, you can check the KNIME Hub or run a search on `nodepit.com`, a search engine for KNIME workflows, components, and nodes.

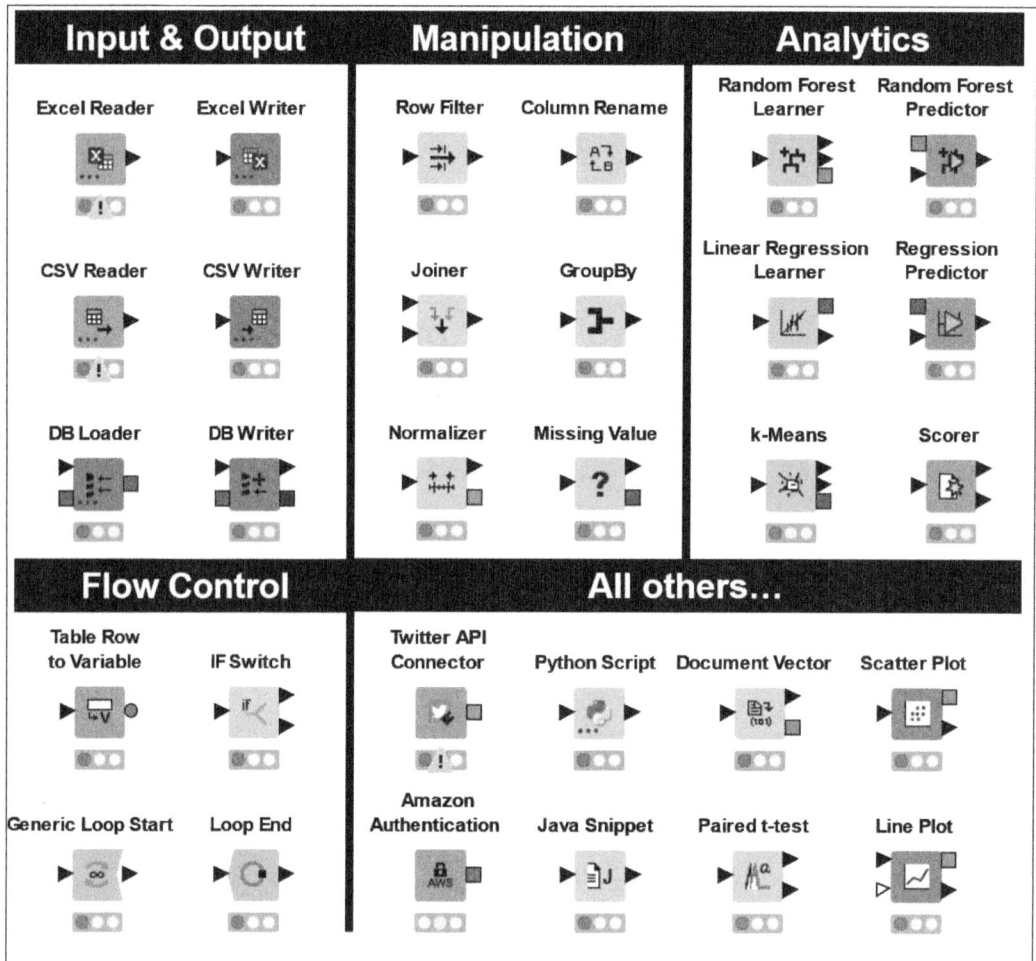

Figure 2.4: A selection of KNIME nodes by type: these are the LEGO® bricks of your data analytics flow

I hope that reading about the broad variety of things you can do with nodes has whetted your appetite for more. It's finally time to see nodes in action and build a simple KNIME workflow.

Hello World in KNIME

As you put together your first workflow, you will learn how to interact with KNIME's user interface to connect, configure, and execute nodes: this is the bread and butter of any KNIME user, which you are about to become.

> The title of this section is a thing for geeks: in fact, when you learn a new programming language, "Hello, World!" is the first program you get to write. It is very simple and is meant to illustrate the basic syntax of a language.

Let's imagine we have a simple and repetitive data operation to perform regularly: every day we receive a text file in **Comma-Separated Value (CSV)** format, which reports the cumulative sales generated by country in the year to date. The original file has some unnecessary columns and the order of rows is random. We need to apply some basic transformation steps so that we end up with a simple table showing just two columns: one is the name of the country and the other the amount of generated sales. We also want the rows to be sorted by decreasing sales. Lastly, we need to convert the file into Excel as it is a format that's easier to read for our colleagues. We can build a KNIME workflow that does exactly that once, in a way that we don't need to repeat the tedious task manually every day. Let's open KNIME Analytics Platform and build our time-saving workflow.

To keep our workflows tidy, we can organize them hierarchically, in folders: in KNIME, folders are called **Workflow Groups**. So, let's start by creating a workflow group that will host our first piece of work:

1. Right-click on the **LOCAL** entry in the KNIME Explorer section (top-left) and then click on **New Workflow Group...** in the pop-up menu.

2. Enter the name of your new folder (you can call it Chapter 2) and click on
    Finish:

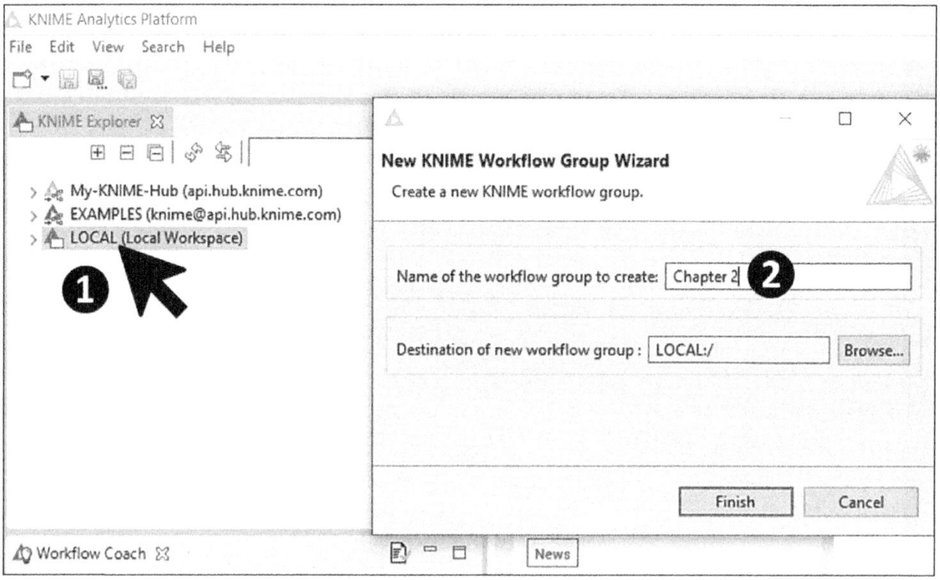

Figure 2.5: Creating a Workflow Group in KNIME: keep your work tidy by organizing it in folders

You will see that the new folder has appeared in your local workspace. Now we can
finally create a new workflow within this group. Similar to what you just did when
creating a group, you just need to follow a few more steps:

3. Right-click on the newly created workflow group and then on **New KNIME
    Workflow...**.

4. Enter the name of your new workflow (how about Hello World?) and then
    click **Finish**. Your workflow will appear in the editor, which at this point will
    look like a sheet of squared paper.

5. It's time to load our CSV file into KNIME, using the proper input node. The
    fastest way to do so is to drag and drop the file directly into the Workflow
    Editor: just grab the file named raw_sales_country.csv from the folder
    where it is located and drop it anywhere on the blank editor. KNIME will
    recognize the type of file and automatically implement the right node for
    reading it: in this case, CSV Reader. As you drop the file, its configuration
    dialog will appear. If at any point you need to revise its configuration, you
    can just double-click on the node to obtain the same dialog.

Like we will do every time we meet a new KNIME node on our journey, let's quickly discover how it works and how to configure it.

CSV Reader

This node (available in the repository under the path **IO > Reader**) reads data from a text file stored in a CSV format and makes it available as a table in KNIME. This node is pretty handy: it attempts to detect the format of the file and recognizes the type of data stored in each column, allowing you to manually change it if needed. It also lets you run some basic reformatting on the fly, like changing the names of columns. As you see in *Figure 2.6*, its configuration window displays multiple tabs, whose headers appear at the top. The first tab (**Settings**) lets you set the fundamentals:

- In the first section at the top, you can specify the path of the file to be read: to do so, just click on the **Browse...** button and select the file. If you dragged and dropped your file in the Workflow Editor, this field is pre-populated. The node lets you also read multiple files in a folder having the same format, by selecting the **Files in folder** mode.

- In the middle section, you can specify the format of the file, like the characters used to delimit rows and columns and if it has column headers. All these parameters get automatically guessed by the node when a new file is loaded (you can click on **Autodetect format** to force a new attempt). One useful option is **Support short data rows**: if this box is ticked, the node will keep working even if some rows have incomplete data points. The good news is that in most cases you will not need to change any of these parameters manually as the automatic detection feature is pretty robust.

- At the bottom of the tab, you find the **Preview** of the table read in the file. This lets you check that the format has been determined correctly.

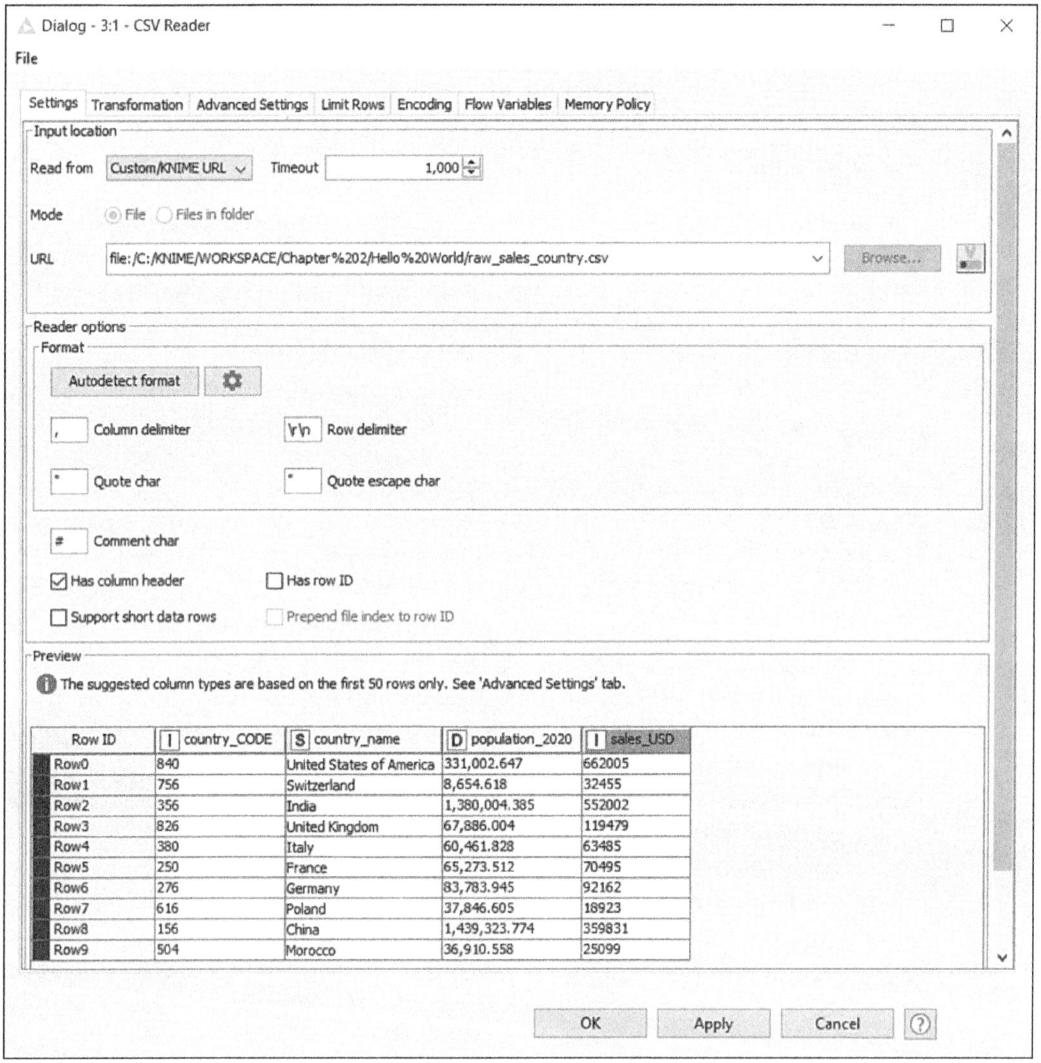

Figure 2.6: Configuration dialog of the CSV Reader node: you can specify which file to read and how

If you move to the second tab of the window (called **Transformation**) you will have the opportunity to apply some simple reformatting to your table as it gets loaded. For instance, you can: change the name of columns (just write the new one in the **New name** column), drop some columns you don't need (untick the box on the left of their name), change the column order (drag and drop them using your mouse), and change their data type (for instance, from text to numbers).

> Every column in a KNIME table is associated with a **data type**, indicated by a squared letter beside the name of the column. The most common data types are strings (indicated by the letter S, which are sets of text characters), decimal numbers (letter D), integer numbers (I), long integers (L, like integers but able to store more digits), and Boolean values (B, which can be only FALSE or TRUE).

You can check the results of your transformation in the preview section at the bottom. To be clear, you could do these transformations later in your workflow (you have specific KNIME nodes for renaming columns, changing their orders, and so on) but it might be just faster and easier to make these changes here on the spot, using one single node.

> In case the CSV Reader node fails in reading your data as you required, try another node called File Reader. Especially with ill-formatted files, the latter node is more robust than CSV Reader, although it cannot transform the structure of the table on the fly.

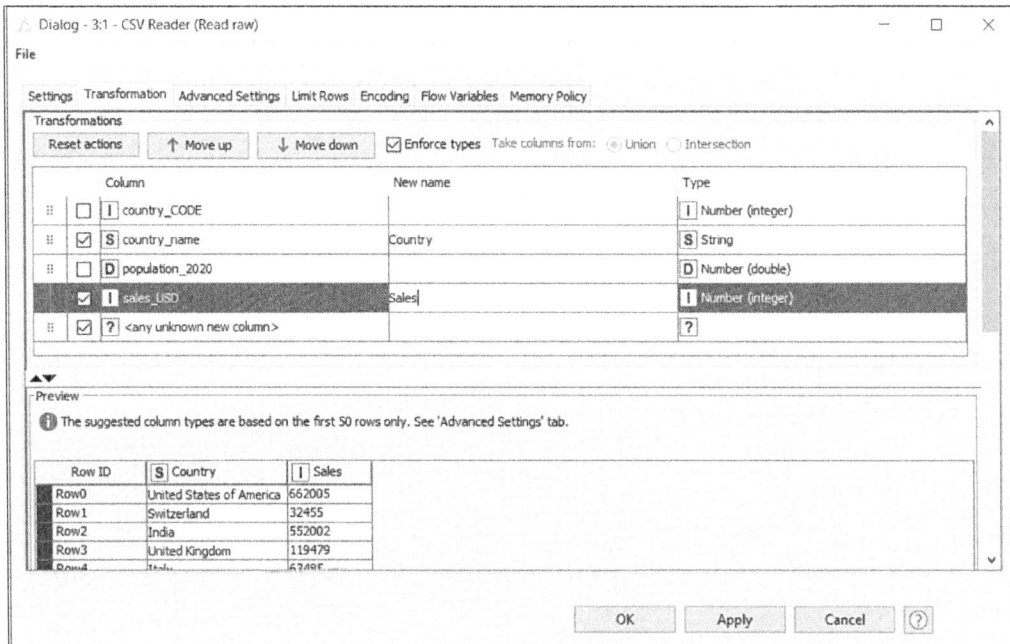

Figure 2.7: The transformation tab of the CSV Reader node: reformat your table on the fly

6. Looking at the preview of the table in the **Settings** tab, it looks like the node has done a good job of interpreting the format of the file. We just noticed that there are some columns we don't need to carry and they can be dropped (specifically, country_CODE and population_2020) and, also, that we can simplify some of the column names by renaming them. To do this, we need to move to the **Transformation** tab: just click on its name at the top of the window.

7. Let's first remove the columns we don't need, by just unticking the boxes beside their names, as shown in *Figure 2.7.*

8. Let's also assign more friendly titles to the other two columns by typing them in the **New name** section: let's rename country_name to Country and sales_USD to Sales.

9. The preview of the transformed table looks exactly like we wanted; this means we are done with the configuration of this node, and we can close it by clicking on the **OK** button.

10. To keep things clear to ourselves and others we want to comment on every node in our workflows. Let's start from this very first node. If we double-click on the label underneath (which by default will read **Node 1**), we can change it to something more meaningful, like Read raw data. From this point on, I will not mention every time we need to comment on each node — just make it become a habit.

11. Our node is displaying an encouraging yellow traffic light: it means it has all it needs to fulfill its duty — we just need to say the word. To execute a node in KNIME, we can either select it and press *F7* on our keyboard or right-click on the node to obtain the pop-up menu, as shown in *Figure 2.8.* When it appears, click on **Execute**:

CSV Reader			
		Configure...	F6
		Execute	F7
		Execute and Open Views	Shift+F10
		Cancel	F9
Read raw data		Reset	F8
		Edit Node Description...	Alt+F2
		New Workflow Annotation	
		Connect selected nodes	Ctrl+L
		Disconnect selected nodes	Ctrl+Shift+L
		Create Metanode...	
		Create Component...	
		Compare Nodes	
		Show Flow Variable Ports	
		Add File System Connection port	
		Remove File System Connection port	
		Cut	
		Copy	
		Paste	
		Undo	
		Redo	
		Delete	
		File Table	

Figure 2.8: The pop-up menu in the Workflow Editor: right-click on any node to make it appear

12. The traffic light turning green is a good sign: our node was successfully executed. A useful feature of KNIME is that you can easily inspect what's going on at each step of the flow, by viewing what data is available at the output ports of every node. In the pop-up menu obtained by right-clicking on a node, you will find one or more icons showing a magnifying lens (normally one for each output port, at the bottom of the menu). By clicking on these icons, you will open a window showing the data you are after. Let's do so now: right-click to make the pop-up menu appear and then click on **File Table** at the bottom of the menu (alternatively you can check out the Node Monitor or use the keyboard shortcut to open the first output view of a node, which is *Shift + F6*). Not surprisingly, we obtain the same table we had in preview in the preview step. It seems that, so far, everything is working right. We can click **OK** and move on.

13. The next step is to sort rows by decreasing amounts of sales. We can use a node that is meant to do exactly that: Sorter. Let's add our Sorter node to the workflow, pulling it from the Node Repository at the bottom left. You can either look it up by typing Sorter in the search box or find it in the hierarchy by clicking first on **Manipulation**, then **Row**, and — finally — **Transform**. When you see the Sorter node, grab it with your mouse and drop it on the workflow, at the right of the CSV Reader node.

14. Your node is now lying alone in the workflow while we want it to be cooperating with other nodes. In fact, we need it to sort the table output by the CSV Reader, so we need to create a connection between the two nodes. In KNIME, we create connections by just drawing them with the mouse. Click on the output port of the CSV Reader (the little arrow on its right) and while keeping the mouse button pressed, go to the input port of the Sorter node. When you release the button, you will see a connection appearing between the nodes. This is exactly what we wanted, the table given in the output by the CSV Reader has now become an input for the Sorter.

We are now ready to configure the Sorter: let's learn about our new node.

▶ ⇅ ▶ *Sorter*

This node (available in the repository in **Manipulation > Row > Transform**) can sort the rows of a table according to a set of criteria defined by the user. Its configuration is self-explanatory: from the drop-down menu, you can select the column you wish to sort by. The radio buttons on the right let you choose whether the sorting shall follow an **Ascending** (A to Z or 1 to 9) or **Descending** (the other way around) order. You can add additional rules on other columns that will come to play to *break the ties* in case multiple rows carry the same value in a column. To do so, just click on the **Add Rule** button and you will see further drop-down menus appearing. You can change the order of precedence among multiple rules by using the ↑ and ↓ arrows:

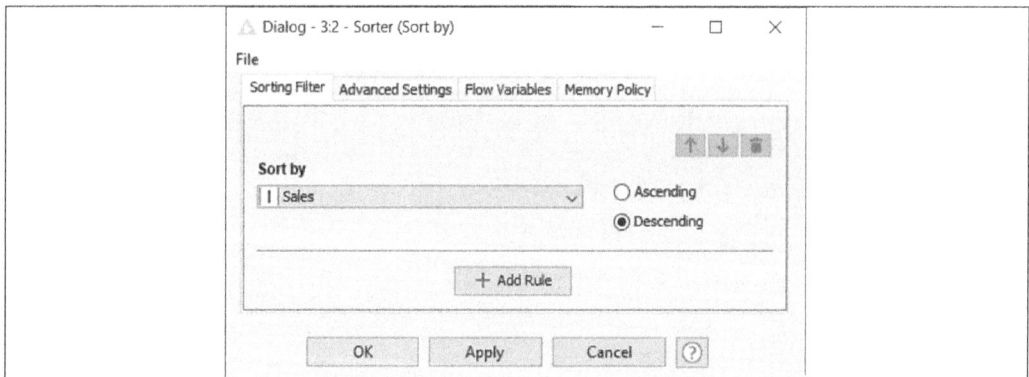

Figure 2.9: Configuration window of the node Sorter: define the desired order of your rows

15. To open the configuration window of Sorter, you can either double-click on the node or right-click on it and then press **Configure...**. You could also just press *F6* on your keyboard after selecting the node with your mouse.

16. Given our needs, the configuration of the node is straightforward: just select Sales in the drop-down menu and then click on the second radio button to apply a descending order. Press **OK** to close the window.

17. The Sorter node is now clear about the input table to use and about the way we want the sorting to happen: it is all ready to go. Let's execute it (*F7* or right-click and select **Execute**) and open the view showing its output (*Shift + F6* or right-click and select **Sorted Table**, the last icon with the magnifying lens):

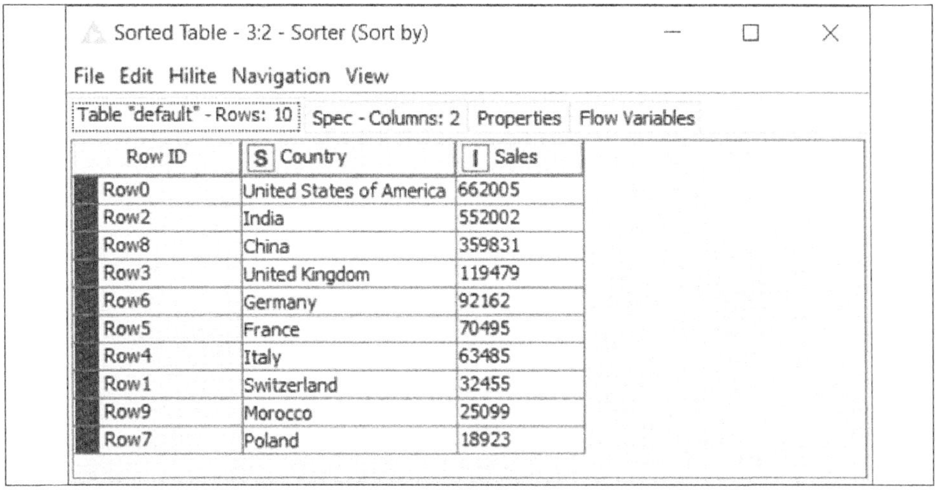

Row ID	S Country	I Sales
Row0	United States of America	662005
Row2	India	552002
Row8	China	359831
Row3	United Kingdom	119479
Row6	Germany	92162
Row5	France	70495
Row4	Italy	63485
Row1	Switzerland	32455
Row9	Morocco	25099
Row7	Poland	18923

Sorted Table - 3:2 - Sorter (Sort by)

File Edit Hilite Navigation View

Table "default" - Rows: 10 Spec - Columns: 2 Properties Flow Variables

Figure 2.10: Output of Sorter node: our countries are now showing by decreasing sales

Every row in a KNIME table is associated with a unique label called **Row ID**. When a table is created, row IDs are normally generated in the form of a counter (Row0, Row1, Row2, and so on) and are preserved along the workflow. That's why in the output of the Sorter node you can still find the original row position by looking at the Row IDs on the left.

It looks like we have our countries sorted in the right order and we can proceed to the last step: exporting our table as an Excel file.

► Excel Writer

This node (available within **IO > Write** in the repository) saves data as Excel worksheets. The configuration dialog will let you first select the format of the file to create (the legacy .xls or the latest .xlsx one) and where to save it (click on the **Browse...** button to select a path). By selecting the **if exists** radio buttons, you can specify what to do if a file with that name is already there where you want to save it: you can overwrite the old data, append the new data as additional rows, or preserve the original file. An important option to check is **Write column headers**: when selected, the column names of your table are added as headers in the first row of your Excel file.

> Although we don't need to do that now, it's useful to know that some KNIME nodes can also save files on cloud-based file systems, like Google Drive or Microsoft Sharepoint. This is why you also see the option **Add ports | File System Connection** when you click on the three dots (...) at the bottom left of the node. Another useful feature of the node is that it can manage multiple input tables and save them as separate worksheets in the same Excel file. To do so, you need to click on the three dots on the node and click on **Add ports > Sheet Input Ports**. You can give different names to the various sheets by typing in the **Sheets** section of the configuration window.

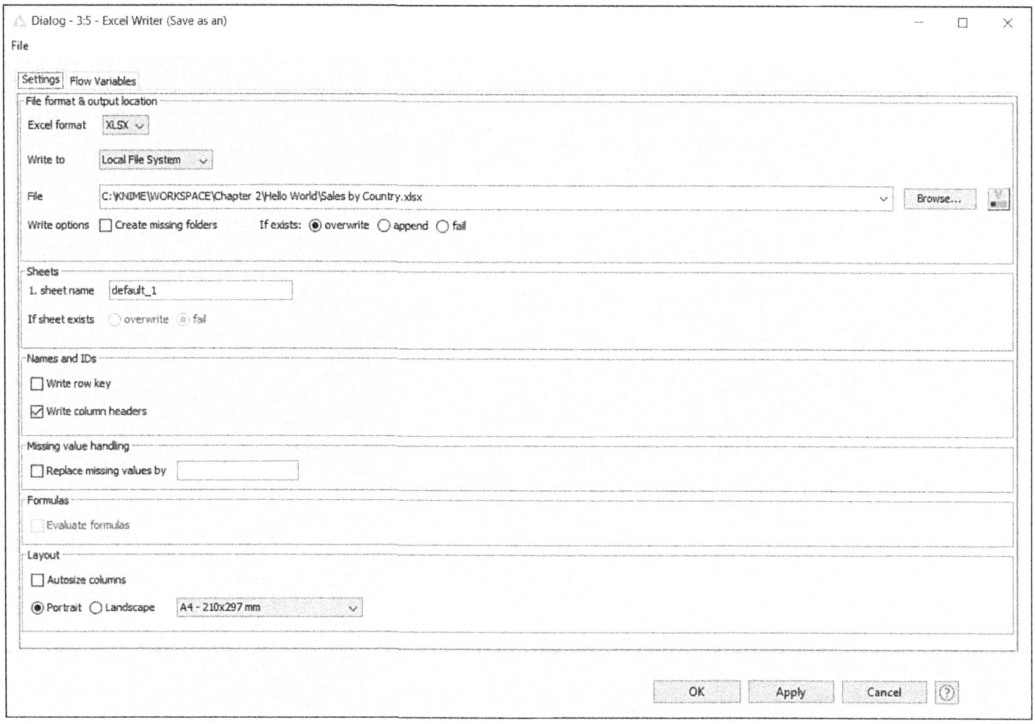

Figure 2.11: Configuration window of Excel Writer: select where to save your output file

18. Let's add the Excel Writer node to our workflow, dragging it from the Node Repository, and then create a connection between the output port of the Sorter and the input node of the Excel Writer.

19. Open the configuration window of the Excel Writer (double-click on it). The only configurations we need to add in this case are the location and the name of the output file (click on the **Browse...** button, go to the desired folder, and type the name of the new file) and, since we might need to repeat this process regularly, select the **overwrite** option using the radio button below.

20. It's time to run the node (*F7* or right-click and select **Execute**) and open the new file in Excel. You'll be pleased to see that the new file looks exactly how we wanted.

Congratulations on creating your first KNIME workflow! By combining three nodes and configuring them appropriately, you implemented a simple data transformation routine that you can now repeat in a matter of seconds, whenever it's needed. More importantly, we used this first tutorial to get acquainted with the fundamental operations you need to build any workflow, such as pulling the right nodes, configuring and executing them, and checking that all works as it should:

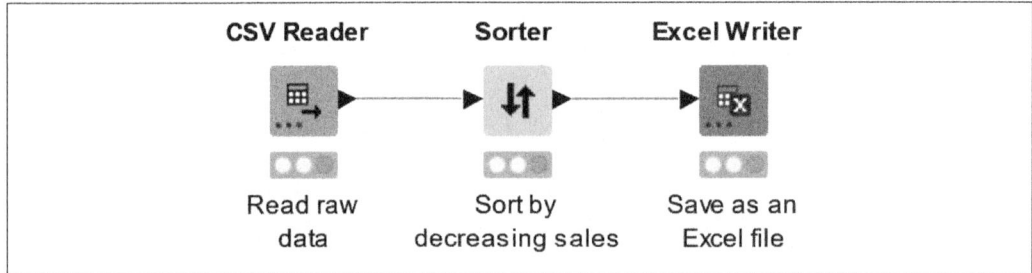

Figure 2.12: Hello World: your first workflow in KNIME

We now have all we need to start building more complex data operations, discovering what other KNIME nodes can do, and this is exactly what we will do in the next few pages. Since we don't want to lose our precious Hello World workflow, it would be a good idea to save it: just press *Ctrl + S* on your keyboard or click on the disk icon at the top left of your screen. If you want to share your workflow with others, you first need to export it as a standalone file. To do so, right-click on the name of the workflow within the KNIME Explorer panel on the left and then select **Export KNIME Workflow...**:

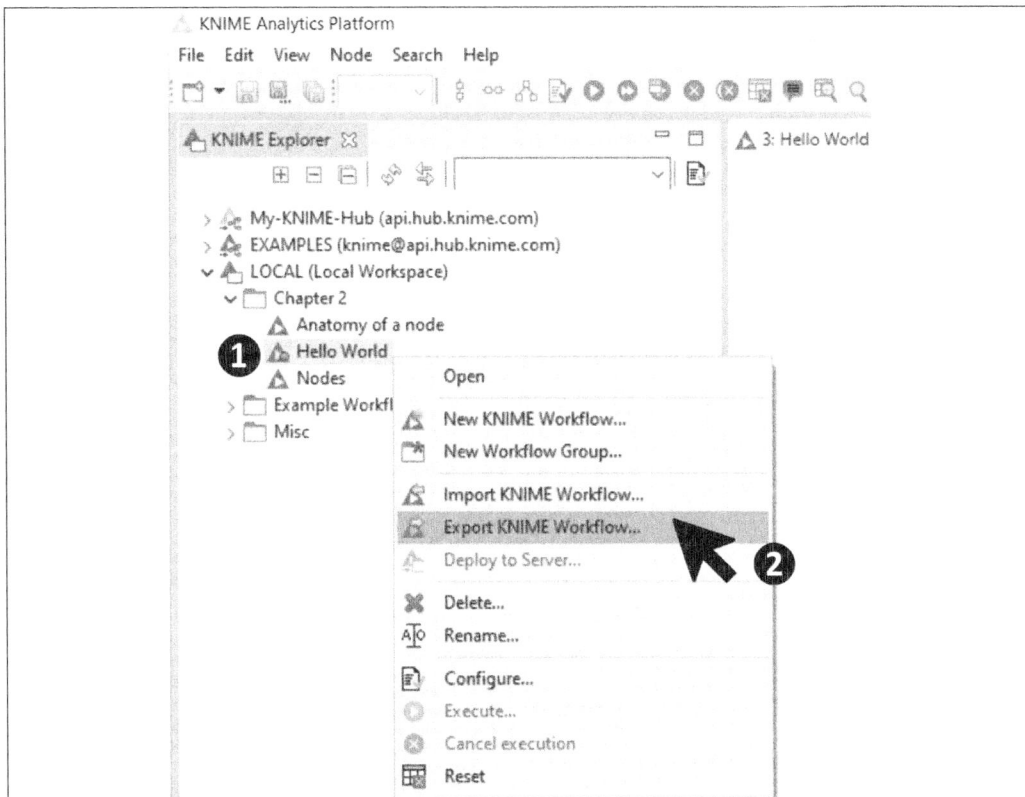

Figure 2.13: How to export a KNIME workflow: you can then share it with whoever you like

In the window that appears, you will have to specify the location and name of the file with your workflow by clicking on the **Browse...** button. If you keep the **Reset Workflow(s) before export** option checked, KNIME will only export the definition of the workflow (the nodes' structure and their configuration) without any data in it. If you untick it, the data stored in every executed node will be exported as well (making your export much larger in size). You can now send the resulting file (with .KNWF as an extension) via email or save it in a safe place. Whoever receives it can import it back in their KNIME installation by clicking on **File | Import KNIME Workflow...** and selecting the location of the file to import and the destination of the workflow.

Cleaning data

Often, when we deal with real-world data analytics, we face a reality that is as annoying as ubiquitous: data can be dirty. The format of text and numbers, the order of rows and columns, the presence of undesired data points, and the lack of some expected values are all possible glitches that can slow down or even jeopardize the process of creating some value from data. Indeed, the lower the quality of the input data, the less useful the resulting output will be. This inconvenient truth is often summarized with the acronym **GIGO**: **Garbage In, Garbage Out**. As a consequence, one of the preliminary phases of a data analytics workflow is **Data Cleaning**, meaning the process of systematically identifying and correcting inaccurate or corrupt data points. Let's learn how to build a full set of data cleaning steps in KNIME through a realistic example.

In this tutorial, we are going to clean a table that captures information on the users of an e-commerce website, such as name, age, email address, available credit, and so on. This table has been generated by pulling directly from the webserver all the available raw data. Our ultimate objective is to create a clean list of contactable users, which we can leverage as a mailing list for sending email newsletters. Since the list of users constantly changes (as some subscribe and unregister themselves every day), we want to build a KNIME workflow that systematically cleans the latest data for us every time we want to update our mailing list:

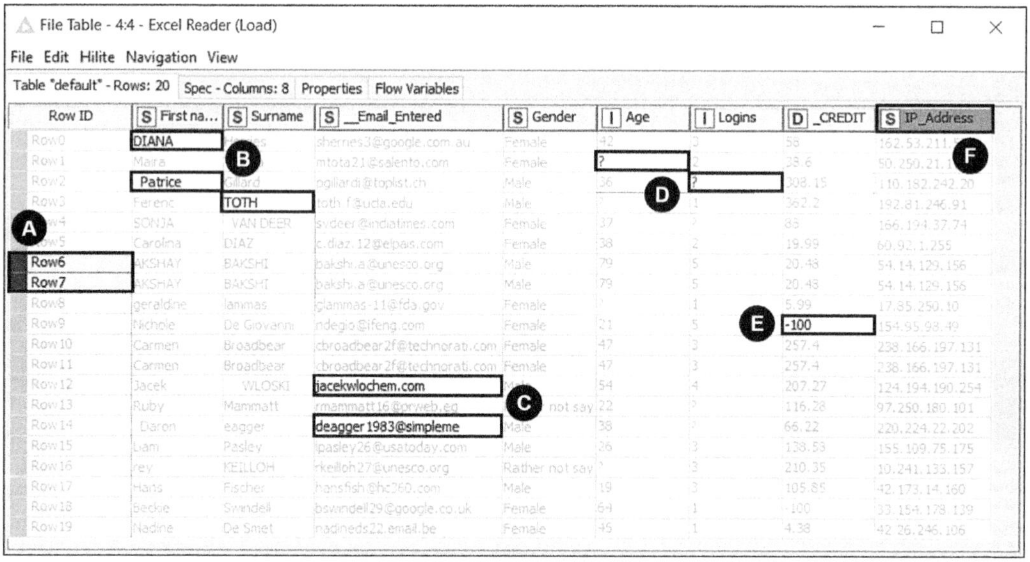

Figure 2.14: The raw data: we certainly have some cleaning chores ahead

As you can see from *Figure 2.14*, a first look at the raw table unveils a series of data quality flaws to be looked after. For instance:

A. Some rows appear to be duplicated.

B. Names and surnames have inconsistent capitalization and some unpleasant blank characters. Additionally, instead of having two separate fields for the name, we would prefer to have a single column (currently missing) with the full name of each person.

C. Some email addresses are wrongly formatted (as they miss the @ symbol or the full domain), making the respective users not contactable.

D. Various values are missing, leaving the cell empty.

> In KNIME, missing values are indicated with a red question mark symbol, ?. For reference, in computer science, a missing value is referred to with the expression NULL.

E. Some credit values are negative. We know that according to company policy these users should be considered inactive and shall not be contacted, so we can remove them from the list.

F. Some columns are not needed. In this case, we can drop the column holding the IP address of the user since it cannot be used for sending a newsletter or to personalize its content.

We have an Excel file (DirtyData.xlsx) with an excerpt of the raw data, showing samples of all those issues listed above. By using this file as a base, we can build a KNIME workflow that polishes the data and exports a good-looking and ready-to-use mailing list. Let's do this one step at a time:

1. First of all, we need to create a blank workflow (you can do this as seen in the previous example or — alternatively — you can go to **File | New...** and then select **New KNIME Workflow**): we can call it Cleaning data.

2. To load the data, we can either drag and drop the source file on the Workflow Editor or grab the Excel Reader node from the repository and place it in the blank editor space.

► *Excel Reader*

This node (**IO > Read**) opens Excel files, reads the content of the specified worksheet, and makes it available as a table at its output port. In the main tab of the configuration dialog, after indicating which file or folder to open (click on **Browse...** to change), you can specify (**Sheet selection**) the worksheet to consider: by default, the node will read the first sheet available in the workbook but you can indicate the name of a specific sheet or its position. If your sheet includes the column headers, you can ask KNIME to use them as column names in the resulting table: in the section **Column Header**, you can select which row contains the column headers. You can also restrict the reading to a portion of the sheet, by specifying the range of columns and rows to read within the **Sheet area** section. You can check whether the node is configured correctly by looking at the bottom of the window, which gives you a preview of what KNIME is reading from the file:

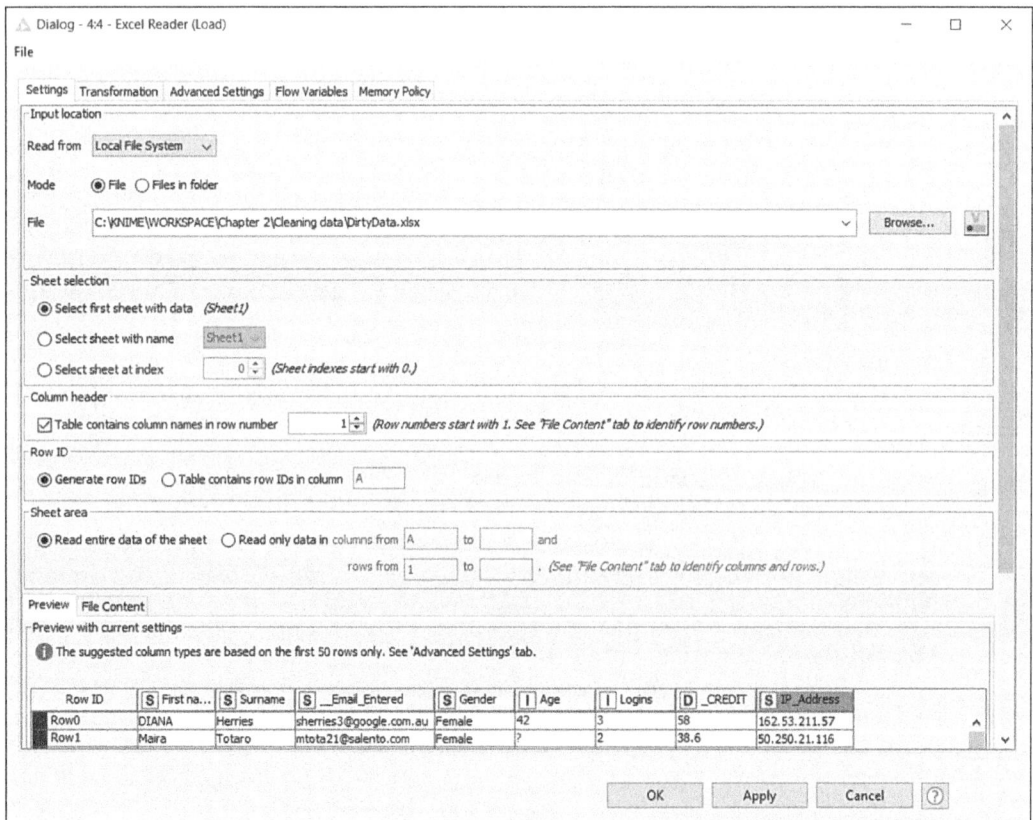

Figure 2.15: Configuration of the Excel Reader node: select file, sheets, and areas to read

If you want to apply some transformations (like renaming columns, reordering them, and so on) as the data gets read, you can use the **Transformation** tab, which works the same as in the CSV Reader node we have already met.

3. Configuring this node will be pretty simple in our case: we should just select the file to open and leave all other parameters unchanged as the default selection looks good for us. We could use the **Transformation** tab to make some adjustments to the format but we will do it later using the appropriate nodes, so we can keep it easy for now.

To remove the duplicated rows we can use a new node that does exactly that: its name is Duplicate Row Filter.

► ⁞ ► *Duplicate Row Filter*

This node (**Manipulation > Row > Filter**) identifies rows having the same values in selected columns and manages them accordingly. In the first tab of the configuration window, you select which columns should be considered for the search of duplicates.

If more than one column is selected, the node will consider duplicates as only rows that have exactly the same values across all the selected columns. In the configuration of many KNIME nodes, we will be asked to select a subset of columns, so it makes sense to spend some time on becoming acquainted with the interface:

- The panel on the right (having a green border) contains the columns included in your selection while the one on the left (red-bordered) displays the excluded columns.

- By double-clicking on the names of the columns or by using the four arrow buttons in the middle, you can transfer the columns across panes.

- If you have many columns, you can look them up by name using the **Filter** textboxes at the top of each pane.

- If you want to select columns by patterns in their names (like the ones starting with an A) or by type (integers, decimal numbers, strings, and so on), you can select the other options available on the radio selector on top (**Wildcard/Regex Selection** or **Type Selection**).

The second tab in the configuration window (titled **Advanced**) lets you decide what to do with the duplicate rows once identified (by default, they get removed but you can also keep them and add an extra column specifying whether they are duplicates or not) and which rows should be kept among the duplicates (by default, the first row is kept and all others are removed, but other strategies are available):

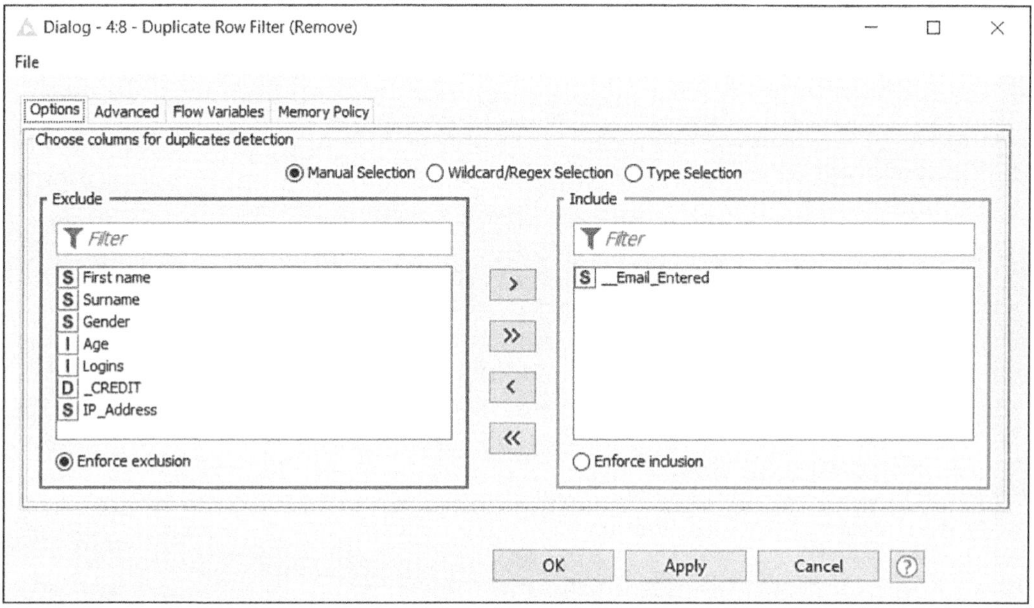

Figure 2.16: Configuration of the Duplicate Row Filter: select which columns to use for detecting duplicate rows

4. Let's implement the Duplicate Row Filter node and connect it with the output port of the Excel Reader. The new node will now show an amber status light, signaling that it can run with its default behavior, although we want to do some configuration first.

5. Double-click on the node to enter its configuration window. Since we don't want to bombard the same user with multiple emails, we should keep one entry per email address, removing all rows having a duplicate address. Hence, from the configuration window, we move all columns to the left and we keep only __Email_Entered on the right. We click on OK and run the node (*F7*).

6. Our curiosity makes it impossible to refrain from checking whether this node has worked well. So, we have a look at the data appearing on its output port (right-click and the last icon with the magnifying lens or *Shift + F6*) and we notice that a couple of rows having duplicated email addresses were removed as expected.

We can now proceed to fix the formatting of names and surnames. To do so, we will start using a very versatile node for working on textual data called String Manipulation.

▶ r[s] ▶ *String Manipulation*

This node (**Manipulation > Column > Convert & Replace**) applies transformations to strings, making it possible to reformat textual data as needed. The node includes a large set of pre-built functions for text manipulation, such as replacement, capitalization, and concatenation, among others:

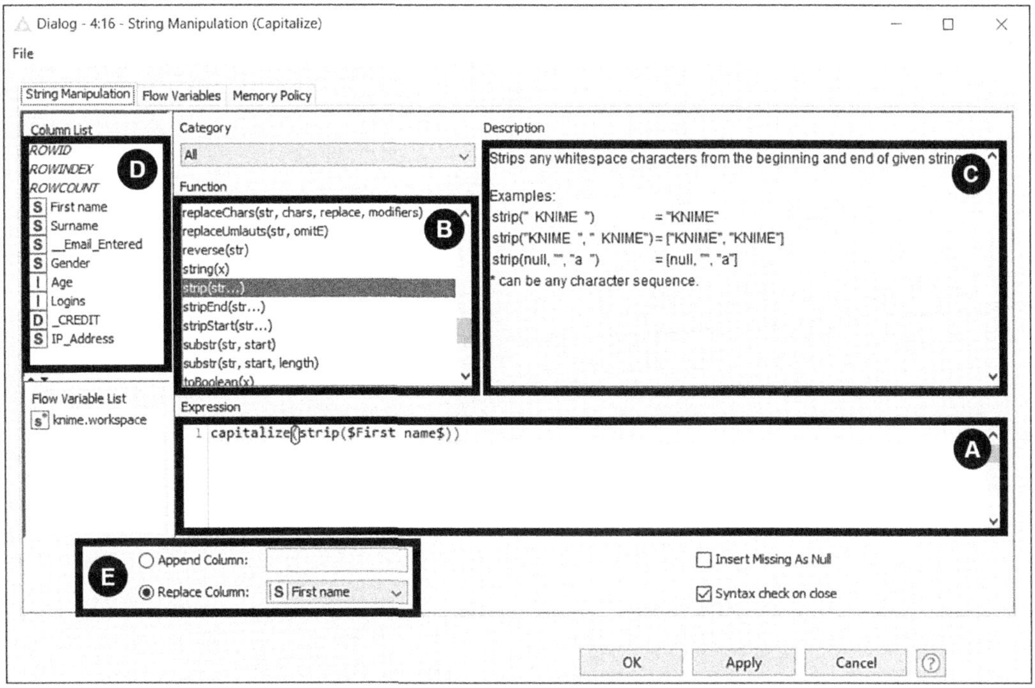

Figure 2.17: String Manipulation: build your text transformation selecting functions and columns to use

The configuration window provides several panels:

A. The **Expression** box is used to specify the overall formula that implements the desired transformation. In most cases, you can build the expression by just using your mouse, clicking on the functions to use and on the columns upon which to apply them.

B. The **Function** list includes all available transformations. For instance, the function upperCase() will convert a string in all-capital letters. When you double-click on a function here, it will get added to your expression.

C. The **Description** box is a handy source of help, showing a description and some examples for each available function as soon as you select it from the list.

D. The **Column List** will show you all available columns in the table. By double-clicking on them, you add them to the expression: they will show with a dollar sign character ($) on either side to indicate a column.

E. At the bottom, you find a radio button to decide where to store your result. You can either **Append** it as a new column or **Replace** an existing one.

Table 2.1 summarizes the most useful functions available within this node.

Function	Description	Example	Result
strip(*x*)	Removes any whitespace from the beginning and the end of a string.	strip(" Hi! ")	"Hi!"
upperCase(*x*), **lowerCase**(*x*)	Converts all characters to upper or lower case.	upperCase("Leonardo")	"LEONARDO"
capitalize(*x*)	Converts first letters of all words in a string to upper case.	capitalize("bill kiddo")	"Bill Kiddo"
compare(*x,y*)	Compares two strings and returns 0 if they are equal and -1 or 1 if they differ, depending on their alphabetical sorting.	compare("Budd","Budd")	0
replace(*x,y,z*)	Replaces all occurrences of substring y within x with z.	replace("cool goose","oo","u")	"cul guse"
removeChars(*x,y*)	Removes from string x all characters included in y.	removeChars("No vowels!","aeiou")	"N wwls!"
join(*x,y,...*)	Concatenates any number of strings in a single string.	join("Hi ","the","re")	"Hi there"
length(*x*)	Counts the number of characters in a string.	length("Analytics is for everyone!")	26

Table 2.1: Useful functions within String Manipulation

This node is perfect for our needs as we have a few strings to manipulate. We need to fix the capitalization of names and surnames, remove those bad-looking whitespaces, and create a new column with the full name:

7. Let's implement the String Manipulation node, dragging it from the repository and connecting the output of the previous node with the input of this new one. Double-click on the node and its configuration dialog appears. Let's start with the column `First name`. We want to see a nice upper-case character at the beginning of every word and we also require whitespaces to be stripped from both ends of the string. Let's build the expression by double-clicking first on `capitalize()` and `strip()` from the **Function** box and then on `First name` from the **Column list**. By clicking in this order, we should have obtained the expression `capitalize(strip($First name$))`, which is exactly what we wanted. In this case, we want to substitute the raw version of the first name with the result of this expression, so we need to select **Replace column** and then `First name`. We are all set so we can click on **OK** and close the window.

8. Now we want to repeat the same for the surname. We'll use another String Manipulation node for it. To make it faster we can also copy and paste the icon of the node from the Workflow Editor, with the usual *Ctrl* + *C* and *Ctrl* + *V* key combinations. We need to repeat the configuration described in the previous step: the only difference is that now we apply it to column `Surname` instead of `First name`. Just make sure that both the expression and the **Replace column** setting refer to `Surname` this time.

9. Both parts of the name look fine now as they show no extra spaces and boast good-looking capitalization. As required by our business case, we need to create a new column carrying the full name of each user, combining first name and surname. Once again, we can use the String Manipulation node for this: let's get one more node of these in the Workflow Editor, make the connection, and open the configuration page. This time, we need to concatenate two strings so we can leverage the `join()` function. Let's double-click first on `join()` from the **Function** box and then on `First name` from the **Column list**. Since we want names and surnames to be separated by a blank space, we need to add this character on the expression, by typing the sequence `," ",` in the expression box just after `$First name$`. We complete the expression by double-clicking on the column `Surname` and we are done. The overall expression should be: `join($First name$," ",$Surname$)`. Before closing, we need to decide where to store the result. This time we want to create a new column so we select **Append** and then type the name of the new column, which could be Full name. Click on **OK** and check the results.

> Since in the end, we are going to keep only the `Full name` column, we could have combined the last three nodes in a single one. In fact, `Full name` can be created at once with the expression: `join(capitalize(strip($First name$))," ",capitalize(strip($Surname$)))`.
>
> We took the longer route to get some practice with the node. It's up to you to decide which version to keep in your workflow.

With all names fixed, we can move on to the next hurdle and remove the ill-formatted email addresses. It's time to introduce a new node that will be ubiquitous in our future KNIME workflows: Row Filter.

► ⇌ ► *Row Filter*

This node (**Manipulation > Row > Filter**) applies filters on rows according to the criteria you specify. Such criteria can either be based on values of a specific column to test (like *all strings starting with A* or *all numbers greater than 5.2*) or on the position of the row in the table (for instance *only the top 20 rows*). To configure the node, you need to first specify the type of criteria you would like to apply using the selector on the left. You also need to specify if those rows that match your criteria should be kept in your workflow (**Include rows...**) or should be dropped, keeping all others (**Exclude rows...**). You have multiple ways to specify the criteria behind your filtering:

- Filter by **attribute value**: In this case, you will be presented on the right with the full list of columns available so that you can pick the one to consider for the filtering (**Column to test**). Once you pick the column, you need to describe the logic for the selection in the box below (**Matching criteria**). You have three options:

- The first one (**use pattern matching**) will check if the value (considered as a string) adheres to the pattern you specify in the textbox. You can enter a specific value like maria: this will match rows like "MARIA" or "Maria," unless you check the **case sensitive match** option, which would consider the lower and upper cases as different. Another option is to use wild cards in your search pattern (remember to tick **contains wild cards**): in this case, the star character "*" will stand for any sequence of characters (so "M*" selects all names starting with "M" like "Mary" and "Mario") while the question mark "?" will match any single character ("H?" refers to any string of two characters starting with "H," so it will include "Hi" and exclude "Hello"). If you want to implement more complex searches, you could also use the powerful **Regular Expressions (RegEx)**, which offer great flexibility in setting criteria.

- The second one (**use range checking**) is great with numbers as it lets you set any kind of interval: you can specify a lower bound (including all numbers that are greater or equal than that) or an upper bound (lower or equal) or both (making it a closed interval).

> Remember that bounds are always considered as included in the interval. If you want to exclude the endpoint of an interval, you need to reverse the logic of your filtering. For instance, if you want to include all non-zero, positive numbers you need to select the option **Exclude rows by attribute value** and set 0 as the upper bound.

- The third option is to match only the rows that have a missing value in the column under test.

- Filter by **row number**: This way you can specify which is the first and the last row to match, considering the current sorting order in the table. So if you put 1 in the **First row number** selector and then 1 in **Last row number**, you will match only the top 10 rows of the table. If you want to match only the rows after a certain position, like from the 100th onwards, you can set the threshold in the first selector (100) and tick the check box below (**to the end of the table**).

- Filter by **row ID**: You could test row IDs against some regular expressions as well, although this route is rarely used:

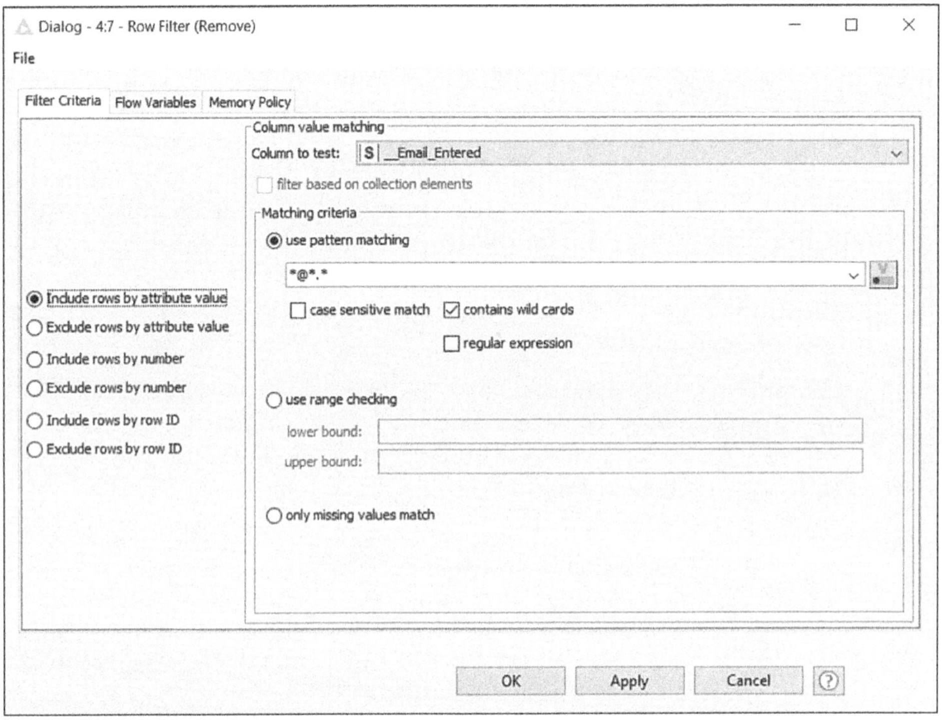

Figure 2.18: Configuration dialog for Row Filter: specify which rows to keep or remove from your table

If your filtering criteria require several columns to be tested, you can use multiple instances of this node in a series, each time looking at a different column. An alternative is to use a different node called Rule-based Row Filter, which lets you define several rules for filtering at once. Other nodes, such as **Row Filter (Labs)** and **Rule-based Row Filter (Dictionary)**, can do more sophisticated filtering if needed. Check them out if you need to.

Let's see our new node in action straight away as we filter out all the email addresses that do not look valid:

10. Implement the **Row Filter** node, connect it downstream, and open its configuration dialog by double-clicking on it. Since we want to keep only the rows matching certain column criteria, let's select the first option from the radio button on the left (**Include rows by attribute value**) and, on the right, pick the column with the email address __Email_Entered. One simple pattern we can use for checking the validity of an email address is the wild card expression *@*.*. This will check for all strings that have at least an @ symbol followed by a dot . with some text in between. This is not going to be the most thorough validity check for email addresses, but it will certainly spot the ones that are clearly irregular and is good enough for us at this stage. Remember to tick the **contains wild cards** checkbox and click **OK** to move on.

11. We have yet more filtering to be done. We want to remove all rows displaying a negative credit: those users are inactive and should not be added to our mailing list. Let's implement an additional Row Filter node and put it next to the previous one, creating the right connections across the ports. We will again use the **Include rows by attribute value** option but the matching criteria will be set as range checking (second radio button on the right). By setting 0 as **Lower bound**, we are good to go since all negative values will be filtered out. We can click **OK** and move on to the next challenge.

At this point, we want to manage the little red question marks appearing here and there in the table, signaling that some values are missing. Also, in this case, KNIME offers a powerful node to manage this situation quickly, with a couple of clicks.

► ? ► *Missing Value*

The node (**Manipulation > Column > Transform**) handles missing values (NULLs) in a table, offering multiple methods for imputing the best available replacement. In the first tab of the configuration window (**Default**), you can define a default treatment option for all columns of a certain data type (strings, integer, and double) by selecting it in the dropdown menus. The second tab (**Column settings**) allows you to set a specific strategy for each individual column by double-clicking on the name of the column from the list on the left and setting the strategy through the menu that will appear.

> Unless you have a large number of columns that you want to treat with the same missing value strategy, it's best to be explicit and use the second tab. That way you only impute missing values for the precise columns specified.

You have a vast list of possible methods to treat your missing values. The most useful ones are:

- **Remove Row**: Gets rid of the row altogether if the value is missing.

- **Fix Value**: Replaces the NULL with a specific value you have to enter in the box that will appear below. All rows with missing values will get the same fix replacement.

- **Minimum/Maximum/Mean/Median/Most Frequent Value**: Calculates a summary statistic on the distribution over all existing values in the column and uses it as a fixed replacement value.

> If you substitute missing values with the median of a numeric column, your imputed values are going to stick "in the middle" of the existing distribution, making your inference less disruptive and more robust. Of course, this will depend on your business cases and on the actual distribution of data, but it's worth giving this approach a try.

- **Previous/Next**: Replaces the missing value with the previous or the next non-missing value in the column, using the current order of rows in the table.

- **Linear Interpolation**: Substitutes missing values with the linear interpolation between the previous and the next non-missing values in the column. If your column represents values changing over time (we call them time series), this handler might offer a smooth way to fill the gaps.

- **Moving Average**: Substitutes the missing values with a moving average calculated over a certain number of non-missing values appearing in the table just before the missing value (**lookbehind window**) or after it (**lookahead window**). For instance, if you have for a column a sequence of values such as [2, 3, 4, NULL] and you apply a lookbehind window of size 2, the NULL value will be substituted for 3.5, which is the average of 3 and 4. For this and the previous handlers, you want to make sure your table is properly sorted (like, in a time series, by increasing time).

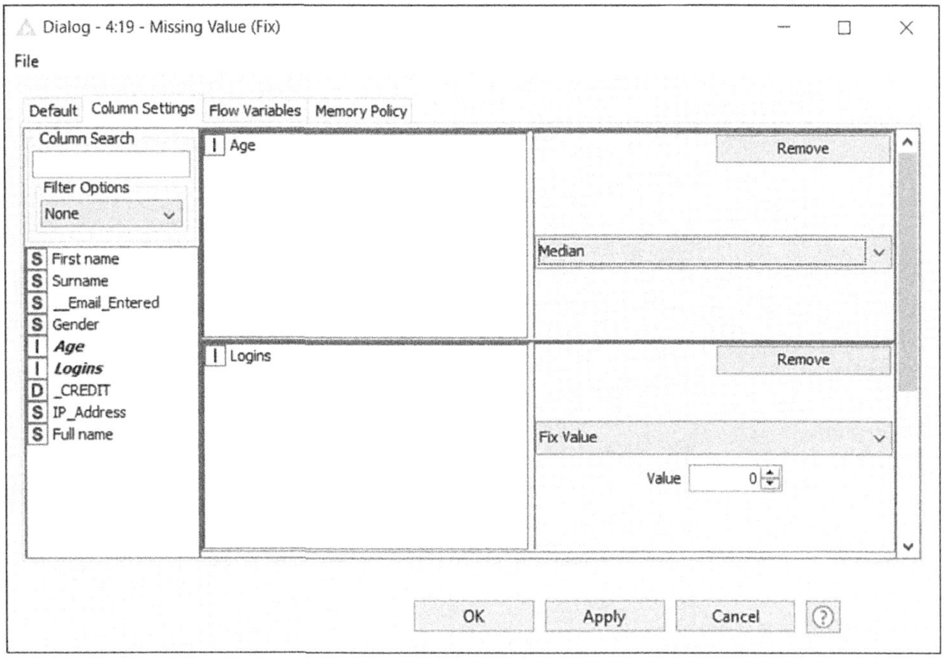

Figure 2.19: Configuration of Missing Value: decide how to manage the empty spots of your table

Going back to our case, we noticed that we have two columns displaying some question marks. Let's manage them appropriately by leveraging the Missing Value node:

12. Drag the Missing Value node on your workflow and connect it properly. Let's jump straight to the second tab of its configuration window (**Column settings**), as we want to keep control of which handling strategy we shall adopt for each column in need. For column Age (double-click on it from the list on the left), we can select **Median**: by doing so, we will assign an age to those users missing one that is not "far off" the age that most users tend to have in our table. When it comes to the number of times users have logged in (Logins column) we assume that the lack of a value means that they haven't logged in yet. So the best strategy to select will be **Fix Value**, keeping 0 as a default value for all. We can click on OK and close this dialog.

13. Let's check how our chain of transformations is looking at the minute. If we click on the last node, execute it (*F7*), and check its output port view (*Shift + F6*), we can breathe a sigh of relief: no missing values, no negative credits, and both names and email addresses look reasonably formatted.

The only steps left ahead of us are of an aesthetic nature: we want to drop the columns we don't need, sort the ones remaining, and give them a more intuitive name, before finally saving the output file. We are going to need a few more nodes to complete this last bit.

▶ 🔀 ▶ *Column Filter*

This node (**Manipulation > Column > Filter**) drops unneeded columns in a table. The only required step for its configuration is to select which columns to keep at the output port (the green box on the right) and which ones to filter out (the red box on the left):

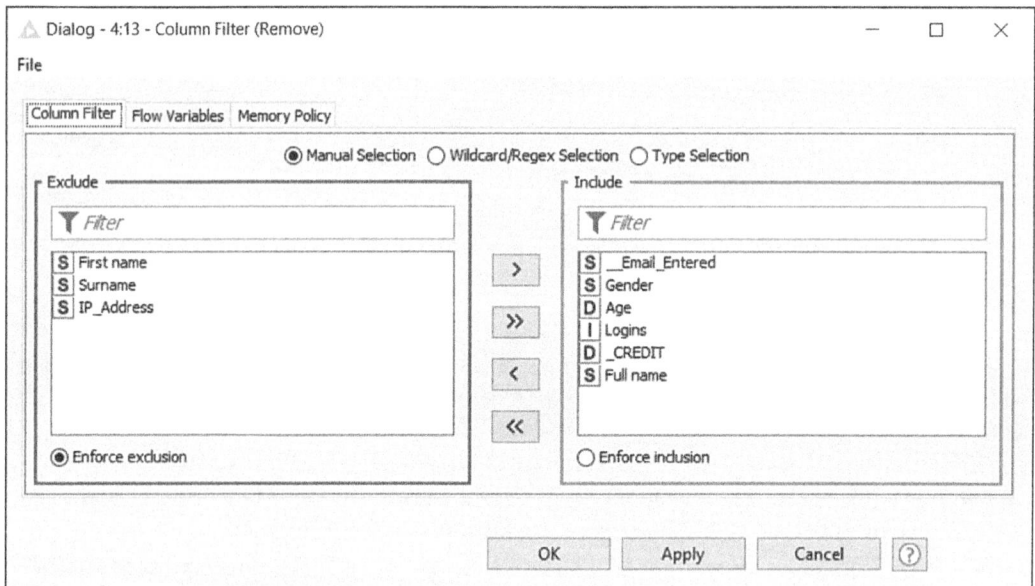

Figure 2.20: Configuration of Column Filter: which columns would you like to keep?

14. Add the Column Filter node to the workflow and exclude the columns we no longer need (First Name, Surname, and IP_Address) by moving them onto the left panel.

► ᴀ⅂ ► *Column Rename*

The node lets you change the names and the data types of columns. To configure it, double-click on the columns you would like to edit (you'll find a list on the left) and tick the **Change** box: you will then be able to enter the new names in the box beside. To change the data type of a column and convert all its values, you can use the drop-down menu on the right. The menu will be prepopulated with a list of possible data types each column can be safely converted into:

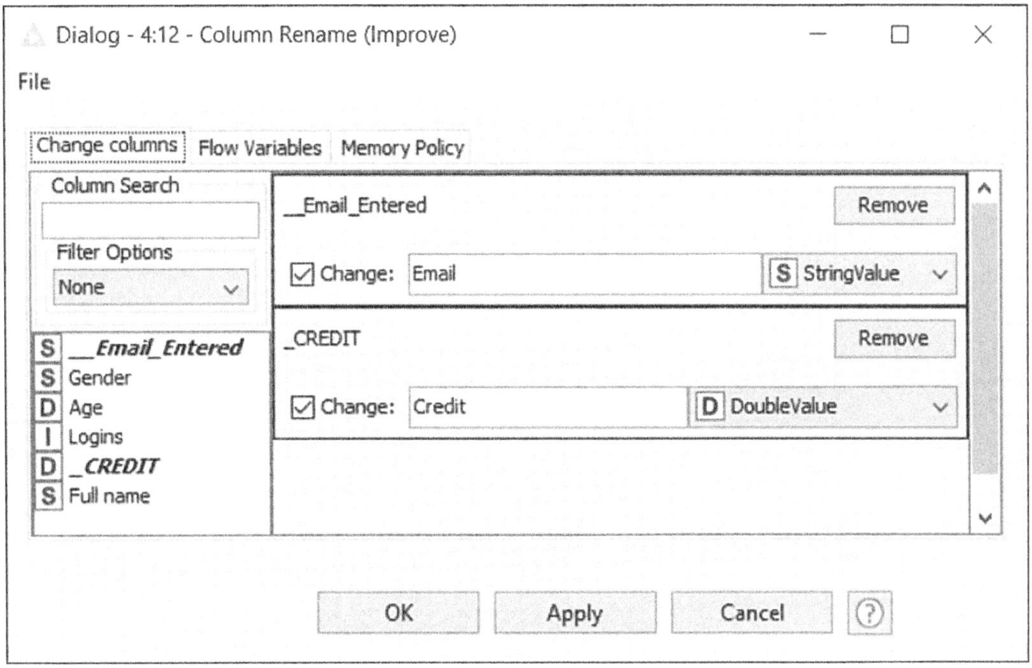

Figure 2.21: Configuration of Column Rename: pick the best names for your columns

15. We can now use the Column Rename node to change the headers in our table. The only ones that need some makeup are __Email_Entered, which can become simply Email, and _Credit, which can be renamed to Credit.

► ⊞ ► *Column Resorter*

This node (available in **Manipulation > Column > Transform**) changes the order of columns in a table. In the configuration window, you will find, on the left, all columns available at the input port, and on the right, a series of buttons to move them around. Select the column you wish to move across and then click on the different buttons to move columns up or down, place columns first or last in the table, or sort them in alphabetical order. If different columns appear at the input port (imagine the case where your source file is coming in with some new columns), they will be placed where the **<any unknown new column>** placeholder lies:

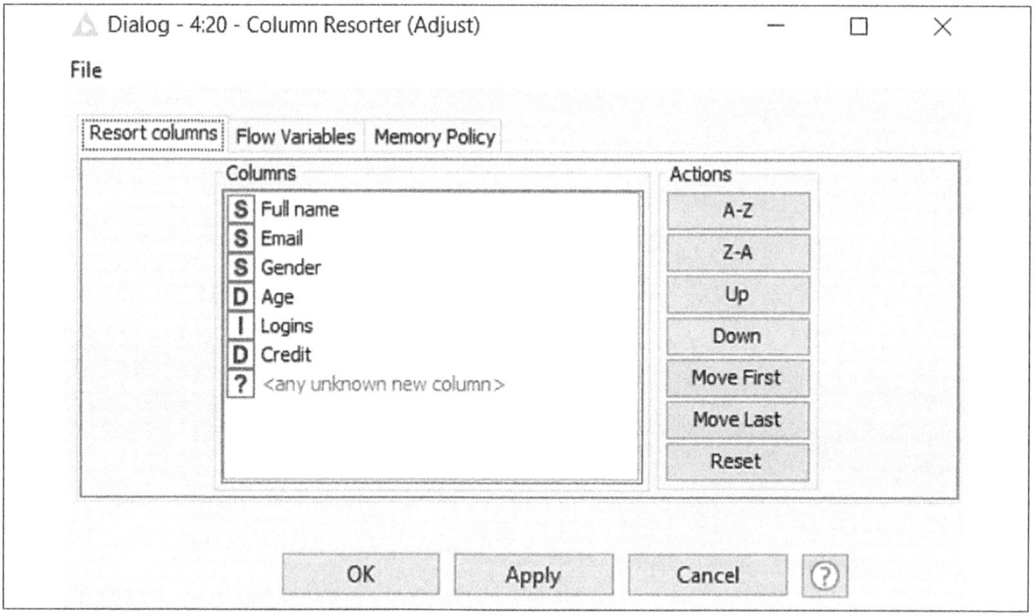

Figure 2.22: Configuration of Column Resorter: shuffle your columns to the desired order

16. The last transformation required is to slightly change the order of columns in the table. In fact, the **Full name** column was added earlier in the process and ended up appearing as the last column while we would like it to be the first. Just select the column and click on **Move First** to fix it as needed.

⊞ *CSV Writer*

This node (**IO > Write**) saves the input data table into a CSV file on the local disk or to a remote location. The only required configuration step is to specify the full path of the file to create: you can click on the **Browse...** button to select the desired folder. The other configuration steps (not required) let you: change the format of the resulting CSV file like column delimiters (**Format** section), keep or remove headers as the first row (**Write column header**), and compress the newly generated file in .gzip format to save space on disk (go to the **Advanced Settings** tab for this):

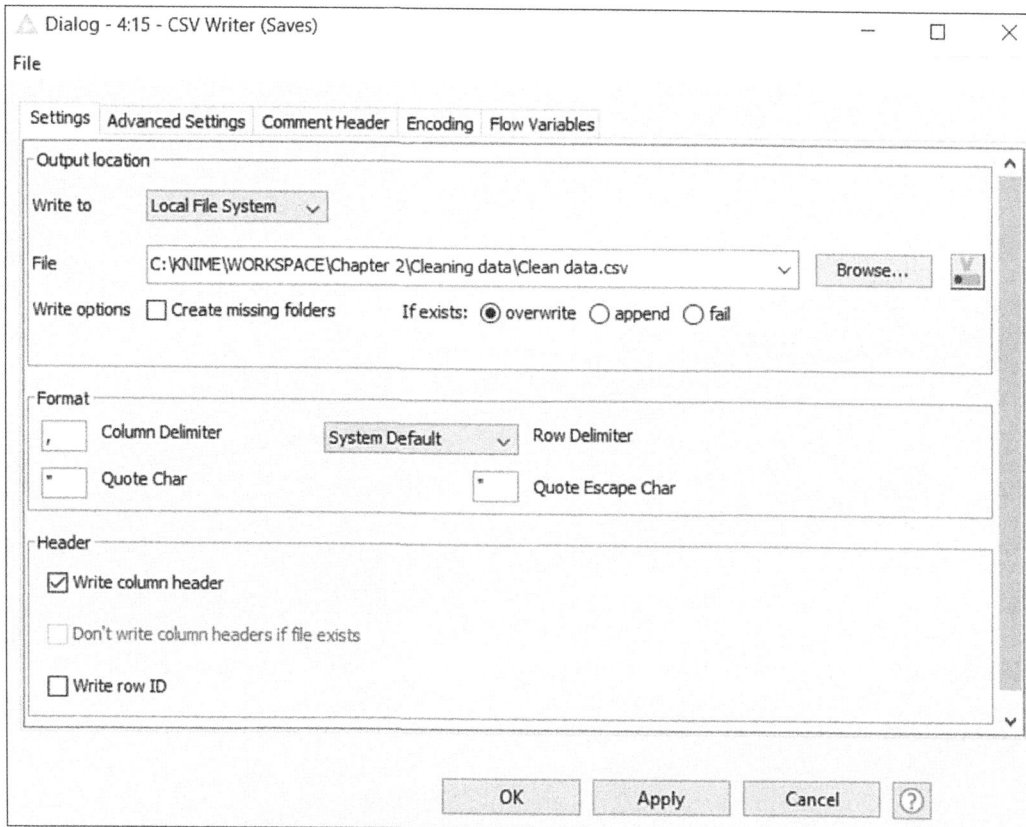

Figure 2.23: Configuration of CSV Writer: save your table as a text file

17. The very last step of our process is to save our good-looking table as a CSV file. We implement the CSV Writer node, connect it, and do the only piece of required configuration, which is to specify where to save the new file and how to name it. Click **OK** to close the window and execute the node to finally write the file on your disk.

Well done for completing your second data workflow! The routine required for building a clean mailing list out of a messy raw dataset required a dozen nodes and some of our time, but the effort was certainly worth it. Now we can clean up any number of records whenever we like by just re-running the same workflow, making sure that the name of the input file and its path stay the same. To do so, you will just need to: reset the workflow (right-click on the name of the workflow in the Explorer on the left and then click on **Reset** or just reset the first node pressing *F8* after having selected it), and execute it again (the simplest way is to just press *Shift + F7* on your keyboard or execute the last node with a right-click and select **Execute**):

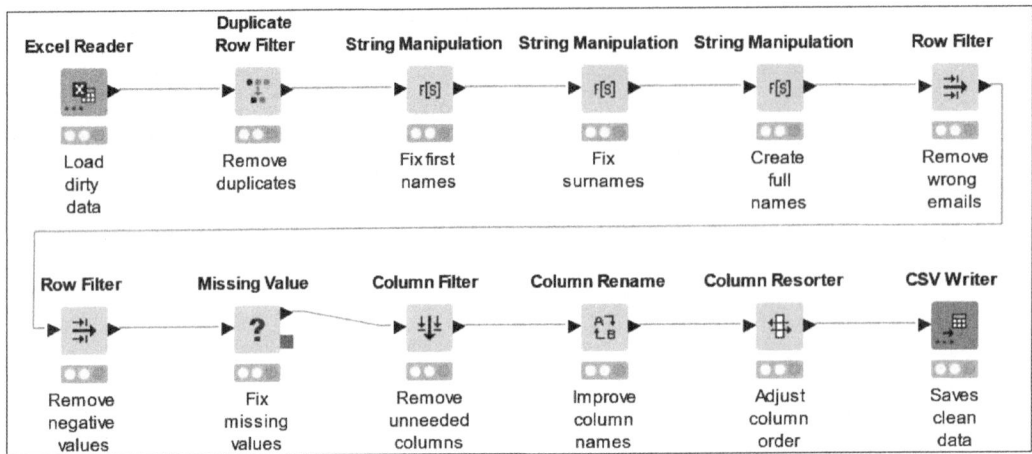

Figure 2.24: The full data cleaning workflow: twelve nodes to make our user data spotless

Summary

This chapter introduced us to KNIME, the new addition to our data analytics toolbox. We learned what KNIME is in a nutshell and got started with its user interface, which enables us to combine simple computation units (nodes) into more complex analytical routines (workflows) with speed and agility, without having to write extensive code. We got started with the ever-present preliminary steps of any data work: loading and cleaning up data to make it usable for doing analytics. We got acquainted with twelve basic nodes in KNIME that empowered us to create repeatable routines, which include: opening files in different formats, sorting and filtering data following some logic, manipulating strings, and managing missing values and duplicate rows. Not bad for being just on the second chapter!

Having the basics clearly explained, we can now dare to go further with KNIME. In the next chapter, *Chapter 3, Transforming Data*, we will learn how to work on multiple data tables and to build more complex data workflows for analyzing real-world data feeds.

3
Transforming Data

Now that we have the basics of KNIME at hand, we can move to the next level. In this chapter, we will learn how to transform data to make the best out of it systematically. The following pages will show how to work with multiple tables, aggregate data points, apply expressions, and iterate through your workflows to automating their execution. All these new skills will make you an autonomous user of KNIME when manipulating real-world data.

This chapter will answer the following questions:

- What is a data model, and how can I visualize it?
- How can I combine several data tables?
- How can I aggregate data points and calculate formulas?
- How can KNIME automate the creation of summary reports?
- What do variables and loops look like in KNIME?

This chapter will end with a full tutorial based on real data and a very realistic business case: it will be an opportunity to put into practice all you've learned so far about KNIME while confronting the complexity of data you will face in your work. Before diving into the concrete ways to transform data, let's invest a few minutes in the fundamentals of relational databases and data models.

Modeling your data

Data tables are hardly useful when they lie apart. In fact, by organizing them together in a database, we amplify their overall value as we unveil patterns and connections across data points. That is why data is typically stored in an ensemble of different tables connected with each other to virtually form a single body called a **Data Model**. When you work with multiple tables, it is beneficial to "visualize" what the underlying data model looks like: this gives you the ability to anticipate ways to leverage the data and interpret it correctly.

We shall bring the concept of a data model to life by going through a business example. Let's imagine that we own a small store selling musical instruments. Our business model is pretty simple: we order instruments from manufacturers and store them in a warehouse. Customers call at our shop and get the chance to try a few instruments before deciding whether to purchase or not. Our most loyal customers sign up and get a membership card: occasionally, they receive a newsletter with new arrivals and special offers.

To manage our store's activities, we use a simple information system that keeps track of products, sales, inventory, and customers. Data is organized in a simple database, made of four different tables, each having multiple columns, whose names are — fortunately — self-explanatory:

- **Product Master Data**: This stores the list of products we buy and sell. For each product, we have a unique *Product_ID*, a *Category* (like Guitars, Violins, and Pianos), a short *Description* (which includes the model of the instrument), the *Brand*, and the *List_price*.

- **Sales Transactions**: This records all sales. Every row includes the *Date* of purchase, the *Receipt_ID* (counting the number of receipts created during each day), the *Product_ID*, the *Quantity* (number of items purchased), the *Discount_rate* that was applied (if any), the overall *Amount* paid, and — if the customers are members of our loyalty card program — their *Customer_ID*.

- **Customer Master Data**: This carries preferences and contact details related to our loyalty card members. It includes the unique *Customer_ID*, *Full_Name*, *ZIP_Code* of where they live, *Email_Address*, *Telephone* number, and their primary *Instrument*.

- **Inventory Transactions**: This accounts for all product movements in our warehouse, such as the loading of the items as they arrive and transferring them to the shop floor. Its columns are *Date* (which includes the time when it happened), *Product_ID*, and *Quantity* (this will be positive when items are loaded in and negative when they leave the warehouse).

By looking at this simple example, we can observe a few features that are worth elaborating on as they apply to most databases we would encounter in our work:

- We see two different types of tables fulfilling two different needs: **Master Data** and **Transactional** tables. Master data tables aim at describing entities of business relevance, such as products, customers, suppliers, employees, and so on. In these kinds of tables, each row corresponds to an instance of the entity (for example, a specific product, or an individual customer), while every column describes a different aspect of the entity (like its name or description). On the other hand, transactional tables record events (like a monetary transaction, a sale, an order) occurring at a specific point in time. Every row corresponds to an event, while columns describe the event's features and the entities that took part in it. Master data and transactional data tend to be updated and used in different fashions: master data tables are touched more rarely than transactional tables. Think about the frequency of adding a new product to the catalog or hiring an employee: these events occur much less often than regular sales or inventory movements do.

- The tables are clearly connected to each other. In fact, many of their columns represent the same thing. For instance, *Product_ID*s of sold items are the same *Product_ID*s we find in the product master data. The two tables are related and, indeed, databases of this kind — omnipresent in firms — are called **Relational Databases**. The columns used to connect multiple tables are called **Keys**: when the rows of two tables have matching values in their keys, it means that these rows are connected and refer to the same event or entity. This means that all rows in the sales transactional table having a specific value in the column *Product_ID* (let's say *PS012*) refer to sales of the same product. Thanks to the relationship occurring across the tables, you can then find the product's description by looking up the value of *Product_ID* in the product master data (where you will find that *PS012* refers to — in this case — a *Steinway piano*).

A simple and effective way of describing the underlying data model of a relational database is through the **Entity-Relationship (ER) Diagram**. The ER diagram looks like a series of boxes connected with each other: each box is a table and displays its columns while the connections show the existing relationships across keys. *Figure 3.1* represents a simplified rendering of the ER diagram of our music store database: keys are highlighted with a bold font and a little icon:

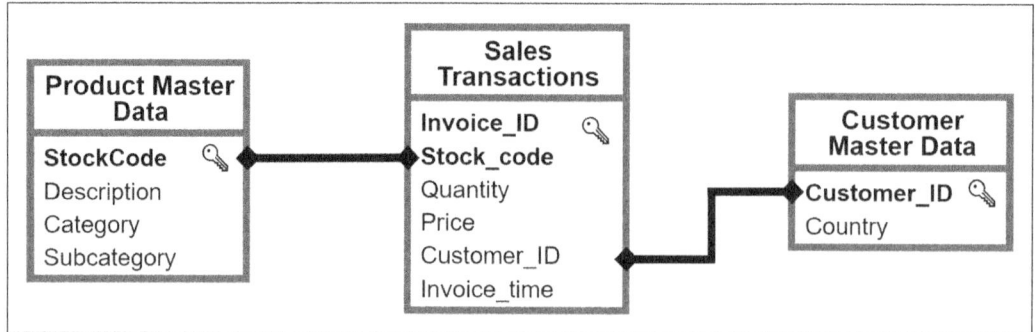

Figure 3.1: The Entity-Relationship diagram of the music store database

We will encounter diagrams of this kind throughout this book. I suggest you make the effort to sketch the ER diagrams of those tables you use at work the most, as it will simplify your thinking on how to best leverage them. In fact, mapping all the data available in the various systems of a firm is a tough but worthwhile exercise.

Keeping this mapping up to date and — in general — managing data assets in a firm requires discipline and a set of formal roles, processes, and standards called **Data Governance**. A good (and often underestimated) practice of data governance is, indeed, to create a **Data Inventory**: this is a systematic description of all information assets in a company. As you build an inventory, you are forced to map master data and transactional tables correctly, spotting duplications and missing keys.

A data inventory includes information about the data stored in tables, such as content, source, owners, and licensing: these are all examples of **Metadata**, a word that literally means "data about data."

Combining tables

Data models show us how data points within separate tables are logically connected with each other. In the practice of data analytics, we often need to combine data together by leveraging the logic relationships which the data model describes. The most common operation for combining two tables into a third one is called **Join**. By combining two tables together, we cross-enrich them as we merge all the information we have on a specific event or entity. The join operation will take the two tables and match the rows that have the same values in the columns we specify (**Matching Columns**). Let's imagine we have the following two tables, which refer to sales transactions and to the product master data:

Sales		
Product	Date	Amount
Gibson Explorer B-2	21-Dec	1040
Squier Affinity	21-Dec	249
Yamaha YDP-164	22-Dec	1499
Squier Affinity	22-Dec	249

Table 3.1: Sales table

Products	
Product	Category
Gibson Explorer B-2	Guitars
Squier Affinity	Guitars
Yamaha YDP-164	Pianos

Table 3.2: Products table

What if we need to calculate the overall sales generated by each product category? The first table tells us the amount of sales for each transaction but misses the category information so we cannot aggregate those sales accordingly. The second table has the category bit but doesn't tell us anything about sales. Each table is missing something, so we need to combine them by means of a join. The good news is that the two tables share a column (*Product*), which could serve for doing the matching. Let's join them together using *Product* as a matching column:

Join of the two tables above			
Product	Date	Amount	Category
Gibson Explorer B-2	21-Dec	1040	Guitars
Squier Affinity	21-Dec	449	Guitars
Yamaha YDP-164	22-Dec	1499	Piano
Squier Affinity	22-Dec	249	Guitars

Table 3.3: Joining the Products table and the Sales table

See what happens? By joining the two tables, we obtain a third one as an output where we have, for each transaction, not only the product name, date, and amount (which would only be available in the first table) but also the category of each product (which is only available in the second table). This table can now be used for calculating how much sales are generated by each product category by just running the right aggregations (which we'll learn how to do in a few pages).

To complete our introduction to joins, let's consider one last aspect. Even if two tables have some columns in common (which could be leveraged for our matching), they will not necessarily have a correspondence between every row of their own and a row in the other table. In the earlier example, we might have, for instance, some transactions that refer to instruments not included in the product master data (maybe they are new arrivals and haven't been categorized yet) or the other way around (products available in the master data that haven't sold yet). If we combine tables without a perfect matching of the rows, the output might carry some blanks (the famous NULL values we met in the previous chapter) since we don't have a corresponding value to use. Depending on our strategy to manage such missing matches (and the resulting incomplete rows in the output), we can implement different types of joins. Let's imagine that we want to join the following two tables (by convention, the two tables combined in a join operation are called **Left** and **Right** table, hence the name of the headers in the following tables):

Left table: Sales		
Product	**Date**	**Amount**
Gibson Explorer B-2	21-Dec	1040
Squier Affinity	21-Dec	249
Korg B2	21-Dec	499
Yamaha YDP-164	22-Dec	1274
Squier Affinity	22-Dec	249
Didgeridoo Black 2	22-Dec	459

Table 3.4: Left table

Right table: Products	
Product	**Category**
Gibson Explorer B-2	Guitars
Squier Affinity	Guitars
Yamaha YDP-164	Pianos
Korg B2	Pianos
Steinway B-211	Pianos
American Jazz-5	Basses

Table 3.5: Right table

Notice that some products have no corresponding matches in the other table, as the following Venn diagram intuitively displays:

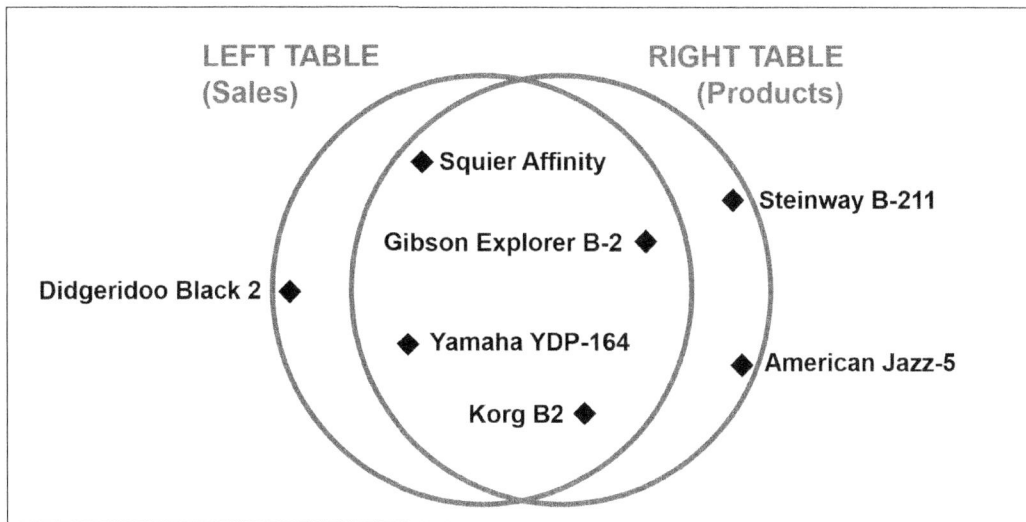

Figure 3.2: Venn diagram of Sales and Product tables: not all instruments are present in both tables

Depending on how we prefer to manage the "non-matching" rows in the resulting output table, we have four different types of joins:

- **Inner Join**: In this case, we only keep the rows with a match in both tables. We focus on the intersection of the keys across the two columns. By doing so, we avoid generating any NULL value due to non-matching keys. On the other side, we might be neglecting some rows which — even if incomplete — carry some valuable information, like sales of products not yet categorized.

- **Left Outer Join**: This type of join will keep all the rows existing in the left table, even those that have no match in the right table. In this way, we might incur some NULL values in the output, but we "preserve" the information stored in the left table.

- **Right Outer Join**: This one is just the opposite of the previous one and will preserve all the rows in the right table, including the ones without a match in the left one.

- **Full Outer Join**: We go for this option when we cannot afford to lose anything! All rows in the two tables will be kept, even if they don't have a match. This is the option that could potentially create most NULL values: it's the price to pay to conserve all data.

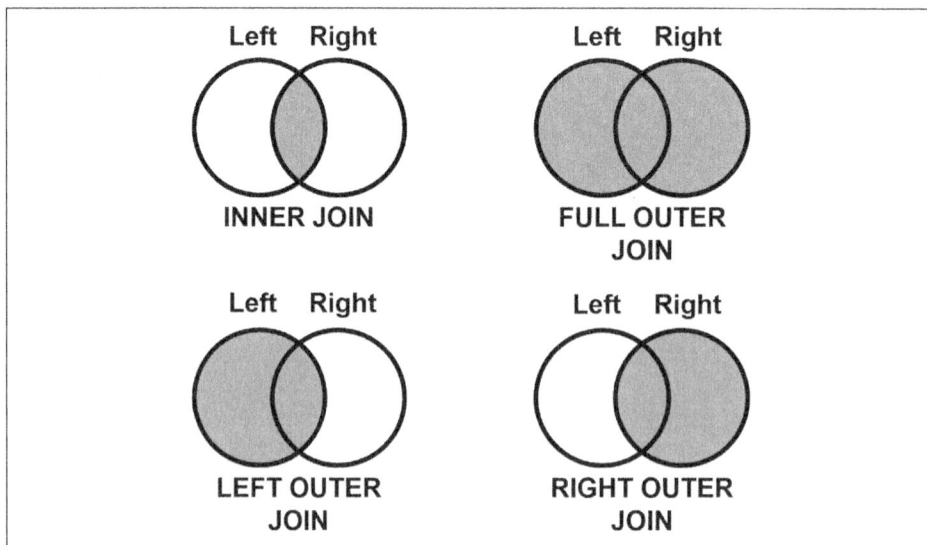

Figure 3.3: The four types of join: decide which rows you want to keep in the output

In *Table 3.6*, you will find the results of applying the four types of joins: the NULL values are displayed as a question mark, as you would find in KNIME. The Inner Join has no NULL values, as anticipated:

Inner Join			
Product	**Date**	**Amount**	**Category**
Gibson Explorer B-2	21-Dec	1040	Guitars
Squier Affinity	21-Dec	249	Guitars
Korg B2	21-Dec	499	Piano
Yamaha YDP-164	22-Dec	1274	Piano
Squier Affinity	22-Dec	249	Guitars

Table 3.6: Inner Join

In the Left Outer Join, we will have a row referring to the Didgeridoo sales, even if it is yet uncategorized. What probably happened with this peculiar Aboriginal instrument is that it is a new shiny arrival that attracted the attention of a customer quickly, before we had the time to update the product master table by adding it:

Left Outer Join			
Product	**Date**	**Amount**	**Category**
Gibson Explorer B-2	21-Dec	1040	Guitars
Squier Affinity	21-Dec	249	Guitars
Korg B2	21-Dec	499	Piano
Yamaha YDP-164	22-Dec	1499	Piano
Squier Affinity	22-Dec	249	Guitars
Didgeridoo Black 2	22-Dec	459	?

Table 3.7: Left Outer Join

In the Right Outer Join, we are also forcing a row for those instruments that, given their price, have not sold yet. This view can be beneficial to discover products that might require some more advertisement in our next newsletters:

Right Outer Join			
Product	**Date**	**Amount**	**Category**
Gibson Explorer B-2	21-Dec	1040	Guitars
Squier Affinity	21-Dec	249	Guitars
Korg B2	21-Dec	499	Piano
Yamaha YDP-164	22-Dec	1499	Piano
Squier Affinity	22-Dec	249	Guitars
Steinway B-211	?	?	Pianos
American Jazz-5	?	?	Basses

Table 3.8: Right Outer Join

The Full Outer Join will contain not only the products that never sold but also the ones that haven't been categorized yet. Creating such a table can help us summarize sales by category and spot uncategorized and unsold products all at once:

Full Outer Join			
Product	**Date**	**Amount**	**Category**
Gibson Explorer B-2	21-Dec	1040	Guitars
Squier Affinity	21-Dec	249	Guitars
Korg B2	21-Dec	499	Piano
Yamaha YDP-164	22-Dec	1499	Piano
Squier Affinity	22-Dec	249	Guitars
Didgeridoo Black 2	22-Dec	459	?
Steinway B-211	?	?	Pianos
American Jazz-5	?	?	Basses

Table 3.9: Full Outer Join

As this simple example unveiled for us, there might be value in any type of join. As data practitioners, we want to know what options we have available so that we can select which one to use, depending on the business case we face.

To perform joins in KNIME, we can leverage a very useful node which is called — unsurprisingly, we shall admit — **Joiner**.

Joiner

The node (available in **Manipulation > Column > Split & Combine**) joins the two tables connected at its input ports according to the user-provided matching criteria. To con-figure it (*Figure 3.4*), you first need to specify the criteria for the join by choosing the couple of columns in the two tables that are related and should match. To add the first couple of columns, click on the button labeled **Add matching criterion**. You will find two drop-down menus with the available columns of the tables connected with the upper and the lower input ports (by convention, they refer, to the **left** and the **right** tables of the join operation, respectively). You can add or remove columns to be matched by clicking on the + and the – buttons on the right. By default, all the couples of columns you enter here need to have matching values for rows to be matched. They also need to be of the same type (integers matching with integers, string match-ing with strings, and so on).

> To solve unmatching data types, the node allows you to convert the data types of the columns before assessing the matching criteria. For example, from the selector labeled as **Compare value in join columns by**, you can pick **string representation** to convert all values to strings before checking if they match.

After clarifying the matching criteria, you need to decide the type of join operation you would like to perform (**Inner**, **Left outer**, **Right outer**, or **Full outer**). To do so, use the Venn diagrams you find in *Figure 3.3* as a guide. If you want an inner join, only the **Matching rows** box needs to stay selected. For the left or right outer joins, you have to tick also the Left or the **Right unmatched rows**, respectively. For the full outer, all box-es should be selected. As you noticed from its icon, the node has three outputs. The first output port on the top carries the result of the join. You can also decide to review the rows that did not find any match in the other table and place them in the second and third output ports. If you are interested in viewing the unmatched rows as well (it might be useful sometimes to understand why not all rows match), you need to tick the **Route unmatched rows to separate ports** box: this will activate the second and third ports which would — otherwise — stay inactive and marked with a red cross.

One last option that you would select in most cases is **Merge joining columns**: by doing so, you keep only one "copy" of the pair of columns used to assess the matching. If you leave it unticked, you will keep both the two columns which were coming from the left and the right input tables: in most cases you don't want that so this box should be al-ways selected.

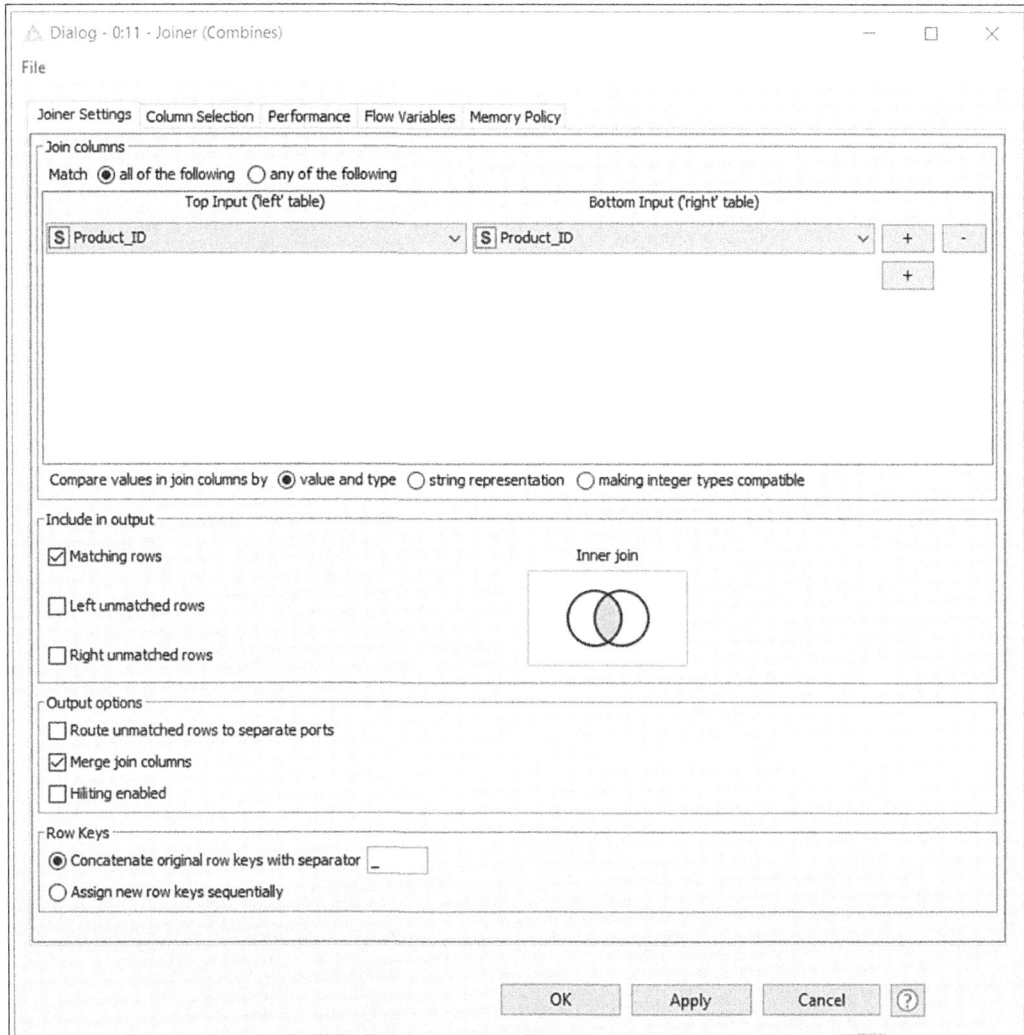

Figure 3.4: Configuration dialog of Joiner: select which columns should match

In the second tab of the configuration dialog (**Column Selection**), you can specify which columns resulting from the join operation should be kept at the output port of the node. This might be handy when you know you will not need some of the columns in the subsequent steps of your workflow: in this case, just go through the columns in the boxes on the right and double-click on the ones to remove:

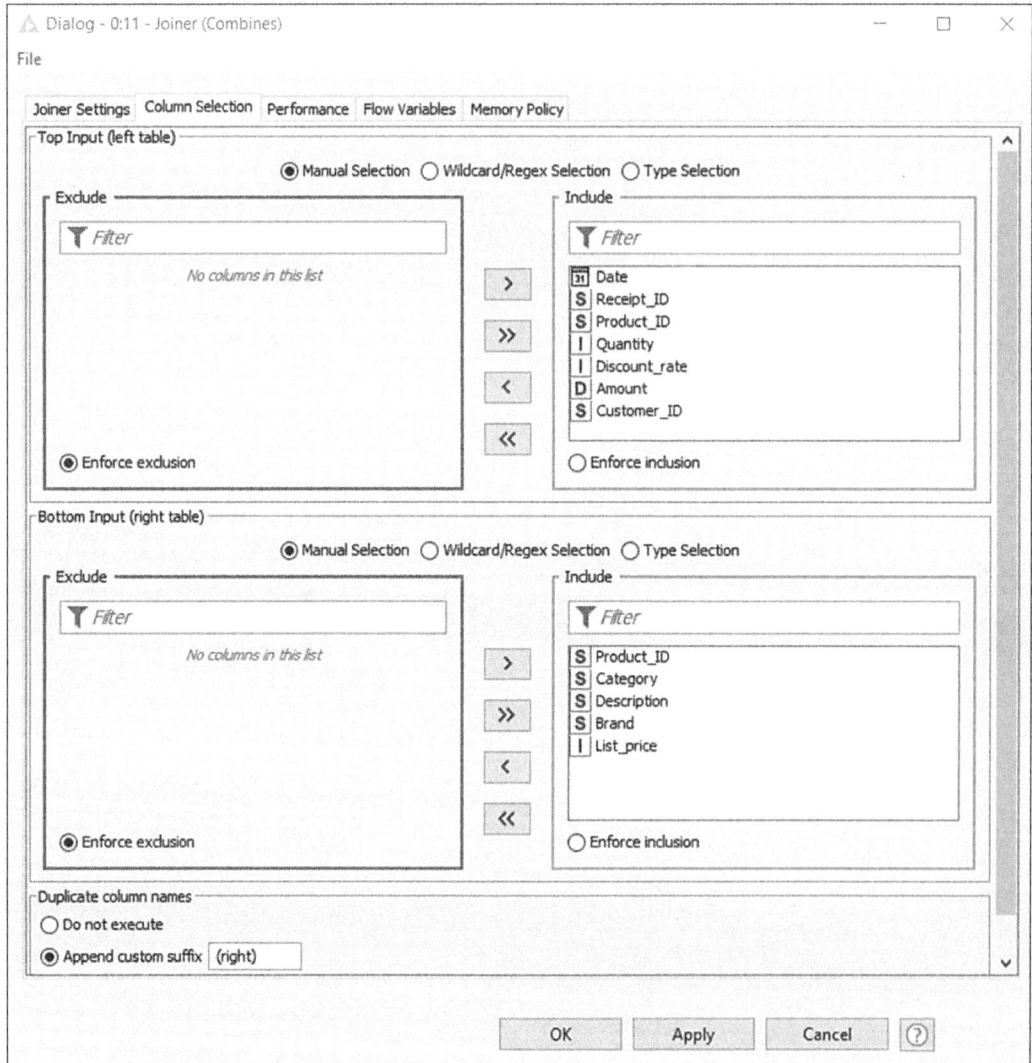

Figure 3.5: Configuration dialog of Joiner: select which columns should match

> For those of you using Microsoft Excel, you will notice that you can implement a Left Outer Join in Excel with functions such as `vlookup()`. By using KNIME instead of Excel, you can run all types of join (not just the left outer) and easily define matching criteria on multiple columns (which in Excel would require some workarounds).

For completeness, there are a couple of other ways to combine tables beyond the join operator. If you don't need to take care of any matching criteria and you just want to "stitch together" tables that have the same size in one dimension, you can:

- Append columns across two tables that have the same number of rows. You will obtain the columns of the first table just beside the second table columns, in whatever order they have in the original table. You can do so in KNIME by using the **Column Appender** node.

- Concatenate rows of two tables having the same columns, putting the rows of the first table on top of the ones coming from the second table. The node for this is called just **Concatenate**.

Figure 3.6 give you an idea of how these two nodes would work:

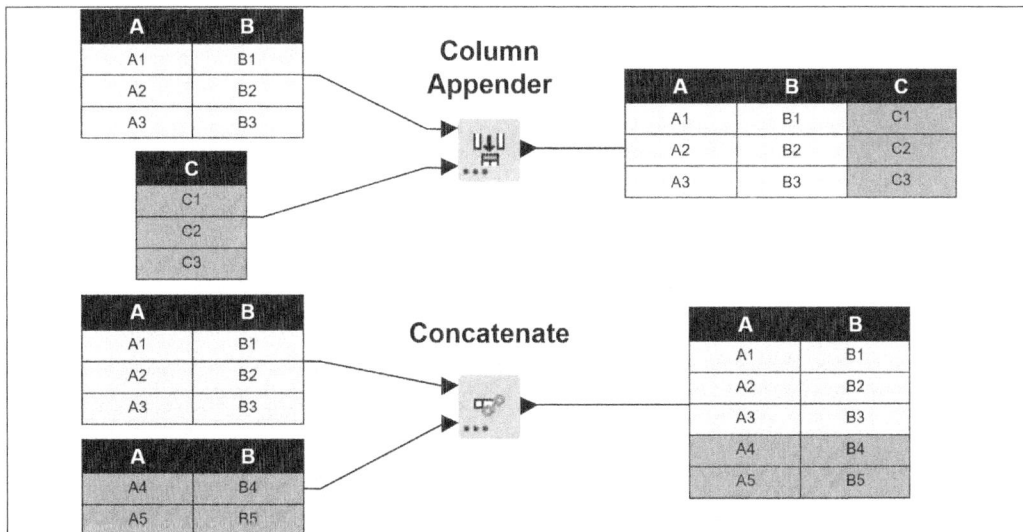

Figure 3.6: Combining tables without matching criteria: you can append columns or concatenate rows with these two nodes

Now we are clear on the many ways available to us to combine several tables into one. Let's move to the other omnipresent data transformation need: aggregating values to create summary views of a table.

Aggregating values

The information contained in a raw data table lies dispersed across all its rows. Often, we need to condense a large table into a smaller and more readable one where its values get aggregated or summarized following a given logic. For instance, if we have a table including all orders received in the last year and want to make sense of our sales' evolution over time, we might prefer to calculate a simpler table that shows the total number of orders generated every month. Instead of having a long table with as many rows as orders, we prefer scanning through its aggregation showing only twelve rows, one for each month.

The simpler way of aggregating data is by using a rather popular database operation called **Group By**: it combines rows in various groups and aggregates their values within each group. To perform a Group By, you will need to decide two things:

- First, you must declare which columns define a **group**. All the rows showing the same values in the columns defining the group will be combined together into a single row in the output. Let's take *Table 3.6* as an example. If you defined our group using column *Category*, the result of the Group By will have only two rows: one with the total sales of guitars and the other one with the total sales of pianos. You can define groups by multiple columns: in this case, you will get an aggregated row for each combination of unique values in the group columns. For example, if you selected both *Date* and *Category* as group definition, you will obtain multiple output rows for each category, one for each different day of sales.

- Second, you need to decide how to summarize rows across, meaning which **aggregation function** to use. For instance, you could simply count all rows appearing in a group, summing up their values or calculating their average. In the case of the sales summary table, we decided to count the number of sales transactions, but we could have calculated the overall income generated each month by using the sum as an aggregation function instead.

It's time to see the Group By operation in action on our music store example. Let's use as input the result of the Inner Join in *Table 3.6*. We want to summarize our sales by product category, calculating the income generated by each category and the number of items sold in total:

Sales, group by Category		
Category	Sales	Quantity
Guitars	1538	3
Pianos	1773	2

Table 3.10: Summary of sales by category

As we would expect, the resulting table has just two rows, one for each category present in the original table. Let's meet the node that can perform aggregation of this kind in KNIME.

⊡ GroupBy

This node (**Manipulation > Row > Transform**) aggregates rows of a table by groups, defined by means of a subset of columns. Its basic configuration requires two steps. In the **Groups** panel, you need to select which columns define the groups by moving them to the list on the right, bordered in green. You can choose multiple columns: the output table will have one row for each unique combination of different values in all of the columns you specify here. If you don't select a column, you will aggregate all rows at the input into one single grand total row at the output:

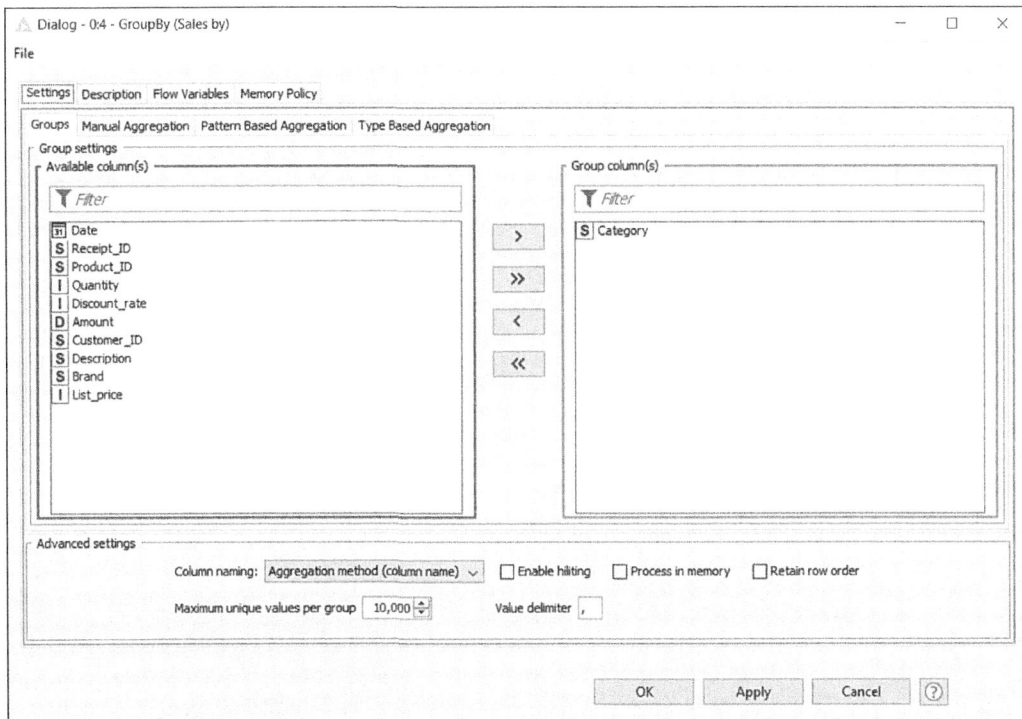

Figure 3.7: Group settings for a Group By: decide what columns define a group

The second step is to declare which columns should be summarized and using which aggregation function. You can define the columns to aggregate upon by double-clicking on their name from the left list. Then, you can specify the aggregation function by selecting it from the drop-down menu under **Aggregation**. You can select the same column multiple times and aggregate it with different functions. In the drop-down menu at the bottom (**Column naming**), you can specify the naming convention to be used for the aggregate columns. The default option is **Aggregation method (column name)**, which will create headers like *Sum(Quantity)*:

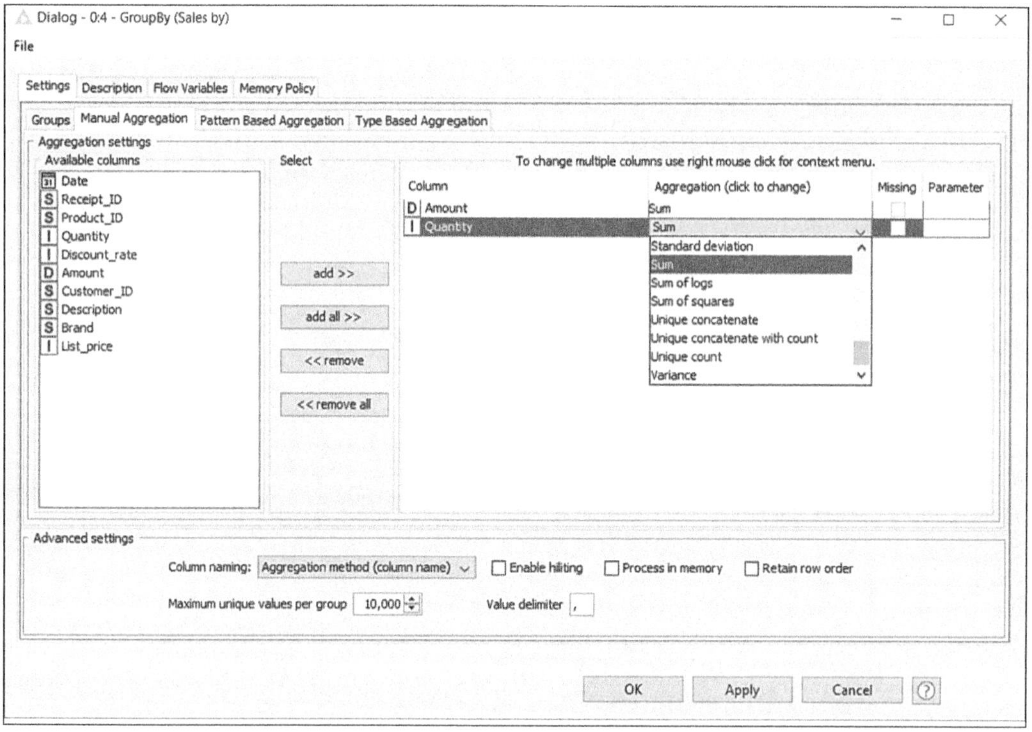

Figure 3.8: Aggregation settings for a Group By: decide how to summarize your rows within each group

In *Table 3.11*, you find the most popular functions you can use for summarizing your rows within each group. For some of these functions, like Count or First, you need to decide whether to consider NULLs as values like all others or ignore them. If you want them to be ignored (focusing the aggregation on actual values only), tick the **Missing** checkbox on the right:

Aggregation Function	Description
Sum	Sums all values in a group, returning the total.
Count/Unique Count	Counts all rows within each group. Unique Count ignores duplicates and counts only distinct values.
Mean/Median	Calculates averages and the median value within each group.
Mode	Takes the value with the highest number of occurrences in a group.
First/Last	Takes the first/last value appearing in each group, depending on their sorting when input. Make sure you sort rows accordingly before.
Minimum/Maximum	Takes the minimum and the maximum values within the group.
Concatenate/Unique Concatenate	Joins all values in a single string, using the delimiter indicated in the text box at the bottom. Unique Concatenate ignores duplicates.
Correlation	Calculates correlation with another column (you can select it by clicking on the **Edit** button), across elements of each group.

Table 3.11: Summarizing functions

Another way of aggregating data is by using the **Pivot** operation. While the Group By groups up being rows in the output table, with this operation, we can "rotate" some groups (that we call pivots) to appear vertically, as columns, in the output table. You can think of a pivot as a 2-dimensional matrix showing aggregations across horizontal groups (which will ultimately appear as rows of the pivot) and pivoted vertical groups (appearing as columns in the output matrix).

Let's see the Pivot operation in use on our music store example. Starting again from the Inner Join result, we would like to summarize our sales in a single table showing sums for each combination of categories (horizontal groups) and dates (vertical groups, or pivots):

Sales, pivot by Category and Dates				
Date	21-Dec		22-Dec	
Category	Sales	Quantity	Sales	Quantity
Guitars	1289	2	249	1
Pianos	499	1	1274	1

Table 3.12: Sales pivot by category and dates

The resulting pivot table has two rows, one for each of the categories (like with Group By), and multiple columns showing the aggregations for each available date. In KNIME, we can use the **Pivoting** node to create such summaries.

▶ 🔁 *Pivoting*

This node (**Manipulation > Row > Transform**) aggregates values by creating a pivot table. Its configuration dialog is similar to that of **GroupBy**, but contains an additional **Pivots** panel, as the following shows:

- In the **Groups** panel, you specify the input columns that define the horizontal groups, which will show as rows in the output pivot table.

- In the **Pivots** panel, you specify instead which input columns to use for creating the vertical groups, appearing as columns in the resulting table.

- Finally, in the **Aggregation** panel, you can select the input columns to summarize and the aggregation method to use.

Similar to what we have seen for the **GroupBy** node, the two drop-down menus at the bottom (**Column name** and **Aggregation name**) can be used to specify the naming convention for the columns of the resulting pivot. By default, you will have headers concatenating the name of each pivot with the aggregation method, like *21-Dec+Sum(Amount)*:

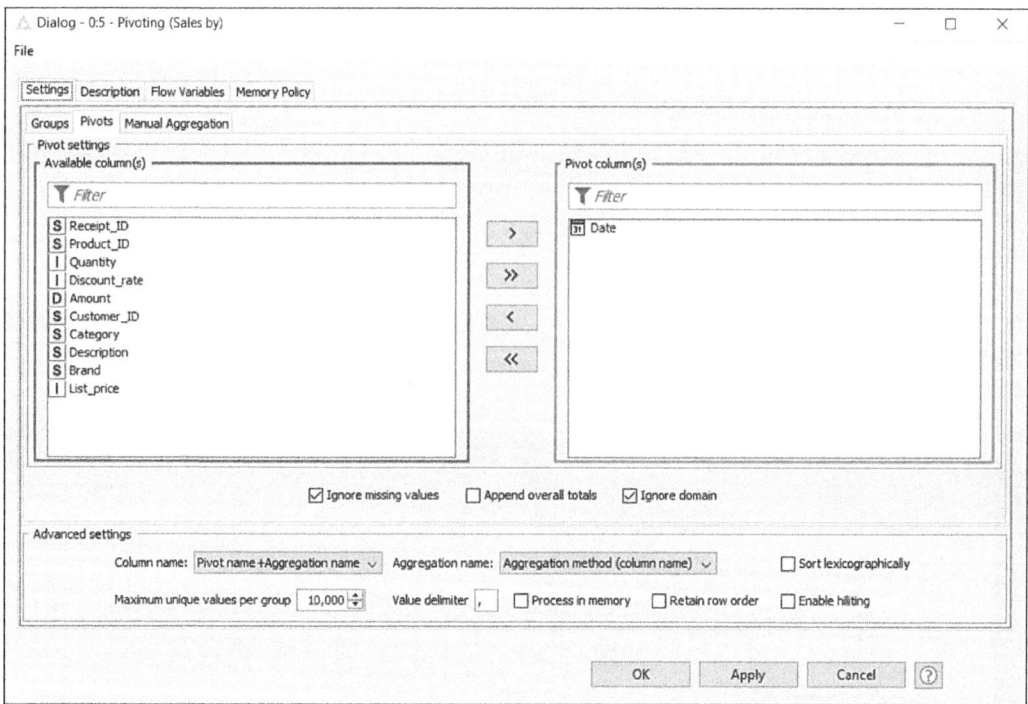

Figure 3.9: Pivot setting: select the columns to use for the vertical groups (pivots)

The **Pivoting** node has not one but three output ports: you can view them by selecting one of the last three magnifying lens icons at the bottom of the pop-up menu after right-clicking on the node. The first output is the pivot matrix (most of the time, you will only need this one), the second one is the total aggregation of the horizontal groups only (pivots are ignored), while the third one is the grand total across all rows of the pivot (groups are ignored).

> The concept of pivot tables has been popularized in Microsoft Excel. Knowing how to build a pivot in KNIME, you now have access to a broader range of aggregation methods, and you will be able to make the pivot operation part of a more extended, automated workflow of steps, removing all manual interventions such as refreshes and copy/paste.

In some cases, you want to run the reverse operation, called **Unpivoting**: this will place the columns of a table to appear as multiple rows in the output table. If you want to perform this transformation in KNIME, check out the **Unpivoting** node.

In *Figure 3.10*, you see a summary of the three table aggregations and disaggregation methods we have seen:

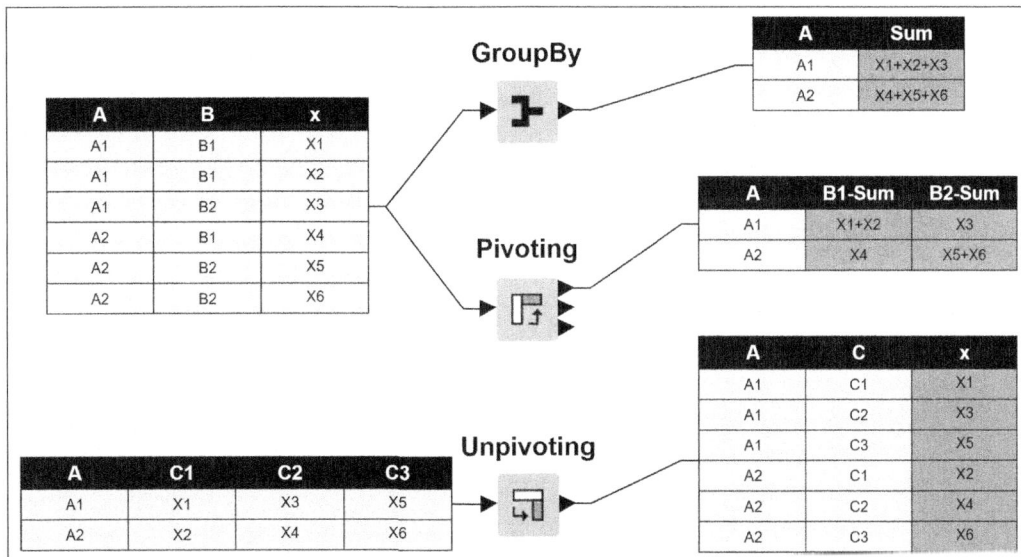

Figure 3.10: Transforming tables by aggregating and disaggregating: a summary of the most useful operations

Combining tables and aggregating values are the fundamental data transformations you can do. Let's see them in action in a full tutorial, which will be an opportunity to learn a few more tricks about KNIME, like calculating formulas, visualizing data, and using loops and variables.

Tutorial: Sales report automation

In this tutorial, you will impersonate the role of a business analyst working for a UK-based online retailer, selling all-occasion gifts. You are intrigued by data analytics and are reading a few (good) books about its potential. You have set for yourself the ambition of progressively amplifying the role of data analytics in the company by leveraging your new skills. You decide to start from something relatively simple: automate and improve the reporting of sales data. By doing so, you want to make a quick and visible impact and instill an *appetite* for more advanced analytics in your colleagues and managers, unlocking interest and investments.

The company you work for has grown quickly and didn't have the opportunity to adopt a sustainable business intelligence solution. The regular reporting is managed manually using Excel. The poor finance analyst responsible for it pulls data from the company website every Friday and, after a couple of hours of boring manual steps, sends an email with the latest status. Due to the manual nature of the activity, the reports are prone to human error, and almost every week this causes several *back and forth* emails, which leave no time for identifying business-meaningful patterns in the data and creating real value. You empathize with the finance analyst and decide to set aside a few hours to automate the full reporting process in KNIME.

First of all, you manage to retrieve a list of the most important business questions people ask about sales evolution. This initial list will be a good base for your initial endeavor:

1. What are the top ten products in our assortment, meaning the ones that generate the most significant number of sales?

2. What are the top three products within each subcategory?

3. To which country do we sell the most?

4. During the current calendar year to date, how much revenue was generated within each product category?

5. What's the relative footprint of each category out of the total portfolio of products for the current year?

6. In which months should we expect a peak in sales for our seasonal categories?

You decide that your first automated report shall include a tabular view answering the first five business questions appearing above. For the last one, since the seasonal behavior of the business is not going to change significantly on a weekly basis, it will be enough to build a chart that depicts the patterns of sales by month as a one-off exercise. Having defined the minimum set of deliverables that your work should cover, you are ready to go to the next step and assess what data is required to make it happen.

> Always start any data work by clarifying the business questions you are after. Many analytics initiatives fail because there is a lack of understanding of what the ultimate objective looks like. Make sure you always "visualize" what you want to obtain from your data analytics capabilities and how you expect it to practically affect your business. If possible, put it in writing, as we just did with the six questions above.

With the help of the finance analyst (who is already getting very excited about your initiative), you retrieve the latest data required for the regular sales reporting and discover that it is scattered across three different tables.

- **Product Master Data**: This includes a unique alphanumeric code (column *StockCode*), which serves as a product ID, a short *Description*, and two columns to locate each item within the two-level product hierarchy used in the company, namely *Category* and *Subcategory*. For example, within the category "Stationery," we find the subcategories "Notebooks" and "Stickers," while within "Home," we have "Clocks" and "Furniture."

- **Customer Master Data**: For each customer who has signed up to the website, it includes an identifier (*Customer_ID*) and the *Country* of residence.

- **Sales Transactions**: This is the biggest table as it records all sales. For every invoice (identified with column *Invoice_ID*), this table can host multiple rows, one for each product (described through its *StockCode*) included within the transaction. For each row, we also have the number of purchased items (*Quantity*), the unit *Price*, the *Customer_ID* (which can be empty, if the customer hasn't signed up), and a string describing the date and time of the purchase (*Invoice_time*).

The product and customer master data tables are available in two text files (named `productMD.csv` and `customerMD.csv`) extracted from the order management system. Transactions are stored, instead, in two separate Excel files (`TransactionL3M.xlsx` and `TransactionsHistory.xlsx`): the first one contains only the most recent sales, covering the latest three months of transactions, while the second one has the remainder of the transactions' history:

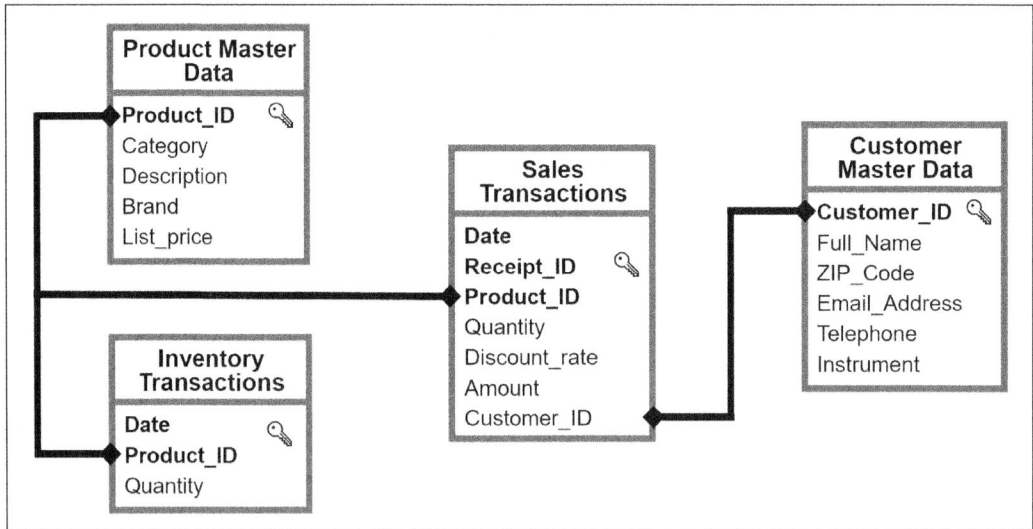

Figure 3.11: An Entity-Relationship diagram of the online retailer database

We now have enough knowledge to get started: should we realize we need more info on the data and the business needs, we can always go back to our finance analyst and ask for extra help. By looking at the list of business questions, we notice that we will need to aggregate our transactions using fields (such as *Category*, *Country*), which **are** in different master data tables, so we will need to load all of them and combine them. Let's open KNIME, create a new workflow (**File | New...** and **New KNIME Workflow**), and begin to build it.

1. As a first step, we load the transactional data, which is contained in two separate Excel files. Let's start from the history, dragging `TransactionsHistory.xlsx` on the blank workflow or implementing the **Excel Reader** node. In the configuration window, we notice that the preview includes all the columns we anticipated being there, so we can close it, leaving the options unchanged. We repeat the same for the other file (`TransactionsL3M.xlsx`) and run both nodes.

The two tables we have loaded so far refer to transactions and share exactly the same columns. We can combine them and stack one on top of the other by using the **Concatenate** node.

► Concatenate

The node (**Manipulation > Row > Transform**) concatenates two tables by adding the rows of the second table at the bottom of the rows of the first table. The node will combine the columns if they have the same header. You can use its configuration window to decide how to handle the columns that do not appear in both input tables. By default, all columns will be kept (the **Use union of columns** option from the **Column handling** section): this means that, if a column only exists in one table, it will show in the output as NULL values for all the rows coming from the other table. If instead, you go for the alternative option (**Use intersection of columns**), all non-matching columns will be discarded at the output:

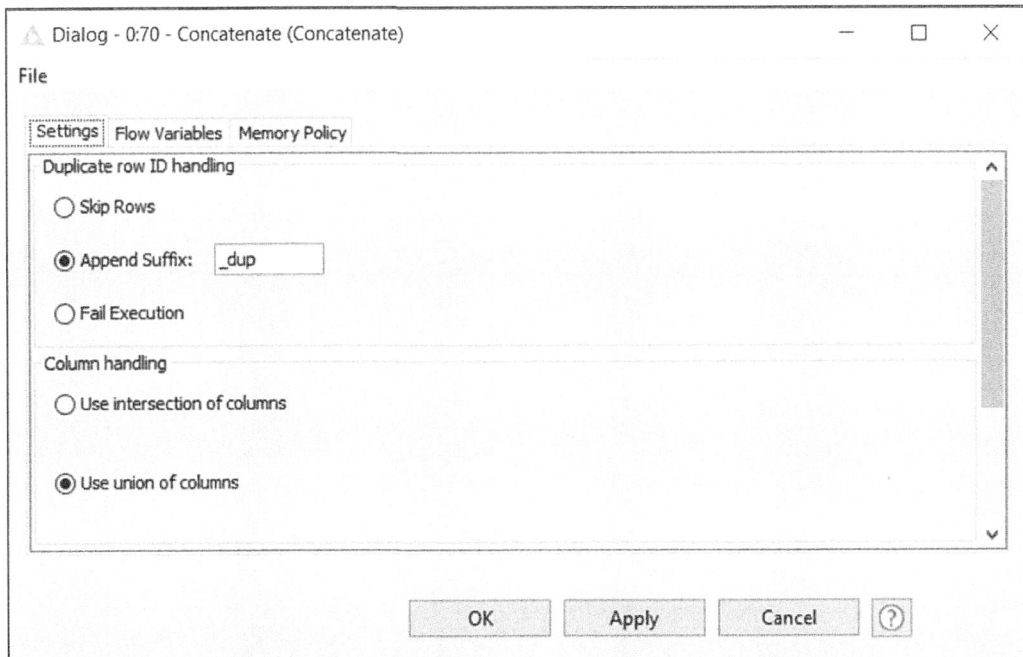

Figure 3.12: Configuration window of the Concatenate node:
choose how to manage duplicate and non-matching columns

2. We can combine the two transaction tables and connect the outputs of the two **Excel Readers** as inputs to a **Concatenate** node. Since the two input tables share precisely the same columns (having identical names), we don't need to care about the configuration of the node and stick with its default behavior. As we run the node, we obtain at the output the full **Sales Transactions** table with more than 600,000 rows.

3. Let's now load the **Customer Master Data** table, stored in the customerMD.csv file. We can either drag and drop the file on the editor or implement a **CSV Reader** node and configure it by specifying the file's path. Double-check in the configuration window that the node has rightly captured the column delimiter (in this case, a semicolon): you can always click on **Autodetect format** to get KNIME to guess it.

4. We can now combine the sales table with the customer master data to enrich each transaction with the information on the *Country* where it was generated. Let's connect the outputs of the **Concatenate** and **CSV Reader** nodes as inputs to a **Joiner** node. By double-clicking on the latter, we can configure it. First, we need to set the conditions for matching rows. We click on the **Add matching criterion** button and select *Customer_ID* from both tables. The second configuration step is to specify the type of join to make. We want to maintain all transactions (left table) even if they don't have a corresponding match on the customer master data (right table), so we decide to go for a left outer join. In fact, our colleague (who is starting to admire our agility in KNIME) confirms that, although not all customers are included in the customer master data, we should consider transactions coming from all product sales. To obtain a left outer join, we need to tick both the **Matching rows** and the **Left unmatched rows**. The Left outer join title on top of the white and yellow Venn diagram confirms that we did well. The last configuration step is to select **Merge joining columns** option so that we don't carry two copies of the *Customer_ID* columns.

When we close the configuration window and run the node, we notice that none of the rows got matched: in fact, the output table has got null values (the '?' cells) in all rows. by reopening the configuration of the Joiner (*Figure 3.13*) we realize what happened: the *Customer_ID* columns in the two tables we are joining refer to the same attribute but have a different data type (string in transactions and integer in the customer master data). These things happen: given the different formats of the files carrying the tables, data types might have been interpreted differently.

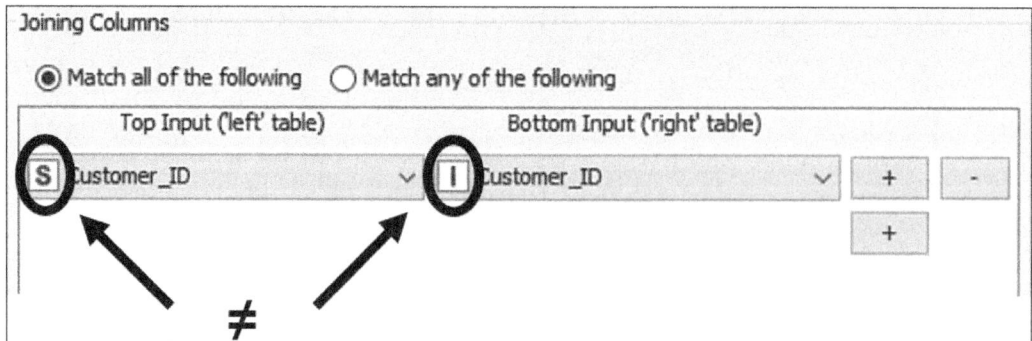

Figure 3.13: Non-matching joining columns: same content but different data types

► 2►S ► *Number To String*

This node (**Manipulation > Column > Convert & Replace**) converts numeric columns (like integers and decimal numbers) intro strings of text. Its configuration is trivial: you just need to select which numeric columns should be converted by keeping or removing them from the right selection panel:

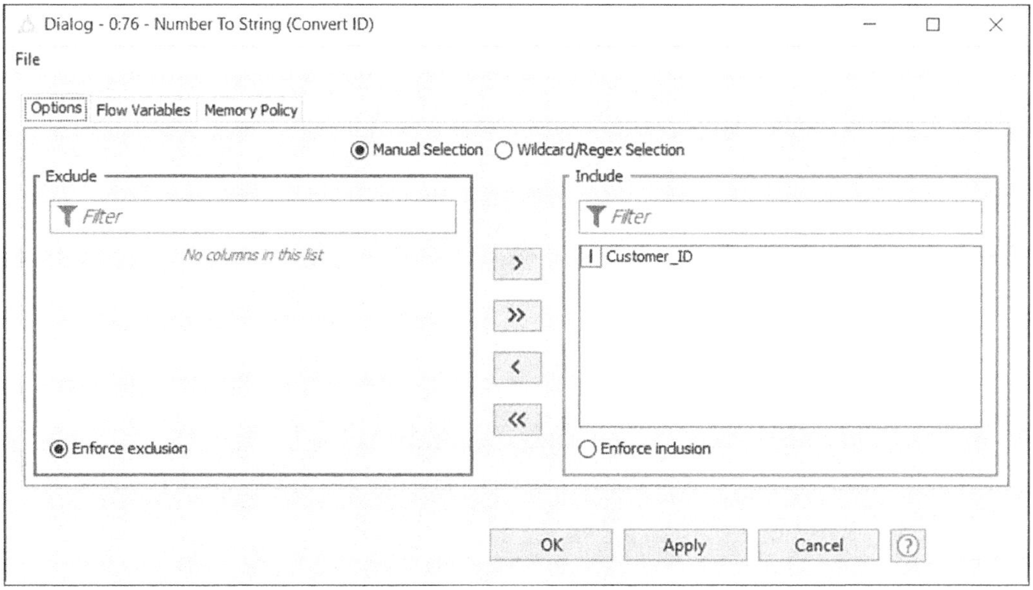

Figure 3.14: Number To String configuration: which numbers do you want to convert into text?

5. To convert the *Customer_ID* column from the master data into a string, we add a **Number To String** node between **CSV Reader** and **Joiner**. The fastest way to do that is to drag the node from the repository and, by clicking the mouse button pressed, drop it on the connector which already exists between the two nodes (which will turn red when selected). We can now execute the **Joiner** node and notice that at its output (*Shift+F6* to open the view) we do not have any more NULL value. Instead, we read all transactions, enriched with an additional column (*Country*) at the right end, which is exactly what we were aiming at.

6. It's now time to load the **Product Master Data** table by loading the `productMD.csv` file through the usual CSV Reader node.

7. We can now add an additional **Joiner** downstream: the first input port should be connected with the first output of the previous **Joiner's** node while the second port should get the product master data from the latest **CSV Reader**. In its configuration, we first select *StockCode* as matching columns from both the left and right tables: the data types nicely match so no conversion is needed. This time we want to run an inner join because we don't want to carry sales from products that are not included in the product master data as they would not belong to any product category, making the reporting less readable. Thus, in the **Joiner's** configuration window, we only keep the **Matching rows** box selected. Lastly, tick the **Merge joining columns** box so that we don't carry two copies of the *StockCode* column. When we execute the node, we obtain a table indicating for each row the description of the product being sold and its classification within the hierarchy.

All the data has now been loaded and combined in a single table: we can proceed in preparing this table, generating the reports we need. We notice that all the business questions require aggregating sales in terms of generated income, while our table displays *Quantity* and *Price* for each line item in an invoice. To calculate the resulting income generated by each transaction, we need to implement a simple mathematical formula, which is what the next node is all about.

► f(x) ► *Math Formula*

This node (**Manipulation > Column > Convert & Replace**) evaluates an expression for each row of a table, returning its result in a given column. The configuration dialog looks very familiar: indeed, it is structured in the same way as for the **String Manipulation** node we met in *Chapter 2, Getting Started with KNIME*. The only difference is that here, you can use functions working on numbers, like `ceil()` or `floor()` to round up or down a decimal number to the nearest integer or `sqrt()` to calculate the square root. You find all the available functions in the list in the middle and, by selecting them, you will read their description and an example appearing in the text box on the right.

The easiest way to build an expression is to double-click on the available columns on the right (only the numeric ones will show up) and create your expression using the central text box. In here, you can add all math operators you need, like +, -, *, /, and parentheses. The result of the expression for each row will be saved either in a new column (**Append Column**) or will substitute the content of an existing one (**Replace Column**), as you can select with the radio button at the bottom:

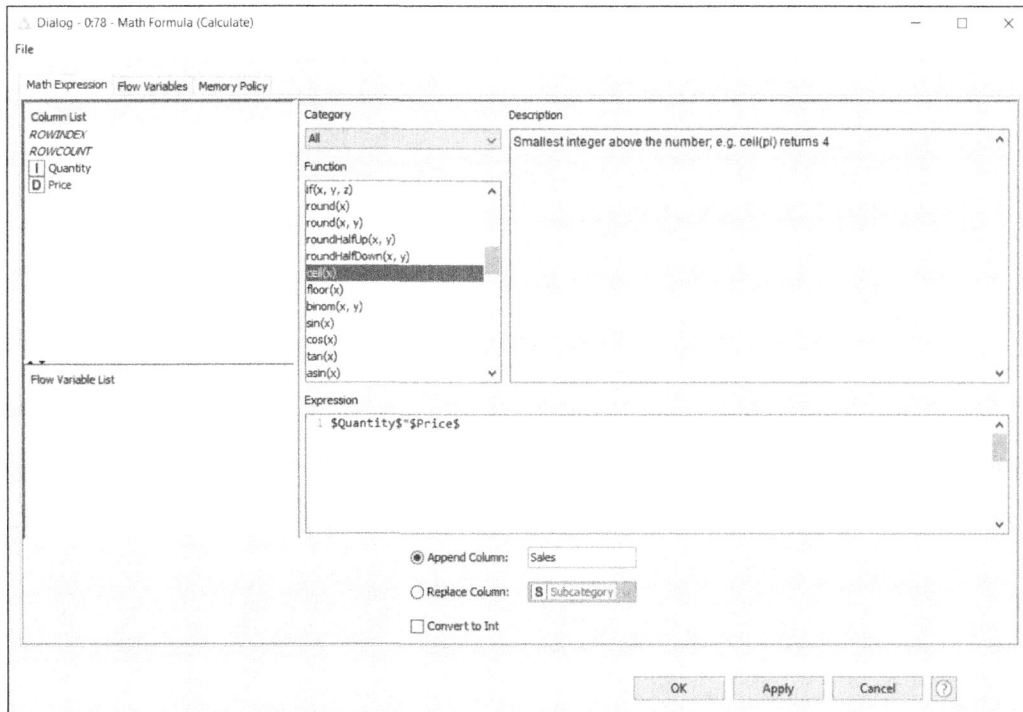

Figure 3.15: Math Formula dialog: build your numeric expression by combining the columns you need

8. To calculate the revenues generated by each transaction, we implement a Math Formula and create a connection between this and the previous node (the **Joiner's** upper output port). In the configuration window, we build the expression: $Quantity$*$Price$, select the option Append Column and give it the name Sales.

By looking at the resulting table, we observe a couple of opportunities for cleaning it up. First, we notice that the column *Country* has some missing values because some customers were missing in the master data. We should substitute it with the default value we use when a country is missing, which is the Unspecified string. Second, we find the category "Others" doesn't refer to actual product sales as it describes additional fees (like postage and bank commissions) and manual adjustments. The finance analyst confirms that all sales generated within "Others" should be excluded from any reporting.

9. To manage the missing countries, add the **Missing Value** node and configure it by using its second tab (**Column Settings**). Double-click on the column *Country*, which you find on the left, and select **Fix Value** in the dropdown that appears. Then, type Unspecified in the text box and click on **OK** to close the window.

10. To remove the rows referring to the "Others" category, we can use a **Row Filter** node. To configure it, select **Exclude rows by attribute value** on the right, then *Category* in the **Column to test** selector and, lastly, "Others" from the **use pattern matching** drop-down menu:

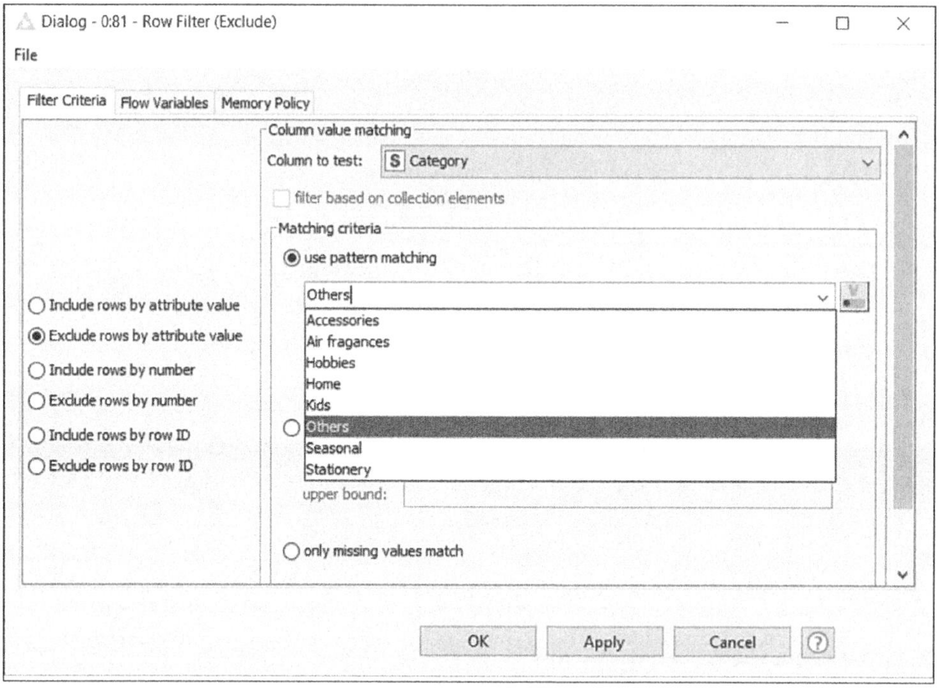

Figure 3.16: Row Filter dialog: exclude the rows having a specific value in a given column

Having the table cleaned up (you should by now have 672,104 rows and 11 columns at the output port of the last node), we are finally able to generate the tables that answer each of our business questions. The first one asks for a list of the products that have generated the most significant amount of sales. At this point, the sales related to a product are scattered across multiple rows, one for each invoice that included the product. Hence, we will need to aggregate sales by product.

11. To obtain the total sales generated by each product, we implement a **GroupBy** node. In the configuration window, we select the columns that define the unique groups at the output. Since we want to have one row for each product and we also want to carry in the report the columns that describe it, in the **Groups** tab, we select the columns *StockCode, Description, Category,* and *Subcategory,* making sure they all end up in the green-bordered list on the right. The **GroupBy** node will create a row for each combination of values in the group columns but, since we know that for each *StockCode,* we have one single *Description, Category,* and *Subcategory,* we can safely keep all of them in the group description, to keep them in our output table, which will result in them being more informative. In the **Manual Aggregation** tab, we double-click on the columns *Sales* and *Quantity* and specify for both of them the option **Sum** as **Aggregation function**. To make our report more readable and avoid bulky column names, we select **Keep original name(s)** in the bottom dropdown labeled as **Column naming**. We can then click on **OK** and move to the next step.

12. Since we want to show only the products generating the most sales, we need to sort the table by decreasing *Sales,* using the **Sorter** node. After implementing the node and making a connection with the previous one, we can select *Sales* in the drop-down menu and pick the **Descending** order.

13. The last step for answering this business question is to limit our ranked list of products to the top ten entries. Using the **Row Filter** node, we **select Include rows by number** on the left and then input 1 as **First row number** and 10 as **Last row number**.

After executing the last node and checking the resulting table, we are positively impressed as the screen displays the ten biggest selling products. This positive intermediate result encourages us to move ahead in our challenge:

Row ID	StockCode	Description	Category	Subcat...	Sales	Quantity
Row1375	22423	REGENCY CAKESTAND 3 TIER	Home	Kitchen	265,295.62	23063
Row3160	85123A	WHITE HANGING HEART T-LIGHT HOLDER	Air fragances	Candles	240,707.67	89264
Row3144	85099B	JUMBO BAG RED RETROSPOT	Accessories	Bags	166,451.16	92726
Row2979	84879	ASSORTED COLOUR BIRD ORNAMENT	Home	Decoration	124,354.72	78160
Row2443	47566	PARTY BUNTING	Kids	Party	102,220.93	23241
Row1128	22086	PAPER CHAIN KIT 50'S CHRISTMAS	Seasonal	Christmas	74,510.46	27608
Row2637	79321	CHILLI LIGHTS	Home	Furniture	70,118.67	15172
Row1355	22386	JUMBO BAG PINK POLKADOT	Accessories	Bags	66,771.74	36801
Row2474	48138	DOORMAT UNION FLAG	Home	Furniture	64,128.57	9857
Row3146	85099F	JUMBO BAG STRAWBERRY	Accessories	Bags	63,526.31	35515

Figure 3.17: Top ten products by sales: who would have thought that a cake stand could make so much money?

The next question asks us to report the top-selling products within each subcategory. Similar to what we already did for the previous question, we apply a filter to the products list, keeping only the ones appearing on top of the sorted list. However, this time, we need to repeat the filtering multiple times, once for each subcategory.

In KNIME, you can *repeat* the execution of a portion of a workflow by creating a **Loop**. Implementing a loop in KNIME is quite simple: you have a set of start and end loop nodes (you find them in **Workflow Control > Loop Support**), which you can use to define the segment of the workflow to be repeated (the **Loop Body**). Depending on the type of **Loop Start** node you pick, you can decide the logic to follow for the repetition. Once the loop is executed, you will find the concatenated results of your loops at the output port of the **Loop End** node, with an extra column telling you the loop number each row refers to. It looks simple, and it actually is!

You will find a graphical summary of the most popular loop nodes below. More specifically:

- **Counting Loop Start**: Use this if you want to repeat a portion of a workflow a given number of times (which you can specify in the configuration dialog).

- **Chunk Loop Start**: The loop will be repeated once for every fixed-size chunk of consecutive rows in the input table. You can decide the number of total loops or chunk size per loop to use. If you select a chunk size of 1, you will repeat a portion of the workflow for each individual row of the input table.

- **Group Loop Start**: The loop will be repeated for every group of rows, defined by each combination of unique values in the columns you decide. Remember the **GroupBy** node? In that case, you obtained an aggregated row for each group: in this case, you will repeat a portion of the workflow for each group. We'll use this node shortly, which will make its behavior clearer.

> There are other nodes for starting and ending loops, which would extend the flexibility you have for repeating some sets of operations in your workflows. Have a look at the **Recursive Loop** nodes: with these you can *bring back* the output of a loop to the start node, to repeat it over and over on the same rows.

Figure 3.18 shows a summary of possible loop setups for your workflow. Remember: you can only have a single **Loop Start** and a **Loop End** node working together on the same loop body. The dashed lines in the figure show you three plausible options for **Loop Start** nodes:

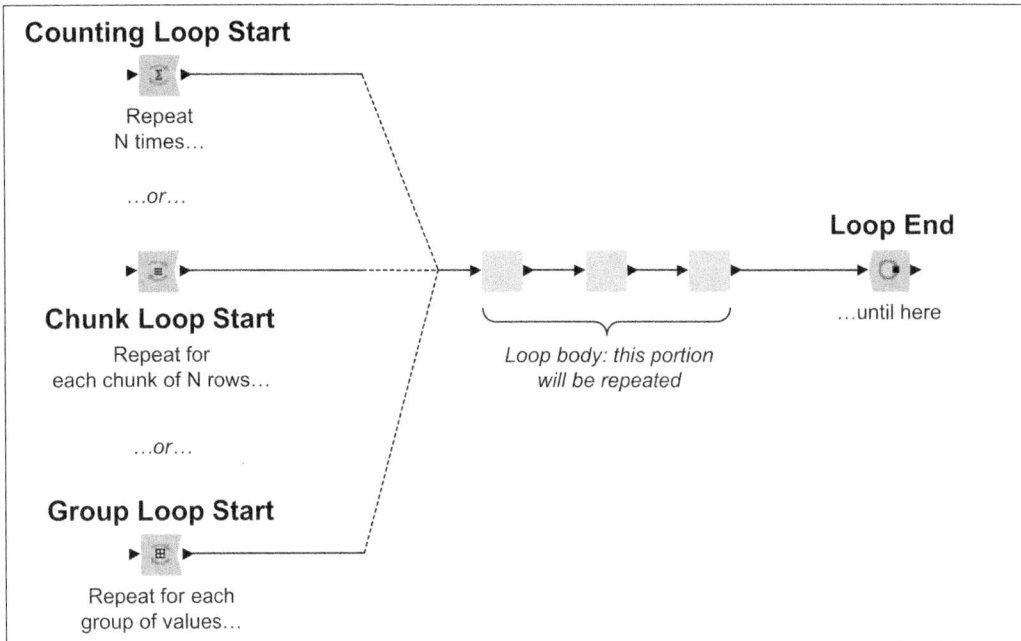

Figure 3.18: Loop nodes in KNIME: repeat a portion of the workflow as many times as you need

After this short digression on creating loops in KNIME, let's go back to our business case. We want to repeat the filtering of the top products for each subcategory, so we should implement a group loop, where the group is simply defined by the column *Subcategory*. Here's how the **Group Loop Start** node works.

▶ ⊞ ▶ *Group Loop Start*

This node (available in **Workflow Control > Loop Support**) marks the starting point of the portion of workflow which will be repeated for each group. All the input rows showing the same values in the columns defining the group will be returned to the downstream loop for execution, one group at a time. Its configuration requires you to specify the columns that define each group. Using this node will require the implementation of a **Loop End** node, which will mark the end of the segment of nodes for which to repeat the execution:

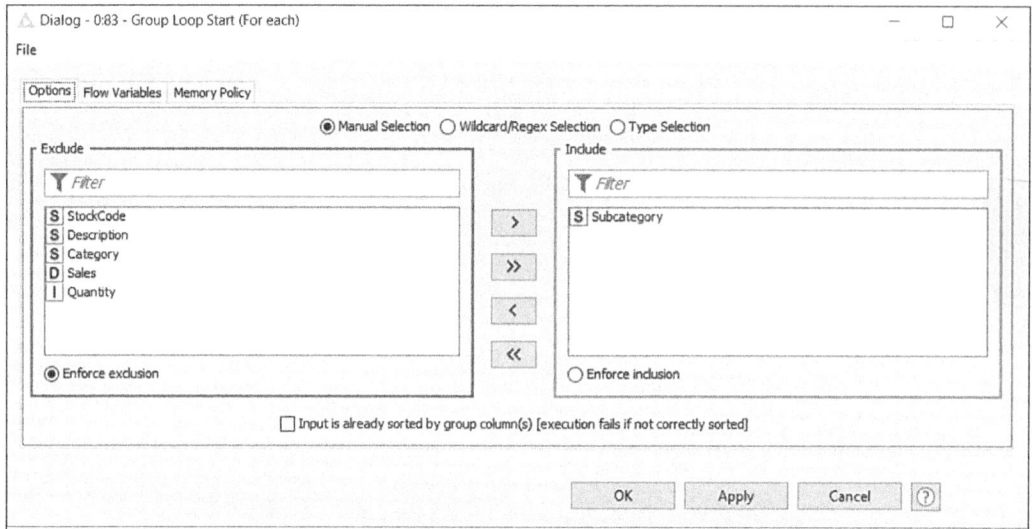

Figure 3.19: Configuration window of the Group Loop Start node:
decide which columns define the group through which you want to iterate

Let's create our first loop in KNIME to answer our current business question.

14. We can reuse the sorted list of products we created for the previous question as a base for our grouped filtering. Drag and drop the **Group Loop Start** node and connect it downstream to the **Sorter** node. In its configuration window, select only *Subcategory* to appear in the **Include** panel on the right.

15. The loop will only have to select the top three products appearing in each group. To do so, we can replicate what we did for the overall top list of products. Let's implement a **Row Filter** node, select **Include rows by number**, and then input 1 as **First row number** and, in this case, 3 as **Last row number**.

To close a loop in a workflow, we need to indicate its end point by using the appropriate node.

▶ ◉ ▶ *Loop End*

This node (**Workflow Control > Loop Support**) marks the end of a workflow loop. At each execution of a loop, it collects the intermediate results by storing the rows arriving at the input port. At the end of the last loop execution, it will return the intermediate results' full concatenation. In its configuration window, you can decide whether or not to add an extra column that counts the loop number in which each intermediate row was generated (**Add iteration column**). In this node's pop-up menu (right-click on the node once implemented), you will find additional options for executing it. If you click on **Step Loop Execution**, you will ask KNIME to run only one single iteration of the loop so you can check intermediate results:

> The coders among you will recognize that this step execution acts as a *breakpoint* that can be used to investigate and debug the way your loop is working. You can also set individual breakpoints at any point within your loop: check out the **Breakpoint** node for doing this.

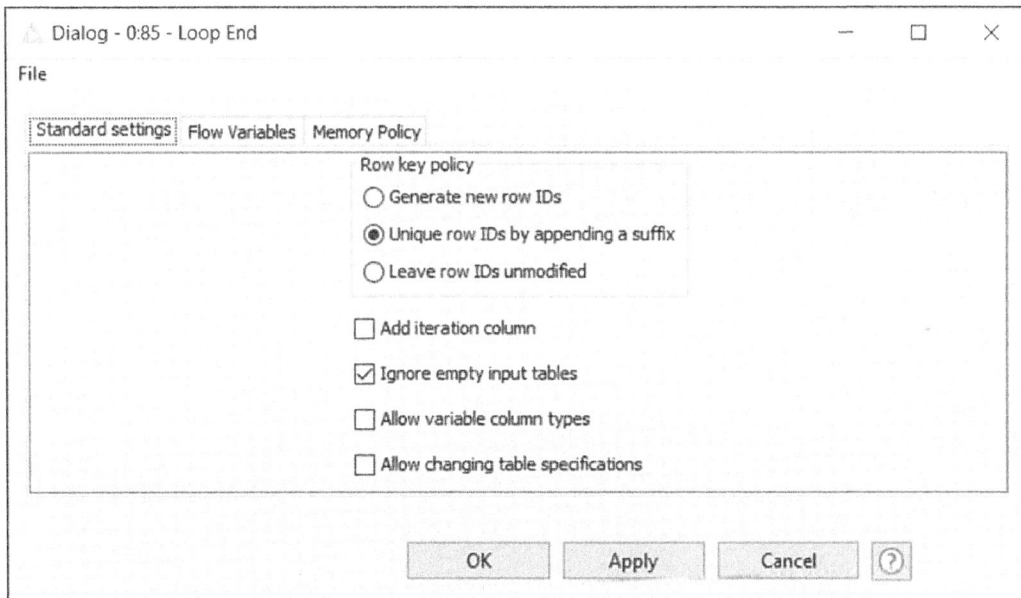

Figure 3.20: Loop End node dialog: do you want to add an iteration column?

> Sometimes, you need to collect multiple tables (with different columns) for each iteration of your loop. In this case, you can use the 2-port version of the **Loop End** node, which you will find in the same repository folder.

16. Let's implement a **Loop End** node, after the **Row Filter**, and untick the **Add iteration column** option: we don't need it, as we keep the name of the *Subcategory* to indicate what we are referring to. The node's output shows three rows for each subcategory, which is exactly what we needed to answer the business question:

Row ID	S StockCode	S Description	S Category	S Subcat...	D Sales	I Quantity
Row3144#0	85099B	JUMBO BAG RED RETROSPOT	Accessories	Bags	166,451.16	92726
Row1355#0	22386	JUMBO BAG PINK POLKADOT	Accessories	Bags	66,771.74	36801
Row3146#0	85099F	JUMBO BAG STRAWBERRY	Accessories	Bags	63,526.31	35515
Row2622#1	75049L	LARGE CIRCULAR MIRROR ...	Home	Bathroom	11,377.25	12673
Row738#1	21463	MIRRORED DISCO BALL	Home	Bathroom	6,671.65	1250
Row1554#1	22672	FRENCH BATHROOM SIGN ...	Home	Bathroom	4,310.07	2679
Row565#2	21232	STRAWBERRY CERAMIC TR...	Accessories	Bijoux	40,357.5	34355
Row386#2	20972	PINK CREAM FELT CRAFT T...	Accessories	Bijoux	22,310.42	18609
Row564#2	21231	SWEETHEART CERAMIC TR...	Accessories	Bijoux	21,576.14	18307
Row3160#3	85123A	WHITE HANGING HEART T-...	Air fragances	Candles	240,707.67	89264
Row2747#3	84347	ROTATING SILVER ANGELS ...	Air fragances	Candles	55,430.84	10041
Row927#3	21733	RED HANGING HEART T-LIG...	Air fragances	Candles	48,188.87	16961

Table "default" - Rows: 75   Spec - Columns: 6   Properties   Flow Variables

Figure 3.21: Top products for each subcategory: each iteration of the loop returned three rows, which have been stitched together by the Loop End node to appear in the same table

The next question asks us to report sales by country, identifying the ones we ship the most to. It will be enough to aggregate, once again, the sales table, this time grouping by country instead of grouping by product as we've done so far. We can reuse the **Row Filter's** output (which excluded the "Others" category) as a starting point for this new branch of the workflow.

17. We need to implement a new **GroupBy** node, having a similar configuration to the first **GroupBy** we used earlier to aggregate by product but with a different definition of groups. Time is money, so let's copy and paste the previous **GroupBy** and connect it with the first **Row Filter**, as anticipated above. In its configuration, let's just work on the **Groups** panel: this time, we want *Country* to be the only column defining groups. We can leave the **Manual aggregation** tab unaltered, as we still want to sum revenues and quantities.

18. To make our output clearer, let's use the **Sorter** node to order rows by decreasing *Sales*, similar to what we did in the earlier branch.

As shown in *Figure 3.22*, we ascertain that most sales are made by UK-based customers, which makes sense, considering that we are talking about a British company:

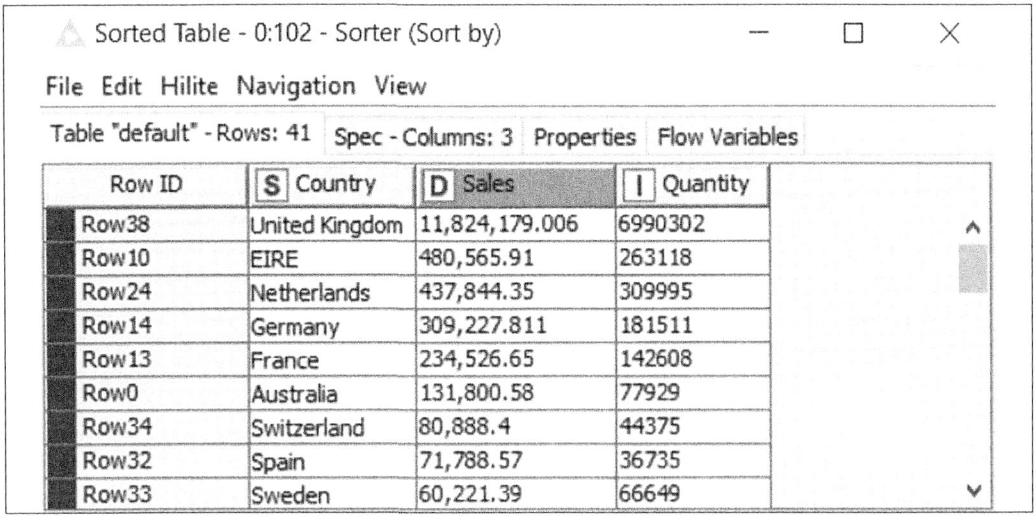

Row ID	S Country	D Sales	I Quantity
Row38	United Kingdom	11,824,179.006	6990302
Row10	EIRE	480,565.91	263118
Row24	Netherlands	437,844.35	309995
Row14	Germany	309,227.811	181511
Row13	France	234,526.65	142608
Row0	Australia	131,800.58	77929
Row34	Switzerland	80,888.4	44375
Row32	Spain	71,788.57	36735
Row33	Sweden	60,221.39	66649

Sorted Table - 0:102 - Sorter (Sort by)

File Edit Hilite Navigation View

Table "default" - Rows: 41 Spec - Columns: 3 Properties Flow Variables

Figure 3.22: Top products for each subcategory: each iteration of the loop returned three rows, which have been stitched together by the Loop End node to appear in the same table

As we move to the next business questions, we notice that they all make reference to a dimension that, so far, we've ignored—time. To proceed in the creation of our reports, we will need to filter by date (two questions ask us to focus on the calendar year to date time frame) and reaggregate by month (to spot seasonal patterns). Managing time-related data in KNIME is relatively easy thanks to a set of nodes that are specifically designed for doing that. We have nodes that convert text to Date&Time data types (**String to Date&Time**), nodes that extract specific elements from a Date&Time data point like hour, month, or day of the week (**Extract Date&Time Fields**), and nodes that will filter rows according to some *temporal* logic (**Date&Time-based Row Filter**). In the next few pages, we will learn how to use such handy nodes one by one.

► String to Date&Time

This node (**Other Data Types > Time Series > Transform**) converts text columns into Date&Time values so that they can be used in time-related nodes. The node attempts to automatically recognize the format of Date&Time fields within strings, leaving the user the possibility to input the text field's expected format manually. In its configuration window, you can first specify which string columns should be converted (ensure you keep on the right only the ones that include Date&Time).

In the **Replace/Append Selection** panel, you can decide whether to replace columns with their converted version or to add them, adding a fixed suffix to their headers. In the last panel, you can enter a string that explains the expected **Date format**: for instance, strings like 16/02/2023 will be correctly parsed using the format string dd/MM/yyyy. By clicking on the button **Guess data type and format**, KNIME will try to recognize the format by analyzing the first cell's content, which you can read in the label below. If the automatic guess doesn't work, you can enter your own string using characters like d, M, y, h, m, and s, which stand for day, month, year, hour, minutes, and seconds (check out the node description for the full list of format placeholders). You can also select a regional setting (called **Locale**, like **en-US** or **it-CH**) to determine the language expected for fields such as month or weekday names:

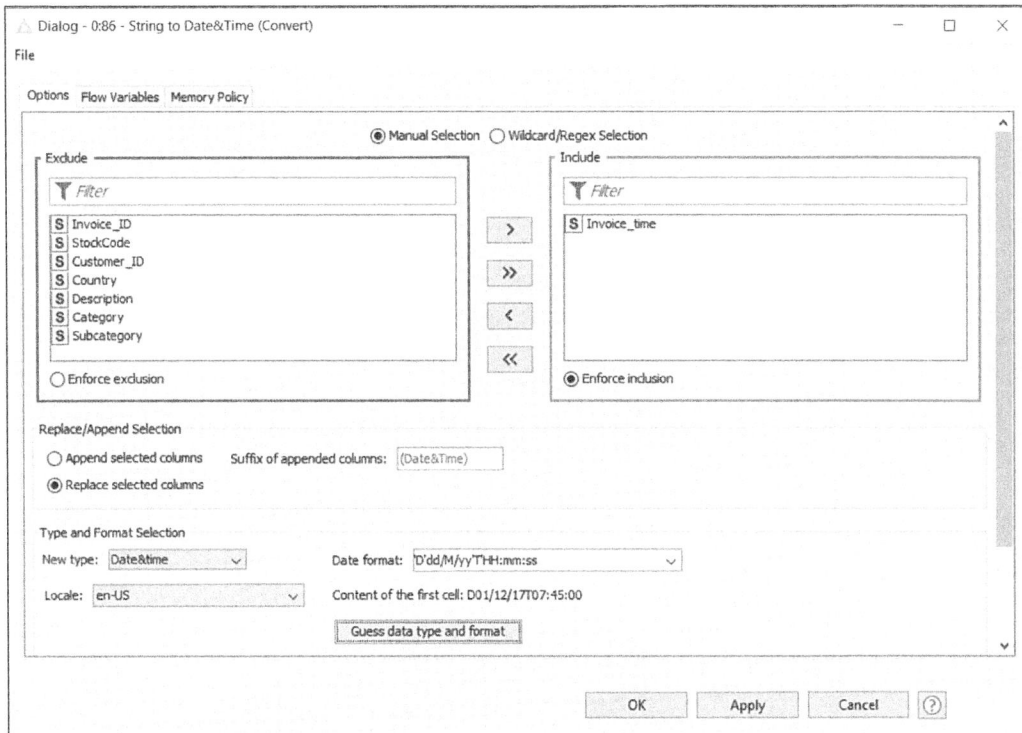

Figure 3.23: String to Date&Time configuration windows: convert a string of text into a Date&Time value

19. Let's implement a **String to Date&Time** node and plug inside it the output of the first **Row Filter** (we can still reuse that one as it carries a cleaned version of the table). Let's keep only the column *Invoice_time* on the right selection panel and click on **Guess data type and format** to let KNIME find a way to interpret the string. We obtain the format string `'D'dd/M/yy'T'HH:mm:ss`, which perfectly matches the content of the first value in our table (`D01/12/17T07:45:00`).

After we run the node, we notice in the output table that the icon on top of the *Invoice_time* column is not an "S" any longer but a calendar picture: KNIME is now going to treat that column as a Date&Time field and we can use all the other time-related nodes for its manipulation. Since the business question focuses on the calendar year to date, we need to find a way to filter rows by dates, exactly what our next node is specialized in.

▸ ⌗ ▸ *Date&Time-based Row Filter*

This node (**Other Data Types > Time Series > Transform**) applies row-level filtering based on a specified time range. To configure it, you first need to select the column that shall be used for the filtering (it must be of Date&Time type). Then you can declare the interval of the rows to keep: you do so by specifying a lower bound (including all values happening later than the point in time you declare in the **Start** panel), an upper bound (keeping everything that occurs before what is declared in the **End** panel), or both (making it a closed interval). The upper bound can be defined either by inputting a specific point in time (option **Date&Time**), a composite interval from the start time (option **Duration**, which can be like 2y 1M, meaning two years and one month from the start), or a specific number of time periods from the start (option **Numerical**, like plus or minus 10 hours from the start). By ticking the **Inclusive** checkbox, every value that is equal to the start (or the end) date will be kept in the output:

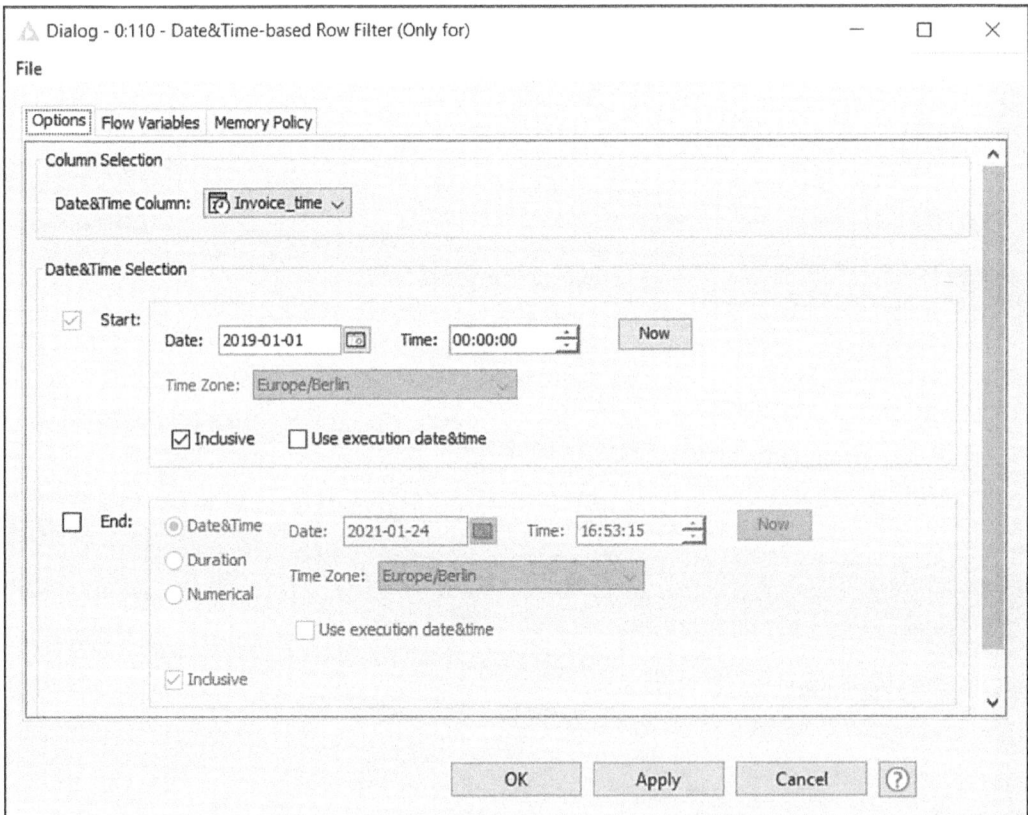

Figure 3.24: Configuration of Date&Time-based Row Filter node:
keep only the rows referring to a specific time range

20. Since the business question refers to the latest calendar year only (which in our dataset is 2019), we need to implement a **Date&Time-based Row Filter** node to remove all earlier rows. For its configuration, we can untick the **End** box (we know that the date doesn't go beyond 2019) and input `2019-01-01` as **Date** and `00:00:00` as **Time** in the **Start** box.

21. Since the question asks how much revenue was generated within each product category, we just need to group the resulting rows (now referring to 2019 only) by *Category*. Implement a **GroupBy** node, keep only *Category* in the definition of **Groups**, and the usual sum of *Sales* and *Quantity* in the **Manual Aggregation** panel. Also, this time, we want to keep the naming simple and select **Keep original name(s)** in the dropdown at the bottom:

Row ID	S Category	D Sales	I Quantity	D Price
Row6	Stationery	604,042.53	661011	1.72
Row5	Seasonal	420,546.18	298003	2.367
Row4	Kids	497,427.07	298060	2.735
Row3	Home	3,008,831.653	1417220	3.664
Row2	Hobbies	393,853.83	132076	4.429
Row1	Air fragances	453,675.36	311514	2.047
Row0	Accessories	948,680	600812	1.93

Figure 3.25: Sales by Category in 2019

Another question is answered! We managed to limit our sales to the time frame of interest and summarize sales at the granularity we need. For the next question, we have to deal with a slight complication: we are asked to compute each category's relative footprint out of the total revenues. This means that we should divide the sales generated in the various categories by the grand total of sales. We can use the **Math Formula** node to implement this division: the numerator of the division is readily available (it's the **Sales** column obtained after the **GroupBy** summarization we already did to answer the previous question). However, the denominator should be calculated separately and somehow included in the formula. This is where **variables** come in handy. Although not every user will need to use variables in KNIME, let's go through the fundamentals. You can consider the next couple of pages as optional in your path to becoming an autonomous KNIME user.

Variables in KNIME can be used to control the configuration of any node dynamically. So far, we've always customized a node's behavior by manually operating on its configuration window. In most cases, this will be enough. However, sometimes we want to configure a node's parameter through a variable that might be, in turn, the output of some calculation executed in another node. For instance, in the case of our sales footprint calculation, we want to use the aggregation of total sales as a variable in our formula.

> In general, any configuration parameter of a node can be controlled by a variable. If you open the configuration window of any node and go to the tab called **Flow Variables** (which we have not used so far), you find a list of the parameters needed by that node, and you can select which variables (if available at that point in the workflow) should be used to control them.

To make variables available, you need to inject them into the workflow. The easiest way to do so is to transform the values of a data table into variables, using a special node called **Table Row to Variable**.

Table Row to Variable

This node (**Workflow Control > Variables**) takes all the values in the first row of the input table and transforms them into individual variables, each one named after the corresponding input column. Its configuration window lets you select the columns whose first row's value should be transformed into variables:

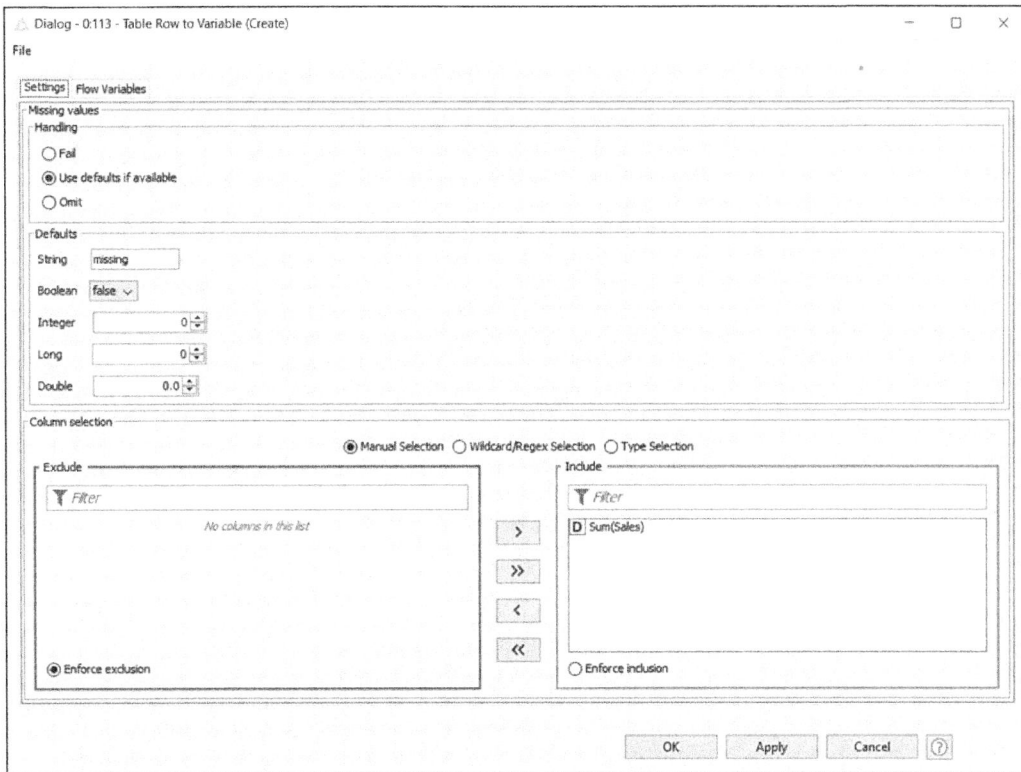

Figure 3.26: Configuration of Table Row to Variable node: select the values to be transformed into variables

The output port of this node is a red circle, which indicates flow variables. You can inject the variables into any node by just connecting this output port with the receiving node's body.

> Every node in KNIME has flow variable ports available. They are hidden by default. To unhide them, just right-click on the node and then click on **Show Flow Variable Ports**.

It's important to clarify that this node will only transform the *values in the first row* of a table into variables. If you need to iterate through different values, you can use **Table Row To Variable Loop Start**. Using this node (for example, in conjunction with a **Loop End** node, which you have already seen), you can create a loop where, at every iteration, the variables assume the value included in each of the input rows.

Now that we know how to implement variables in KNIME, we can create a variable that contains the total aggregation of sales, which we will then use in the **Math Formula** node, to calculate the sales footprint. Let's use **GroupBy** to aggregate total sales and then a **Table Row to Variable** node to transform that number into a variable.

22. We need to aggregate all the sales that happened in 2019 into one single row, holding the grand total of generated revenues. Let's implement **GroupBy** and connect it to the output port of the **Date&Time-based Row Filter** node. Since we only need a row with the grand total, we can leave the **Group** panel empty: this will generate a warning on our node, but we know why we are doing this, so we can ignore it. On the **Manual Aggregation** panel, let's add the usual *Sales* column and aggregate through the **Sum** function. To avoid any confusion with the variable name, let's select **Aggregation method (column name)** as the naming convention this time (the menu at the bottom). Once we run the node, we obtain a simple output, which is exactly what we were after: a table with one row and one column, displaying the grand total of sales in 2019.

23. We are now ready to transform this value into a variable by implementing the **Table Row to Variable** node right after the **GroupBy**. No configuration is needed for this node, as we can transform all columns (just one in our case) into variables.

24. It's finally time to make the footprint calculation. Let's implement a **Math Formula** node and make the two connections we need. First, this node should receive as an input table the result of the **GroupBy** that we used a few steps ago to calculate the total sales by category. Second, we should inject the variable with the grand total of sales, by creating a connection between the red port of the **Table Row to Variable** node and the **Math Formula** node. To do so, you can click on the red circle, keep the button pressed, and release it on the **Math Formula** node icon.

> Although this is not needed, if you want to view any node's variable ports, just open the pop-up menu (right-click on the node) and then click on **Show Flow Variable Ports**.

The node configuration dialog now allows us to use the flow variable we have just injected. You will notice the variable (called *Sum(Sales)*) on the right within the **Flow Variable List**. We can calculate the footprint by using the mouse and keyboard and obtaining the expression: $Sales$/$${DSum(Sales)}$$*100. We can append the resulting column, assigning it the name *Footprint* and, for simplicity, converting it to an integer number by ticking the last checkbox at the bottom:

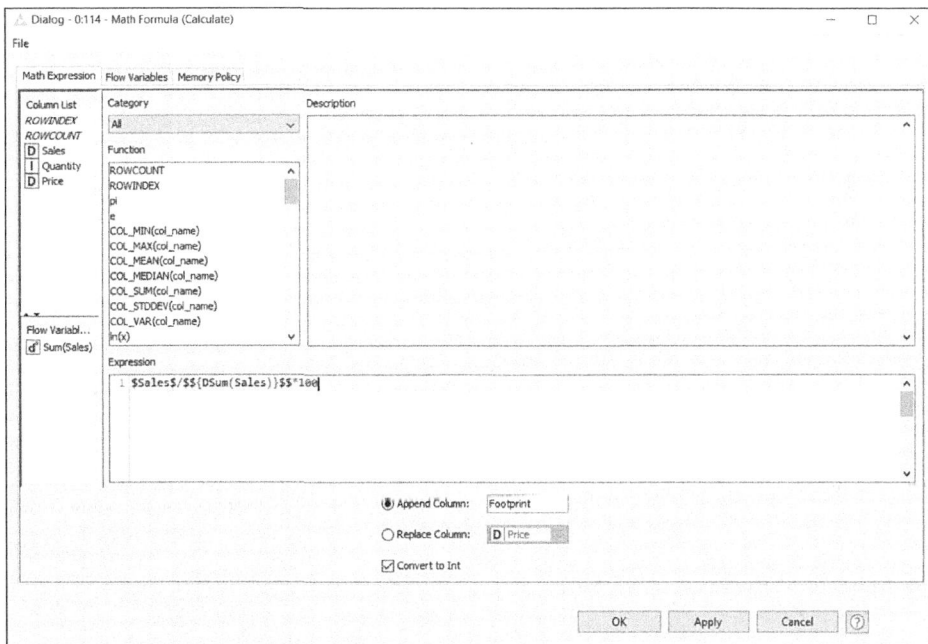

Figure 3.27: Configuration of the Math Formula node for the footprint calculation: we found both columns and variables on the left, ready to be used in the expression

Also, this business question has now found a proper answer: the output of Math Formula includes both the footprint of each category and its total sales, answering two questions at once. We have one last question to manage, which will require producing a chart. For all the previous ones, we have produced some tables: it would be nice to collect all these tables in a single Excel file with multiple tabs so we can disseminate our report easily and in a compact form.

25. Let's implement an **Excel Writer** node. Since this time we need to save four different tables in a single Excel file, we need to add three input ports to the node. To do so, click on the three dots appearing at the bottom left of the node icon and then **Add ports | Sheet Input Ports**. Repeat this, two more times, to obtain four input ports in total. Connect the output ports of the nodes providing the *answers* to the five questions we have managed so far (the overall top ten products, the top three by subcategory, the sales by country, and the output of the last Math Formula having both footprint and sales by category in 2019). In the **Excel Writer**'s configuration, this time we find four textboxes in the **Sheets** panel: we can use them to assign a meaningful name to guide whoever is reading the report. After declaring the full path and the name of the output file (click on the **Browse...** button to select it), we are ready to close the configuration and execute the node:

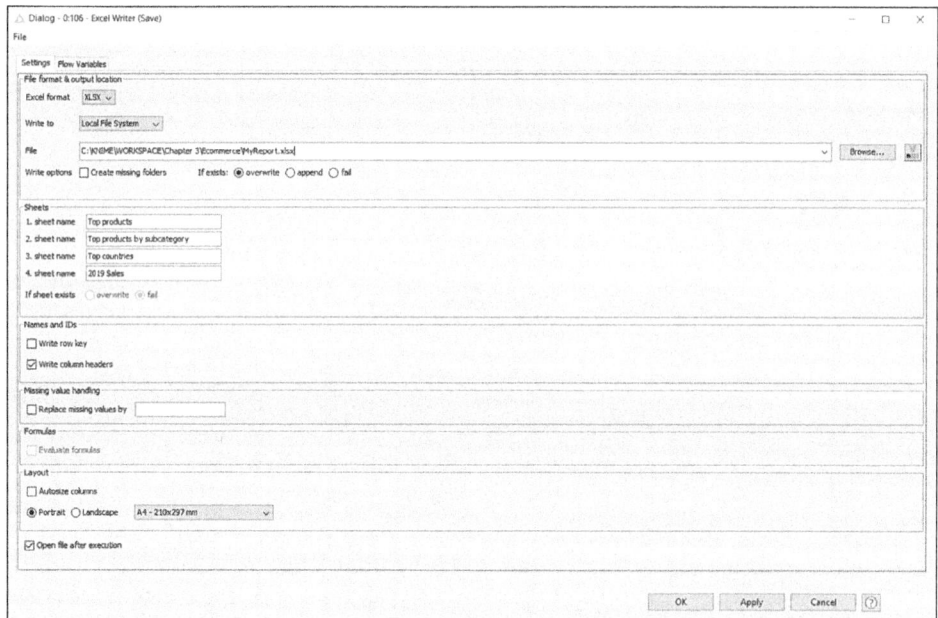

Figure 3.28: Configuration of the Excel Writer: you can name each sheet differently

The resulting Excel file looks exactly as we expected: we have four tabs, each looking after a different aspect of our business, providing straightforward answers to the common questions we had:

	A	B	C	D	E	F		C	D	E	F	G	H	I	J	K	L
1	StockCode	Description	Category	Subcatego	Sales	Quantity	1	Category	Subcatego	Sales	Quantity						
2	22423	REGENCY CAKESTAND 3 TIER	Home	Kitchen	265295.6	23063	2	Accessories	Bags	166451.2	92726						
3	85123A	WHITE HANGING HEART T-LIGHT HOLDER	Air fragances	Candles	240707.7	89264	3	Accessories	Bags	66771.74	36801						
4	85099B	JUMBO BAG RED RETROSPOT	Accessories	Bags	166451.2	92726	4	Accessories	Bags	63526.31	35515						
5	84879	ASSORTED COLOUR BIRD ORNAMENT	Home	Decoratio	124354.7	78160	5	Home	Bathroom	11377.25	12673						
6	47566	PARTY BUNTING	Kids	Party	102220.9	23241	6	Home	Bathroom	6671.65	1250						
7	22086	PAPER CHAIN KIT 50'S CHRISTMAS	Seasonal	Christmas	74510.46	27608	7	Home	Bathroom	4310.07	2679						
8	79321	CHILLI LIGHTS	Home	Furniture	70118.67	15172	8	Accessories	Bijoux	40357.5	34355						
9	22386	JUMBO BAG PINK POLKADOT	Accessories	Bags	66771.74	36801	9	Accessories	Bijoux	22310.42	18609						
10	48138	DOORMAT UNION FLAG	Home	Furniture	64128.57	9857	10	Accessories	Bijoux	21576.14	18307						
11	85099F	JUMBO BAG STRAWBERRY	Accessories	Bags	63526.31	35515	11	Air fragances	Candles	240707.7	89264						
12							12	Air fragances	Candles	55430.84	10041						
13							13	Air fragances	Candles	48188.87	16961						

Top products | Top products by subcate ...   Top products by subcategory | Top cou ...

	A	B	C	D	E	F	G	H	I		A	B	C	D	E	F	G	H	I
1	Country	Sales	Quantity							1	Category	Sales	Quantity	Price	Footprint				
2	United Kingdom	11824179	6990302							2	Accessories	948680	600812	1.930299	15				
3	EIRE	480565.9	263118							3	Air fragances	453675.4	311514	2.047196	7				
4	Netherlands	437844.4	309995							4	Hobbies	393853.8	132076	4.428578	6				
5	Germany	309227.8	181511							5	Home	3008832	1417220	3.663905	48				
6	France	234526.6	142608							6	Kids	497427.1	298060	2.735283	8				
7	Australia	131800.6	77929							7	Seasonal	420546.2	298003	2.36662	7				
8	Switzerland	80888.4	44375							8	Stationery	604042.5	661011	1.719668	10				
9	Spain	71788.57	36735							9									
10	Sweden	60221.39	66649							10									
11	Unspecified	54542.72	34309							11									
12	Denmark	53714.02	218817							12									
13	Belgium	45959.56	28324							13									

Top countries | 2019 Sales   Top countries | 2019 Sales

Figure 3.29: The output file in Excel has four sheets to answer five business questions

It's time to move on to the last and final business question, which is about monthly peaks of sales across our seasonal subcategories, which are "Christmas", "Summer", and "Easter". To show seasonal patterns across the year, we decide to aggregate sales by month/subcategory combinations. A pivot table will enable such bidimensional aggregation, which will be easy to display on a line chart. The only outstanding intricacy to solve is related to the aggregation by month. At this point, in fact, we do not have months indicated in a separate column, so we cannot perform the aggregation straightaway. Fortunately, there is a node that enables us the extraction of any temporal field from a Date&Time column.

▶ ② ▶ *Extract Date&Time Fields*

This node (**Other Data Types > Time Series > Transform**) creates a separate column for each date or time field (such as Year, Month, Day of week, Hour, Minute, and so on), extracting it from a given Date&Time input column. Its configuration requires us to select the Date&Time source column and then tick the boxes of the fields to extract. Since some fields are prone to regional and language differences, you can specify the **Locale** you prefer to use. For instance, if you extract Month (name) for a date in December, with the **es-ES** locale (Spanish), you will get `diciembre`:

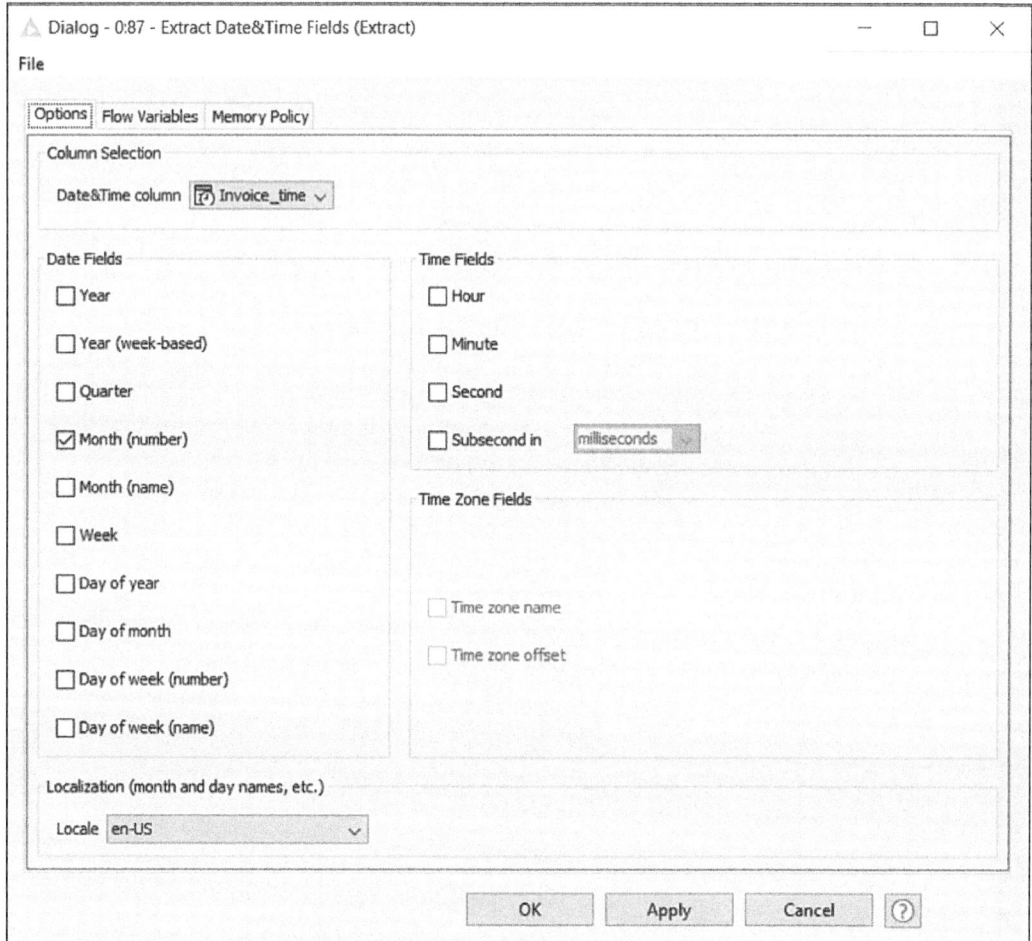

Figure 3.30: Configuration of Extract Date&Time Fields node:
select the fields you want to appear as a separate column

26. Let's implement an **Extract Date&Time Fields** node and connect the **String to Date&Time** output port to it (we want to consider the full dataset—not just 2019—so we want to build a separate branch). The configuration is straightforward: we only have one Data&Time field in the input table so we find it already selected in the drop-down selection at the top. We only need to extract **Month (number)**, so this will be the only box to tick.

27. We can now summarize sales by month and subcategory: add a **Pivoting** node and configure it so that **Groups** are defined by the newly created column (*Month (number)*), **Pivots** are defined by the column *Subcategory*, and the **Manual Aggregation** is on **Sum** of *Sales*. To keep the headers clean, let's select **Pivot name** as **Column name** and **Keep original name(s)** as **Aggregation name** in the drop-down menus at the bottom.

Seasonality can be explained better through a nice chart instead of a table. To build a chart in KNIME, you can use one of the visualization nodes (check them out in the repository in **View > JavaScript**), like the one we will use for our line chart.

Line Plot

This node (**View > JavaScript**) generates a line plot based on the data given at the input port. When configuring the node, you need to specify what column to use for the horizontal axis (**x-axis**) and what columns to visualize as separate lines (**y-axis**). Additionally, you can generate a static vectorial image (in SVG format) at the node's output port: to enable this, tick the **Create image at outport** box at the top:

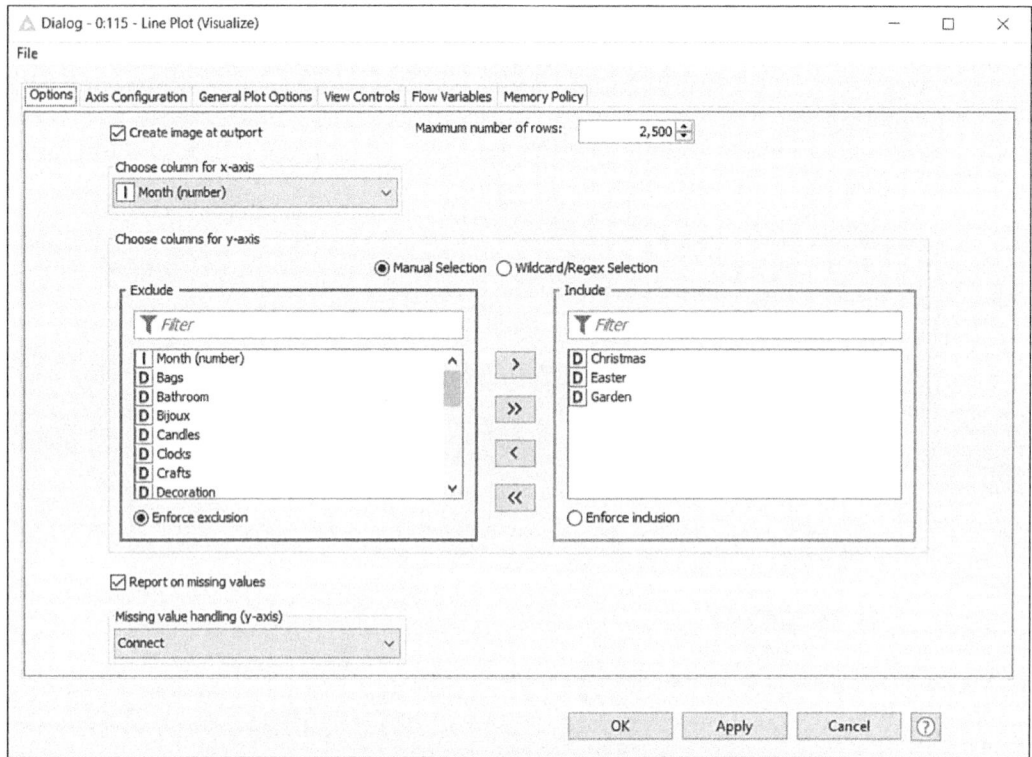

Figure 3.31: Configuration of Line Plot node:
select which columns to use on the horizontal and vertical axes of your chart

In the **Axis Configuration** panel, you can specify the titles of the horizontal and vertical axes, while in the **General Plot Options**, you can set **Chart title**, **Chart subtitle**, and the size of the output image.

28. Let's implement a Line Plot chart (pick the JavaScript version from the node repository) and connect the first output of the **Pivoting** node with it. For its configuration, let's choose *Month (number)* for the **x-axis** and the columns related to the seasonal subcategories (*Christmas*, *Easter*, and *Garden*) for the **y-axis**. Let's also check the first option box so we generate the vectorial image at the outport. To make the chart more readable, we can add also the names of the axis (Sales and Month will do) using the **Axis Configuration** panel. To execute the node and open its output straightaway, right-click on the node and then select **Execute and Open Views** (or *Shift + F10*):

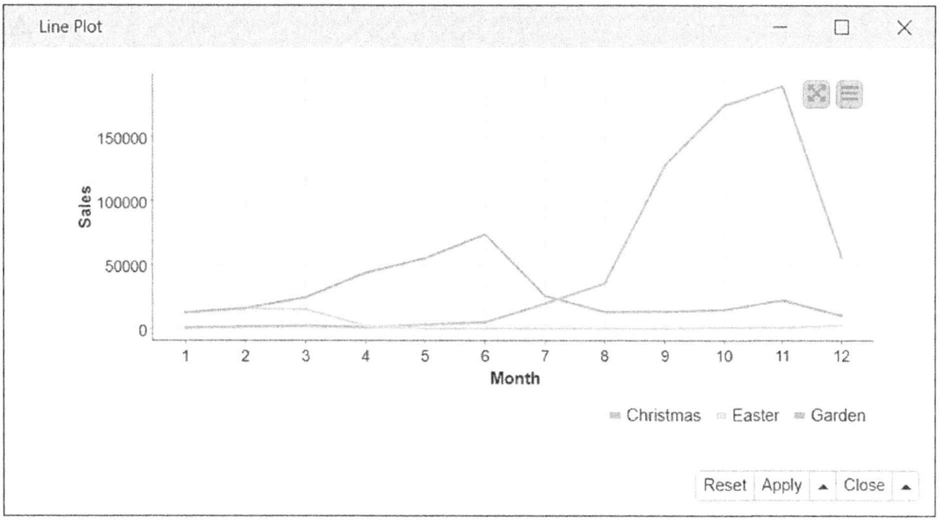

Figure 3.32: Output of the Line Plot node: our seasonal subcategories
display an unsurprising monthly pattern

The chart's output confirms to us the seasonality patterns that we would expect from our subcategories: the shape of the lines can help us to best plan for the demand that we will encounter in the coming years. It would be nice to export this chart as a vectorial file so that we can include it in shiny presentations and—most importantly, as we will learn—build an engaging story out of it!

Image Writer (Port)

This node (**IO > Write**) saves an image as a separate file. The only configuration needed is to specify the **Output location**. You can select it in your file system by clicking on the **Browse...** button:

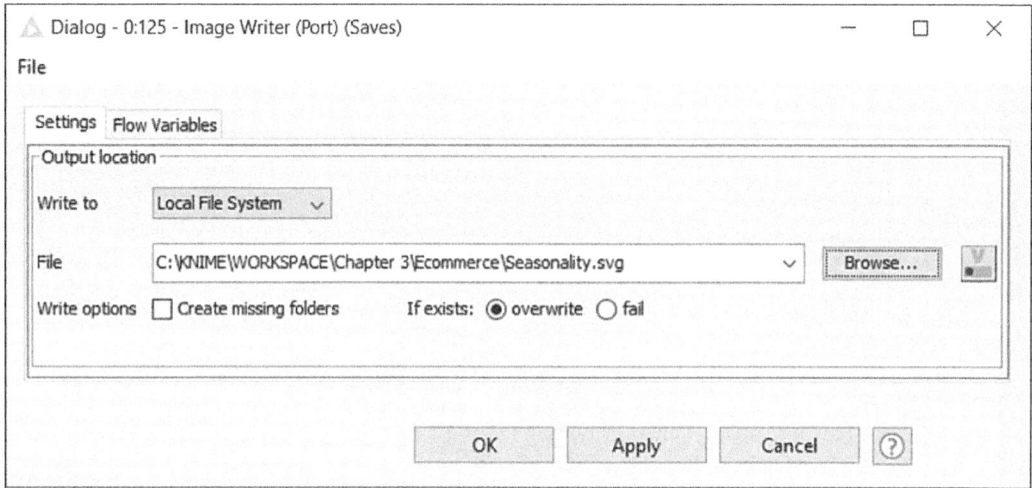

Figure 3.33: Configuration of the Image Writer (Port) node: where do you want your image file to be?

29. Let's implement the **Image Writer (Port)** node; connect the output of the **Line Plot** node with it (the green square connectors indicate that we are transferring images here), and configure it by specifying the location of the output file (make sure you indicate the full file name, including the .svg extension at the end).

You made it! It took some time, but the investment was entirely worth it: your workflow is now able to generate a multi-page report (and, when needed, visual proof of the seasonal patterns) in a matter of seconds. Every time new data becomes available, the full workflow can be reset (select the initial nodes and press *F8*) and re-run by just executing the final nodes (or *Shift + F7* to execute all nodes at once): no more human error or tedious manual steps with Excel. The finance analyst is very thankful, as she can now reinvest the time she used to spend every Friday pulling together the reports in something more value adding, like analyzing the numbers in depth, offering a relevant interpretation of data evidence, and providing some recommendations for improving the business results moving forward.

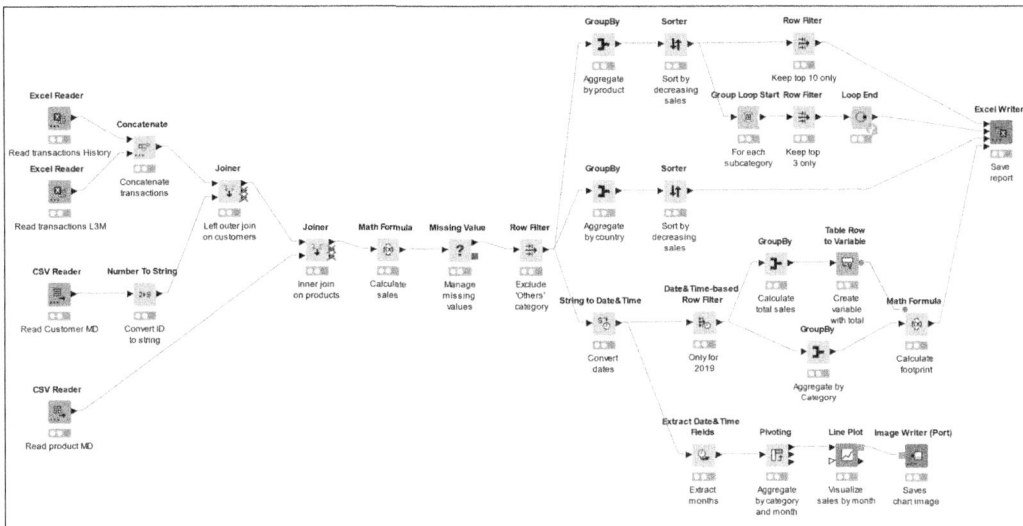

Figure 3.34: It looks like a fish, but it's a workflow that automates sales reporting

After admiring you in action, she is now intrigued by KNIME and wants to learn how to automate her data work by herself in the future. You have successfully planted a seed of enthusiasm for data analytics in your workplace, and it seems it is contagiously propagating further.

Summary

By completing this chapter, you have made decisive progress in becoming a confident user of data analytics. You have learned how to provide some logic structure to your database by creating a simple entity-relationship model. You have also experienced the essential operations for transforming data assets, such as combining tables and aggregating values as needed. Your analytics toolbox is getting fatter: with fourteen more KNIME nodes at your disposal, you can now build some simple descriptive analytics workflows and automate their executions through loops and variables. The full tutorial has allowed you to gather first-person experience in building a machine that provides systemic answers to recurring needs, starting from a set of business questions and delivering a repeatable process to answer them.

In the next chapter, we will get all of this to the next level by introducing the fundamental concepts of artificial intelligence: we will soon discover how to build machines that can autonomously learn from data and support our work.

4

What is Machine Learning?

Autonomous self-driving cars, ultraprecise robot surgeons, impeccable virtual assistants, fully automated financial traders: some of the most promising AI applications seem more like sci-fi material than prospects to an imminent reality. We could fill entire books by just collecting and presenting sensational stories of algorithmic wonders. If we manage — instead — to keep both feet firmly on the present ground and recognize how intelligent algorithms can *already* support our everyday work needs, then we start unlocking tangible value for us and our business. This is what this chapter is all about: stripping away the myth from reality by meeting in person the main machine learning algorithms and techniques. The end objective is to start counting on them as everyday companions rather than out-of-reach, futuristic possibilities.

In this chapter, we will find answers to the following questions:

- What are AI and machine learning?
- What is the "machine learning way" to solve business problems? What's the difference between this approach and the traditional approach?
- How can machines learn? Which algorithms are available out there for making this happen? How do they work?
- What tradeoffs do I need to consider when selecting the right model for my business need?
- How can I assess the performance of a machine learning solution?

Although this chapter is the most "analytical" one of the book, you will find only a handful of math formulas involved. The point is to give you an intuitive understanding of how machine learning works versus providing the whole theoretical background behind it.

Think about it: you don't need to be a mathematician to use math, and you don't have to become a computer scientist or an expert coder to use a computer! Similarly, the next few pages will not make you able to recreate from scratch full modeling procedures: it will, instead, show you how to utilize the ones that—spoiler alert— are already conveniently implemented in software platforms like KNIME. In this chapter, we will learn the unmissable foundations needed to make you a user of machine learning, while in the next one, we will put them into practice using KNIME nodes through full tutorials. You might be impatient to jump into the practice, but I strongly recommend you go through this chapter first and feel confident about it before moving on. Buckle up: let's talk AI!

Introducing artificial intelligence and machine learning

Can machines think? This is what English polymath and wartime codebreaker Alan Turing asked himself in his seminal 1950 paper that would lay the groundwork for AI. Although Turing does not use the term "artificial intelligence" (it would be introduced as a research discipline only six years later), he was convinced that machines would eventually compete with human beings in *all purely intellectual fields*.

Using technology devices to extend and partially replace human intellect was not a new quest. Back in the 17th century, French mathematician and philosopher Blaise Pascal invented the **Pascaline** (*Figure 4.1*), a fully working mechanical computer that could do addition and subtraction of numbers entered by rotating its dials.

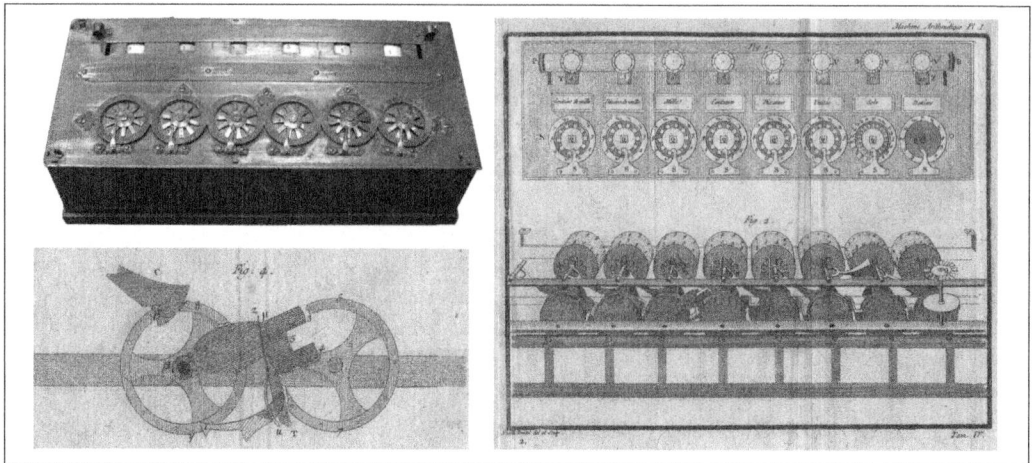

Figure 4.1: Pascal's arithmetic machine, a.k.a. the Pascaline. From the top left, clockwise: an original device built in 1652; a view of the underlying system of gears; the detailed plan of the sautoir, the ingenious mechanism enabling the carryover in additions. The photograph is by Rama, Wikimedia Commons, Cc-by-sa-2.0-fr.

Calculating mathematical operations is a very specific intellectual task. Still, the Pascaline was early proof that technology can replicate and amplify people's capacity to do brain work, not just physical activities. This is what AI is all about: **Artificial Intelligence (AI)** is defined as the ability of machines to perform actions that display *some* form of human intelligence, such as solving logical problems, using language to communicate, recognizing visual and auditory patterns, making sense of the environment, or coordinating physical movements. Within the broader field of AI, **Machine Learning (ML)** focuses on the artificial replication of a *specific* aspect of human intelligence: the ability to learn.

The faculty of learning has immense potential value when applied to any business. If a machine can autonomously learn from data for us, we can use it to consistently grow our knowledge on customers, competitors, and our own operations. We can reduce costs, simplify processes, grow revenue thanks to better decisions, proactively prepare for the future, and even improve the experience — and so the loyalty — of our customers. ML algorithms are tireless partners in growing our business: they can extend our team's overall intelligence, leveraging the extensive computational capacity of digital technology (which gets increasingly cheaper over time) and the massive amount of data that would be otherwise largely lying unused in a corporate database. The strong potential of autonomous learning explains why, in the last few years, ML has grown so much in popularity to unseat its conceptual parent, AI, as the trendiest technology phenomenon on everyone's lips. Today, AI and ML are often used as synonyms, and in the rest of the book, we will primarily refer to the latter. To avoid confusion in your further readings, just remember: AI looks at the full scope of human intelligence, ML concentrates on the autonomous learning bit.

> An **Algorithm** is a problem-solving procedure or, in other words, a series of pre-defined steps that can be followed to solve a specific task. The steps required by a machine to multiply two numbers or to make a prediction based on previous values are both examples of algorithms. Computers are often able to solve complex problems, provided that a human equips them with the right algorithm to follow.

One important clarification is needed on the nature of the tasks that we can solve with AI and the classification that derives from it. In fact, researchers postulate the existence of two types of AI: strong and weak:

- **Strong AI** (or **AGI**, **Artificial General Intelligence**) is the hypothetical aptitude of machines to potentially understand and execute *any* intellectual task. A strong AI would autonomously "understand what's needed" and then "go for it," even displaying those features that make us human, such as consciousness, self-awareness, creativity, intentionality, and sentience. However fascinating (and scary) the concept of strong AI appears, today it still mainly falls into the realm of theoretical speculation or fictional exploration. Many researchers argue that AGI is decades away, while some believe it will never become a reality. In any case, we are not going to investigate it further in this book: here we will focus, instead, on the other type of AI, which is undoubtedly more in reach.

- **Weak AI** refers to machines' ability to solve *pre-determined* and specific tasks, like predicting future sales, anticipating the behavior of a user in a given situation, or unveiling ways to optimize a particular business process. To make weak AI happen, there is always a fundamental role for human operators to play when setting things up: algorithms will need to be guided to the problem to solve and initially tweaked for operating at their best. In the upcoming part of the book, we will learn how to do precisely that: to make AI drive value in our everyday work, by setting up the right algorithms in the right way, so as to make them operate at best for our advantage.

Since strong AI is nowhere close to us and weak AI is clearly dependent on the people that set it up correctly, one thing is clear: humans and machines are not in conflict with each other, fighting for supremacy in the workforce arena and protecting their jobs. Actually, it is quite the opposite: the magic happens when humans collaborate with machines by "coaching" them properly in their learning endeavors. When this happens, intelligent machines show their full value, ultimately benefitting their human companions. Having this in mind, let's start to learn how to coach the AI properly, by recognizing the business situations where the right algorithm can make the difference.

The machine learning way

Ironically, one of the foremost barriers preventing the exploitation of ML in a business is neither the implementation of the algorithm nor the retrieval of the data (the *how*): the toughest part is to recognize the right occasion to use it (the *why*)! We need to identify within the complex map of business processes (the operating model of the company) the specific steps where algorithms can bring real value if adopted. If we develop our sensitivity to recognize such leverage points, then we will be able to find in our work the first opportunities to put ML into practice.

There is a machine learning way (we can call it the **ML way**) to operate business processes. Let's go through three sample scenarios to distinguish between the traditional and the ML ways to create value with data.

Scenario #1: Predicting market prices

You work for a car dealership, specializing in multibrand, used vehicles. You notice that some cars take much longer to sell because their initial listing price was too high versus customers' expectations. To improve this situation, you want to implement a technical solution to guide the price-setting process in a data-based manner: the objective is to anticipate the actual market price of each car to keep inventory under control while maximizing revenues.

Here are two possible approaches to solve this:

- The traditional way is to codify a set of rules that define how the car's features impact the market price and build a "calculator" that implements these rules. The calculator will leverage a mix of available data points (like the starting price of new cars by brand and model, or the cost of accessories) and some thumb-rules defined thanks to common sense and to the expertise of those who have been for some time in the business. For example, some rules can be: *the car depreciates by 20% during its first year and then by an additional 15% every further year of age*, or *cars that run for more than 10,000 miles/year are high-mileage and their value is reduced by a further 15%*, and so on. To build this calculator, you will need to implement these if-then rules using a programming language, which means that you also need a programmer to develop and maintain the code over time.

- The ML way is to get an algorithm to analyze all the data related to previous sales and autonomously "learn" the rules that connect the car features (like mileage, age, make, model, accessories, and so on) with the actual price at which the car sold. The algorithm can identify some recurrent patterns, which are partly confirming the rules we already had in mind (maybe adding a further level of precision to those approximate thumb rules), and partly identify new and unexpected connections, which humans failed to recognize and summarize in a simple rule (like, for instance, *model X depreciates 37% more slowly when equipped with this rare optional*). Using this approach, the machine can keep learning over time: the rules underlying the price will evolve and get automatically updated as new sales happen and new car models enter the market.

The main difference is that in the traditional approach, our price prediction will leverage the existing human knowledge on the matter (if adequately documented and codified), while the ML way provides for that knowledge (and possibly more) to be autonomously learned from data by the machine.

Scenario #2: Segmenting customers

You work in the marketing team of a local supermarket chain. You are responsible for preparing a weekly newsletter to be sent to those customers who signed up for the loyalty program and opted in to receive emails from you. Instead of sending a one-size-fits-all newsletter to everyone, you want to create a reasonable number of different versions and distribute them accordingly to the various groups. By selecting key messages and special offers that are closer to each group's needs, you aim to maximize the engagement and loyalty of your entire customer base.

There are at least two ways to create such groups:

- The traditional way is to use common sense and your existing knowledge to select the features that can reasonably discriminate across different types of customers, each having a more specific set of needs. For instance, you can decide to use the age of household members and average income level to define different groups: you will end up with groups like the *affluent families with children* (to whom you might talk about premium-quality products for kids) and *low-income 60+ empty nesters* (more interested in high-value deals). This traditional approach assumes that the needs within each group—in this case, solely defined by age and income—are homogeneous: we might end up ignoring some meaningful differences across other dimensions.

- The ML way is to ask an algorithm to identify for us a number of homogeneous groups of customers that systematically display similar shopping behavior. Not being restricted by the cognitive capacity of humans (who would struggle to take into account dozens of variables at once) and their personal biases (driven by their individual and specific experiences), the algorithm can come up with groups that are specific and more closely connected to the actual preferences of each customer, like *food lovers who shop at the weekend* (to whom we might send some fancy recipes every Saturday morning) and *high-income pet owners* (wanting to take care of their beloved furry companions).

Traditionally, we would differentiate actions by considering apparent—and, sometimes, naïve—differences, while the ML way goes straight to the core of the matter and identifies those homogeneous groups that best describe the diversity of our customer base, keeping everyone included and engaged.

Scenario #3: Finding the best ad strategy

You work in the digital marketing department of a mid-sized company providing online photo printing services. Your responsibility is to define and execute digital advertising campaigns with the ultimate objective of maximizing their return. Instead of having a single campaign based on the same content, you want to optimize your strategy by testing different digital assets and seeing what works best. For example, you might have banners showing different products (like photo books and cheesy mugs with a portrait on them), various colors and fonts, or alternate versions of the tagline text. You can post your ads on social media and search engines, and you can control the available budget and duration of each test.

Also in this case, we can recognize two possible approaches to make this happen:

- The traditional way is to run the so-called A/B/n testing: you define several alternative executions (for instance, three similar ads with the same graphic but three different call-to-action texts like *buy me now*, *check it out*, or *click to learn more*), run each of them — let's imagine — 10,000 times, and calculate their individual return by counting, for example, the number of orders generated by each execution. You will need to repeat the test over time to check if it's still valid and, if you want to optimize across other dimensions (like the time of day at which the ad is served, or the location of users, and so on) you will end up with a growing number of combinations to test (and a larger cost of the experiment).

- The ML way is to let an algorithm dynamically decide what to test and how, moving progressively toward the path leading to the best combinations of variable aspects. At first, the algorithm will start similarly as in an A/B/n test, trying some random combinations: this will be enough to grasp some first knowledge on the most promising directions to take. Over time, the algorithm will focus its attention (and budget) more and more on the few paths that are working best, finetuning and enriching them with an increasingly larger number of factors. In the end, the algorithm might end up with some very specific choices like *use a pink font and display a photo mug for people in their 50s who are connecting through a laptop*.

In both approaches, we have used tests to learn what the best ad strategy was. However, in the traditional A/B/n testing approach, we had to define test settings based on prior knowledge and common sense. In the ML way, we put the machine in the driving seat and let it interact with the environment, learn progressively, and dynamically adjust the testing strategy, so as to minimize costs and get higher returns.

The business value of learning machines

These three scenarios unveil some recurrent differences between the traditional and the ML way to operate business processes. Let's have a look at the incremental benefits we get from ML:

- Both approaches rely on technology and data, but the ML way leverages them *more extensively*. Suppose you allow algorithms to explore the full information content of a large database. In that case, you capitalize on the massive horsepower of digital technologies and avoid hitting the bottleneck of human cognitive limitation. With ML, more data will be considered at once (think about the many attributes of customers to be segmented or the factors that differentiate digital ads), which is likely to end up in better business outcomes. In other words, the ML way tends to be **more accurate and effective** than traditional approaches, leading to an economic advantage for the company relying on it.

- Once it is correctly set up, the ML way can operate *independently* and with *minimal supervision* from its human companion. This means driving automation of intellectual tasks and, as a result, incremental **efficiency** and productivity for the business. Because of this automation, ML algorithms can stay **always on** and keep learning unceasingly on a 24/7 schedule. This means that they will get better and better at what they do over time, as more data comes in, without necessarily having to invest in further upgrades or human improvements. Think about the new car models appearing in the market or the evolving preferences of customers served by a digital ad: algorithms will observe reality vigilantly, spot trend breakers, and react accordingly to keep the business going.

- The traditional approach relies on *previous* human knowledge while the ML way generates *additional* knowledge. This is a game-changing and fascinating benefit of ML called **Knowledge Discovery**: learning algorithms can provide a better and sometimes insightful understanding of reality (think about the subtle rules that explain car price formation, or the unexpected connections pulling together consumers in homogeneous groups) that can't be spotted by just looking at the data. It is the capacity to *hack* reality by finding unexpected patterns in the way things work. If the learning algorithm provides for its outcome to be humanly intelligible (and many of them do), this knowledge will go and accrue to the overall know-how of the organization in terms of customer understanding, market dynamics, operating model, and more: this can be as valuable as gold, if used well!

Making processes more efficient and effective, plus systematically acquiring an additional understanding of the business, these benefits by themselves are enough to explain why ML is currently exploding in modern business, making it a competitive advantage that nobody wants the risk of not having. Let's now meet the types of algorithms that can enable all of this.

Three types of learning algorithms

The scenarios we have seen in the previous section were not selected at random. They match the standard categorization of ML algorithms that provides for three fundamental types: **Supervised Learning**, **Unsupervised Learning**, and **Reinforcement Learning**. When we want to apply the ML way, we need to select one of these three routes: our choice will depend on the nature of the problem we need to solve. Let's now go through each group to understand what they are made of and what types of tasks they fulfill.

Supervised learning

In supervised learning, your objective is to predict something "unknown" by learning from some "known" pieces of information. The easiest way to make sense of the supervised learning approach is to think about how it differs from traditional programming. In *Figure 4.2*, you will find on the left a very familiar setup. In plain computer programming, we need some input *data*, a *program,* and a *computer* to generate some *results*. The program is a series of instructions — described in a machine-intelligible idiom, called the **Programming Language** — which the computer will apply to the input data to return the desired results as an output. In supervised ML, we keep all these four elements (data, program, computer, and results) but change the order of two of them. As you can see from the right part of *Figure 4.2*, in supervised learning, you give data and results — as inputs — to a computer that will return — as output — the program that "connects" the results to the data.

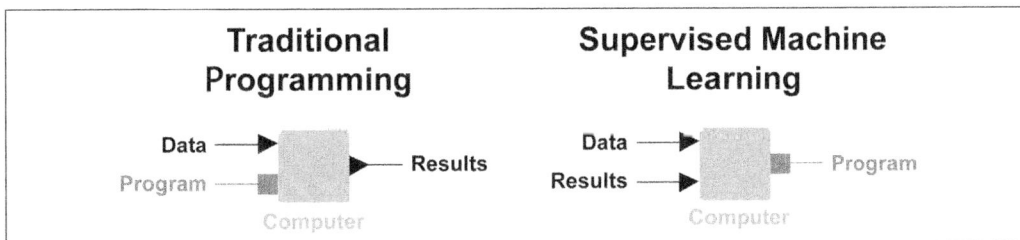

Figure 4.2: Traditional programming compared with the supervised ML approach.
The ingredients are the same, but the order differs.

What empowers the computer to make this "magic" happen is the supervised ML algorithm: this algorithm is a series of steps that can find out the set of transformations (mathematically described as a **Statistical Model**) that you can apply to some input data to obtain something close to the desired results. Thanks to these algorithms, the computer will "learn" from past data (for which we know the results) to unveil the approximate mechanism connecting input data to the unknown results.

This will be even clearer if we apply it to **Scenario #1** introduced in the *The Machine learning way* section: the car price predictions. In this case, our input data is the known attributes of the cars sold in the past. The result that we want to get is the price of those cars. If we leverage the supervised ML approach, we can use our known *past data* (features of previously sold cars) and *past results* (previous sale prices) to infer such transformation steps (the *program*, or model) that, once applied to *future data* (features of the next cars to be sold), will return the *future results* (predicted prices). In this setup (see *Figure 4.3*), the ML algorithm is implemented in the **Learner** block. The **Predictor** block will just "execute" on new data points from the program that is provided by the learner block.

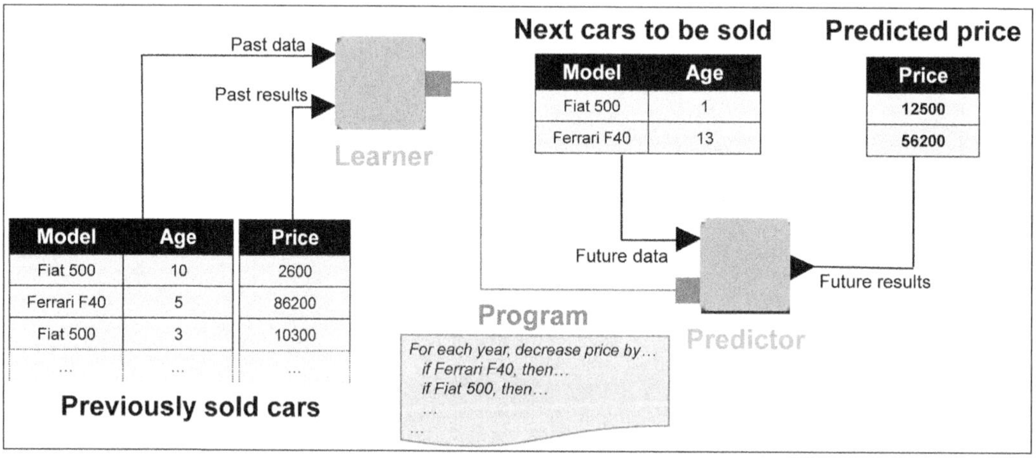

Figure 4.3: Supervised ML in action: learning from previously sold cars to understand the unwritten rules of how the features of the cars define their prices

Thanks to the supervised ML algorithm, which empowers the learner, we can find out the "hidden rules" of price formation. Ferraris will have a much higher starting point and follow a different price decay over time than Fiat 500s: the algorithm will find those rules out.

It is important to recognize that in supervised learning, you always have a specific measure to be predicted: this is called the **Target** (or **Dependent** variable). In the previous example, the price of the car was the target variable of our learning. All other variables — the ones used to predict what the target will be — are called **Features** (or **Independent** variables). The model and the age of cars in *Figure 4.3* were the two features used in the learning.

When input data is enriched with "results" (also known as **labels**), it is called **labeled data**. For simplicity, think about this: a labeled data table will always have multiple columns containing the features and a specific column containing the target. Labeled data is an unmissable ingredient of supervised ML.

Depending on the nature of the target variable, you can identify two scenarios of learning, which require different learning algorithms within the supervised family:

- When the target variable is a numeric measure (like *5.21* or *$23,000*), then you need a **Regression** algorithm. Linear Regression is the easiest and most common example of algorithms able to predict numbers.

- When the target variable is a categorical measure (like a string of text indicating to which category or class an element belongs), you will need a **Classification** algorithm. Examples of classes are *red*, *blue*, and *green*, or binary categories like *true* and *false*, or labels identifying a specific behavior, such as *will buy this product* and *will not buy this product*. Decision Trees, Random Forests, and Support Vector Machines are just some of the many algorithms available to you when you want to predict to which classes the elements of a table belong. You will learn how to use some of them in the next chapter.

Some supervised algorithms can be used for both regression and classification. This is true of Neural Networks, which can predict either numbers or classes.

The Logistic Regression algorithm (a variation of Linear Regression) can predict the likelihood of belonging to binary classes. Hence, as confusing as it is, Logistic Regression is a classification algorithm even if the name suggests the contrary.

Before we move on to the following type of learning algorithms, it is worth thinking about why this one is called supervised. The analogy we can strike is with a teacher who gives a lesson by providing multiple examples of how something works, hoping that the student will grasp the concept by noticing connections. When sharing various illustrations of a concept (the labeled data), the teacher *supervises* the student's learning. Without those examples for which we knew the outcome (the target variable), the teacher would have been unable to guide the student. That's why in supervised learning, you always have a target variable, and you always need to start from some labeled data.

Let's move on to the next type of ML algorithm, where you don't need any labeled data to start learning.

Unsupervised learning

In this case, your objective is not to make a prediction but to unveil some hidden structure in your data. Unsupervised ML algorithms are capable of *exploring* your data table to find out some interesting patterns in the way rows and columns are connected to each other.

There is a broad series of use case scenarios where unsupervised learning can be of great value:

- The simplest case is **Clustering**. This is about aggregating your data points to create homogeneous groups, called clusters. Each group will contain points that are "similar" to each other. This is exactly what we needed to do in **Scenario #2**, where we had to build groups of similar supermarket customers to send each of them a meaningful and personalized newsletter. Algorithms like K-means and Hierarchical Clustering are good examples of unsupervised ML algorithms dedicated to identifying clusters.

> An interesting extension of clustering in the world of text mining is **Topic Modeling**, meaning the identification of topics (groups of conceptually related words) in text documents. One of the most popular algorithms for topic modeling is **Latent Dirichlet Allocation (LDA)**.

- Finding **Association Rules** is another common need covered by unsupervised learning. Let's imagine that you have an extensive database containing a description of all the receipts generated in a supermarket. Some products might frequently "end up" together in the same receipt: think about milk and coffee or pasta and tomato sauce. Algorithms like Apriori and FP-Growth will scout for several meaningful and statistically significant rules, such as *customers buying pasta will likely also buy tomato sauce*. These rules can be insightful information to leverage when optimizing a store's assortment or defining which products should be on adjacent shelves (**Market Basket Analysis**).

- Another typical usage of unsupervised learning is called **Dimensionality Reduction**. If you have a table with many columns, it could be that some of them are correlated to each other: as a consequence, your table will be redundant since the information carried by one column might be already present in other columns. To avoid all the drawbacks linked to redundancy (such as performance degradation and loss of accuracy), it is worth reducing the number of columns of the table without losing the overall information contained in it. The algorithms dedicated to dimensionality reduction, such as **Principal Component Analysis (PCA)**, can explore the structure of the table and produce a "narrower" version of it (with fewer columns, so a lower dimensionality) carrying similar informative content.

Let's now compare this unsupervised approach with the supervised one we discussed earlier. The critical difference is that in unsupervised learning, we are not after the connections between features and target: as a matter of fact, we don't have a target column in the first place! Indeed, the input data for an unsupervised algorithm is *unlabeled*: no target variable and no labels are required. Following the previous analogy, the student here will not need any "supervision" from the teacher, based on previous examples. The learning happens by exploring the data as-is and looking for patterns that are intrinsic to the data itself (like clusters of items or associations between elements).

While in supervised learning, we could easily understand whether a prediction was robust or not (by comparing it with the "real" value), in unsupervised learning, it is more difficult to assess how good the job of the algorithm was. In other words, there is not a definite good or wrong answer in unsupervised learning, only more or less valuable structures unveiled. We will have to measure its effectiveness by looking at how it fits the original purpose we aimed at. We will look more into this complexity later.

Let's now move on to the third and last class of ML algorithms.

Reinforcement learning

When adopting the reinforcement learning approach, you learn by repeatedly interacting with the environment in a "trial and error" fashion. The fundamental difference with the earlier types of learning methodologies is that, in this case, the algorithm acts as an autonomous *agent*: based on the current *state*, it will decide what *action* to take, execute it in either the real world or in a simulated *environment*, and then — depending on the outcome of its action — update its strategy to maximize the total *reward*. As you can see in *Figure 4.4*, these steps go through a loop of progressive improvements of the strategy, following a simple, common-sense base logic: if the state resulting from my action brings a positive reward, then the behavior leading to that action is positively reinforced (hence the name). If instead, that action brought a negative reward, then that behavior should be penalized so that it doesn't happen again.

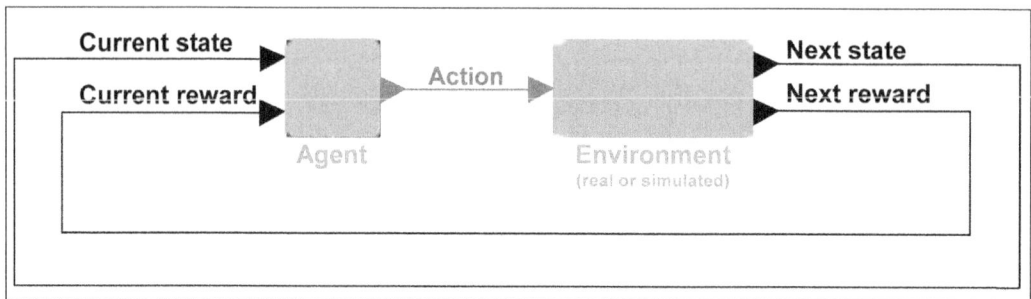

Figure 4.4: Reinforcement learning: an autonomous agent freely interacts with the environment and learns as it goes

We can recognize two use case scenarios where reinforcement learning is used:

- You can let the agent interact directly with the **external environment**, like in the case of **Scenario #3**, the digital advertising strategy for the photo printing company. Employing a series of iterations (testing different types of ads) and moving through a path of gradually increasing rewards (higher media ROI), we will end up having a robust strategy to adopt in our campaigns. The interaction can happen with the physical, real-world environment too: for instance, a robotic arm can learn how to best move some packages using the state captured through its camera sensors and continuously improving the way its engines respond to reach that objective. Reinforcement learning algorithms such as Q-learning are great for maximizing the total rewards of systems like these.

- An alternative approach is to provide a **simulated environment** for one or multiple agents to interact virtually and progressively learn from what happens. This is the case of algorithms like **Monte Carlo Tree Search (MCTS)** and its most famous implementation, Google AlphaZero, which proved able to learn from scratch and become a champion in virtually any game solely through "self-playing." The only external input required by the algorithm to get started is the list of formal rules of the games: then it proceeds as a true self-learner, playing alone with itself and swapping sides if needed. Let's take the game of chess as an example: at first, the agent will play very silly games made of random (but formally correct) moves. Then, little by little, it will learn that, by making some smart openings and defending some critical positions on the board, the chances of winning will increase. After a few hours of learning (and millions of games played), the agent will have finetuned its strategy of the most advantageous moves and will have become unbeatable by any human chess grandmaster.

Reinforcement learning has the great advantage of not requiring any labeled data to start: the agent will autonomously decide which route of experimentation to take and pursue it, accruing new data points at each step of the path. While potentially quite powerful, reinforcement learning is still not widely used in business applications because of the practical challenges of implementation such as building a working "interface" with the real world or satisfying all safety constraints—like making sure the agent doesn't cause any "damage" as it wanders around during the learning process. For this reason, in the rest of the book, we will focus on supervised and unsupervised learning algorithms: they can enable you to create value for your job quickly before moving onto more sophisticated quests.

Selecting the right learning algorithm

In the last few pages, we have heard the name of several different algorithms: this gave us a glimpse of the vast (and continuously growing) selection of ML algorithms that we could use to "go the ML way" when solving a problem. *Figure 4.5* offers a view of the catalog of ML algorithms organized by type of learning (supervised, unsupervised, and reinforcement) and objective. For each scenario, we have a choice of alternative algorithms that could do the job for you: a selection of the most commonly used algorithms are on the right-hand side of *Figure 4.5*:

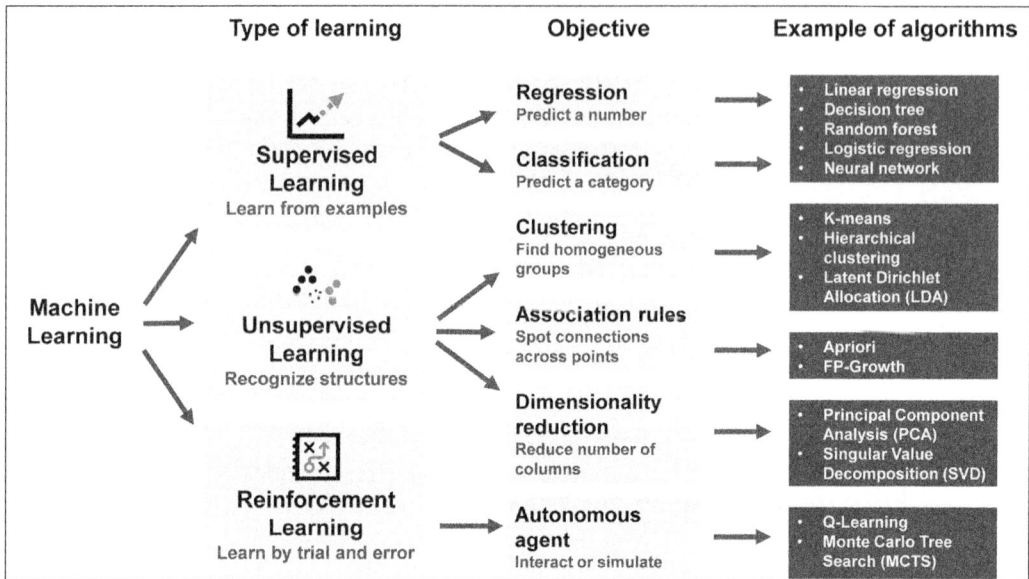

Figure 4.5: Catalog of ML algorithms: depending on your need, you select which route to take

As a user of ML, you will need to decide which algorithms, out of the many alternatives, are best suited for the task you want to accomplish. Each algorithm adopts its own logic, carrying specific strengths and weaknesses: as you select among them, you need to strike a good trade-off between their characteristics. For example, a good algorithm might be very accurate but extremely slow and expensive to run, while another one is the opposite: which one is best for you? Let's start familiarizing ourselves with the most essential attributes that define the various algorithms:

- **Performance**. Possibly the most important one to consider, this tells us "how well" the algorithm accomplishes its job and "how robust" we expect it to be in the future. For instance, in the case of supervised learning, we would measure how accurate our predictions are or, in other words, how "close" they fall to reality. This is a complex issue to consider: later we will go into more depth regarding the many measures that we can use to assess how accurate and robust an algorithm is.

- **Speed**. Depending on how many "iterations" are needed to run the full procedure, algorithms might be slow and resource-greedy or fast and light.

- **Explainability**. Some algorithms offer an easily interpretable output by human beings: this is strictly required when you want to uncover new knowledge from data and transfer it to other people or when you want to give a solid explanation of why the algorithm suggested something. In other cases, we don't need to comprehend how the algorithm operates, and we are OK to receive a complex (but accurate) *Black Box* output, impenetrable by human cognition.

- **Amount of data required**. Some algorithms perform well only with a large number of previous data points to start from. Others can be robust already with dozens of rows and do not require any big data to work.

- **Prior knowledge required**. In some cases, the algorithm requires you to make assumptions about the data you expect or the environment you operate in. Other procedures will be more agnostic toward their domain of application and do not require any prior knowledge.

These five points are just some of the many attributes you can consider when selecting the right algorithm. The good news is that these algorithms are already conveniently implemented in data analytics software platforms, for example, as KNIME nodes or as libraries in Python. Having them readily available lets you "try a few" and decide accordingly.

> In some cases, you can combine different algorithms together in a single learning procedure. In this way, you will take the best of both, collectively smoothing the edges of their individual behavior: this is called **Stacking**.

One thing is sure: there is not a "one size fits all" approach to use ML, and you need to become acquainted with a selection of alternative procedures. All these algorithms are like utensils to keep in your backpack so that you can leverage them depending on the need. By knowing several algorithms, you are free to set the right trade-offs between their contrasting attributes and do the best to solve most business cases you will find on your way.

Since performance measures are fundamental, let's get into more details on how we can assess them in machine learning algorithms.

Evaluating performance

Measuring how good an algorithm is at doing its job is not always an easy task. Take the case of unsupervised learning: we expect a good unsupervised algorithm to unveil the most interesting and useful structures from data. The assessment on what makes them *interesting* or *useful*, however, will depend on your specific end goal and often requires some human judgment as well. In reinforcement learning, a good algorithm will be able to come back with a sizeable total reward, unlocking the opportunity to keep maximizing the return of our continuous interaction with the environment. Also in this case, the concept of *reward* will depend on a specific definition of value, determined by the case we are solving.

If we stay, instead, in the area of supervised learning, the performance evaluation is more straightforward: since our objective is to predict something (numbers or categories), we can assess the performance by measuring the differences between predicted and known samples. The results of this comparison between prediction and actual values can be condensed into summary scores. Let's learn about these scores for both regression and classification.

Regression

Since regression is all about predicting numeric values, scoring its performance means assessing the overall distance of the results of the prediction from the actual values we were trying to predict: the smaller the distance, the smaller the error, and the smaller the error, the better. In the case of the simple Linear Regression you see in *Figure 4.6*, we are trying to predict the price of second-hand cars (target variable) based solely on their age (our only independent variable). The dotted line shows the result of our model, which gives us a prediction of the price given the age: of course, as the age increases, the price decreases. Hence our line goes down as we move to the right. The circles represent the cars' actual prices, so the error that we make in our prediction is the distance between each circle and the dotted line: this "gap" from reality is called **residual**. By properly aggregating residuals, we can obtain a single performance metric for any regression.

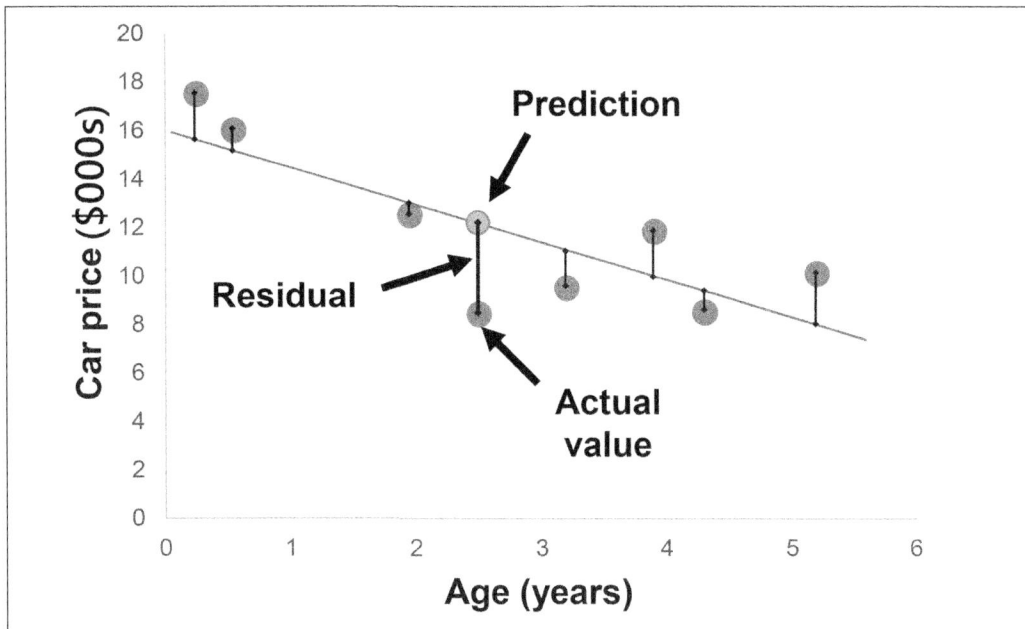

Figure 4.6: Assessing the regression performance: how much error did we make in the prediction?

One way to do so is to average them out. However, we should consider that residuals can be positive or negative quantities depending on whether the prediction is lower or higher than the actual values (see both cases in *Figure 4.6*). To avoid that negative residuals counterbalance (and, so, "mask out") positive residuals, we can calculate their squares, average them out, and then put that under a square root sign so as to bring this metric to the same unit of measure of the predicted quantity (like dollars, in the car example). This is how we obtain one of the most popular scoring metrics for regression: it's called **Root Mean Squared Error**, or **RMSE**. Its formula is:

$$RMSE = \sqrt{\frac{\sum_{i=1}^{N}(a_i - p_i)^2}{N}}$$

where a_i is the ith actual value, p_i is its corresponding prediction, and N is —simply — the total number of points in your data set. RMSE gives us an immediate indication of the confidence interval we can use together with our prediction. Given its formula, the RMSE is also the standard deviation of the residuals: consequently, we can interpret it as the maximum error to expect in 68% of the predictions. To be on the safer side, we can multiply the RMSE by 2, obtaining broader intervals and an extended level of confidence: we can presume that our error will be lower than twice the RMSE 95% of the time. Let's imagine that we predict a car price to be $16,000 using a regression model with an RMSE of $1,200: we can state that we are 95% confident that the actual price of that car will lie between $13,600 and $18,400, which is $16,000 ± $2,400 (twice the RMSE). Of course, the lower the RMSE, the better the model, as we can boast narrower confidence intervals for our predictions.

Using RMSE to build confidence intervals is not always mathematically correct. In fact, this holds true only under the assumption that residuals follow a normal distribution (the typical Gauss bell curve), which might not always be the case. Still, it's a handy rule of thumb that I recommend keeping in mind when evaluating regressions.

An alternative summary metric for evaluating the performance of regressions is the **Coefficient of Determination**, R^2. It can be calculated using the following formula:

$$R^2 = 1 - \frac{\sum_{i=1}^{N}(a_i - p_i)^2}{\sum_{i=1}^{N}(a_i - \bar{a})^2}$$

where we find, on top of the measures encountered above, $\bar{a}$, which is the average of the actual values. Look at the fraction in the formula: we are comparing the squared errors of our model (the same quantity we found in RMSE) with the square error of a *baseline* model, which would naively use as a constant prediction the average of the observed values. If our model is similar to this baseline, R^2 will end up being close to zero, indicating that our model is quite useless. If, instead, our model generates much smaller errors than what the baseline does, then we obtain an R^2 close to 1. In this case, the higher the R^2, the better.

One intuitive way to interpret the coefficient of determination is to look at it as the proportion of the variation observed in our target variable, which is actually explained by the model. If in our car price prediction, we obtain $R^2=0.75$; we can say that our model, solely based on the age of the car, explains 75% of the variability in car price, leaving the remaining 25% unaccounted for. If we built a more accurate model or added some additional features, such as mileage and accessories, we will probably be able to explain a larger proportion of the price variability, and our R^2 will get closer to 1.

> There are no specific R^2 reference thresholds that can always tell us if a model is "good" or "bad." Think about an apparently chaotic signal, such as the fluctuation of currency exchange rates. If we built a regression model that explained only 25% of the variability in future exchange rates, we could make a lot of money out of it! It's better not to fix static thresholds of R^2.

Differently from RMSE, R^2 is a dimensionless metric. This means that we can compare the goodness of regression models even if they predict values lying on different scales. For instance, we can compare a model predicting house prices (in the range of a hundred thousand dollars) with another model predicting motorbike prices (which are typically much cheaper), by juxtaposing their R^2 values: the higher the R^2, the better.

Classification

The job of classification algorithms is to assign each item of a data set to a class, predicting a specific value of the target variable. Out of all possible classes, only one is right and matches with reality. Hence, a simple way to measure the performance of a classifier will be to "count" the number of times the algorithm got it right out of the total number of predictions. However, this simple performance score might not tell us the full story. Let's see this concept come to life with an example.

You want to assess the performance of an image classification model: however random this task might look (and—in all fairness—it does), the job of your binary classifier is to assign a label that differentiates the content of the image between dogs and muffins. When it comes to Chihuahua and blueberry muffins, your classifier struggles a bit, predicting the content as displayed in *Figure 4.7*:

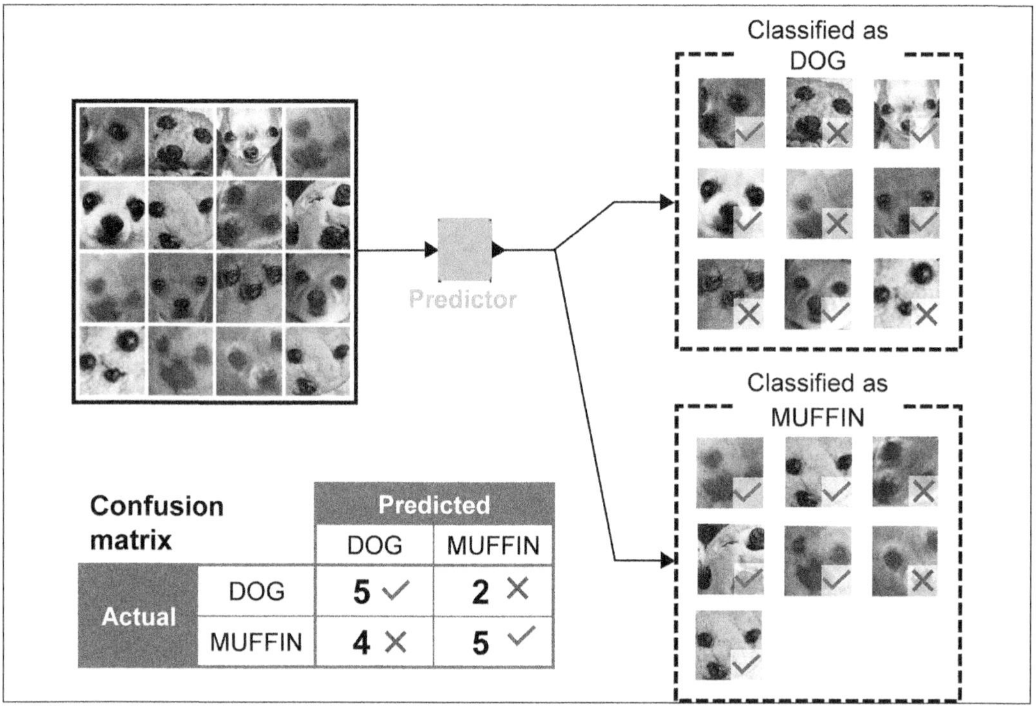

Figure 4.7: Is that a Chihuahua or a blueberry muffin? This classifier got it right 10 times out of 16.

The table you find on the bottom left of *Figure 4.7* is called a **Confusion Matrix**: it has the benefit of showing the full picture of the classification outcome, highlighting the number of instances where the classifier got "confused" and assigned the wrong label to the pictures. The confusion matrix counts all the combinations between any predicted class value (columns) and the reality, so the actual class (rows). The cells on the main diagonal will tell us how many times the classifier got it right, while all other cells count the errors. In this case, it looks like our model had an "unbalanced" performance as it had a harder time recognizing the dogs, while it was a bit more robust in spotting muffins. In the case of Chihuahuas and blueberry muffins we are not very worried about this asymmetry; however, in other cases, this might be a big deal, generating very different outcomes.

Let's move on to a more serious case: a classifier that predicts whether a patient is infected by a contagious virus by analyzing a series of features coming from a blood test exam. Also in this case, there are two classes, positive and negative, and we have two different types of classification errors we can make. One is about assigning the class positive to a patient who, in reality, is healthy: this is called a **False Positive**. The outcome of this error is that we communicate the result to the patient, who will immediately start a quarantine, and run some more accurate tests to confirm our findings. The other type of error we can make is when we assign the class negative to a patient who is actually infected by the virus: this is a **False Negative**. Of course, the outcome of this error is much more impactful than the previous case: we would send the patient home, allowing a further spread of the virus due to the contamination of other people and failing to start any early treatment for the person. To summarize: not all errors are born equal when it comes to classification. As a consequence, one single number might not be enough to explain the full situation. That is why it is wise to calculate the confusion matrix and select among multiple metrics the most appropriate to your needs. Depending on the case you are solving, you should pick one of the summary metrics shown on the right-hand side of *Figure 4.8* as the most important one to assess performance with. Let's go through each of them:

- **Accuracy** is telling you the percentage of good predictions versus the total ones. When the type of error does not matter, you can use this "balanced" measure to explain the overall performance of a classifier.

- **Precision** will tell you how confident the classifier is when it labels a case as positive. You can use this metric when you need to avoid at all costs the situation where a case predicted to be positive turns out to be negative. If a very precise classifier tells you that a case is positive, it is most likely right.

- **Sensitivity** tells you how confidently the classifier can rule out the possibility that a positive case is not classified as such. You need to use this metric when you want to avoid false negatives. If a very sensitive classifier tells you that a case is negative, it is most likely right. Diagnostic classifiers in medicine are typically built so as to maximize sensitivity at all costs, as you want to be sure to send home without a cure only patients that are really negative.

> The classes names positive and negative are just conventional. Depending on your case, you can decide which class is positive and calculate all the scoring metrics accordingly. In the case of more than two classes, it works like that: you select the single positive class, and then the metrics are calculated considering any other class as negative. It's just a convention.

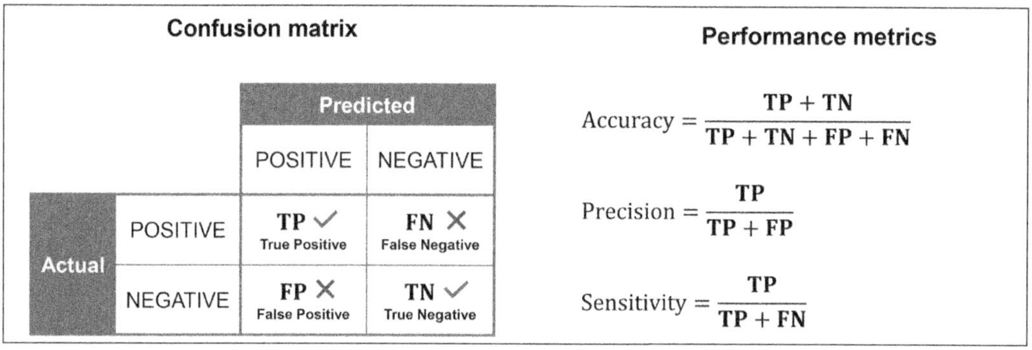

Confusion matrix				Performance metrics

Figure 4.8: Assessing performance in classification: pick the metric that makes the most sense in your case

With this, we have seen the most popular ways we can use to evaluate the performance of supervised learning predictors. Before building our first ML model, we need to go through one last fundamental concept and learn how to manage it: overfitting.

Underfitting and overfitting

American mathematician John Nash received the 1994 Nobel Prize for Economics for his landmark work on game theory. His "Nash equilibrium" has become the foundation of how economists predict the outcome of non-cooperative strategic interactions. The story of John Nash has been popularized by the Academy Award-winning movie *A Beautiful Mind* starring Russell Crowe as Nash. In the movie, John Nash is portrayed in his life-long struggle with paranoid schizophrenia: his condition brought him to believe he had found "secret messages" hidden in the text of regular magazine articles, supposedly added by Soviet spies for covert communication. Perceiving meaningful connections between unrelated things is a typical tendency of early-stage delusional thought, a condition that psychiatrists call *apophenia*. Now, think about it: when you have (a lot of) data and (massive) computing power available, it is likely to fall into the trap of thinking that you have found some interesting patterns of general validity. In reality, you might have just found a spurious, random connection as a consequence of the vast extent of availability of resources.

This will become clearer with an example: let's imagine we have a large database containing all sorts of information on the ticket holders of a nationwide annual lottery. We have two years of history available, and we want to use the information on the past two winners to predict the future ones by identifying the recurrent features. We decide to use a supervised ML algorithm to do so. After some heavy calculation, the algorithm comes up with a complex series of apparently "winning" rules that are shared only by the lucky winners of the two previous editions.

These rules are like: *the 4th digit of their telephone numbers is a 7, their ticket numbers include exactly 3 odd digits, they were born on a Tuesday*, and many others. Clearly, these rules are not going to be able to predict anything meaningful: they are just artificially "connecting" two specific points through a series of meaningless factors that happen to be in common for the winners. As the example shows, when the haystack is large enough, it is easy to find something very similar to a needle! Similarly, when you have a massive amount of data, if you look long enough, you can find any connection, although this doesn't make it meaningful. This is comparable to the apophenia condition we encountered in John Nash's story. We need to avoid at any cost falling into this trap of "analytical fallacy": it is just a deception caused by our desire to find connections at all costs, even if they do not actually exist, by using artificially overcomplicated models. This condition is called **overfitting**, and it's a problem that can potentially arise when attempting any prediction. Hence, we need to systematically avoid it when building a supervised ML model which generates predictions.

Let's see overfitting in action in our car price example. *Figure 4.9* shows the Polynomial Regression for different degrees, represented by the parameter **N**.

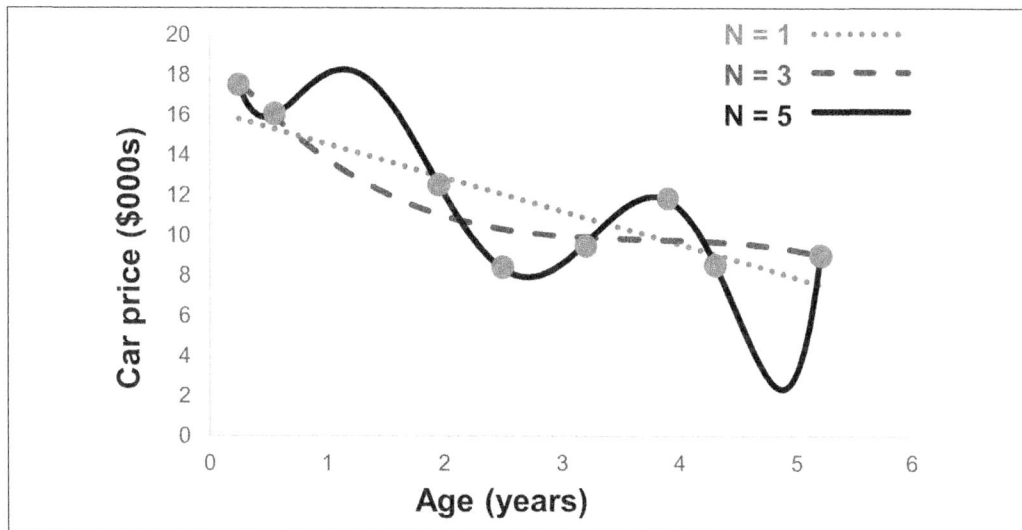

Figure 4.9: Regression models to predict car prices with different polynomial degrees N. Which one would you pick?

As **N** grows from 1 to 5, the fitting line shows a more convoluted path: this signifies that the underlying model becomes more complex. By looking at the three curves, we can notice the following:

- When **N = 1** (dotted line), our model is exactly the same as the simple Linear Regression model we encountered earlier. Although it is a good starting point, it looks a bit too "simple" as it fails to consider the stronger devaluation of car prices happening in the first few months of age.

- When **N = 3** (dashed line), we get a more encouraging fit, as we clearly see a stronger erosion of price in the early life of a car and a subsequent flattening of the curve. This looks solid, as it is in line with what our business understanding suggests.

- When **N = 5** (continuous line), we have a nearly perfect fit with the existing points. However, this sounds "too good to be true" and, indeed, the shape of the curve is artificially built in a way that meets the points, without providing solid modeling of the price evolution over age. There are some weird bumps like the one happening at around 1.5 years of age, where the price is supposed to be inexplicably higher than what we have with new cars. It looks like we have just "forced" the curve to touch the few "past" points, which is a short-sighted objective. Instead, our real purpose was to find a robust model able to predict the price of the "next" cars coming to market.

From this example, we can start seeing that the level of complexity of a supervised model needs some finetuning: if the model is too basic, its predictive performance will be necessarily low. On the other extreme, if the model is too complex, we might have just "connected the previous dots": we end up in the delusional state of weaving together coincidences into an apparent general pattern.

Let's build on this concept by bringing an additional supervised example: this time, we deal with classification. As you can see in *Figure 4.10*, you have a number of elements on a plate that could be either dots or crosses. You want to predict their class (being a dot or a cross) based on their position by drawing a continuous line that differentiates across elements, leaving dots on the top-right side of the plate and crosses on the bottom-left side. By applying a non-linear **Support Vector Machine (SVM)** learning algorithm, you obtain three different curves of progressively increasing complexity.

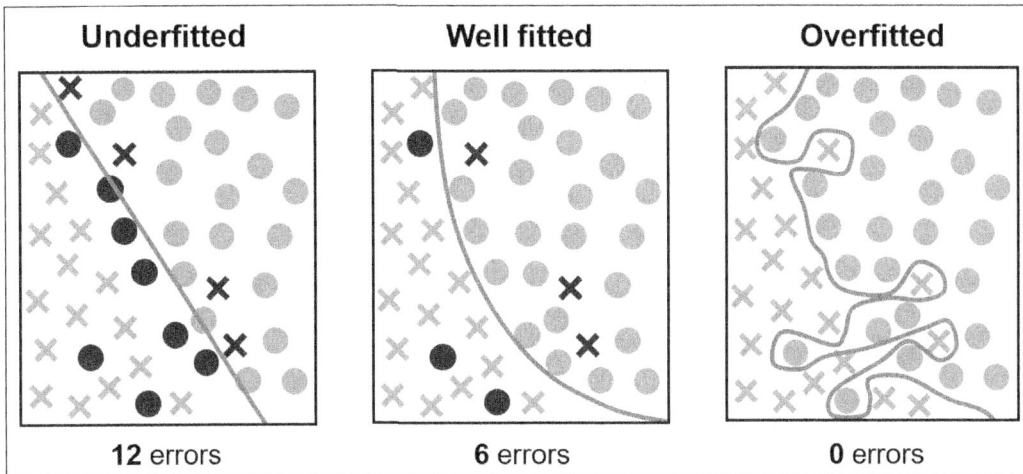

Figure 4.10: We want to draw a line able to differentiate dots (top-right side) and crosses (bottom-left side). Misclassified elements are in darker gray. Which line is likely to do the job better with future elements?

Let's have a look at the three cases:

- The model on the left is a straight line that looks like a very rudimentary way to differentiate between dots and crosses. It seems that we are consistently missing some dots in the middle area of the chart, which happen to be just outside the region where they should. Overall, our accuracy level is near 75%, as we made 12 misclassifications.

- The model in the middle is slightly more complex than the previous one but also more accurate (only six errors this time). The curvature we now have on the line accounts well for the dots we were consistently missing before. Intuitively, the six misclassifications we made (they are in darker gray in the picture) look more like "exceptions": the curved line seems close to a general rule that is likely to repeat in the future when new elements will land on the plate.

- The model on the right is apparently the best: it nailed the class of all elements on the plate, reaching an accuracy of 100%. However, this complex model is unlikely to have a general validity: the curve is zigzagging through the current elements to avoid any misclassification, but we can expect that, if new elements show up, they will be misclassified as a consequence of all these artificial bends.

These examples have illustrated an important property of supervised ML: if we want to build models that perform well in predicting "future" cases, we need to strike the right balance of complexity when learning. We can recognize three cases, as summarized in *Table 4.1*. Let's go through each of them, starting from the extremes:

- **Underfitted models**. Like in the Polynomial Regression with **N = 1** and the first plate of the classification, an underfitted model is just not good enough to predict anything. This naïve model will generate large error rates (higher residuals or many misclassifications) even when asked to fit the known data points. As a logical consequence, we cannot expect the same model to magically start working well on future cases: this makes underfitted model pretty useless for making any prediction.

- **Overfitted models**. These models sit at the opposite extreme of underfitted models and are as bad as the former. The mathematical complexity of the model lets it adapt very well to known data points, introducing unrealistic elements like the many bumps of the regression with **N = 5** or the zigzags across elements in the classification. We "believe" to have reached a high level of accuracy, but this is just a self-inflicted delusion: whenever new points arrive, our accuracy level will dramatically drop as a consequence of those artificial complexities we have allowed.

- **Well-fitted models**. As for many other things in life: *virtue lies in the middle ground*. Well-fitted models will be less accurate than overfitted ones when fitting data points. However, given the limitations they had in capturing the complexity of a phenomenon, they will tend to focus on the (fewer) connections that matter most, ignoring the excessively complex paths that fitted models used. Well-fitted models are best suited for predicting the "unknown," which is exactly the point of why we wanted to build a supervised model.

	Underfitted	Well-fitted	Overfitted
Model complexity	Low	Mid	High
Performance on past cases	Low	Mid	High
Performance on future cases	Low	Mid	Low
Description	The model is too naïve, and the resulting predictions are not accurate. It is unable to describe well the modeled phenomenon.	The model is well balanced. It grasps patterns of general validity that are likely to repeat in future cases.	The model is complex and works well only on the very specific points used to learn. It is unable to predict the outcome of future cases.

Table 4.1: Typical characteristics of under-, well-, and overfitted models.

The good news is that ML models can be "tuned" for complexity by changing a set of values, called **Hyperparameters**, that modulate their learning behavior. For example, in the Polynomial Regression, **N** is nothing more than a hyperparameter of the model: by making **N** vary from 1 to 5 (or more), we can control how complex the model is and, by making some attempts, we can try to find the well-fitted level. We will learn about hyperparameters more when talking through the specific learning algorithms later in the book.

> Another way to reduce the complexity of a model is to reduce the number of features. The fewer the features, the simpler the model, and the lower the chances to overfit. This is another motive for doing dimensionality reduction, one of the unsupervised scenarios we have previously introduced.

Now we are clear on the pathological condition of overfitted models: it's time to move on and talk about how to diagnose it and what a possible cure can look like.

Validating a model

By looking once again at *Table 4.1* and, more specifically, at its third row, we find that the only way to spot a well-fitted model is to evaluate its performance on "unseen" samples. Both under- and overfitted models will underperform versus a well-fitted model when it comes to the level of accuracy of future cases. But what if we do not yet have any future cases to use for this purpose?

A fundamental "trick" we use in supervised ML is to randomly split the data set of known samples into two subsets: a **training set**, which normally covers 70 to 80% of the original data, and a **test set**, which keeps the remainder of the data. *Figure 4.11* shows this operation, called **Partitioning**, in action. Then, we use *only* the training set for performing the actual learning, which will generate the model. Finally, we will evaluate the model's performance on the test set: this is data that the algorithm has *not* seen yet when learning. This means that, if the model grew overcomplex by creating many bumps and zigzags to adapt to the training set, we would get low-performance scores on the test set. In other words, if the model is overfitted to the training set, then it will perform very badly on the test set. With this trick, we have assessed the accuracy of "future" samples without doing any time travel!

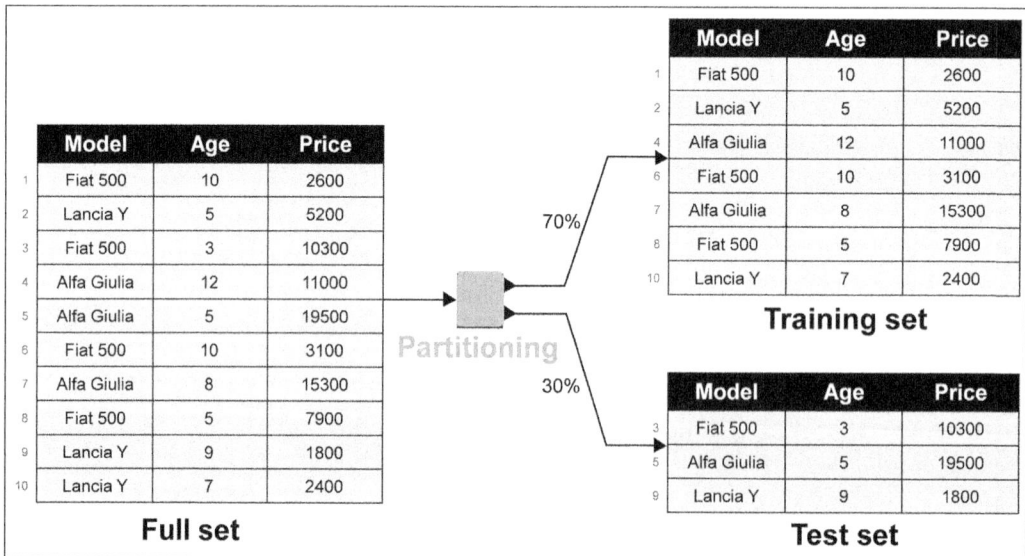

Figure 4.11: Partitioning a full set in training and test subsets. Rows are randomly sampled and distributed to the two subsets, according to the desired proportion

Figure 4.12 shows the expected amount of prediction error in test and training sets by increasing levels of complexity. The amount of error obtained on the samples included in the training set can be lowered progressively by working on the hyperparameters of the model in a way to increase its complexity. For example, in the Polynomial Regression case, as we move from left to right, we are growing the value of **N**: with a high-complexity model (**N = 5**, we are on the far right), the error of the training line is almost zero. If you look at the error calculated on the test set (the U-shaped curve), you will face the reality and recognize that the true predictive power of the model is much lower: only a well-fitted model can ensure good performance on "unseen" data points.

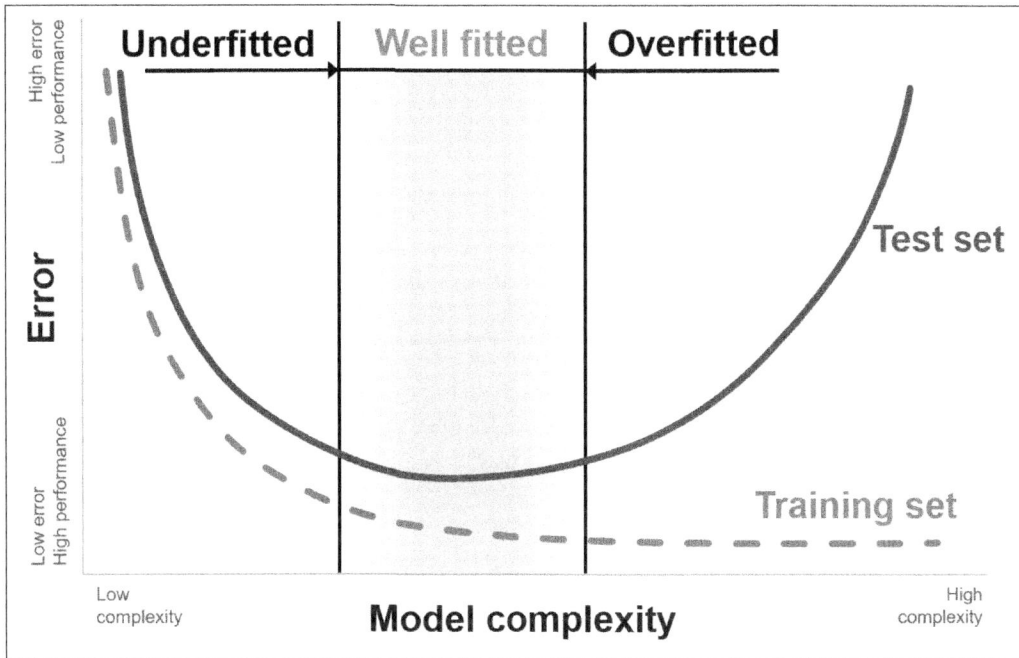

Figure 4.12: The amount of error produced by a supervised ML model as complexity grows: for the test set, it follows a U-shaped curve

Pulling it all together

We finally have all the ingredients for building and validating a well-fitted supervised ML model. Let's see now what the recipe looks like. We can visualize a recurrent "structure" made of four fundamental blocks that collectively define our basic flow for supervised learning:

1. **Partitioning**. To avoid overfitting, we need to leverage a validation mechanism that prevents us from scoring a model on the same data used for learning. Thus, the first step we always do in supervised learning is to partition the full set of labeled data points to obtain a training and a test data set. In most cases, the split happens through random sampling.

2. **Learner**. The training data set can be used to train a model by leveraging the learning algorithm. The output of this operation will be the statistical model (defined through a set of parameters), which can be applied to different data so to obtain a prediction.

3. **Predictor**. We can now "run" the model learned in the previous step on the test set, which has been kept out of the training process. The output of the predictor will be the test set enriched with an additional column: the predicted value of the target for each row.

4. **Scorer**. The output of the predictor contains *both* the observed target (the actual value we aimed at predicting) and its model-generated prediction. By comparing the values of these two columns, we can assess the performance of the prediction. It will be enough to calculate one or more summary metric scores, like the ones we introduced a few pages ago, like RMSE, R^2, sensitivity, or the full confusion matrix.

That's it! By following this logic flow, described in *Figure 4.13*, you can build a supervised model and assess its true performance, avoiding the risk of overfitting.

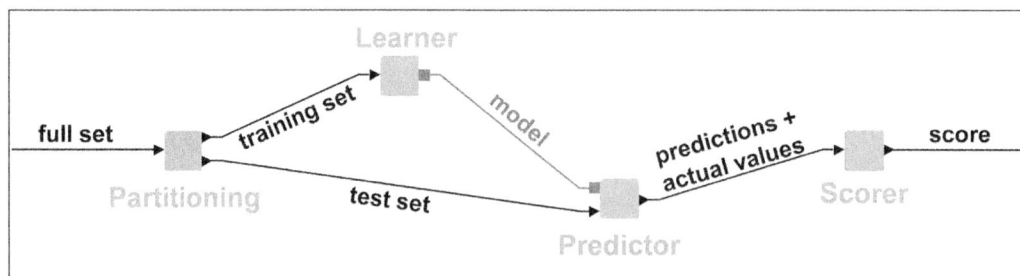

Figure 4.13: The typical flow for validating a supervised ML model. To prevent overfitting, you need to partition the data, learn on the training portion, and finally predict and score on the test partition only.

Of course, once you have a validated model, you can confidently apply it to all "future" data points, finally unlocking the real value of ML predictions. Let's take the example of the second-hand cars price prediction: you used your full database containing the historical sales to build and validate a model. Once you have a validated model and you are sure it does not overfit, you are ready for prime time: every time you need to estimate the price of a car, you can now execute the model on the car's features and obtain the predicted price. Of course, this time, you will not have the "real value" to compare it with, but you can use the confidence interval of your prediction (like the RMSE for regression) to anticipate the range of expected errors you are going to get.

It's worth spending a few last thoughts on the flow portrayed in *Figure 4.13*: this is the "base" process you can adopt when building and validating a supervised ML model. Many improvements can be incrementally applied to make your models better and better. Just to give you some perspective on the many additions we can make, let's mention a few that leverage iterations for improving the process:

- The partitioning trick has some limitations: for example, if you have a relatively small data set to start from and hold 30% out from learning, you might end up with an inadequate validation since the model had too few points to learn from. One alternative route, called **k-Fold Cross Validation**, is to split your full set into k folds (usually 5 or 10) and iterate multiple times, using each fold as a test set to be held out each time. In the end, you will get k different models and scores. By averaging them out, you will obtain a much more robust validation than having just a one-off partitioning.

- As we saw earlier, you can "tune" the hyperparameters of a model to maximize the performance score obtained on the test set (which will, in turn, ensure maximum accuracy on the future predictions and prove the general validity of your model). You can loop through different hyperparameters, managing them as variables, and spot the set of values that put you at the bottom of the U-shaped curve we saw in *Figure 4.12*. This procedure is called **Hyperparameter optimization** and can be implemented by using loops and variables.

- As mentioned before, if you have uninformative or redundant features in a data set, your model will be unnecessarily complex. There are many techniques used for identifying the best subset of features to use in your learning: they go under the general name of **Feature Selection**. One simple iterative technique for selecting features is called **Backward Elimination**: you start with having all features selected. Then, at each iteration, you remove one feature—the one that induces the smallest decline (or the biggest increase) of performance if removed from the set. At some point, you will have "tried" multiple combinations of features, and you can pick the one that maximizes the overall predictive performance.

These are just some of the many possible techniques you can use and creatively combine to improve the quality of your modeling. Hopefully, this shows you a hint of the fascinating reality of the world you are getting into: the practice of ML is a mix of art and science, and you can always look for some more ingenious ways to squeeze incremental value from data and algorithms.

Summary

In this chapter, you were introduced to the fundamental concepts behind machines that can learn from data. After stripping away the futuristic gloss of AI, we went through a series of practical business scenarios where we saw intelligent algorithms at work. These examples showed us how, if we look carefully, we can often recognize occasions to leverage machines for getting intellectual work done. We saw that, as an alternative to the traditional mode of operating, there is an ML way to get things done: whether we are predicting prices, segmenting consumers, or optimizing a digital advertising strategy, learning algorithms can be our tireless companions. If we coach them well, they can extend human intelligence and provide a sound competitive advantage to our business. We explored the differences among the three types of learning algorithms (supervised, unsupervised, and reinforcement) and understood the fundamental drivers that can guide us in selecting which algorithms to use. We have then learned what needs to happen to build a robust predictive model and properly assess its performance while staying away from the menace of overfitting. It was a long journey in the captivating world of statistical learning, but, as promised, we didn't need to go through many formulas or complex math. This chapter enabled you to get the intuition behind the vital concepts of ML so that you can move quickly to practice and keep learning while doing.

It's now time to put our hands back onto KNIME and build (and validate) a few ML models based on real-world data: get ready because this is what the next chapter is all about.

5

Applying Machine Learning at Work

You've heard a lot about creating business value with intelligent algorithms: it's finally time to roll up our sleeves and make it happen. In this chapter, we are going to experience what it means to apply machine learning to tangible cases by going through a few step-by-step tutorials. Our companion KNIME is back on stage: we will learn how to build workflows for implementing machine learning models using real-world data. We are going to meet a few specific algorithms and learn the intuitive mechanisms behind how they operate. We'll glimpse into their underlying mathematical models, focusing on the basics to comprehend their results and leverage them in our work.

This practical chapter will answer several questions, including:

- How do I make predictions using supervised machine learning algorithms in KNIME?
- How can I check whether a model is performing well?
- How do we avoid the risk of overfitting?
- What techniques can I use to improve the performance of a model?
- How can I group similar elements together using clustering algorithms?

The tutorials included in this chapter cover three of the most recurrent cases when you can rely on machine learning as part of your work: predicting numbers, classifying entities, and grouping elements. Think of them as "templates" that you can widely reapply after you reach the last page of the chapter and that you are likely to keep using as a reference. The steps of the tutorials are also organized in the same order they would unfold in everyday practice, including the "back and forth" iterations required for improving the performance of your model. This will prepare you to face the actual use of real-life machine learning, which often follows a circuitous route made of trial and error attempts.

Within each tutorial, you will encounter one or two machine learning algorithms (specifically, **linear regression** in the first, **decision tree** and **random forest** in the second, and **k-means** in the third) that will be introduced and explained before being seen in action. Let's get started with some first predictions!

Predicting numbers through regressions

For this tutorial, you will assume the—somewhat—enviable role of a real estate agent based in Rome, Italy. The company you work for owns multiple agencies specialized in rentals of properties located in the broader metropolitan area of the Eternal City. Your passion for data analytics got you noticed by the CEO: she asked you to figure out a way to support agents in objectively evaluating the fair monthly rent of a property based on its features. She noticed that the business greatly suffers when the rent set for a property is not aligned with the market. In fact, if the rent is too low, the agency fee (which is a fixed percentage of the agreed rent) will end up being lower than what it could have been, leaving profit on the table. On the other hand, if the ask is too high, revenues for the agency will take longer to materialize, causing a substantial impact on the cash flow. The traditional approach to set the monthly rent for new properties is a "negotiation" between owners and agents, who will use their market understanding (and sometimes the benchmark of similar properties) to convince the owners about the right rent to ask for.

You are sure that machine learning has the potential to make a difference, and you are resolute in finding an ML way to improve this business process. The idea that comes to mind is to use the database of the monthly rent of previously rented properties (for which we have available their full description) to predict the right monthly rent of future properties based on their objective characteristics. Such a data-driven approach, if well communicated, can ease the price-setting process and result in a mutual advantage for all the parties involved: the landlord and the agency will get a quick and profitable transaction, and the tenant will obtain a fair rent.

The prospect of building a machine able to predict rental prices is exhilarating and makes you impatient to start. You manage to obtain an extraction of the last 4,000 rental agreements signed at the agency (RomeHousing-History.xlsx). The table contains, for each property:

- *House_ID*: a unique identifier of the property.

- *Neighborhood*: the name of the area where the property lies, ranging from the fancy surroundings of Piazza Navona to the tranquil, lakeside towns of Castelli Romani. *Figure 5.1* shows a map of the Rome area with some of these neighborhoods.

- *Property_type*: a string clarifying if the property is a flat, a house, a villa, or a penthouse.

- *Rooms*: the number of available rooms in the property, including bathrooms.

- *Surface*: the usable floor area of the property in square meters.

- *Elevator*: a binary category indicating if an elevator is available (1) or not (0).

- *Floor_type*: a category showing if the property is on a Mezzanine, a Ground floor, or an Upper level.

- *Floor_number*: the floor number on which the property is situated, based on the European convention (0 is for the ground floor, 0.5 is the mezzanine, 1 is for the first level above the ground, and so on).

- *Rent*: the all-inclusive, monthly rent in euros on the final rental agreement.

Figure 5.1: The Rome neighborhoods covered by our real estate.
Have you visited any of these places already?

Before building the model, you wisely stop for a second and think through the ways you are going to practically leverage it once ready. You realize that the potential business value for completing this endeavor is two-fold:

1. First, by interpreting how the model works, you can find out some insightful evidence on the market price formation mechanisms. You might be able to find answers to the questions: *what features really do make a difference in the pricing?*, *does the floor number impact the value greatly?*, and *which neighborhoods prove to be most expensive ones, at parity of all other characteristics of the property?*. Some of the answers will reinforce the market understanding that your agency already has, adding the benefit of making this knowledge explicit and formally described. More interestingly, other findings might be truly unexpected and unveil original dynamics you did not know about.

2. Second, your model can be used to generate data-based recommendations on the rent to be set for new properties as they go on the market and enter the portfolio of the agency. To make things more interesting on this front, the owner shares with you a list (RomeHousing-NewProperties.xlsx) of 10 incoming properties for which the rental price has not been fixed yet, using the same features (such as *Neighborhood*, *Property_type*, and so on) available in the historical database. Once ready, you will apply your model to these sample properties as an illustration of how it works.

You are now clear on what the business requires, and you can finally translate it into definite machine learning terms, building on what we have learned in the previous chapter. You need to build a machine that predicts "unknown" rental prices by learning from some "known" examples: the database of previously rented properties is your *labeled* dataset, as it has examples of your target variable, in this case, the *Rent*. Going through the catalog of machine learning algorithms (*Figure 4.5*), you realize we are clearly in the category of *supervised* machine learning. More specifically, you need to predict numbers (rent in euros), so you definitely need to leverage an algorithm for doing a *regression*.

The ML way to solve this business opportunity is now clear in front of your eyes: you can finally get KNIME started and create a new workflow (**File | New… | New KNIME Workflow**):

1. As a very first step, you load your labeled dataset by dragging and dropping the file (RomeHousing-History.xlsx) into your blank workflow or by implementing the **Excel Reader** node. In either case, KNIME will have recognized the structure of the file, and you just need to accept its default configuration. After running the node, you obtain the dataset shown in *Figure 5.2*, where you find the nine columns you expected:

File Table - 9:1 - Excel Reader (Load)

File Edit Hilite Navigation View

Table "default" - Rows: 4000   Spec - Columns: 9   Properties   Flow Variables

Row ID	House_ID	Neighborhood	Property_type	Rooms	Surface	Elevator	Floor_type	Floor_number	Rent
Row0	103501	Cassia	Flat	2	65	0	Upper	2	900
Row1	105122	Collatino	Flat	2	30	1	Ground floor	0	500
Row2	104125	Collatino	Flat	3	80	1	Upper	4	950
Row3	104675	Infernetto	Flat	3	75	0	Upper	2	800
Row4	102481	Ostia	Flat	3	70	1	Ground floor	0	800
Row5	103133	Magliana	Flat	2	60	1	Upper	3	650
Row6	103095	Cassia	Flat	3	85	1	Upper	2	1150
Row7	104367	Prati	Flat	5	130	0	Upper	5	2000
Row8	104969	Cinecittà	House	3	70	1	Upper	1	800
Row9	102566	Cinecittà	Flat	2	50	0	Ground floor	0	550
Row10	104696	Piazza Navona	Flat	2	60	1	Upper	2	1500
Row11	103742	Castelli Romani	Flat	4	95	1	Upper	3	1000
Row12	103705	Piazza Navona	Flat	3	60	1	Ground floor	0	1600
Row13	105117	Trastevere	Flat	2	65	0	Upper	1	1400
Row14	103961	Piazza Navona	Flat	3	65	1	Upper	6	1550
Row15	104144	Cinecittà	Flat	2	60	0	Upper	4	700
Row16	105578	Castelli Romani	Flat	5	65	1	Upper	1	700
Row17	103889	Piazza Navona	Flat	3	70	0	Upper	1	1500
Row18	103551	Piazza Navona	Flat	3	80	0	Upper	3	1650
Row19	105950	Montagnola	Flat	4	135	0	Upper	3	1350

Figure 5.2: Historical rental data loaded into KNIME: 4,000 properties to learn from

When you build a machine learning model, you will interact in various ways with the columns of your data table. It is sensible to get an understanding of what you are going to deal with by exploring the columns right at the beginning. Fortunately, the **Statistics** node helps as it displays at once the most important things you need to know about your columns.

►◄ ⊨ *Statistics*

This node (**Analytics > Statistics**) calculates summary statistics for each column available in the input table. The checkbox appearing at the top of its configuration dialog (*Figure 5.3*) lets you decide whether to **Calculate median values** of the numeric columns: this calculation might be computationally expensive for large datasets, so you will tick it only if necessary. The column selector in the middle lets you decide which columns should be treated as **Nominal**. For these columns, the node will count the number of instances of each unique value: this is useful for categorical columns when you want to quickly assess the relative footprint of every category in a table. The main summary metrics calculated by the node are minimum (**Min**), average (**Mean**), **Median**, maximum (**Max**), standard deviations (**Std. Dev.**), **Skewness**, **Kurtosis**, count of non-numeric values such as missing values (**No. Missing**), and plus or minus infinite (**No. +∞**, **No. –∞**). The node will also output the histograms showing the distributions of the values and, for nominal columns, the list of the most and least numerous categories identified in the dataset:

> **Skewness** and **Kurtosis** are certainly the least known summary statistics among the ones mentioned above. However, they are useful in telling you quickly how much the shape of a distribution differs from the iconic bell-shaped curve of a pure Gaussian distribution. Skewness tells you about the symmetry of the distribution: if it has a positive value, it is skewed on the left while if it has a negative value, it is skewed on the right. Kurtosis tells you about the flatness of the distribution: if negative it is flatter than a bell curve, while if positive it shows a sharper peak.

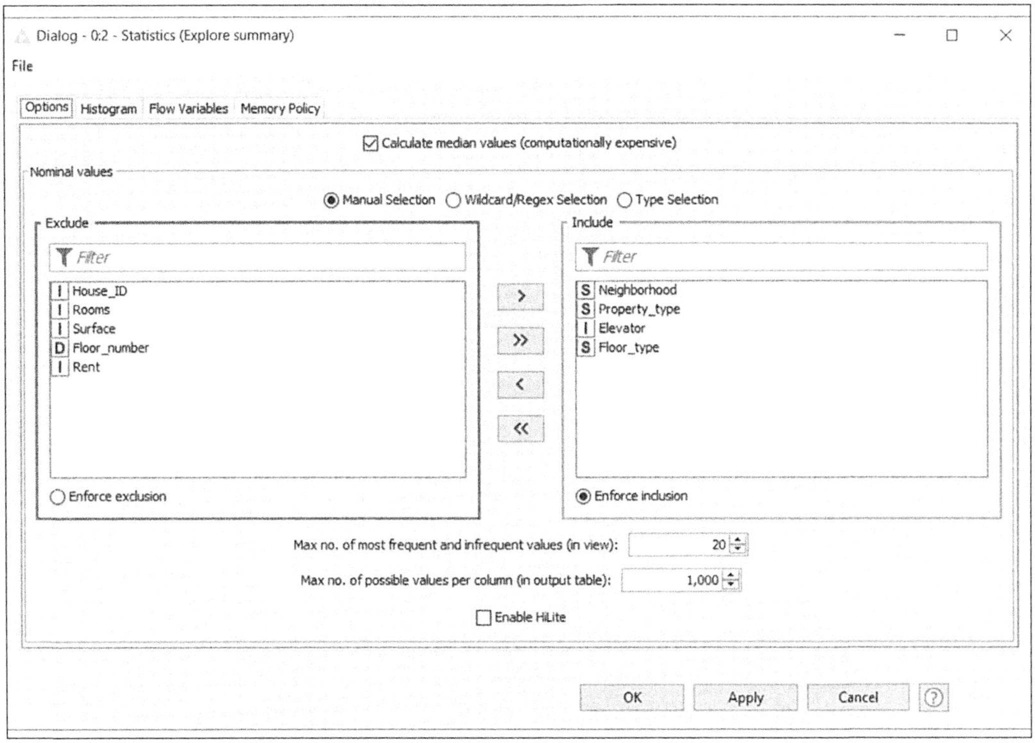

Figure 5.3: Configuration of Statistics: explore the data with its summary statistics

2. Implement the **Statistics** node and connect it with the previous one. When configuring it, check the first box so we can have a look at the median values of the numeric columns. In the selector of the nominal values, keep only the string-typed columns (*Neighborhood*, *Property_type*, and *Floor_type*) plus *Elevator*. Although formally numeric, this latter column splits our samples into two categories, the properties equipped with the elevator and the ones missing it: it will be interesting to read a count of how many properties fall into each category, so we shall treat this column as nominal. If you run the node and display its main output (just press *Shift + 10* or, after you execute the node, right-click on it and select **View: Statistics View**) you will obtain a window with three useful tabs. The first one (*Figure 5.4*) gives you all the highlights on the numeric columns: we learn that the average rent of the properties in our database is slightly above €1,000 and that the median floor surface is around 70 square meters. We also learn that there are no missing values: this is good news as we don't need to engage in clean up chores:

Column	Min	Mean	Median	Max	Std. Dev.	Skewness	Kurtosis	No. Missing	No. +∞	No. -∞	Histogram
House_ID	101,983	103,982.5	103,982.5	105,982	1,154.8449	-8.55E-15	-1.2	0	0	0	
Rooms	2	2.6712	3	6	0.7999	1.2029	1.459	0	0	0	
Surface	15	73.125	70	200	24.975	1.3864	3.3338	0	0	0	
Elevator	0.0	0.7035	1	1	0.4568	-0.8915	-1.2059	0	0	0	
Floor_number	0.0	2.2006	2	10	1.887	0.9846	0.6121	0	0	0	
Rent	300	1,010.3625	900	3,000	415.1401	1.0673	1.1327	0	0	0	

Figure 5.4: Numeric panel within the Statistics output: how are my numeric features distributed?

The second and third (*Figure 5.5*) tabs tell you about the nominal columns: we learn that some neighborhoods (such as `Magliana` and `Portuense`) are much less represented in our dataset than others. By looking at the values in the *Property_type* column, we also learn that the vast majority of our rented properties have been flats:

Neighborhood	Property_type	Elevator	Floor_type
No. missings: 0	No. missings: 0	No. missings: 0	No. missings: 0
Top 20: Parioli : 492 Castelli Romani : 412 Cinecittà : 366 Prati : 339 Piazza Navona : 330 Collatino : 323 Monte sacro : 285 Cassia : 235 Infernetto : 193 Monti : 185 Trastevere : 147 Termini : 145 Marconi : 107 Montagnola : 98 Ostia : 72 EUR : 65 Trigoria : 59 Aventino : 45 Testaccio : 41 Portuense : 35	Top 20: Flat : 3821 Penthouse : 150 House : 19 Villa : 10	Top 20: 1 : 2814 0 : 1186	Top 20: Upper : 3183 Ground floor : 648 Mezzanine : 169
Bottom 20: Magliana : 26	Bottom 20:	Bottom 20:	Bottom 20:

Figure 5.5: Top/bottom panel within the Statistics output:
check the values of your categorical columns

Now that we have explored the dataset and have become acquainted with the main characteristics of its columns, we can proceed with the fun part and design our model. To build a robust supervised machine learning model, we need to rely on the typical flow that we encountered in the previous chapter. Let's refresh our memory on this critical point: in order to stay away from the trap of overfitting, we need to partition our labeled data into training and test sets, learn on the training set, predict on the test set, and — finally — assess the expected performance of the model by scoring the predicted values. You can go back to *Chapter 4*, *What is Machine Learning?*, and check *Figure 4.13* out to see once again the full process: we are always required to follow this approach when implementing a machine that can predict something useful. So, the very first step is to randomly partition all our labeled data rows into two separate subsets. This is exactly the "specialty" of our next node: **Partitioning**.

⊞ *Partitioning*

This node (**Manipulation > Row > Transform**) performs a row-wise split of the input table into two tables corresponding to the upper (first partition) and lower (second partition) output ports. The selector at the top of its configuration window (*Figure 5.6*) lets you set the size of the first partition (upper output port). You can either specify the number of rows to be included (**Absolute**) or the relative size of the partition in percentage points (**Relative[%]**). The second selector specifies the method used for splitting the rows into the two partitions:

- **Take from top**: if you select this option, the split will happen according to the current sorting order. The top rows of the input table will end up in the first partition while all others, after a certain threshold, will go to the second. The position of the threshold depends on the size of the partition that you have already decided above.

- **Linear sampling**: also, in this case, the order of the input table rows is preserved: every n^{th} row will go to an output port, alternating regularly across the two partitions. If, for instance, you run a linear sampling for creating two equally sized partitions (each having half of the original rows), you will end up with all the odd rows in a partition and all the even ones in the other. If, instead, the split is one-third and two-thirds, you will have every third row in the first partition and all others in the second one. This is particularly useful when your dataset is a time series, with records sorted chronologically.

- **Draw randomly**: if you go for this option, you obtain a random sampling. The only thing you can be sure of is that the number of rows in the first partition will be exactly what you have set in the first selector.

- **Stratified sampling**: in this case, you also run a random sampling but, you force the distribution of a nominal column to be preserved in both output partitions. For example: if you have an input table describing 1,000 patients, out of which 90% are labeled as negative and 10% as positive, you can use stratified sampling to retain the ratio between positive and negative patients in each partition. In this case, if you want to have 700 rows to go to the first partition, you will end up with exactly 630 negative patients and 70 positive ones: the proportion is kept.

If you have selected a splitting method based on a random selection (the last two options in the list above), you can protect the reproducibility of your workflow by ticking the **Use random seed** optional box. When you specify a constant number for initializing the random sampling, you are "fixing" the random behavior: as a result, you will always obtain the same partitions every time you execute the node. This is handy when you want to keep the partitioning constant as you go back and forth in the construction of your workflow or when you want other people to get the same partitioning on their machines:

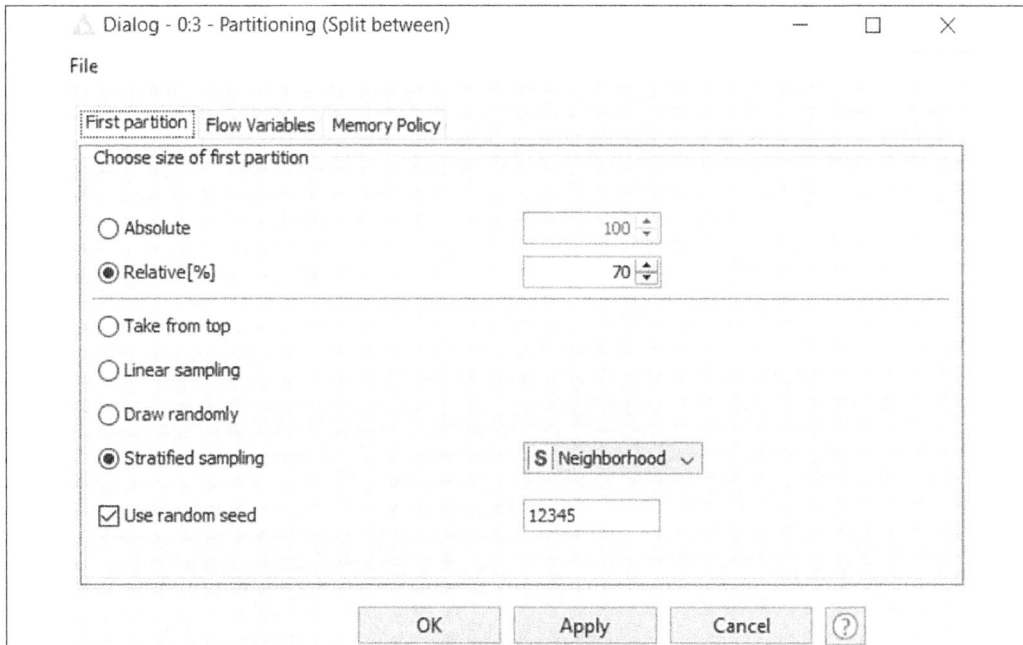

Figure 5.6: Configuration dialog of Partitioning: how do you want to split your dataset?

One thing that computers really struggle with is behaving randomly and doing anything "unexpected" as they are built and programmed to follow a deterministic set of steps. For this reason, computers leverage special algorithms for generating sequences of **pseudo-random numbers** that "look" as if they are truly random. Notably, the starting point of these sequences (the **random seed**) can determine the full progression of numbers. When needed, a computer can still generate a random seed by looking at a quickly changing state (like the number of clock cycles of the CPU from the last boot) or by measuring some microscopic physical quantities (like a voltage on a port) that are affected by uncontrollable phenomena, such as thermal noise and other quantic effects. It's interesting how computers struggle with what would take us just a flip of a coin!

Let's start our supervised learning typical flow and split our full housing dataset into training and test subsets:

3. Let's implement the **Partitioning** node and connect it with the output of the **Excel Reader** output (you can keep the **Statistics** node unhooked as we don't need to use its outputs). In the configuration dialog, let's make sure that we select the **Relative[%]** option with the value 70. This means that, out of the 4,000 properties available at the inputs, 70% of them will be used for training (which is a fair thing to do since, as anticipated in *Chapter 4, What is Machine Learning?*, the training set should normally cover between 70% and 80% of the total full dataset). We want the partitioning to happen randomly. In the previous step, we noticed that some nominal columns (like *Neighborhood*) display an unbalanced distribution across their values. This means that we have the risk of having the very few properties in a smaller neighborhood (like the 26 rows referring to `Magliana`) ending up solely in a partition. Although this is not strictly required, we better avoid any unbalance that can affect our learning and select **Stratified sampling** on *Neighborhood* in the dialog. You can also click on the bottom tick box and, on the right, type in a random seed, like 12345, so that you can count on the same partitioning over and over. When you run the node, you find that in the upper output port (right-click on the node and select **First partition**) you find 2,800 rows that are exactly 70% of the original dataset. This is a good sign and we can move ahead with the learning step.

At this point, we need to add the nodes (both learner and predictor) that implement the specific machine learning algorithm we want to use. The simplest algorithm for predicting numbers is **linear regression,** which is what we are going to use in this tutorial. It's worth introducing first the underlying mathematical model so that we can get ready to interpret its results.

Linear regression algorithm

The linear regression model is a generalization of the simple regression we have used to predict second-hand car prices in *Chapter 4, What is Machine Learning?*. In that case, we modeled the price as a straight line, following the simple equation:

$$y = p_0 + p_1 x$$

where y was the dependent variable, so the target of our prediction (the price of the car), x, was the only independent variable (in that case, the age of the car in years) and p_0 and p_1 were the parameters of the model, defining the *height* of the line (also known as the *offset* or *intercept*) and its *slope*, respectively:

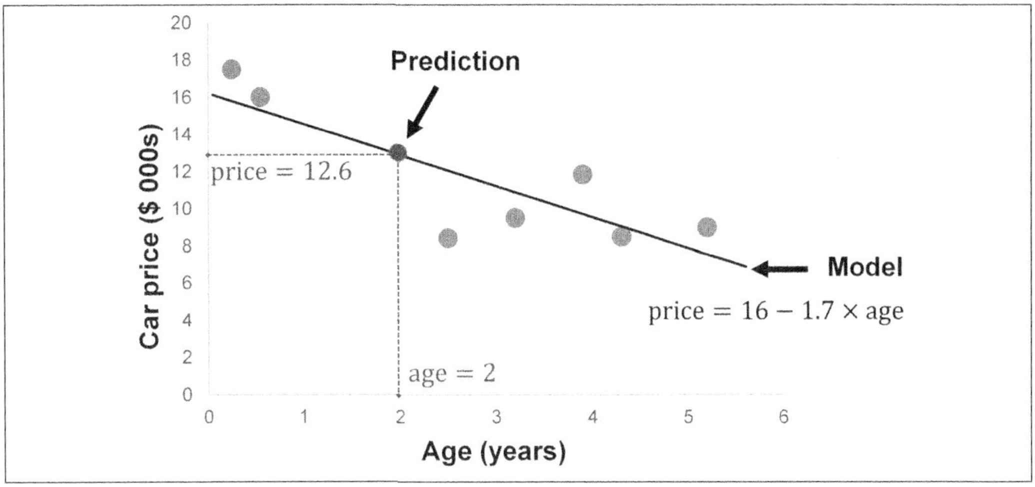

Figure 5.7: Linear regression of car prices: the line shows the prediction as the age varies

Specifically, as you can see in *Figure 5.7*, we have $p_0 = 16$ (it's where the model line encounters the vertical axis) and $p_1 = -1.7$ so the price of the car is predicted through the simple model:

$$price = 16 - 1.7 \times age$$

The price of a 2-year-old car will be estimated to be \$12,600, since:

$$16 - 1.7 \times 2 = 12.6$$

The purpose of the *learner* algorithm of a simple linear regression is to find the right parameters (p_0 and p_1) that minimize the error of a prediction, while the *predictor* algorithm will just apply the model on new numbers, like we did when we came up with the estimated price of a 2-year-old car.

Linear regression is a generalization of the simple model that we have just seen in action. Its underlying mathematical description is:

$$y = p_0 + p_1 x_1 + p_2 x_2 + \cdots + p_N x_N$$

where y is still the (single) target variable that we are trying to predict, the various x_i values represent the (many) independent variables that correspond to the features we have available, and the p_i values are the parameters of the model that define its "shape." Since we have several independent variables this time (for this reason, we call it a **multivariate model**), we cannot "visualize" it any longer with a simple line on a 2D chart. Still, its underlying mathematical model is quite simple because it assumes that every feature is "linearly" connected with the target variable. Here you go: you have just met the multivariate linear regression model.

If we apply this model to the prediction of the rental prices, our target variable is represented by the column *Rent* while the features (independent variables) are all the other columns, like *Rooms*, *Surface*, and so on. The multivariate linear regression model will look like:

$$Rent = p_0 + p_1 \times Rooms + p_2 \times Surface + \cdots$$

and the aim of the learner algorithm implementing this model will be to find the "best" values of p_0, p_1, p_2, and so on that minimize the error produced on the training set.

There are ways to find analytically (meaning through a set of given formulas, nothing overly complex) the set of parameters p_i that minimize the error of a linear regression model. The simplest one is called **Ordinary Least Squares (OLS)**: it minimizes the sum of the squared errors of a linear regression. Do you remember the **Root Mean Squared Error** (**RMSE**) metric introduced in *Chapter 4*? By using the ordinary least squares procedure, we are going to minimize the RMSE, which is exactly what we need to do here.

The model above expects every independent variable to be a number. So, how do we deal with the nominal features we have in our dataset like *Floor_type*? We can solve this apparent limitation with a common trick used in machine learning: creating the so-called **dummy variables**. The idea is very simple: we transform every nominal variable into multiple numerical variables. Let's take the example of *Floor_type*: this is a categorical variable whose value can be either Upper, Mezzanine, or Ground floor. In this case we would replace this categorical variable by creating three numeric dummy variables: *Floor_type=Upper*, *Floor_type=Mezzanine*, and *Floor_type=Ground*. The dummy variables will take as values either 1 or 0, depending on the category: for a given row, only one dummy variable will take 1 and all others will take 0. For example, if a row refers to an Upper floor property, the dummy variable *Floor_type=Upper* will be 1 and the other two will be 0.

Thanks to this trick, we can apply a linear regression model on any categorical variables as well; we just need to "convert" them into multiple additional dummy variables.

We have all we need to give the linear regression model a try by introducing the KNIME node that implements its learning algorithm.

▶ 〰️ *Linear Regression Learner*

This node (**Analytics > Mining > Linear/Polynomial Regression**) trains a multivariate linear regression model for predicting a numeric quantity. For its configuration (see *Figure 5.8*) you will have to specify the numeric column to be predicted by picking it in the **Target** drop-down menu at the top:

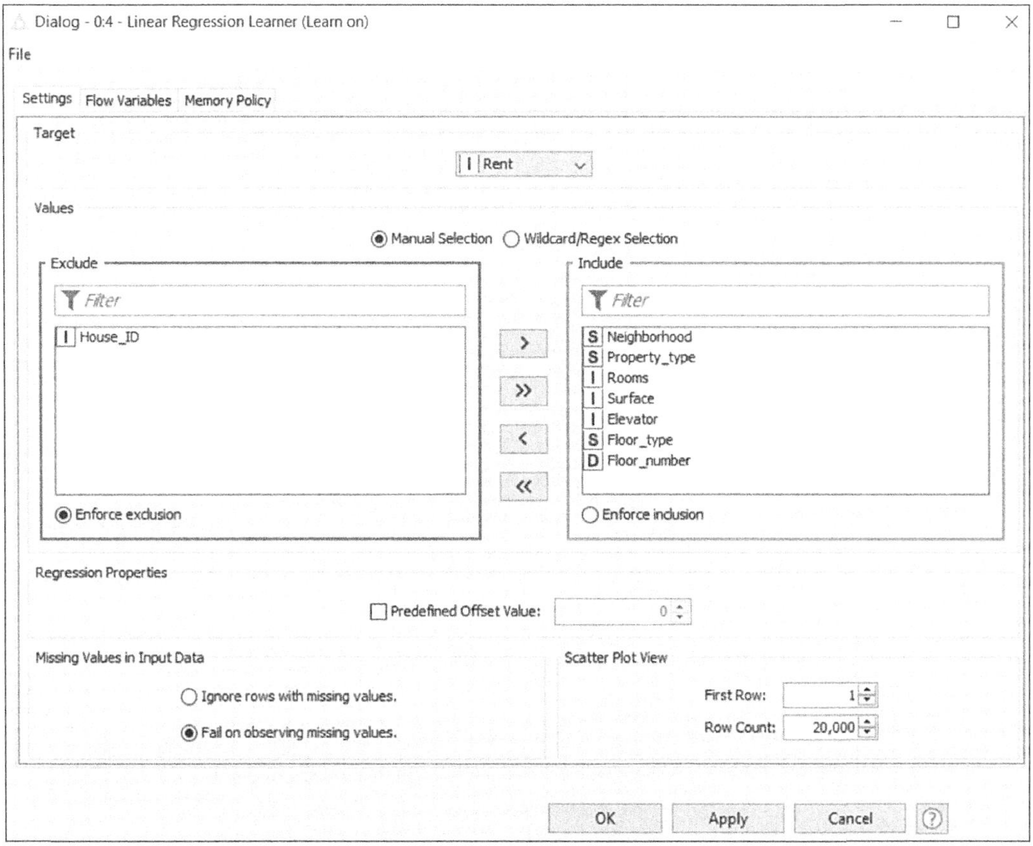

Figure 5.8: Configuration dialog of Linear Regression Learner; choose what to predict and the features to use

Then, in the central box, you can select which columns should be used as features: only the columns that appear on the green box on the right will be considered as independent variables in the model. The nominal columns, such as strings, will be automatically converted by the node into dummy variables.

> If a nominal column (like *Type*) admits N unique values (like A, B, and C), this node will actually create not N, but $N-1$ dummy variables (*Type=A* and *Type=B*). In fact, one of the nominal values can be covered by the combination of all zeros: in our case, if *Type* is C, both *Type=A* and *Type=B* will be zero, implying that the only possible value for that row is C. In this way, we make the model simpler and avoid the so-called dummy variable trap, which might make our model parameters impossible to calculate. The node takes care of this automatically, so you don't have to worry about it: just keep this in mind when reading the model parameters related to dummy variables.

By clicking on the **Predefined Offset Value** tick box, you can "force" the offset value of the linear regression model (we also called it p_0 or intercept earlier) to a certain value or remove it, by setting it to zero. This reduces the "flexibility" of the model to minimize the error so it will reduce its accuracy. However, this trick might be helpful when you are trying to reduce the complexity of the model and improve its explain ability, as we have one less parameter to interpret. By default, this node will fail if there are some missing values in the input data. To manage this, you can either manage them earlier in the workflow, using the **Missing Value** node, or select the **Ignore rows with missing value** option at the bottom-left corner of the configuration dialog.

Once executed, the node will return at its first output port the regression model, which can then be used by a predictor node for making predictions. The second output is a table (*Figure 5.9*) that contains a summary view of the regression model parameters, where for each variable (including the dummy ones) you can find:

- **Coeff.**: this is the **parameter** (also called coefficient) of the variable. This is the p_i parameter we have seen in the regression model formula.

- **Std. Err.**: this is **the standard deviation of the error** expected for this parameter. If you compare it with the value of the parameter, you get a rough idea of how "precise" the estimation of that parameter can be. You can use it also to get a rough confidence interval for the given parameter as we did in *Chapter 4, What is Machine Learning?*, when talking about RMSE. In the case of the car price regression, if the parameter for the variable *Age* is -1.7 and the standard error is 0.1, you can say that 95% of the time, the price of a car declines by $M 1.7 ± 0.2 (2 times the standard error) every year.

- **t-value** and **P>|t|**: these are two summary statistics (**t-value** and **p-value**) generated by the application of the Student test, which clarifies how significant a variable is for the model. The smaller the p-value, the more confident you can be in rejecting the possibility that that parameter looks significant just "by chance" (it's called **null hypothesis**). As a general rule of thumb, when the p-value (the last column in this table) is above 0.05, you should remove that variable from the model, as it is likely insignificant:

Row ID	S Variable	D Coeff.	D Std. Err.	D t-value	D P>|t|
Row1	Neighborhood=Cassia	-361.633	21.98	-16.453	0
Row2	Neighborhood=Castelli Romani	-712.071	21.272	-33.475	0
Row3	Neighborhood=Cinecittà	-583	21.437	-27.196	0
Row4	Neighborhood=Collatino	-561.935	21.655	-25.95	0
Row5	Neighborhood=EUR	-430.322	26.197	-16.427	0
Row6	Neighborhood=Infernetto	-621.998	22.456	-27.699	0
Row7	Neighborhood=Magliana	-608.508	33.284	-18.282	0
Row8	Neighborhood=Marconi	-500.728	24.164	-20.722	0
Row9	Neighborhood=Montagnola	-483.346	24.296	-19.894	0
Row10	Neighborhood=Monte sacro	-530.228	21.723	-24.409	0
Row11	Neighborhood=Monti	-126	22.475	-5.606	0
Row12	Neighborhood=Ostia	-564.32	25.695	-21.962	0
Row13	Neighborhood=Parioli	-215.546	21.139	-10.197	0
Row14	Neighborhood=Piazza Navona	217.836	21.511	10.127	0
Row15	Neighborhood=Portuense	-510.689	30.56	-16.711	0
Row16	Neighborhood=Prati	-177.889	21.515	-8.268	0
Row17	Neighborhood=Termini	-258.655	23.106	-11.194	0
Row18	Neighborhood=Testaccio	-210.036	29.045	-7.231	0
Row19	Neighborhood=Trastevere	-64.205	23.045	-2.786	0.005
Row20	Neighborhood=Trigoria	-534.072	26.809	-19.922	0
Row21	Property_type=House	-22.665	29.391	-0.771	0.441
Row22	Property_type=Penthouse	35.789	12.081	2.962	0.003
Row23	Property_type=Villa	9.072	50.642	0.179	0.858
Row24	Rooms	25.777	4.03	6.397	0
Row25	Surface	9.614	0.133	72.343	0
Row26	Elevator	1.82	4.657	0.391	0.696
Row27	Floor_type=Mezzanine	36.009	11.459	3.142	0.002
Row28	Floor_type=Upper	22.754	7.277	3.127	0.002
Row29	Floor_number	4.354	1.502	2.898	0.004
Row30	Intercept	569.877	21.855	26.075	0

Figure 5.9: The summary output of the Linear Regression Learner node: find out what the parameters of the regression are and if they turn out significant or not

If you right-click on the node after it is executed, you can open an additional graphical view (select **View: Linear Regression Scatterplot View**) where you can visually compare the individual features against the target to look for steep slopes and other patterns.

Let's now put this node to work with our Rome properties and see what it's got:

4. Implement the **Linear Regression Learner** node and connect it with the upper output of the **Partitioning** node, which is the training set (a 70% random sample of the historical database of rents). In the configuration window, double-check that *Rent* is set as the **Target** variable on top. Feature-wise, at this point, we can keep all of them to see if they are significant or not. However, we can already remove one, *House_ID*, as we already know we don't want it to be used. We don't want to make use of the unique identifier of the property to infer the rental price. That number has been assigned artificially when the property was added to the database, and it is not connected with features of the property itself, so we don't want to consider it in a predictive model. Run the model and open the second output port to obtain the summary view of the model parameters.

This summary view will look similar to what is displayed in *Figure 5.9*, although the numbers could differ given that the random partitioning might have generated in your case different partitions: welcome to the world of probabilistic models! However, we can already notice that some parameters display a p-value (the last column of the table, **P>|t|**) higher than 0.05. This means we can come back to this step later and do some cleaning and improve the performance of the model. For now, let's proceed further so that we can make some predictions and score the model.

▶ Regression Predictor

This node (**Analytics > Mining > Linear/Polynomial Regression**) applies a regression model (given as an input in the first blue port on the left) to a dataset (second port) and returns the result of the prediction for each input row. The node does not require any configuration and can be used in conjunction with either the **Linear Regression Learner** node, introduced above, or the **Polynomial Regression Learner** node: you can check this one out by yourself if you want to build linear regressions on different polynomial degrees as we did in *Chapter 4, What is Machine Learning?* (have a look at *Figure 4.9*).

5. Let's add the **Regression Predictor** node to the workflow and make the connections: link the blue square output of the **Linear Regression Learner** to the upper input port of the predictor and connect the bottom output port of the **Partitioning** (the test set) to the second input port. No configuration is needed so you can execute the node and look at the output, which is similar to what you find in *Figure 5.10*:

Row ID	I House_ID	S Neighborhood	S Property_type	I Rooms	I Surface	I Elevator	S Floor_type	D Floor_number	I Rent	D Prediction (Rent)
Row2	104125	Collatino	Flat	3	80	1	Upper	4	950	896.373
Row3	104675	Infernetto	Flat	3	75	0	Upper	2	800	777.714
Row7	104367	Prati	Flat	5	130	0	Upper	5	2000	1,815.203
Row8	104969	Cinecittà	House	3	70	1	Upper	1	800	743.444
Row14	103961	Piazza Navona	Flat	3	65	1	Upper	6	1550	1,540.644
Row17	103889	Piazza Navona	Flat	3	70	0	Upper	1	1500	1,565.125
Row18	103551	Piazza Navona	Flat	3	80	0	Upper	3	1650	1,669.971
Row24	102907	Infernetto	Flat	2	50	1	Upper	1	550	509.056
Row31	105048	Cinecittà	Flat	2	65	1	Upper	1	750	692.262
Row33	103031	Infernetto	Flat	2	60	1	Upper	3	700	613.902
Row36	105191	Parioli	Flat	4	105	1	Upper	3	1500	1,504.534
Row38	103624	Ostia	Flat	3	75	0	Upper	3	750	839.746
Row40	105355	Trastevere	Flat	3	90	1	Upper	1	1350	1,477.181
Row45	105343	Monte sacro	Flat	2	40	0	Upper	7	700	528.991
Row47	103463	Cinecittà	Flat	2	55	0	Upper	3	700	603.011
Row48	104995	Cassia	Flat	3	55	0	Upper	5	800	858.863
Row51	102602	Termini	Flat	2	50	1	Upper	2	900	876.753
Row55	104399	Parioli	Flat	3	85	0	Upper	2	1200	1,280.305
Row57	102437	Piazza Navona	Flat	3	90	1	Upper	1	1800	1,759.222
Row58	104020	Monte sacro	Flat	2	60	0	Upper	1	750	695.145
Row70	105650	Termini	Flat	2	70	1	Mezzanine	0.5	900	1,075.754
Row71	104315	Parioli	Flat	3	100	1	Upper	5	1600	1,439.395
Row80	102050	Monte sacro	Flat	3	70	1	Ground floor	0	750	791.773
Row83	103210	Prati	Flat	2	55	0	Upper	6	1200	1,021.184

Figure 5.10: Output of the Regression Predictor node: we finally have a prediction of the rental price.

You can look with pride at the last column on the right, called *Prediction (Rent)*: for each row in the test set (which has not been "seen" by the learner node) the node has generated a prediction of the rent. This prediction was obtained by just "applying" the parameters of the regression model to the values of the rows in the test set. Let's see how this works with an example: consider the parameters in *Figure 5.9*. In this case the intercept (last row) is 569.9, the parameter of *Rooms* is around 25.8, the one for *Surface* is 9.6, the parameter of the dummy variable associated with the Collatino neighborhood (*Neighborhood=Collatino*) is -561.9, and so on. When the predictor had to come up with a prediction for the first row in the test set (see the first line in *Figure 5.10*), it had to just apply the formula of the regression model, with the parameters found by the learner, to this property (with 3 rooms, 80 square meters, based in Collatino, and so on). Hence, the resulting calculation for the **Regression Predictor** node is:

$$Prediction(rent) = 569.9 + 25.8 \times 3 + 9.6 \times 80 + (-561.9) + \cdots = 896.4$$

In this specific case, if you add all the other features that were not reported in the preceding formula, we come up with a final prediction of €896.4, making around €50 of error versus the actual rental price, which we know is €950: not bad for our first prediction! To have a complete view of the performance of the current model, we would need to check the difference between predicted and real rents for all rows in the test set, using the **Numeric Scorer** node.

► ✦ ► *Numeric Scorer*

This node (**Analytics > Mining > Scoring**) calculates the summary performance metrics of a regression by comparing two numeric columns. Its only required configuration (*Figure 5.11*) is the selection of the two columns to be compared: you can select the target column of the regression, containing the actual values, in the **Reference column** dropdown, and the predictions in the next one, labeled as **Predicted column**. If you want to output the performance scores as variables as well (this is useful when doing hyperparameter optimization), you need to tick the **Output scores as flow variables** box at the bottom. The node outputs the most popular scoring metrics of a regression, including the **Coefficient of Determination, R^2**, and the **RMSE**:

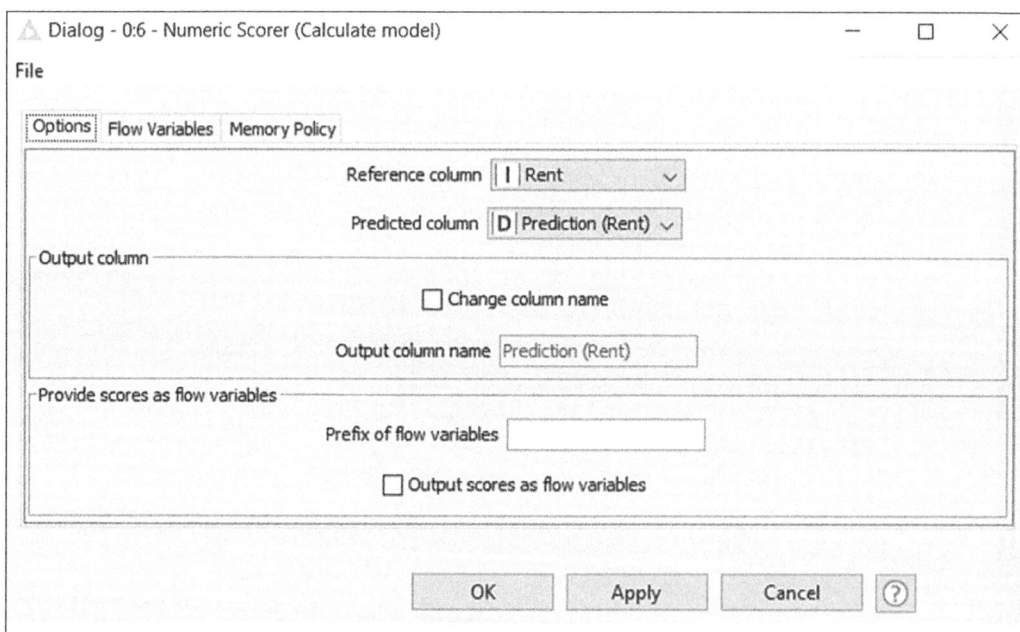

Figure 5.11: Configuration dialog of the Numeric Scorer node: select the columns to compare.

6. Implement the **Numeric Scorer** node (watch out: don't get confused with the **Scorer** node, which is used for classifications) and connect the output of the **Regression Predictor** with its input port. For its configuration, just double-check that you have *Rent* and *Prediction (Rent)* in the drop-down menus at the top and run the node. Its output (*Figure 5.12*) is very encouraging (of course, you can get slightly different results from what you find in these figures and that's normal):

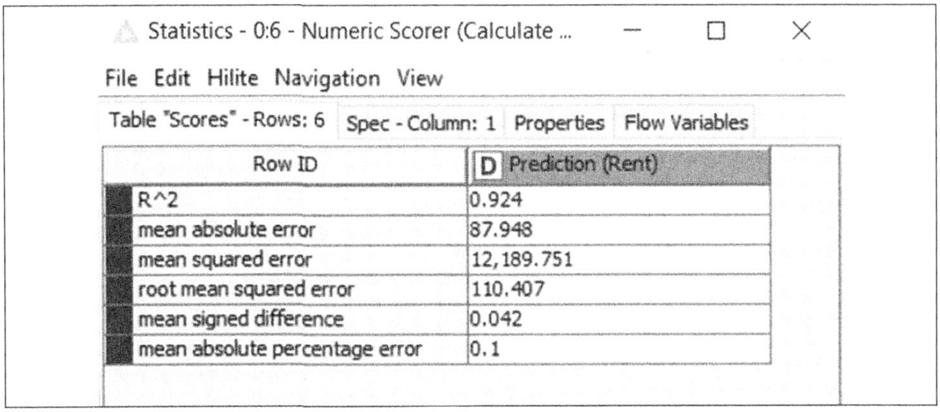
Statistics - 0:6 - Numeric Scorer (Calculate ...

File Edit Hilite Navigation View

Table "Scores" - Rows: 6 | Spec - Column: 1 | Properties | Flow Variables

Row ID	D Prediction (Rent)
R^2	0.924
mean absolute error	87.948
mean squared error	12,189.751
root mean squared error	110.407
mean signed difference	0.042
mean absolute percentage error	0.1

Figure 5.12: Performance metrics as returned by the Numeric Scorer node: not bad for your first regression

We obtained an R^2 of 0.92, which means that our current model accounts for around 92% of the full variability of rental prices in Rome. Considering the limited sample and the few features available, this looks quite good already. Also, the RMSE is €110, which means that 68% of the time (one standard deviation) we will make a prediction error that is, in absolute terms, below €110, and 95% of the time our error will be below €220 (two times the RMSE). The last performance metric, **Mean Absolute Percentage Error** (**MAPE**) tells us that, on average, our predicted rent will differ from the actual rent by around 10%: again, not bad at all.

Still, we strive for the best and question ourselves if we can do anything to improve the model. The simplest thing to do will be to consider whether we can improve the selection of features. Let's go back and have a look at the parameters obtained by the regression (*Figure 5.9*) and if we can remove some unneeded (or damaging) features. When we remove excess features from a model, we obtain at least two advantages: first, we make the model simpler and more explanatory to other human beings, as we have fewer parameters to explain. Secondly, we reduce the possibility for the model to overfit on the training set and, so, we increase its general robustness.

> Another reason for removing features is to avoid the risk of **multicollinearity**, which happens when features are correlated with each other. Correlated features are redundant: they can produce degradation of the predictive performance of your model and should be removed. The **Linear Correlation** node can help you calculate the correlation across all pairs of numeric columns in a table. As an alternative, you can use the **Variance Inflation Filter** (**VIF**) component, available in the KNIME Hub: as a rule of thumb, all variables showing a VIF higher than 5 should be removed.

Let's have a look at the p-values (last column of the table) and see if we can unveil some opportunities. Remember, the higher they are, the less meaningful their associated features proved to be. For sure we notice that the feature *Elevator* should be removed: its p-value is way above the thumb-rule threshold of 0.05 so we can go ahead and remove it. Also, the variable *Property_type* shall be removed: the p-values of their dummy variables are high, with the exception of *Property_type=Penthouse* (indicating that Penthouse is the only type that seems to be significant in affecting the value of the rent). Still, considering how few penthouses we have in the dataset, it's worth removing this feature and further simplifying the model. Let's give this simplification a try and see what happens:

7. Open the configuration dialog of the **Linear Regression Learner** node and move *Elevator* and *Property_type* to the left box of the column selector, so as to remove them as features of the model.

8. Now let's run the full model and see if something changed. To do so, it will be enough to execute the **Numeric Scorer** node: all previous nodes will be forced to run as well.

By removing these two features (see the updated results in *Figure 5.13*), we managed to keep the same performance levels, proving that they were unneeded. Actually, the performance has marginally increased (notice the lower RMSE), probably showing that we were slightly overfitting because of these uninformative variables. Additionally, we simplified the model, making it simpler to explain. Now we can predict the rental price of a property in Rome by knowing only the neighborhood, the number of rooms, the surface, and its floor (number and type):

Coefficients and Statistics - 0:4 - Linear Regression Learn...

Table "Coefficients and Statistics" - Rows: 26   Spec - Columns: 5   Properties   Flow Variables

Row ID	S Variable	D Coeff.	D Std. Err.	D t-value	D P>|t|
Row1	Neighborhood=Cassia	-364.227	21.981	-16.57	0
Row2	Neighborhood=Castelli Romani	-715.227	21.247	-33.663	0
Row3	Neighborhood=Cinecittà	-587.821	21.393	-27.477	0
Row4	Neighborhood=Collatino	-567.392	21.596	-26.273	0
Row5	Neighborhood=EUR	-435.708	26.16	-16.655	0
Row6	Neighborhood=Infernetto	-624.731	22.407	-27.882	0
Row7	Neighborhood=Magliana	-610.913	33.303	-18.344	0
Row8	Neighborhood=Marconi	-506.537	24.103	-21.015	0
Row9	Neighborhood=Montagnola	-486.451	24.293	-20.025	0
Row10	Neighborhood=Monte sacro	-534.179	21.694	-24.623	0
Row11	Neighborhood=Monti	-130.327	22.441	-5.807	0
Row12	Neighborhood=Ostia	-567.884	25.691	-22.104	0
Row13	Neighborhood=Parioli	-219.284	21.11	-10.388	0
Row14	Neighborhood=Piazza Navona	214.887	21.505	9.992	0
Row15	Neighborhood=Portuense	-515.662	30.541	-16.884	0
Row16	Neighborhood=Prati	-181.986	21.49	-8.468	0
Row17	Neighborhood=Termini	-263.534	23.064	-11.426	0
Row18	Neighborhood=Testaccio	-214.694	29.017	-7.399	0
Row19	Neighborhood=Trastevere	-67.706	23.025	-2.941	0.003
Row20	Neighborhood=Trigoria	-538.085	26.787	-20.087	0
Row21	Rooms	26.08	4.032	6.469	0
Row22	Surface	9.604	0.133	72.249	0
Row23	Floor_type=Mezzanine	35.589	11.469	3.103	0.002
Row24	Floor_type=Upper	21.045	7.248	2.904	0.004
Row25	Floor_number	5.609	1.447	3.876	0
Row26	Intercept	574.7	21.654	26.54	0

Statistics - 0:6 - Numeric Scorer (Cal...

Table "Scores" - Rows: 6   Spec - Column: 1   Properties   Flow Variables

Row ID	D Prediction (Rent)
R^2	0.925
mean absolute error	87.294
mean squared error	12,069.083
root mean squared error	109.859
mean signed difference	-0.284
mean absolute percentage error	0.099

Figure 5.13: Updated parameters and performance scores after the removal of two features: every little helps

These last two steps have shown us the value of selecting features wisely. As anticipated in *Chapter 4, What is Machine Learning?*, feature selection is an important practice in machine learning, indeed.

> In this case, we applied feature selection "by hand," checking the parameters manually and selecting the least meaningful ones. There are more systemic and semi-automated techniques to find out the best subset of features to use in a machine learning model. If you are curious, check the KNIME nodes for **Feature Selection** loops and have a look at the sample workflow available on the KNIME Hub called **Performing a Forward Feature Selection**.

Before concluding, we need to do one last thing: it's time to apply our model to the 10 incoming properties for which the rental price is not available yet. This will be a way to illustrate our findings to the owner of the company. It will also be an opportunity for us to understand how predictive models are used in real life after they are built. In fact, once models are constructed (and validated against overfitting, as we did through the partitioning in training and test sets, and so on) they are **operationalized** in a way that they can be applied to future samples (in this case, the 10 new properties) whenever a prediction is needed. Let's see this in action with our properties:

9. Load the Excel file with the new properties (RomeHousing-NewProperties. xlsx) *by dragging and dropping it into your workflow or implementing an* **Excel Reader** *node*. Once executed, you will find a short table that has exactly the same columns as the historical database, but — of course — lacks the *Rent* value.

10. Implement a new **Regression Predictor** node (or copy/paste the existing one) and connect it as displayed in *Figure 5.14*. You should link the output of the **Linear Regression Learner** (yes — we are going to reuse the model we learned earlier) to the first input of the predictor. Then connect the **Excel Reader** output (the 10 new properties) to the second input of the predictor. You can now execute the node and have a look at the output:

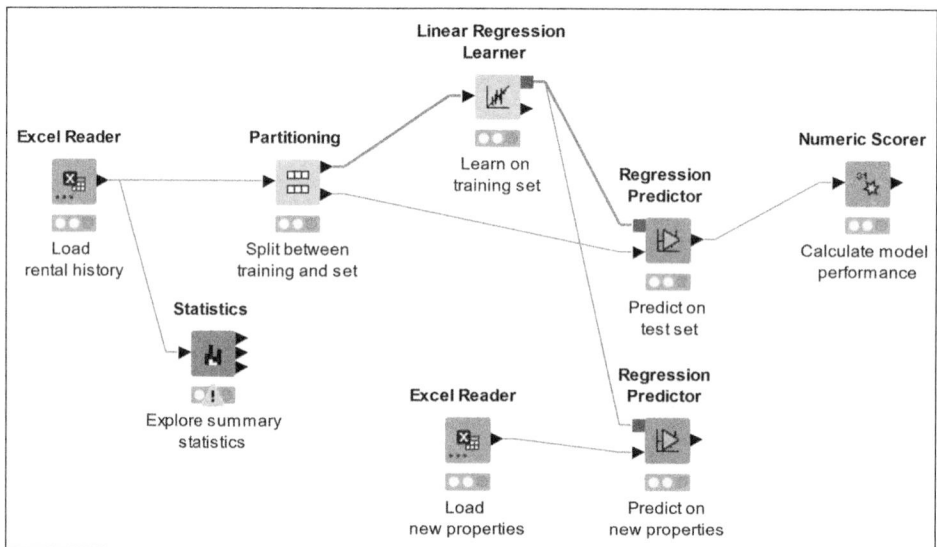

Figure 5.14: Full workflow for the Rome rent prediction

At this point, you have all you need to go back to the owner of the real estate with your output table (which will have a similar format to what you find in *Figure 5.15*) and wait impatiently for her reaction, which turns out to be very positive! She loves it, as she finds that the estimates make, at least at a first glance, a lot of sense:

Row ID	S House_ID	S Neighborhood	S Property_type	I Rooms	I Surface	I Elevator	S Floor_type	I Floor_number	D Prediction (Rent)
Row0	new_001	Trastevere	Villa	2	60	0	Upper	1	1,162.068
Row1	new_002	Infernetto	Flat	2	50	1	Ground floor	0	482.346
Row2	new_003	Castelli Romani	Flat	3	80	1	Upper	2	738.323
Row3	new_004	Termini	Flat	4	90	1	Upper	5	1,328.965
Row4	new_005	Montagnola	Flat	3	80	1	Upper	2	967.099
Row5	new_006	Montagnola	Flat	2	55	0	Ground floor	0	668.648
Row6	new_007	Monti	Flat	3	80	1	Upper	2	1,323.223
Row7	new_008	Aventino	Penthouse	3	90	1	Upper	9	1,588.854
Row8	new_009	Piazza Navona	Flat	4	145	0	Upper	3	2,324.407
Row9	new_010	EUR	Flat	3	100	1	Upper	9	1,249.189

Figure 5.15: The predicted rental prices on the new properties:
do you fancy a 145 square meter flat near Piazza Navona at this price?

The understandable initial stress turns quickly to a broad sense of enthusiasm. The model you created responds to the initial business objectives. In fact:

- The interpretation of the parameters of the model tells us something quite useful about the price formation mechanisms. For instance, you have found that the presence of the elevators and the type of flat doesn't count as much as the surface, the number of rooms, the floors, and, very importantly, the neighborhood to which the property belongs. By looking at the parameters of the neighborhood dummy variables (*Figure 5.13*), you find out what additional value each neighborhood brings (of course to be added to the rest of the components of your regression). For instance, Piazza Navona is by far the most expensive area while Castelli Romani seems to offer (at parity of characteristics) the most accessible rent.

- On top of this, you now have a simple approach to quickly generate a recommendation of what fair rent looks like, which could be the basis for the discussion with the prospective landlord when fixing the rental price. By having a data-based number to start from, the agents can aim at a smoother negotiation session, which will more likely end up with a quicker and more profitable matching of demand and offer in the housing market.

Congratulations on completing your first regression model! It's now time to move on and challenge ourselves with a different undertaking: anticipating consumers' behavior.

Anticipating preferences with classification

In this tutorial, you will step into the role of a marketing analyst working for a mid-sized national consumer bank, offering services such as accounts, personal loans, and mortgages to around 300,000 customers in the country. The bank is currently trying to launch a new type of low-cost savings account, providing essential services and a pre-paid card that can be fully managed online. The product manager of this new account is not very pleased with how things are going and invites you to join a review meeting. You can see he is tense as he presents the outcome of a pilot telemarketing campaign run to support the launch. As part of this pilot, 10,000 people were randomly selected among the full bank customer base and were phoned by an outbound call center. The outcome was apparently not so bad: 1,870 of the contacted customers (19% of the total) signed up for a new account. However, the calculation of the **Return On Investment** (**ROI**) pulled the entire audience back to the unsettling reality. The average cost of attempting to contact a customer through a call center is $15 per person while the incremental revenue resulting from a confirmed sale is estimated to be, on average, $60. The math is simple: the pilot telemarketing campaign cost $150,000 and generated revenues amounting only to $112,200, implying a net loss of $37,800. Now it is clear why the product manager looked disappointed: repeating the same campaign on more customers would be financially devastating.

You timidly raise your hand and ask whether the outcomes of the pilot calls could be used to rethink the campaign target and improve the ROI of the marketing efforts. You explain that some machine learning algorithms might be able to predict whether a customer is willing or not to buy a product by learning from previous examples. As it normally happens in these cases, you instantly earn the opportunity to try what you suggested, and your manager asks you to put together a proposal on an ML way to support the launch of the new savings account.

You have mixed feelings about what just happened: on one hand, you are wondering whether you were a bit too quick in sharing the idea. On the other hand, you are very excited as you get to try leveraging algorithms to impact the business on such an important case. You are impatient to start and ask for all the available information related to the customers that were involved in the pilot. The file you receive (`BankTelemarketing.csv`) contains the following columns:

- *Age*: the age of the customer.
- *Job*: a string describing the job family of the customer, like `blue-collar`, `management`, `student`, `unemployed`, and `retired`.

- *Marital*: the marital status, which could be `married`, `single`, `divorced`, or `unknown`.

- *Education*: the highest education level reached to date by the customer, ranging from `illiterate` and `basic.4y` (4 years of basic education in total) to `university.degree`.

- *Default*: this tells us whether we know that the customer has defaulted due to extended payment delinquency or not. Only a few customers end up being marked as defaulted (yes): most of them either show a good rating history (no) or do not have enough history to be assigned in a category (unknown).

- *Mortgage* and *Loan*: tells us whether the user has ever requested a housing mortgage or a personal loan, respectively.

- *Contact*: indicates if the telephone number provided as a preferred contact method is a `landline` or a `mobile` phone.

- *Outcome*: a string recording the result of the call center contact during the pilot campaign. It can be yes or no, depending on whether the customer opened the new savings account or decided to decline the offer.

Before you get cracking, you have a chat with the product manager to get clear on what would be the most valuable outputs for the business given the situation:

- First of all, it would be very useful to understand and document what characteristics make a customer most likely to buy the new banking product. Given its novelty, it is not clear yet who will find its proposition particularly appealing. Having some more clues on this aspect can help to build more tailored campaigns, personalize their content, and — by doing so — transfer the learnings from the call center pilot to other types of media touchpoints.

- Given that the pilot covered only a relatively small subset of customers — around 3% of the total — it would be useful to identify "who else" to call within the other 97% to maximize the ROI of the marketing initiative. In fact, we can assume that the same features we found in our pilot dataset — such as age, job, marital status, and so on — are available for the entire customer database. If we were able to *score* the remaining customers in terms of their *propensity* to buy the product, we would be focusing our efforts on the most inclined ones and greatly improving the campaign's effectiveness. In other words, we should create a **propensity model** that will score current (and future) customers to enable a better marketing targeting. We will use the propensity scores to "limit" the next marketing efforts to a selected subset of the total customer base where the percentage of people in the new product is higher than 19% (as it was in our pilot): by doing so, we would increase the ROI of our marketing efforts.

From a machine learning standpoint, you need to create a machine able to predict whether a consumer will buy or will not open a savings account before you make the call. This is still a clear case of supervised learning, since you aim at predicting something based on previous examples (the pilot calls). In contrast with the Rome real estate case, where we had to predict a number (the rental price) using *regression* algorithms, here we need to predict the value of the categorical column *Outcome*. We will then need to implement *classification* algorithms, such as decision trees and random forest, which we are going to meet shortly. We are clear on the business need, the available data, and the type of machine learning route we want to take: we have all we need to start getting serious about this challenge. After creating a new workflow in KNIME, we load the data into it:

1. Drag and drop the file `BankTelemarketing.csv` onto the blank workflow. After the **CSV Reader** node dialog appears, we can quickly check that all is in order and close the window by clicking on **OK**. Once executed, the output of the node (*Figure 5.16*) confirms that our dataset is ready to go:

File Table - 3:1 - CSV Reader (Read pilot)   — □ ✕

File Edit Hilite Navigation View

Table "default" - Rows: 10000   Spec - Columns: 9   Properties   Flow Variables

Row ID	I Age	S Job	S Marital	S Education	S Default	S Mortgage	S Loan	S Contact	S Outcome
Row0	37	admin.	married	basic.9y	no	yes	no	mobile	yes
Row1	54	housemaid	married	basic.4y	no	no	no	mobile	yes
Row2	51	management	married	unknown	no	no	no	mobile	yes
Row3	27	services	single	high.school	no	no	yes	mobile	no
Row4	43	blue-collar	married	basic.6y	no	no	no	landline	no
Row5	31	self-employed	married	university.d…	no	no	no	mobile	no
Row6	33	technician	single	university.d…	no	no	no	landline	yes
Row7	28	blue-collar	single	professional…	no	yes	no	mobile	no
Row8	49	entrepreneur	married	university.d…	no	yes	no	landline	no
Row9	48	blue-collar	married	basic.6y	unknown	no	yes	mobile	no
Row10	47	self-employed	married	basic.6y	unknown	no	no	landline	yes
Row11	24	student	single	unknown	no	yes	no	mobile	no
Row12	46	admin.	divorced	university.d…	no	no	no	mobile	no
Row13	42	blue-collar	divorced	basic.4y	no	no	yes	landline	no
Row14	41	services	married	unknown	no	yes	yes	mobile	no
Row15	27	blue-collar	single	basic.9y	unknown	yes	no	mobile	no
Row16	38	blue-collar	married	basic.6y	unknown	no	yes	landline	no
Row17	57	retired	married	basic.4y	no	no	no	mobile	yes
Row18	39	services	married	high.school	unknown	no	no	landline	no

Figure 5.16: The pilot campaign data: 10,000 customers through 8 features and for which we know the outcome of their call center contact

2. As usual, we implement the node **Statistics**, to explore the characteristics of our dataset. After confirming its default configuration, we check the **Top/bottom** tab of its main view (press *F10* or right-click and select **View: Statistics View** to open it). It seems that there are no missing values and that all seems to be in line with what we knew about the pilot campaign: the *Outcome* column shows 1,870 rows with yes, which is what the product manager managed in his presentation. We also notice that the *Default* column has only one row referring to a defaulted customer. This column might still be useful as it differentiates between customers who never defaulted and ones we don't have any certainty about, so we decide to keep it and move on:

Statistics View - 3:13 - Statistics (Explore)							— □ ✕

File

| Numeric | Nominal | Top/bottom | | | | | |

Job	Marital	Education	Default	Mortgage	Loan	Contact	Outcome
No. missings: 0	No. missings: 0	No. missings: 0	No. missings: 0	No. missings: 0	No. missings: 0	No. missings: 0	No. missings: 0
Top 20:	Top 20:	Top 20:	Top 20:	Top 20:	Top 20:	Top 20:	Top 20:
blue-collar : 1938	married : 5667	university.degree : 2360	no : 7281	yes : 4963	no : 7095	mobile : 6061	no : 8130
admin. : 1738	single : 2651	high.school : 2125	unknown : 2718	no : 4517	yes : 2385	landline : 3939	yes : 1870
technician : 1437	divorced : 1640	basic.9y : 1564	yes : 1	unknown : 520	unknown : 520		
services : 1021	unknown : 42	professional.course : 1323					
management : 798		basic.4y : 1183					
retired : 647		unknown : 732					
entrepreneur : 554		basic.6y : 702					
self-employed : 531		illiterate : 11					
housemaid : 462							
unemployed : 444							
student : 272							
unknown : 158							
Bottom 20:	Bottom 20:	Bottom 20:	Bottom 20:	Bottom 20:	Bottom 20:	Bottom 20:	Bottom 20:

Figure 5.17: The Top/bottom output of the Statistics node:
only one person in this sample defaulted – good for everyone!

3. Since we are in the supervised learning scenario, we need to implement the usual partitioning/learn/predict/score structure in order to validate against the risk of overfitting. We start by adding the **Partitioning** node and connecting it downstream to the **CSV Reader** node. In its configuration dialog, we leave the **Relative** 70% size for the training partition and we decide to protect the distribution of the target variable *Outcome* in both partitions, selecting the **Stratified sampling** option. Additionally, we put a static number in the random seed box (you can put 12345 as you see in *Figure 5.18*) and tick the adjacent checkbox:

> As a general rule, always perform a stratified sampling on the target variable of a classification. This will reduce the impact of imbalanced classes when learning and validating your model. There are other ways to restore a balance in the distribution of classes, such as under-sampling the majority class or over-sampling the minority one. One interesting approach is the creation of synthetic (and realistic) additional samples using algorithms like the **Synthetic Minority Over-sampling Technique**: check out the **SMOTE** node to learn more.

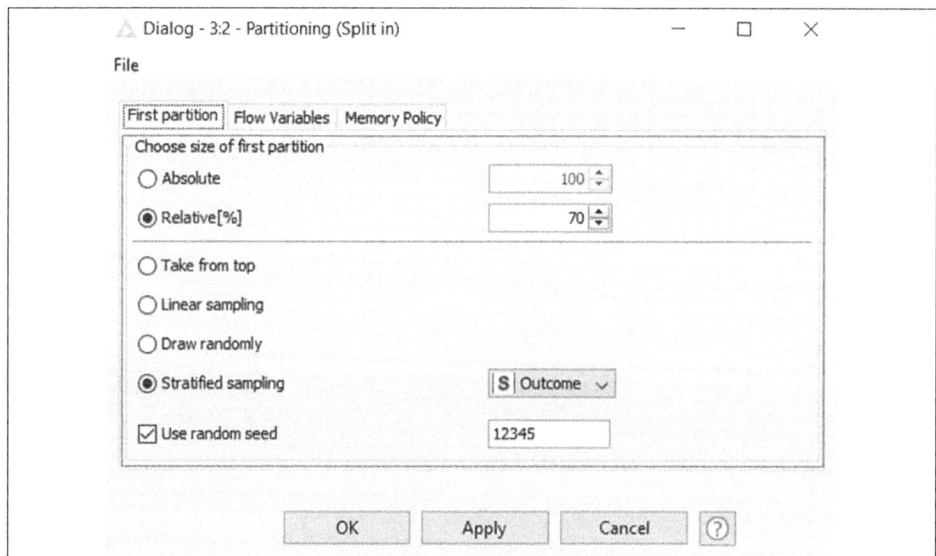

Figure 5.18: Performing a stratified sampling using the Partitioning node: this way, we ensure a fair presence of yes and no customers in each partition

Now that we have a training and test dataset readily available, we can proceed with implementing our first classification algorithm: **decision trees**. Let's get a hint of how it works.

Decision tree algorithm

Decision trees are simple models that describe a decision-making process. Have a look at the tree shown in *Figure 5.19* to get an idea of how they work. Their hierarchical structure resembles an upside-down tree. The root on top corresponds to the first question: according to the possible answers, there is a split between two or more subsequent *branches*. Every branch can either lead to additional questions (and respective splits into more branches) or terminate in *leaves*, indicating the outcome of the decision:

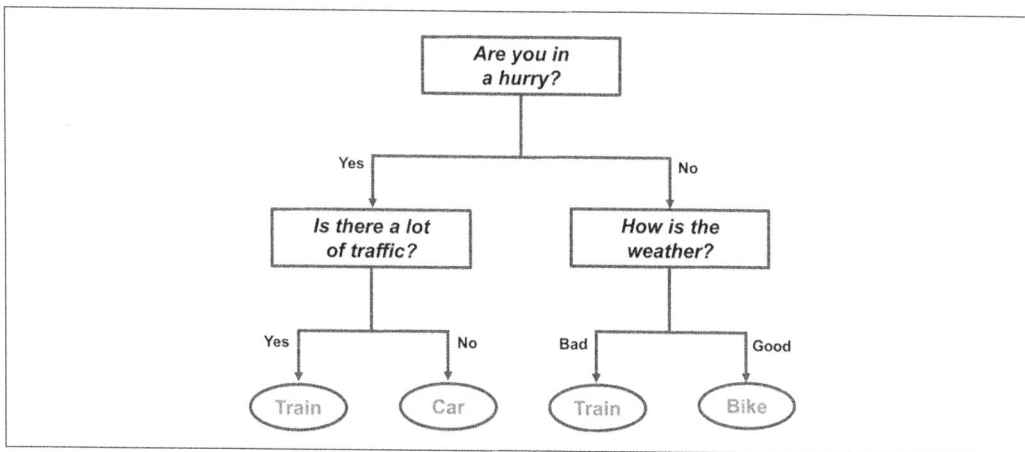

Figure 5.19: How will you go to work tomorrow? A decision tree can help you make up your mind

Decision trees can be used to describe the process that assigns an entity to a class: in this case, we call it a **classification tree**. Think about a table where each entity (corresponding to a row) is described by multiple features (columns) and is assigned to one specific class, among different alternatives. For example, a classification tree that assigns consumers to multiple classes will answer the question *to which class does the consumer belong?*: every branching will correspond to different outcomes of a test on the features (like *is the age of the consumer higher than 35?* or *is the person married?*) while each terminal leaf will be one of the possible classes. Once you have defined the decision tree, you can apply it to all consumers (current and future). For every consumer in the table, you follow the decision tree: the features of the consumer will dictate which specific path to follow and result in a single leaf to be assigned as the class of the consumer.

There are many tree-based learning algorithms available for classification. They are able to "draw" trees by learning from labeled examples. These algorithms can find out the right splits and paths that end up with a decision model able to predict classes of new, unlabeled entities. The simplest version of a decision tree learning algorithm will proceed by iteration, starting from the root of the tree and checking what the "best possible" next split to make is so as to differentiate classes in the least ambiguous way. This concept will become clear by means of a practical example. Let's imagine that we want to build a decision tree in order to predict which drink fast-food customers are going to order (among soda, wine, or beer), based on the food menu they had (the delicious alternatives are pizza, burger, or salad) and the composition of the table (whether it is among kids, couples, or groups of adults). The dataset to learn from will look like the one shown in *Figure 5.20*: we have 36 rows, each referring to a previous customer, and three columns, one for each feature (*Menu* and *Type*) and the target class (the *Favorite drink*).

	Menu	Type	Drink		Menu	Type	Drink
1	Pizza	Kids	Soda	19	Pizza	Kids	Beer
2	Burger	Kids	Soda	20	Burger	Kids	Soda
3	Salad	Kids	Soda	21	Salad	Kids	Soda
4	Pizza	Couples	Wine	22	Pizza	Couples	Beer
5	Burger	Couples	Wine	23	Burger	Couples	Wine
6	Salad	Couples	Beer	24	Salad	Couples	Wine
7	Pizza	Groups	Beer	25	Pizza	Groups	Beer
8	Burger	Groups	Beer	26	Burger	Groups	Wine
9	Salad	Groups	Wine	27	Salad	Groups	Beer
10	Pizza	Kids	Soda	28	Pizza	Kids	Soda
11	Burger	Kids	Beer	29	Burger	Kids	Soda
12	Salad	Kids	Soda	30	Salad	Kids	Soda
13	Pizza	Couples	Beer	31	Pizza	Couples	Beer
14	Burger	Couples	Wine	32	Burger	Couples	Wine
15	Salad	Couples	Wine	33	Salad	Couples	Wine
16	Pizza	Groups	Beer	34	Pizza	Groups	Beer
17	Burger	Groups	Soda	35	Burger	Groups	Beer
18	Salad	Groups	Beer	36	Salad	Groups	Beer

Figure 5.20: Drink preferences for 36 fast-food customers:
can you predict their preferences based on their food menu and type?

Since we have only two features, the resulting decision tree can only have two levels, resulting in two alternative shapes: either the first split is by *Menu* and the second, at the level below, by *Type,* or the other way around. The learning algorithm will pick the split that makes the most sense by looking at the count of the items falling into each branch and checking which splits make the "clearest cut" among classes.

In this specific case, the alternative choices for the first split are the ones drawn in *Figure 5.21*: you can find the number of customers falling into each branch, separated by alternative class (beer, soda, or wine). Have a look at the number and ask yourself: between the *Menu* split on the left and the *Type* split on the right, which one is differentiating in the "purest" way among the three classes?

Drinks by Menu	Burger		Pizza		Salad	
	#	%	#	%	#	%
Beer	3	25%	8	67%	4	33%
Soda	4	33%	3	25%	4	33%
Wine	5	42%	1	8%	4	33%
Total	12	100%	12	100%	12	100%

Drinks by Type	Couples		Groups		Kids	
	#	%	#	%	#	%
Beer	4	33%	9	75%	2	17%
Soda	0	0%	1	8%	10	83%
Wine	8	67%	2	17%	0	0%
Total	12	100%	12	100%	12	100%

Figure 5.21: Which of these two alternative splits gives you the most help in anticipating the choice of drinks?

In this case, it seems that the *Type* split on the right is a no-brainer: kids are consistently going for sodas (with the exception of 2 customers who — hopefully — got served with alcohol-free beer), groups prefer beers, while couples go mainly with wine. The other alternative (split by *Menu*) is messier: for those having salad and, to some extent, burger, there is no such clear cut drinks choice. Our preference for the option on the right is guided by human intuition: for an algorithm, we need to have a more deterministic way to make a decision. Tree learning algorithms use, in fact, metrics to decide which splits are best to pick. One of these metrics is called the **Gini index**, or **Impurity index**. Its formula is quite simple:

$$I_G = 1 - \sum_{i=1}^{M} f_i^2$$

where f_i is the relative frequency of $i\text{-}n^{th}$ class (it's in the % column in *Figure 5.21*), among the M possible classes. The algorithm will calculate the I_G for each possible branching of a split and average the results out. The option with the lowest Gini index (meaning, with the least "impure" cut) will win among the others. In our fast-food case, the overall Gini index for the option on the left will be the average of:

$$I_G(\text{ Menu is Burger}) = 1 - [0.25^2 + 0.33^2 + 0.42^2] = 0.65$$

$$I_G(\text{ Menu is Pizza }) = 1 - [0.67^2 + 0.25^2 + 0.08^2] = 0.49$$

$$I_G(\text{ Menu is Salad }) = 1 - [0.33^2 + 0.33^2 + 0.33^2] = 0.67$$

By averaging them out, we find that the Gini index for the left option is 0.60 while the one for the right option is 0.38. These metrics are confirming our intuition: the option on the right (the split by *Type*) is "purer" as demonstrated by the lower Gini index. Now you have all the elements to see how the decision tree learning algorithm works: it will iteratively calculate the average I_G for all possible splits (at least one for each available feature), pick the one with the lowest index, and repeat the same at the levels below, for all possible branches, until it is not possible to split further. In the end, the leaves are assigned by just looking at where the majority of the known examples fall. For instance, take the branching on the right in *Figure 5.21*: if this was the last level of a tree, kids will be classified with soda, couples with wine, and groups with beer. You can see in *Figure 5.22* the resulting full decision tree you would obtain by using the fast-food data we presented above:

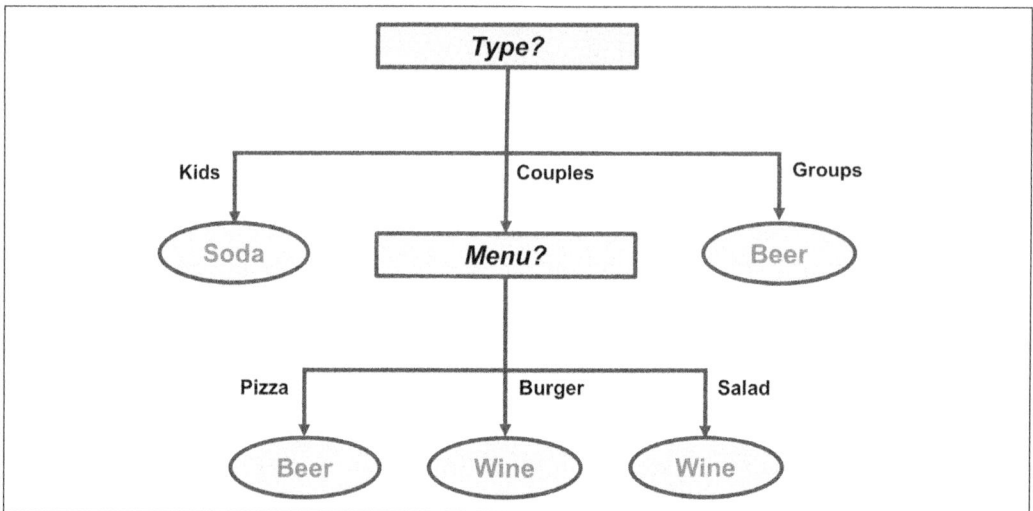

Figure 5.22: Decision tree for classifying fast-food customers according to their favorite drink. In which path would you normally be?

By looking at the obtained decision tree, you will notice that not all branches at the top level incur further splits at the level below. Take the example of the *Type*=Kids branch on the top left: the vast majority of kids (10 out of 12) go for Soda. There are not enough remaining examples to make a meaningful further split by *Menu*, so the tree just stops there. On top of this basic stopping criterion, you can implement additional (and more stringent) conditions that limit the growth of the tree by removing less meaningful branches: these are called – quite appropriately, I must say – **pruning mechanisms**. By pruning a decision tree, you end up with a less complex model: this is very handy to use when you want to avoid model overfitting. Think about this: if you have many features and examples, your tree can grow massively.

Every combination of values might, in theory, produce a very specific path. Chances are that these small branches cover an insignificant case that just happened to be in the training set but has no general value: this is a typical case of overfitting that we want to avoid as much as possible. That is why, as you will soon see in KNIME, you might need to activate some of the pruning mechanisms to avoid overfitting when growing trees.

Let's make another consideration related to numeric features in decision trees. In the fast-food example, we only had nominal features, which make every split quite simple to imagine: every underlying branch covered a possible value of the categorical column. If you have a numeric column to be considered, the algorithm will check what the Gini index would be if you split your samples using a numeric threshold. The algorithm will try multiple thresholds and pick the best split that minimizes impurity. Let's imagine that in our example we had an additional feature, called *Size*, that counts the number of people sitting at each table. The algorithm will test multiple thresholds and will check what the Gini index would be if you divided your samples according to these conditions, which are questions like "is *Size* > 3?", "is *Size* > 5?", and "is *Size* > 7?". If one of these conditions is meaningful, the split will be made according to the numeric variable: all samples having *Size* lower than the threshold will go to the left branch, and all others to the right branch. The Gini indices resulting from all the thresholds on the numeric features will be compared across all other indices coming from the categorical variables as we saw earlier: at each step, the purest split will win, irrespectively of its type. This is how decision trees can cleverly mix all types of features when classifying samples.

> Decision tree models can be extended to predict numbers and, so, become **regression trees**. In these trees, each leaf is labeled with a different value of the target variable. Normally, the value of the leaf is just the average of all the samples that ended up in such a leaf node, after going through a construction mechanism similar to the ones for classification trees (using Gini indices and all that). You can build regression trees in KNIME as well: have a look at the **simple regression tree** nodes in the repository.

Now that we know what decision trees are, let's grow one to classify our bank customers according to the outcome of the telemarketing campaign. We'll use a new node for that: the **Decision Tree Learner**.

▶ 🔲 ■ *Decision Tree Learner*

This node (**Analytics > Mining > Decision tree**) trains a decision tree model for predicting nominal variables (classification). The most important fields to be set in its configuration dialog (see *Figure 5.23*) are:

- **Class column**: you need to specify your nominal target variable to be predicted.

- **Quality measure**: this is the metric used to decide how to make the splits. The default value is the **Gini index** we have encountered above. You can also select the information for **Gain ratio**, which would tend to create more numerous and smaller branches. There is not a good and bad choice, and in most cases both measures generate very similar trees: you can try them both and see which one produces the best results.

- **Pruning method**: you can use this selector to activate a robust pruning technique called **MDL (Minimum Description Length)** that removes the less meaningful branches and generates a balanced tree.

- **Min number records per node**: you can control the tree growth-stopping criterion by setting a minimum number of samples for allowing a further split. By default, this hyperparameter is set to 2: this means that no branch will be generated with less than 2 samples. As you increase this number, you will prune more branches and obtain smaller and smaller trees: this is an effective way for tuning the complexity of the trees and obtaining an optimal, well-fitted model. By activating the MDL technique in the earlier selector, you go the "easy way" as it will automatically guess the right level of pruning.

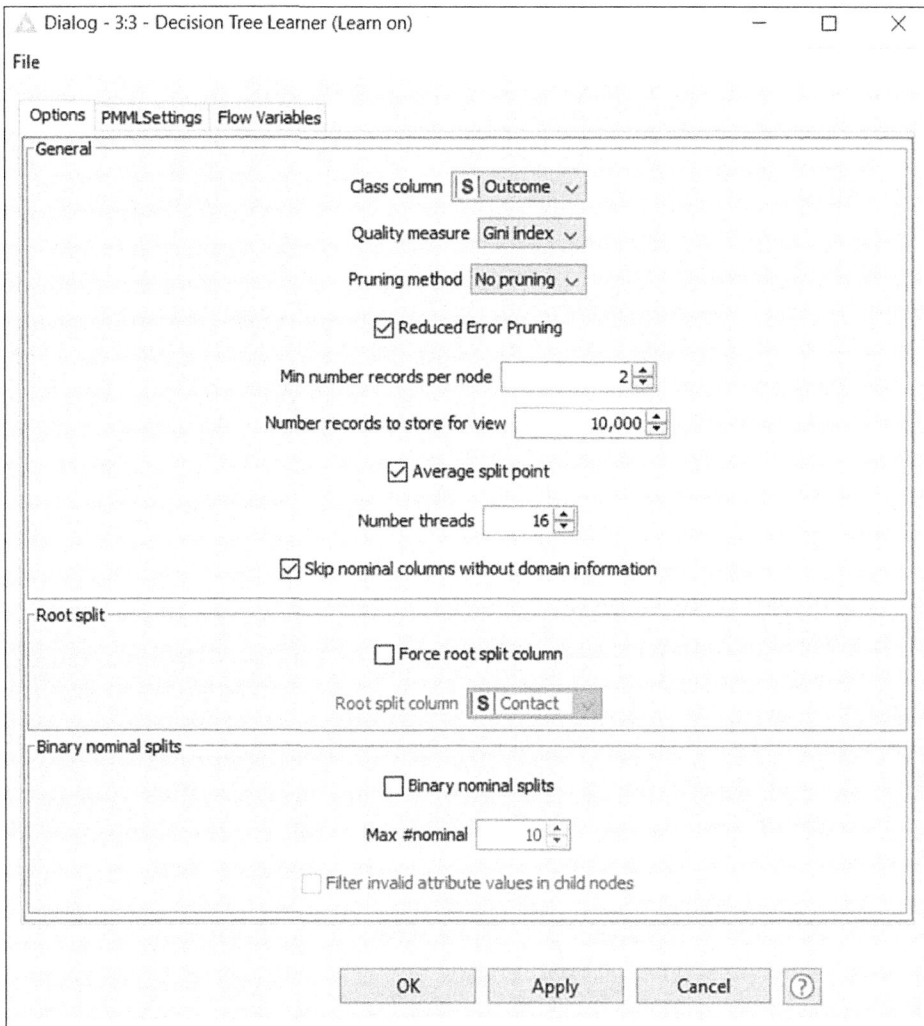

Figure 5.23: Configuration window of the Decision Tree Learner node:
are you up for some pruning today?

The output of the node is the definition of the tree model, which can be explored by opening its main view (right-click on the node and select **View: Decision Tree View**). In *Figure 5.24*, you will find the KNIME output of the fast-food classification tree we obtained earlier (see, for comparison, *Figures 5.22* and *5.21*): at each node of the tree, you find the number of training samples falling into each value of the class. You can expand and collapse the branches by clicking on the circled **+** and **–** signs appearing at each split:

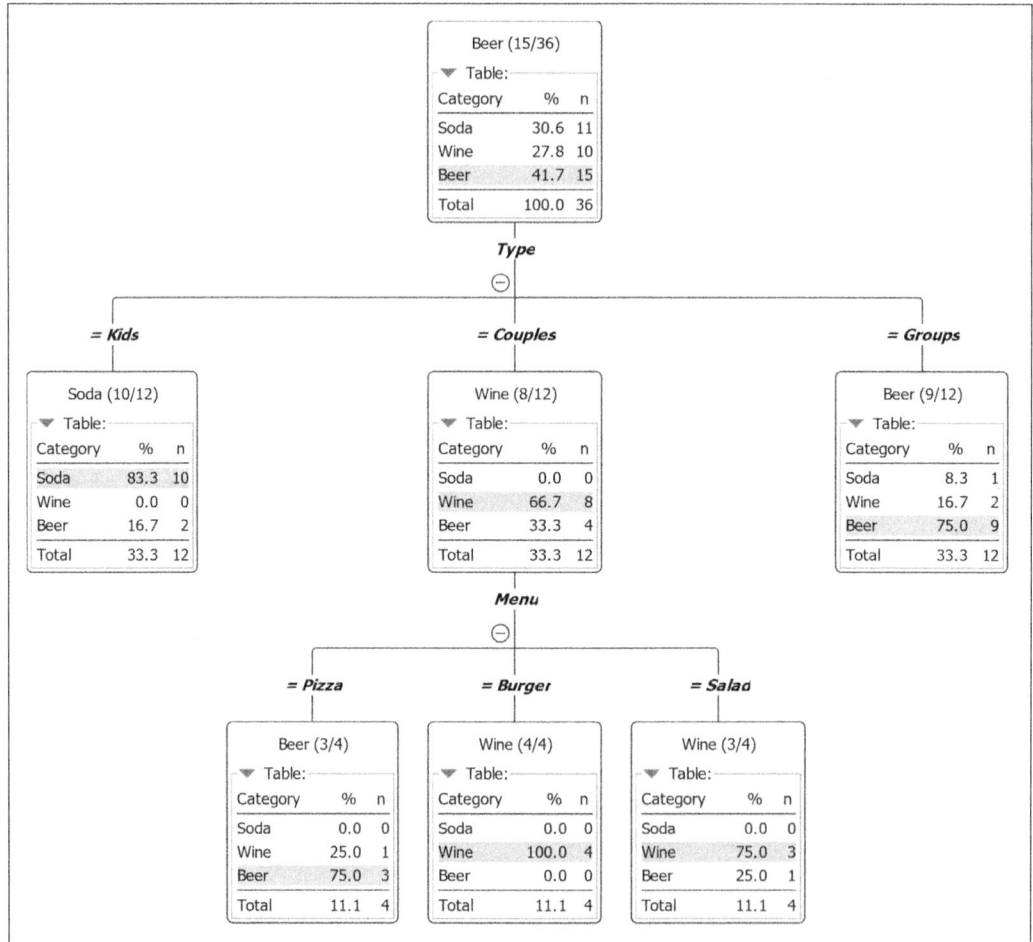

Figure 5.24: The fast-food classification tree, as outputted by the Decision Tree Learner node in KNIME. The gray rows correspond to the majority class

4. Drag and drop the **Decision Tree Learner** node from the repository and connect the upper output of the **Partitioning node** (the training set) with it. Let's leave all the default values for now in its configuration (we will have the opportunity for some pruning later): the only selector to double-check is the one setting the **Class column** that in our case is *Outcome*. If you run the node and open its decision tree view (select the node and press *F10*), you will meet the tree you have just grown:

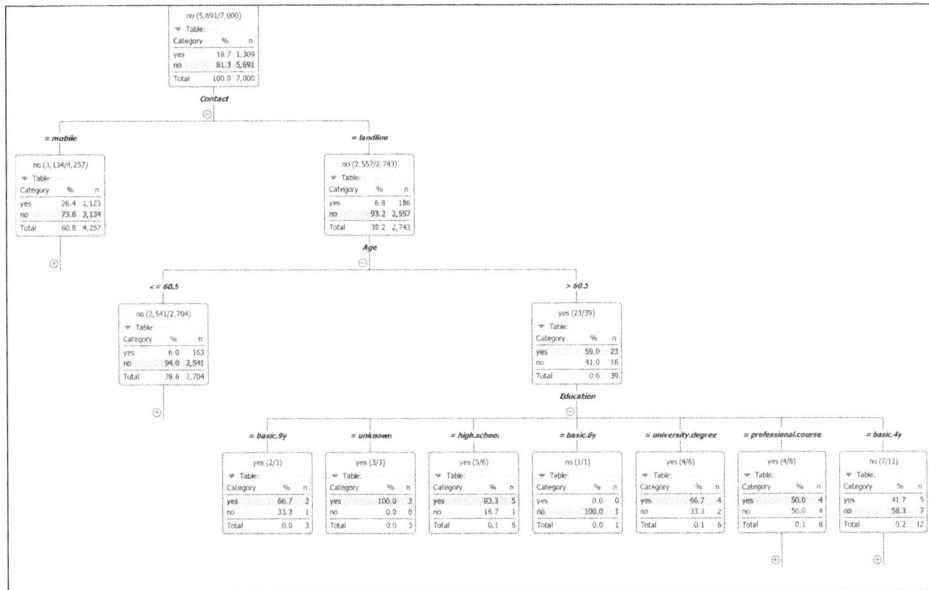

Figure 5.25: A first tree classifying bank customers by Outcome:
this is just a partial view of the many levels and branches available

As you expand some of the branches, you realize that the tree is very wide and deep: *Figure 5.25* shows an excerpt of what the tree might look like (depending on your random partitioning, you might end up with a different tree, which is fine). In this case, we noticed that the top split divided customers into mobile and landline users. This is what happened: the Gini index was calculated across all features and scored the lowest for *Contact*, making this the single most important variable to differentiate customers according to their *Outcome*. Let's see whether this tree is good enough and predict the outcomes in the test set.

Decision Tree Predictor

This (**Analytics > Mining > Decision tree**) applies a decision tree model (provided as an input in the first port) to a dataset (second port) and returns the prediction for each input row. This node will not require any configuration and will produce a similar table to the one provided in the input with an additional column that includes the result of the classification.

5. Let's implement the **Decision Tree Predictor** node and wire it in such a way it gets as inputs the tree model outputted by the **Decision Tree Learner** node and the second outport of the **Partitioning** node, which is our test set. As you execute the node, you will find an output that the precious additional column called *Prediction (Outcome)*.

At this point, we can finally assess the performance of the model by calculating the metrics used for classification. Do you remember the accuracy, precision, sensitivity measures, and confusion matrix we obtained in the cute dog versus muffin example? It's time to calculate these metrics by using the right node: **Scorer**.

Scorer

This node (**Analytics > Mining > Scoring**) calculates the summary performance scores of classification by comparing two nominal columns. The only step required for its configuration (*Figure 5.26*) is the selection of the columns to be compared: you should select the column carrying the observed (actual) values in the **First Column** dropdown, while predictions go in the **Second Column** selector. The node outputs the most important metrics for assessing a classification performance, namely: the Confusion Matrix, provided as a table in the first output (columns will refer to the predictions, while actual values will go as rows) and summary metrics such as **Accuracy**, **Precision**, and **Sensitivity**, which you can find in the second output of the node.

Some of the performance metrics for a classification will depend on which class you decide to be considered as `Positive`: have a look at *Figure 4.8* in the previous chapter to get a refresher. In the second output of the Scorer node, you will find one row for every possible class: each row contains the metrics calculated under the assumption that one specific class is labeled as `Positive` and all the other classes are `Negative`.

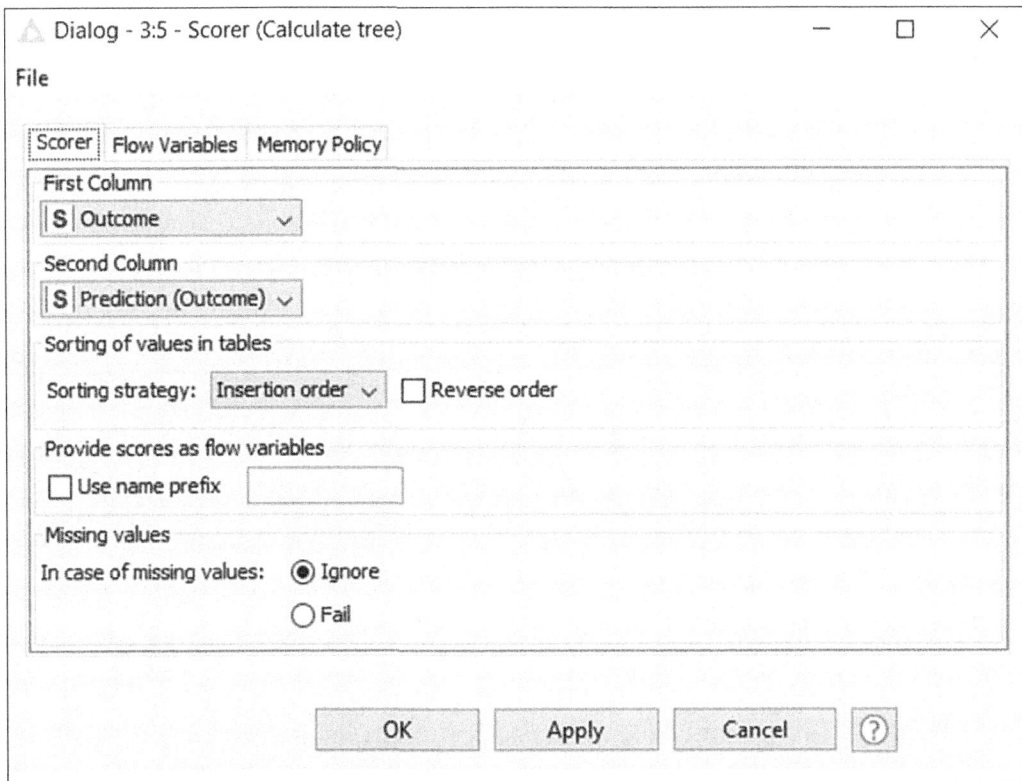

Figure 5.26: The configuration window of the Scorer node: just select the columns to compare across

6. We can now add the **Scorer** node (make sure you don't get confused and pick the **Numeric Scorer** node, which can only be used for regressions) to the workflow and connect it downstream to the **Decision Tree Predictor**. In the configuration window, we can leave everything as it is, just checking that we have *Outcome* as **First Column** and *Prediction (Outcome)* as **Second Column**. Execute the node and open its main view (*F10* or right-click and select **View: Confusion Matrix**).

The output of the **Scorer** node (*Figure 5.27*) tells us that we get an accuracy level of 78.3%: out of 100 predictions, 78 of them turn out to be correct. The confusion matrix helps us understand whether the model can bring value to our business case:

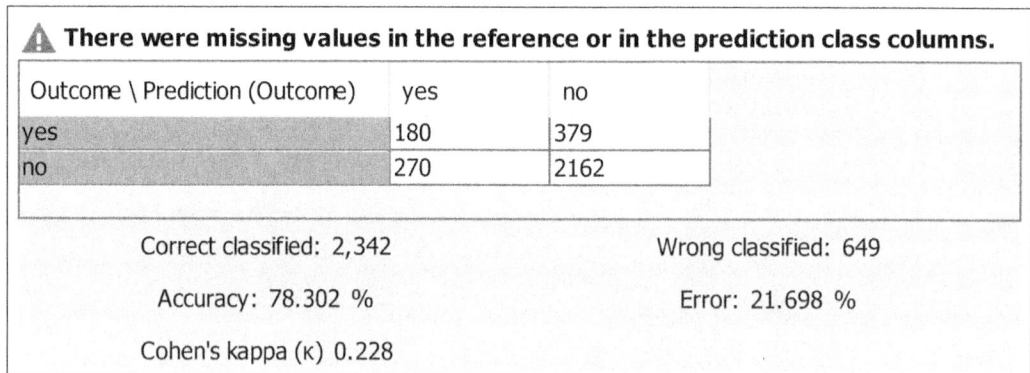

⚠ **There were missing values in the reference or in the prediction class columns.**

Outcome \ Prediction (Outcome)	yes	no
yes	180	379
no	270	2162

Correct classified: 2,342   Wrong classified: 649

Accuracy: 78.302 %   Error: 21.698 %

Cohen's kappa (κ) 0.228

Figure 5.27: The output of the node Scorer after our first classification:
78% accuracy is not bad as a starting point

In the case shown in *Figure 5.27*, we have 450 customers (180 + 270) in the test set that were predicted as interested in the account (*Prediction (Outcome)* = yes). Out of this, only 180 (40%, which corresponds to the precision of our model) were predicted correctly, meaning that these customers ended up buying the product. The number seems to be low, but it is already encouraging: the algorithm can help to find a subset of customers that are more likely to buy the product. If we indiscriminately called every customer—as we know from the pilot—we would have achieved a success rate of 19% while, by focusing on the (fewer) customers that the algorithm identified as potential (*Prediction (Outcome)* = yes), the success rate would double and reach 40%.

Let's now think about what we can do to improve the results of the modeling. We remember that our decision tree was deep and wide: some of the branches were leading to very "specific" cases, which interested only a handful of examples in the training set. This doesn't look right: a decision tree that adapted so closely to the training set might produce high errors in future cases as it is not able to comprehend the essential patterns of general validity. We might be overfitting! Let's equip ourselves with a good pair of pruning shears: we can try to fix the overfitting by reducing the complexity of the tree, making some smart cuts here and there:

> Sometimes, the Decision Tree Predictor node generates null predictions (red ? in KNIME tables, which caused the warning message you see at the top of *Figure 5.27*). This is a sign that the tree might be overfitted: its paths are too "specific" and do not encompass the set of values that require a prediction (this "pathology" is called **No True Child**). Besides taking care of the overfitting, one trick you can apply to solve the missing values is to open the **PMMLSettings** panel (second tab in the **Decision Tree Learner** configuration) and set **No true child strategy** to **returnLastPrediction**.

7. Open the configuration dialog of the **Decision Tree Learner** and select **MDL** as the **Pruning method**. This is the simplest and quickest way to prune our tree: we could have also iterated through higher values of **Min number records per node** (give it a try to check how it works), but MDL is a safe approach to get quick improvements.

8. Let's see if it worked. We don't need to change anything else, so let's just execute the **Scorer** node and open its main view to see what happened.

When you look at the results (*Figure 5.28*) you feel a thrill of excitement: things got better. The accuracy raised to 83% and, most importantly, the precision of the model greatly increased. Out of the 175 customers in the test set who are now predicted as *Outcome*=yes, 117 would have ended up actually buying the product. If we followed the recommendation of the model (which we can assume will keep a similar predictive performance on customers we didn't call yet—so the remaining 97% of our customer base), the success rate of our marketing campaign will move to 67%, which is more than 3 times better than our initial baseline of 19%!

Outcome \ Prediction (Outcome)	yes	no
yes	117	444
no	58	2381

Correct classified: 2,498   Wrong classified: 502

Accuracy: 83.267 %   Error: 16.733 %

Cohen's kappa (κ) 0.251

Figure 5.28: The output of the node Scorer after our tree pruning: the precision

The model was previously overfitting and some pruning clearly helped. If you now open the tree view of the **Decision Tree Learner** node, you will find a much simpler model that can be explored and, finally, interpreted. You can expand all branches at once by selecting the root node (just left-click on it) and then clicking on **Tree | Expand Selected Branch** from the top menu. By looking at the tree, which might be similar to the one shown in *Figure 5.29*, we can finally attempt some interpretation of the model. Look at the different percentages of the yes category within each node: we found some buckets of customers that are disproportionally interested in our product:

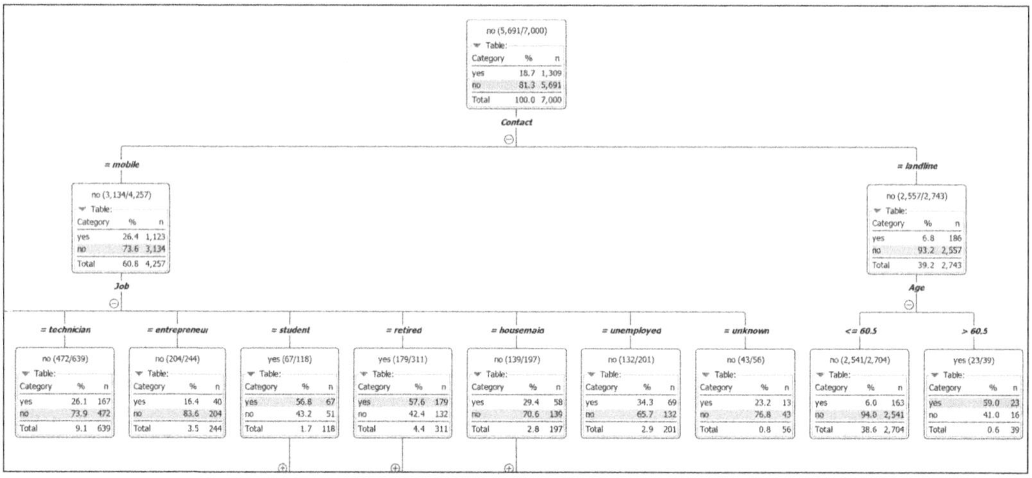

Figure 5.29: An excerpt of the decision tree classifying bank customers by Outcome: students, retired, and 60+ customers using landlines are showing the most interest in our new savings account

For example, we find out that customers falling into these three segments:

- Mobile users who are students
- Mobile users who are retired
- Landline users who are 60+ years old

responded much more to our pilot campaign than all others, having more than 50% of the samples ending up with opening a new savings account. We have a quick chat with the product manager and show these results to him. He is very excited about the findings and, after some thinking, he confirms that what the algorithm spotted makes perfect sense from a business standpoint. The new type of account has less fixed costs than the others, so this explains while its proposition proves more compelling to lower-income customers, such as students and the retired. Additionally, this account includes a free prepaid card, which is a great tool for students, who can get their balance topped up progressively, but also for older customers, who do not fully trust yet the usage of traditional credit cards and prefer keeping the risk of fraud under control. The account manager is very pleased with what you shared with him and does not stop thanking you: by having data-based evidence of the characteristics that make a customer more likely to buy his new product, he can now finetune the marketing concept, highlighting benefits and reinforcing the message to share with prospective customers.

The positive feedback you just received was invigorating and you want to quickly move to the second part of the challenge: building a propensity model able to "score" the 97% of the customers that have not been contacted yet. To do so, we will first need to introduce another classification algorithm particularly well suited for anticipating propensities: **random forest**.

Random forest algorithm

One approach used in machine learning to obtain better performance is **ensemble learning**. The idea behind it is very simple: instead of building a single model, you combine multiple *base* models together and obtain an *ensemble* model that, collectively, produces stronger results than any of the underlying models. If we apply this concept to decision trees, we will grow multiple models in parallel and obtain… a forest. However, if we run the decision tree algorithm we've seen in the previous pages to the same data set multiple times, we will just obtain "copies" of identical trees. Think about it: the procedure we described earlier (with the calculation of the Gini index and the building of subsequent branches) is completely deterministic and will always produce the same outputs when using the same inputs. To encourage "diversity" across the base models, we need to force some variance in the inputs: one way to do so is to randomly sample subsets of rows and columns of our input dataset, and offer them as different training sets to independently growing base models. Then, we will just need to aggregate the results of the several base models into a single ensemble model. This is called **Bagging**, short for **Bootstrap Aggregation**, which is the secret ingredient that we are going to use to move from decision trees to random forests.

To understand how it works, let's visualize it in a practical example: *Figure 5.30* shows both a simple decision tree and a random forest (made of four trees) built on our bank telemarketing example:

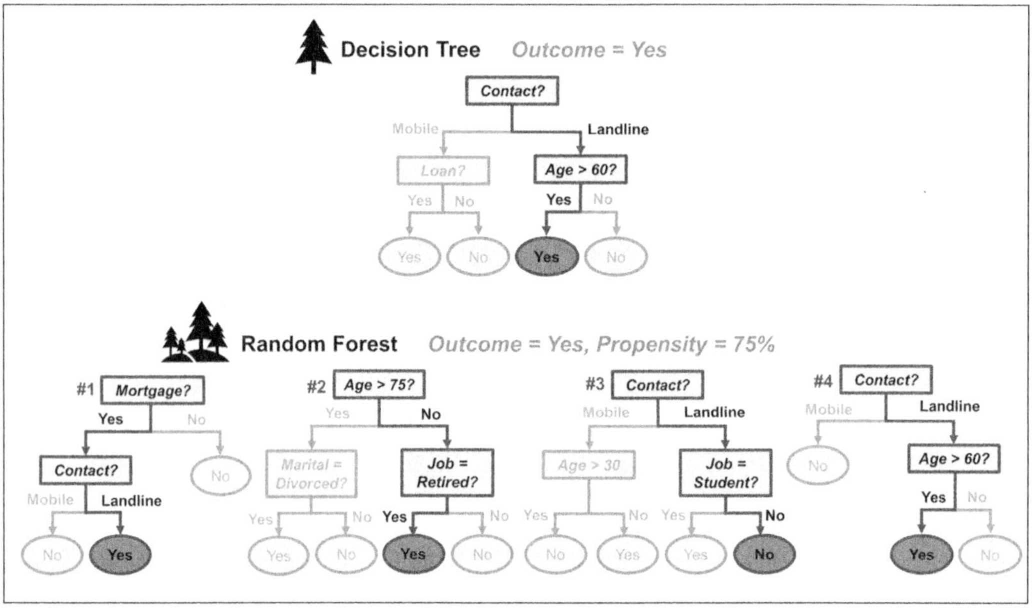

Figure 5.30: A decision tree and random forest compared: with the forest you get a propensity score and higher accuracy

Thanks to a random sampling of rows and columns, we managed to grow four different trees, starting from the same initial dataset. Look at the tree on the bottom left (marked as #1 in the figure): it only had the *Mortgage* and the *Contact* columns available to learn from, as they were the ones randomly sampled in its case. Given the subset of rows that were offered to it (that were also randomly drawn as part of the bootstrap process), the model applies the decision tree algorithm and produces a tree that differs from all other base models (you can check the four trees at the bottom — they are all different). Given the four trees that make our forest, let's imagine that we want to predict the outcome for a 63-year-old retired customer, who has a mortgage and gets contacted by landline. The *same* customer will follow four *different* paths (one for each tree), which will lead to different outcomes. In this case, 3 trees out of 4 agree that the prediction should be yes. The resulting ensemble prediction will be made in a very democratic manner, by voting. Since the majority believes that this customer is a yes, the final outcome will be yes with a **Propensity score** of 0.75 (3 divided by 4).

The assumption we make is that the more trees that are in agreement with a customer being classified as yes, the "closer" the customer is to buying our product. Of course, we normally build many more trees than just four: the diversity of the different branching each tree displays will make our ensemble model more "sensitive" to the smaller nuances of feature combinations that can tell us something useful about the propensity of a customer. Every tree offers a slightly "different" point of view on how to classify a customer: by bringing all these contributions together — in a sort of decisions crowdsourcing — we obtain more robust collective predictions: this is yet another proof of the universal value of diversity in life!

> Although the propensity score is related to the probability that a classification is correct, they are not the same thing. We are still in the uncertain world of probabilistic models: even if 100% of the trees agree on a specific classification, you cannot be 100% sure that the classification is right.

Let's get acquainted with the KNIME node that can grow forests: meet the **Random Forest Learner** node.

Random Forest Learner

This node (**Analytics > Mining > Decision Tree Ensemble > Random Forest > Classification**) trains a random forest model for classification. At the top of its configuration window (*Figure 5.31*) you can select the nominal column to use as the target of the classification (**Target Column**). Then, in the column selector in the middle, you can choose which columns to use as features (the ones appearing on the **Include** box on the right): all others will be ignored by the learning algorithm. The option **Save target distribution...** will record the number of samples that fell into each leaf of the underlying tree models: although it is memory expensive, it can help to generate more accurate propensity scores, by means of the **soft voting** technique, which we will talk about later.

Toward the bottom of the window, you will find also a box that lets you choose how many trees you want to grow (**Number of models**). Lastly, you can decide to check a tick box (labeled as **Use static random seed**) that, similarly to what you found in the **Partitioning** node, lets you "fix" the initialization seed of the pseudo-random number generator used for the random sampling of rows and columns: in this case, you will obtain, at parity of input and configuration parameters, always the same forest generated:

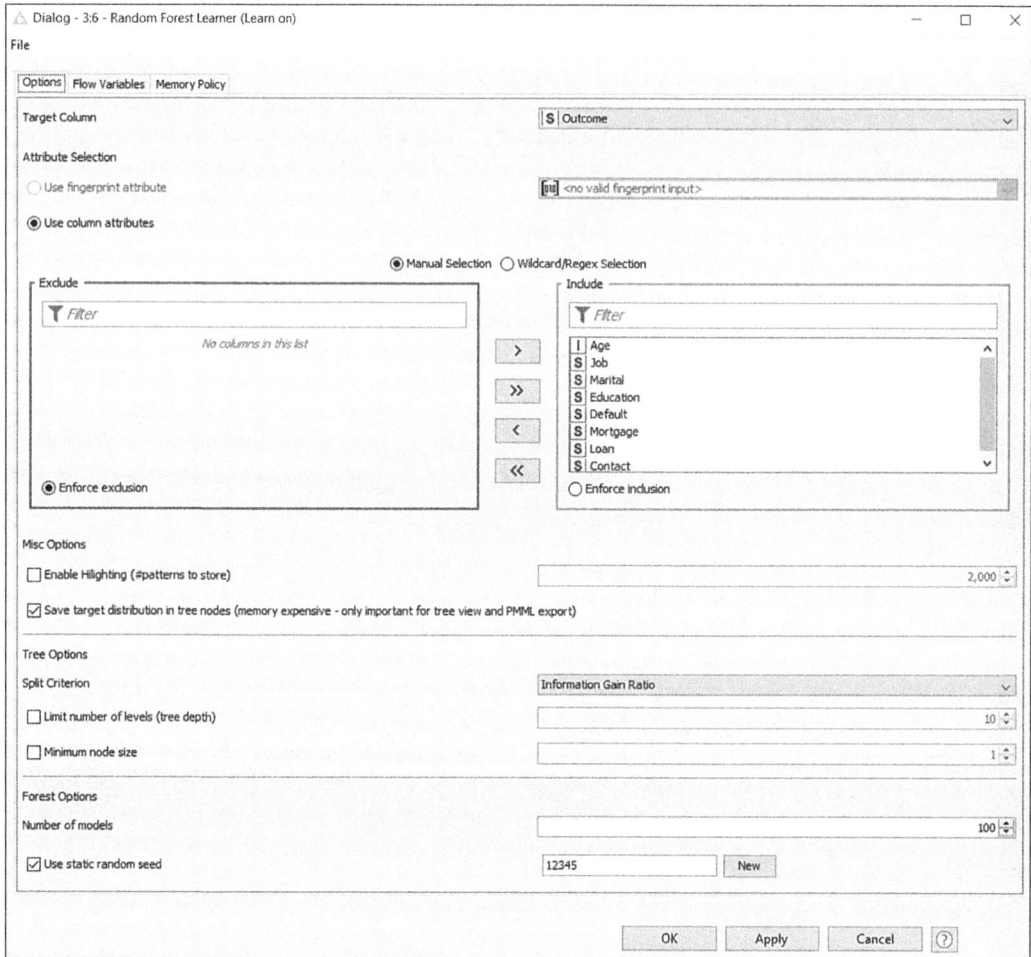

Figure 5.31: Configuration window of the Random Forest Learner node:
how many trees you want to see in the forest?

9. Let's implement the **Random Forest Learner** node and connect the training set (the first output port of the **Partitioning** node) with its input: there is no harm in reusing the same training and test sets used for the decision tree learner. If we execute the node and open its main view (*F10* or right-click and then select **View: Tree Views**), we will find a tree-like output, as in the case of the decision trees: however, this time, we have a little selector at the top that lets us scroll across all 100 trees of the forest.

> Random forests are **black box** models as they are hard to interpret: going through 100 different trees would not offer us a hint for explaining how the predictions are made. However, there is a simple way to check which features proved to be most meaningful. Open the second outport of the **Random Forest Learner** node (right-click and click on **Attribute statistics**). The first column — called *#splits (level 0)* — tells you how many times that feature was selected as the top split of a tree. The higher that number, the more useful that feature has been in the learning process of the model.

Random Forest Predictor

This node (**Analytics > Mining > Decision Tree Ensemble > Random Forest > Classification**) applies a random forest model (which needs to be provided in the first gray input port) to a dataset (second port) and returns the ensemble prediction for each input row. As part of its configuration, you can decide whether you want to output the propensity scores for each individual class (**Append individual class probabilities**). If you tick the **Use soft voting** box, you enable a more accurate estimation of propensity: in this case, the vote of each tree will be weighted by a factor that depends on how many samples fell in each leaf during the learning process. The more samples a leaf has "seen," the more confident we can be about its estimation. To use this feature, you will have to select the option **Save target distribution...** in the **Random Forest Learning** node, which is upstream.

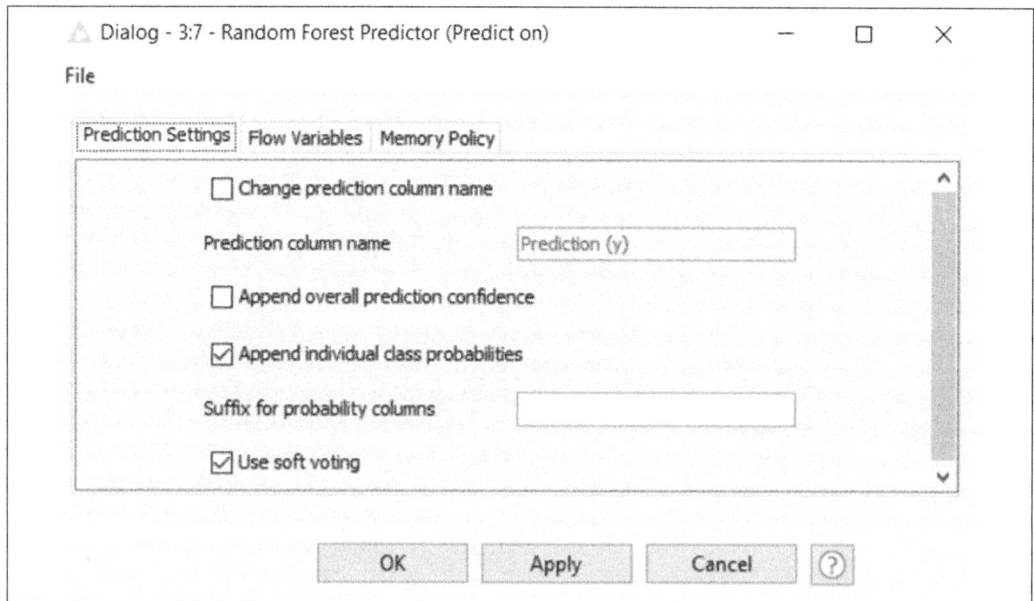

Figure 5.32: The configuration dialog of Random Forest Learner node.
You can decide whether you want to see propensity scores or not.

10. Drag and drop the **Random Forest Predictor** node onto the workflow and connect its inputs with the forest model, outputted by the **Random Forest Learner** and the training set, meaning the bottom outport of the **Partitioning** node. Configure the node by unticking the **Append overall prediction confidence** box, and ticking both the **Append individual class probabilities** (we need the propensity score) and the **Use soft voting** boxes. After you execute it, you will find at its output the test set enriched with the prediction, *Prediction (Outcome)*, and the propensity scores by class. Specifically, the propensity of a customer being interested in our product is *P (Outcome=Yes)*.

11. Implement a new **Scorer** node (for simplicity, you can copy/paste the one you used for the decision tree) and connect it downstream to the **Random Forest Predictor**. For its configuration, just make sure you select *Outcome* and *Prediction (Outcome)* in the first two drop-down menus. Execute it and open its main output view (*F10*).

The results of **Scorer** (*Figure 5.33*) confirm that, at least in this case, the ensemble model comes with better performance metrics. Accuracy has increased by a few decimal points and, most importantly (as it directly affects the ROI of our marketing campaigns), precision has reached 72% (open the **Accuracy statistics** outport to check it or compute it easily from the confusion matrix):

Outcome \ Prediction (Outcome)	yes	no
yes	119	442
no	46	2393

Correct classified: 2,512   Wrong classified: 488

Accuracy: 83.733 %   Error: 16.267 %

Cohen's kappa (κ) 0.265

Figure 5.33: The Scorer node output for our random forest.
Both accuracy and precision increased versus the decision tree: diversity helps

Now that we have confirmation that we have built a robust model at hand, let's concentrate on the propensity score we calculated and see what we can do with it.

Open the output of the **Random Forest Predictor** node and sort the rows by decreasing level of propensity (click on the header of column *P (Outcome=yes)* and then on **Sort Descending**): you will obtain a view similar to the one shown in *Figure 5.34*:

Row ID	Age	Job	Marital	Education	Default	Mortgage	Loan	Contact	Outcome	P (Outcome=yes)	P (Outcome=no)	Prediction (Outcome)
Row4431	74	retired	divorced	unknown	no	yes	no	mobile	yes	0.909	0.091	yes
Row930	78	retired	divorced	basic.4y	no	no	no	mobile	yes	0.861	0.139	yes
Row1971	62	retired	divorced	basic.4y	no	no	no	mobile	yes	0.861	0.139	yes
Row9378	64	admin.	married	basic.4y	unknown	no	no	mobile	yes	0.849	0.151	yes
Row4020	79	housemaid	divorced	basic.4y	no	unknown	unknown	mobile	yes	0.845	0.155	yes
Row4258	48	retired	divorced	professional...	no	yes	no	mobile	yes	0.833	0.167	yes
Row4372	45	retired	divorced	professional...	no	yes	no	mobile	yes	0.833	0.167	yes
Row701	45	retired	divorced	basic.4y	no	yes	no	mobile	yes	0.814	0.186	yes
Row4781	41	retired	married	professional...	no	no	no	mobile	yes	0.812	0.188	yes
Row6928	42	retired	married	professional...	no	no	no	mobile	yes	0.812	0.188	yes
Row6378	71	housemaid	married	unknown	no	yes	no	mobile	no	0.811	0.189	yes
Row7636	62	housemaid	married	basic.4y	no	no	no	mobile	yes	0.809	0.191	yes
Row9183	65	housemaid	married	basic.4y	no	no	no	mobile	no	0.807	0.193	yes
Row9007	80	retired	married	illiterate	unknown	yes	yes	mobile	yes	0.803	0.197	yes
Row9190	64	management	married	basic.4y	unknown	yes	no	mobile	yes	0.798	0.202	yes
Row558	64	retired	married	basic.4y	no	unknown	unknown	landline	no	0.787	0.213	yes
Row9807	66	housemaid	married	basic.4y	no	yes	no	mobile	yes	0.786	0.214	yes
Row3038	64	retired	married	unknown	no	yes	no	mobile	yes	0.784	0.216	yes
Row2115	63	admin.	married	university.d...	no	yes	yes	landline	yes	0.783	0.217	yes
Row9781	71	retired	divorced	basic.4y	no	no	yes	mobile	no	0.782	0.218	yes
Row9557	64	admin.	divorced	high.school	no	no	no	mobile	yes	0.782	0.218	yes
Row5100	44	retired	married	university.d...	no	no	no	mobile	yes	0.781	0.219	yes

Figure 5.34: The predictions generated by the random forest in descending order of propensity, P (Outcome=yes): the more we go down the list, the less interested customers (column Outcome) we find

At the top of the list, we have the customers in the test set that most decision trees identified as interested. In fact, if you look at the column *Outcome*, we find that most rows show a yes, proving that, indeed, these customers were very interested in the product (when called, they agreed to open the savings account). If you scroll down the list, the propensity will go down and you will start finding increasingly more no values in column *Outcome*. Now, let's think about the business case once again: now that we have a model able to predict the level of propensity, we could run it on the other 97% of customers that were not contacted as part of the pilot. If we then sorted our customer list by decreasing level of propensity (as we just did on the test set), we will obtain a prioritized list of the next people to call about our product. We will expect that the first calls (the ones directed to the most inclined people) will end up with a very high success rate (like we noticed in the test set).

Then, little by little, the success rate will decay: more and more people will start saying *no* and, at some point, it will start to become counterproductive to make a call. So, the key question becomes: at what point should we "stop" to get the maximum possible ROI from the initiative? How many calls should we make? What is the minimum level of propensity, below which we should avoid attempting to make a sale? The exciting part of propensity modeling is that you can find an answer to these questions before making *any* call!

In fact, if we assume that the customers that were part of the pilot were a fair sample of the total population, then we can use our test set (which has not been "seen" by the training algorithm, so there is no risk of overfitting) as a base for simulating the ROI of a marketing campaign where we call customers by following a decreasing level of propensity. This is exactly what we are going to do right now: we will need to first sort the test set by decreasing level of propensity (the temporary sorting we did earlier did not impact the permanent order of the rows in the underlying table); then, we calculate the cumulative profit we would make by "going through the list," using the cost and revenue estimates shared by the product manager. We check at which level of propensity we maximized our profit, so that we have a good estimate of the number of calls that we will need to make in total to optimize the ROI. Let's get cracking!

12. Implement a **Sorter** node and connect it at the output of the **Random Forest Predictor** node. We want to sort the customers in the test set by decreasing level of propensity, so select column *P (Outcome=yes)* and go for the **Descending** option.

13. Implement a **Rule Engine** node to calculate the marginal profit we make on each individual customer. We know that every call we make costs us $15, irrespective of its outcome. We also know that every account opening brings an incremental revenue of $60. Hence, every customer that ends up buying the product (*Outcome*=Yes) brings $45 of profit while all others hit us by $–15. Let's create a column (we can call it *Profit*) that implements this simple logic, as shown in *Figure 5.35*:

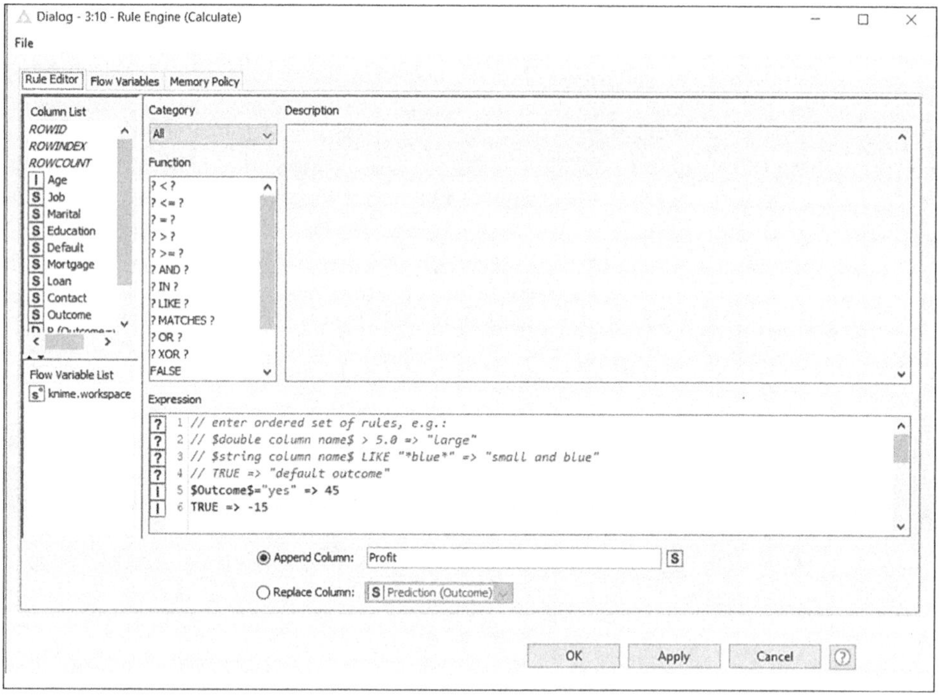

Figure 5.35: The Rule Engine node for calculating the marginal profit for each individual customer

To calculate the cumulative profit we will need to use a new node, called **Moving Aggregation**.

Moving Aggregation

As the name suggests, this node (**Other Data Types > Time Series > Smoothing**) aggregates values on moving windows and calculates cumulative summarizations. To use a moving window, you will have to declare the **Window length** in terms of the number of rows to be considered and the **Window type** (meaning the direction of movement of the window in the table). For example, if you select **3** as the length and **Backward** as the type, the previous 3 rows will be aggregated together. If you want to aggregate by cumulating values from the first row to the last, you need to check the **Cumulative computation** box. Similarly to a Group By node, the **Aggregation settings** tab will let you select which columns should be aggregated and using which method:

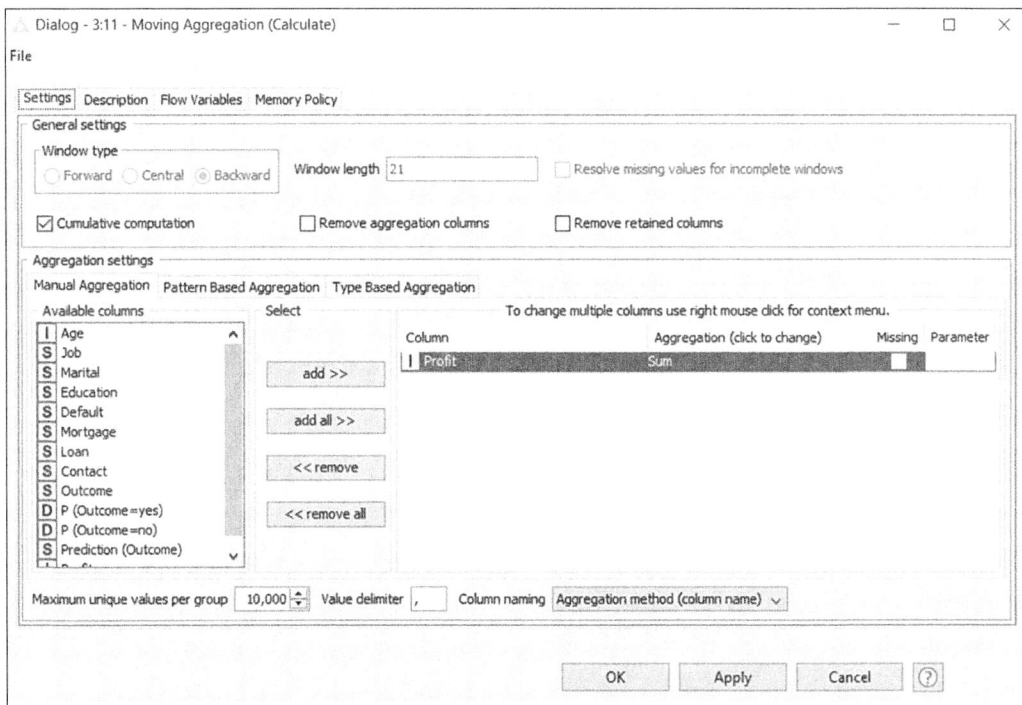

Figure 5.36: Configuration dialog of the Moving Aggregation node: you can aggregate through moving windows or by progressively cumulating

14. Implement the **Moving Aggregation** node and connect it downstream from the **Rule Engine**. Check the **Cumulative Computation** box, double-click on the *Profit* column on the left, and select **Sum** as the aggregation method. Execute the node and open its outport view.

The **Moving Aggregation** node has cumulated the marginal profit generated by each customer. If we scroll the list (similar to the one displayed in *Figure 5.37*) and keep an eye on the last column, *Sum(Profit)*, we noticed that the profit peaks when we are slightly below the first third of the full list. When the *P (Outcome=yes)* propensity is near 0.23, we obtain a profit of around $8,200. This means that by calling only people above this level of propensity (called the **Cutoff** point), we maximize the ROI of our campaign.

Row ID	Age	Job	Marital	Education	Default	Mortgage	Loan	Contact	Outcome	P (Outcome=yes)	P (Outc...	Predicti...	Profit	Sum(Profit)
Row424	46	admin.	single	high.school	no	no	no	mobile	yes	0.231	0.769	no	45	8145
Row55	33	self-employed	single	high.school	no	yes	yes	mobile	no	0.231	0.769	no	-15	8130
Row8763	58	technician	married	professional...	no	yes	no	mobile	no	0.231	0.769	no	-15	8115
Row7139	58	retired	married	university.d...	unknown	no	no	mobile	yes	0.231	0.769	no	45	8160
Row7408	36	admin.	divorced	university.d...	no	yes	yes	mobile	yes	0.231	0.769	no	45	8205
Row2661	28	blue-collar	single	basic.9y	no	yes	no	mobile	no	0.231	0.769	no	-15	8190
Row4242	51	blue-collar	divorced	basic.9y	no	no	no	mobile	no	0.23	0.77	no	-15	8175
Row6490	55	entrepreneur	married	professional...	no	yes	no	mobile	no	0.23	0.77	no	-15	8160
Row8840	29	admin.	married	high.school	no	unknown	unknown	mobile	no	0.23	0.77	no	-15	8145
Row5326	29	entrepreneur	married	university.d...	no	yes	no	mobile	no	0.23	0.77	no	-15	8130
Row8148	39	self-employed	single	university.d...	no	no	no	landline	no	0.229	0.771	no	-15	8115
Row6240	34	technician	married	basic.9y	no	yes	no	mobile	no	0.229	0.771	no	-15	8100
Row8717	39	admin.	divorced	high.school	no	no	no	mobile	no	0.229	0.771	no	-15	8085
Row7337	44	admin.	single	professional...	no	no	no	mobile	no	0.229	0.771	no	-15	8070
Row9829	52	technician	married	basic.9y	no	yes	no	mobile	no	0.229	0.771	no	-15	8055
Row934	41	management	married	university.d...	unknown	yes	no	mobile	no	0.229	0.771	no	-15	8040
Row1962	50	self-employed	single	basic.9y	no	no	no	mobile	no	0.229	0.771	no	-15	8025
Row1925	55	technician	divorced	professional...	no	yes	no	mobile	yes	0.229	0.771	no	45	8070
Row8340	38	services	single	basic.9y	no	no	no	mobile	no	0.229	0.771	no	-15	8055
Row3493	27	admin.	divorced	high.school	no	yes	no	mobile	no	0.228	0.772	no	-15	8040
Row3292	34	blue-collar	single	basic.9y	no	yes	no	mobile	no	0.228	0.772	no	-15	8025

Figure 5.37: The output of the Moving Aggregation node: it seems that we reach maximum profit when we call people having a propensity of around 0.23.

To make this concept clearer, let's visualize the changing profit by employing a line chart.

Line Plot (local)

This node (**View > Local (Swing)**) generates a line plot. The only configuration that might be needed is the box labeled **No. of rows to display**, which you can use to extend the limit of rows considered for creating the plot.

15. Implement a **Line Plot (local)** node, extend the number of rows to display to at least 3,000 (the size of the test set), execute it, and open its view at once (*Shift + F10*). In the **Column Selection** tab, keep only *Sum(Profit)* on the right and remove all other columns.

The output of the chart (shown in *Figure 5.38*) confirms what we noticed in the table and makes it more evident: if we use the propensity score to decide the calling order of customers, our profit will follow the shape of the curve in the figure. We will start with a steep increase of profit (see the first segment on the left), as most of the first people we call (which are top prospects, given their high propensity score) will actually buy the product. Then, at around one-third of the list (when we know that the propensity score is near 0.23), we reach the maximum possible profit. After that, it will drop fast as we will encounter fewer and fewer interested customers. If we called all the people on the list, we will end up with a significant loss, as we have painfully learned as part of the pilot campaign:

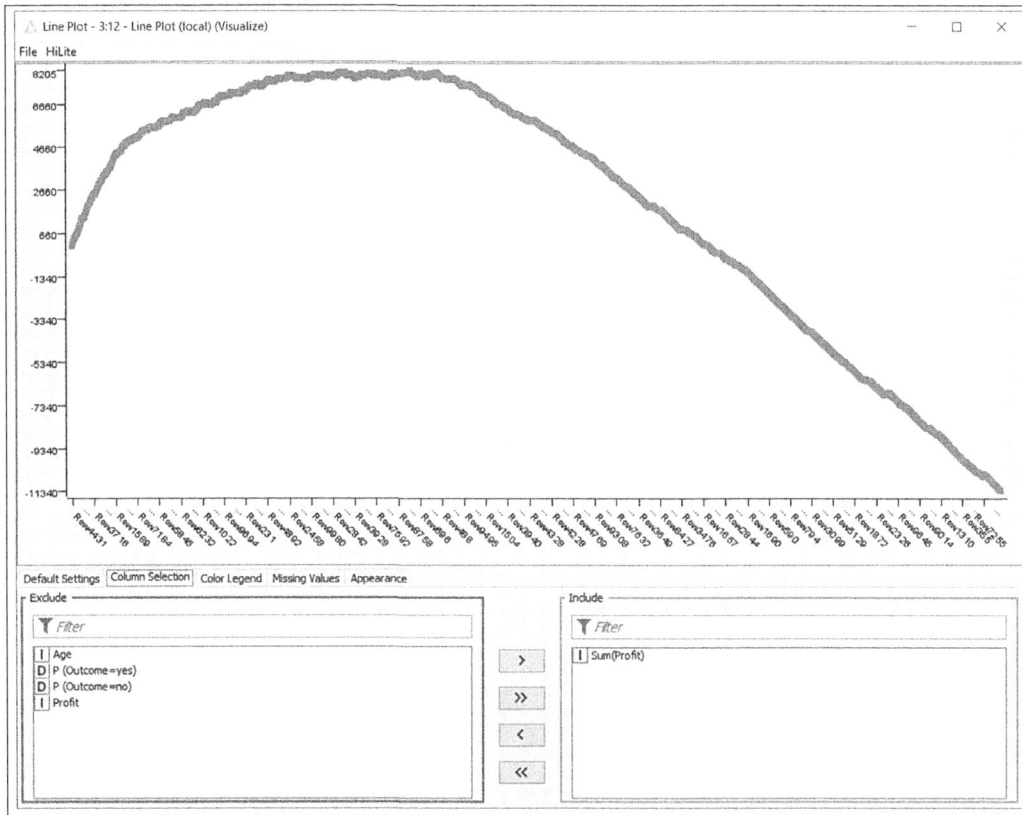

Figure 5.38: The cumulative profit curve for our machine learning-assisted telemarketing campaign: we maximize the ROI at around one-third of the list sorted by propensity

Thanks to this simulation, we have discovered that if we limit our campaign to customers with a propensity score higher than 0.23 (which will be around one-third of the total population), we will maximize our profit. By doing the required proportions (our simulation covered *only* the test set, so 3,000 customers in total), we can estimate how much profit we would make if we applied our propensity model to the *entire* bank database. In this case, we would use the scores to decide who to call within the remaining 97% of the customer base. The overall "size of the prize" of conducting a mass telemarketing campaign will bring around $800,000 of profit, if we were to call one-third of the bank's customers. Considering that it might not be viable to make so many calls, we might stop earlier in the list: in any case, we will make some considerable profit by following the list that our random forest can now generate. The simulation that we just did can be used as a tool for planning the marketing spend and sizing the right level of investment. The product manager and your boss are pleased with the great work you pulled together. You definitely proved that spotting (and following) the ML way can bring sizeable value to the business: in this case, you completely reversed the potential outcome of a marketing campaign. The heavy losses in the pilot can now be transformed into a meaningful value, thanks to data, algorithms, and — most importantly — your expertise in leveraging them. It was a terrific result, and it took only 12 KNIME nodes (*Figure 5.39*) to put all of this together!

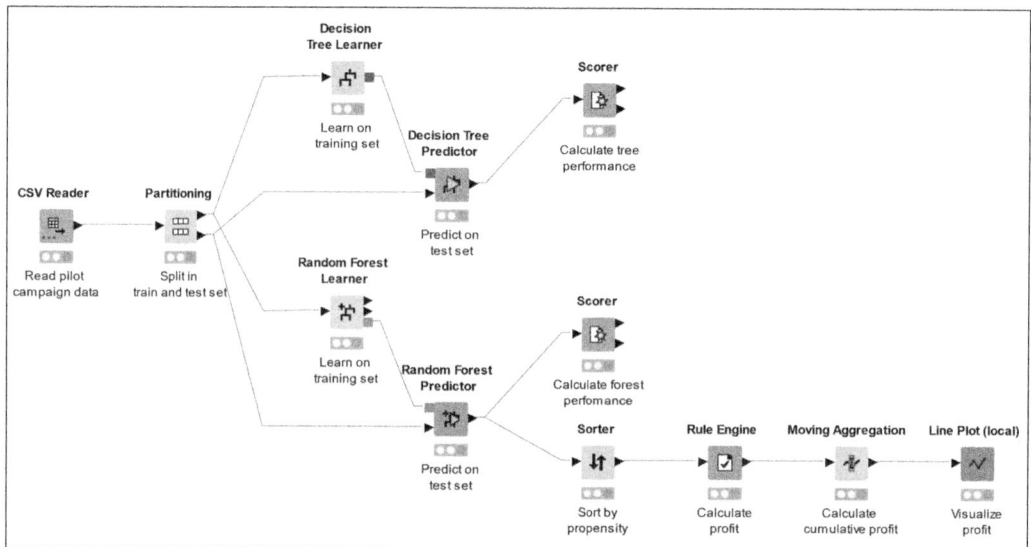

Figure 5.39: Full workflow for the bank telemarketing optimization

Segmenting consumers with clustering

In this tutorial, you will re-enter the shoes of the business analyst working for the online retailer we encountered in *Chapter 3, Transforming Data*. This time, instead of automating the creation of a set of financial reports, you are after a seemingly sexier objective. The **Customer Relationship Management (CRM)** team is looking for a smarter way to communicate with those customers who opted-in to receive regular newsletters. Instead of sending a weekly email equal for all, the CRM manager asked you to find a data-based approach for creating a few meaningful consumer segments. Once segments are defined, the CRM team can build multiple messages, one for each segment. By doing so, they will offer a more personalized (and engaging) experience for the entire customer base, which will ultimately affect customer loyalty and drive sustainable revenue growth.

Unsupervised learning offers a proven methodology that can meet this business need: by using a clustering algorithm, we can create several groups of customers that *look similar* in terms of their characteristics (such as age, family composition, and income level) and the consumption patterns they displayed through previous purchases (like the average price of the products they selected, the overall amount of money they spent, or the frequency of their orders). This is the ML way of helping the business: use clustering to segment consumers appropriately.

The CRM manager has already initiated the gathering of some basic consumer-level data and obtained a CSV file (eCommerce-CRM.csv), which has 4,157 rows — one for each customer — and four columns:

- *Customer_ID*: a unique identifier of the customer.

- *Average Price*: the average unit price for all purchases made by each customer. It gives us a directional view of the "premiumness" of the former shopping choices displayed by the customer.

- *Basket Size*: the average number of units purchased within any single order created by the customers. This measure indicates whether they prefer to go for "bulk" shopping with fat baskets or smaller, occasion-driven purchase acts.

- *Unique Products*: the average number of different articles that the customer buys on each occasion. This metric indicates the breadth of the assortment "tried" by each customer. It gives us an idea of the customer's willingness to explore new products versus their preference of "keep buying" the same articles all the time.

As we exchange thoughts with the CRM manager about this dataset, she confirms what we had already noticed: the three consumption metrics included in the data (the last three columns) are far from giving us a comprehensive picture of each customer's preferences. If we wanted, we could have generated many more columns by aggregating the transactions history: think about the absolute number of purchases by customer, the total generated value, the "mix" of purchased categories and subcategories, the premiumness of the purchased products within each category and subcategory, and also the customer characteristics, like their age, the average income of the neighborhood they live in, and so on. Still, we decide to go ahead and leverage the power of machine learning on this first dataset: we can always increase the level of the model sophistication later if we want. Now, the important thing is to "start rocking" and pragmatically prove some first business value from this new way of operating. In terms of deliverables, you align with your business partner the need to assign each customer to a small number of clusters and put together some visualizations to interpret what differentiates clusters.

It's time to power KNIME on, create a new workflow, and load our CRM extract into it:

1. Load the file eCommerce-CRM.csv onto the workflow editor. As the **CSV Reader** node dialog pops up, we can check that all four columns are showing in the preview and click **OK** to confirm the default setting. After executing the node, we can look at its output view (*Figure 5.40*) and move to the next step:

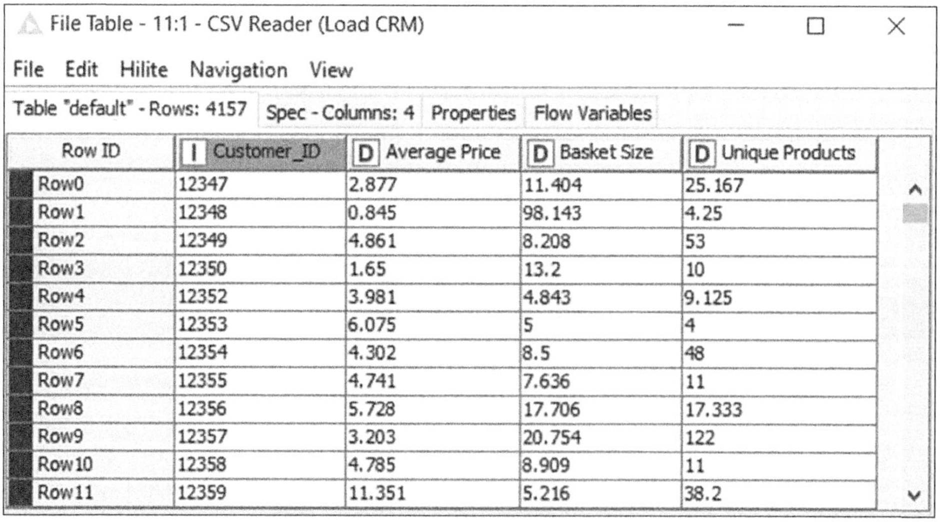

Row ID	I Customer_ID	D Average Price	D Basket Size	D Unique Products
Row0	12347	2.877	11.404	25.167
Row1	12348	0.845	98.143	4.25
Row2	12349	4.861	8.208	53
Row3	12350	1.65	13.2	10
Row4	12352	3.981	4.843	9.125
Row5	12353	6.075	5	4
Row6	12354	4.302	8.5	48
Row7	12355	4.741	7.636	11
Row8	12356	5.728	17.706	17.333
Row9	12357	3.203	20.754	122
Row10	12358	4.785	8.909	11
Row11	12359	11.351	5.216	38.2

File Table - 11:1 - CSV Reader (Load CRM)

File   Edit   Hilite   Navigation   View

Table "default" - Rows: 4157   Spec - Columns: 4   Properties   Flow Variables

Figure 5.40: The CRM extract once loaded:
for every customer, we have three metrics, each one giving us a hint of their shopping habits

Creating homogenous groups of elements, such as customers in our case, requires the use of a clustering algorithm. Let's make acquaintance with possibly the most popular clustering algorithm available today – **k-means**.

K-means algorithm

The k-means algorithm is perhaps the easiest (and yet probably the most used) approach used for clustering. The big idea is elementary and can be summarized in two lines: each element in a dataset is assigned to the closest cluster. At each step of the process, the position of the clusters gets updated, so they become more and more compact.

Let's imagine we want to cluster a set of points displayed on a bi-dimensional scatter plot. Each point is described employing two numbers that represent the horizontal and the vertical coordinates, respectively. The distance between any two points can be easily calculated through the Pythagorean theorem (yes, the same used for calculating the sides of a right triangle — see *Figure 5.41* for a refresher):

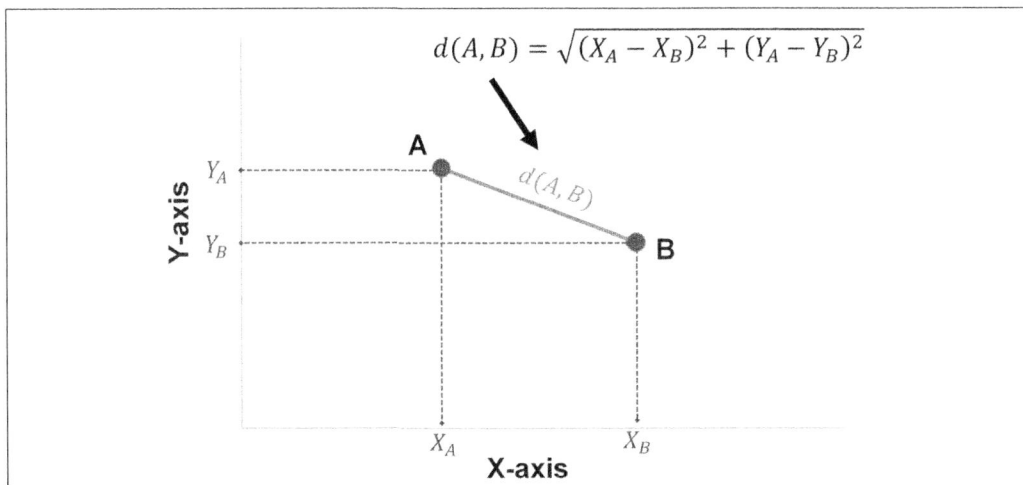

$$d(A, B) = \sqrt{(X_A - X_B)^2 + (Y_A - Y_B)^2}$$

Figure 5.41: Calculating the distance between two points using the Pythagorean theorem: you make the square root of the sum of the squared differences for each coordinate

The goal of the k-means algorithm is to create a given number (k) of homogenous groups formed by points that are relatively close to one another. Like many other machine learning algorithms, k-means has an iterative approach: at each iteration, it groups the points based on their proximity to some special points called the **centroids** of each cluster. Every point is associated with its closest centroid. The algorithm then updates the position of the centroids iteratively: at each iteration, the groups will tend to be more and more homogenous, meaning that the points forming these clusters will be gradually closer and closer to each other.

Let's see in detail the sequence of steps that make the k-means algorithm:

    a.   **Initialization**: the first step of the algorithm is making the initial choice of the centroids, one per cluster. There are different ways to make this choice. The simplest way is to randomly select k points in our dataset.

    b.   **Grouping**: the algorithm now calculates the distance of each point from each centroid (using the Pythagorean theorem), and each point is matched with its closest centroid (the one lying at the smallest distance). In this way, all the points near a centroid are grouped together as they belong to the same cluster.

    c.   **Update**: the algorithm now calculates the centroid of each cluster again by making an average of the coordinates of all the points that belong to the cluster. Basically, the centroid is updated so that it matches the center of mass of the newly formed group.

At this point of the process, we return to step b to start a new iteration and repeat steps b and c as long as it is possible to improve the centroids. At every iteration, the clusters will converge, meaning that they will become increasingly more meaningful. We will stop when the update step produces no change in the way in which points are assigned to clusters. When this happens, the algorithm terminates: a stable solution has been found, and the current definition of clusters is returned as the resulting output. Should this convergence not take place, the algorithm will stop in any case once a preset number of maximum iterations is reached.

This process might still look complicated but let me stress how simple the underlying mathematics is: random draws, averages, squares, and the square roots in the Pythagorean theorem are all the math we need to implement the k-means algorithm.

To better understand how the algorithm works, let's go through a concrete example and use some charts to display the evolution of the various iterations graphically. For the sake of simplicity, we will use a simple dataset formed only by two columns: by having only two columns, we can visualize the distances between the various points on 2-dimensional scatter plots (Cartesian diagrams).

When we work with datasets with more than two columns (as is usually the case), the concept of distance becomes more difficult to visualize in our human mind. While, with three columns, we can still imagine the algorithm working on a 3-dimensional space, with 4, 5, or 10 columns, we will necessarily need to delegate the task to machines. Luckily, they are much more at ease than humans when navigating multidimensional spaces. The good news is that the basic formula for calculating distances (the Pythagorean theorem you found in *Figure 5.41*) stays the same: you will have to calculate the squares of the distances across *all* dimensions—no matter how many they are—and sum them across.

Going back to the real estate sector for a second, let's imagine that we have a dataset describing 16 properties utilizing their price per square meter and their age in years (see *Figure 5.42* on the left). We want to cluster these properties in three homogeneous clusters. The business reason we want to create such a cluster is immediate: should a client show interest in any of these properties, we want to immediately recommend considering all other properties in the same cluster since they should exhibit *similar* features. This example looks naïve with 16 properties: we wouldn't need k-means to identify similarities with so little data involved. However, the beauty of k-means is that it could easily scale to many dimensions and properties, while our human brain would start struggling with a few more data points:

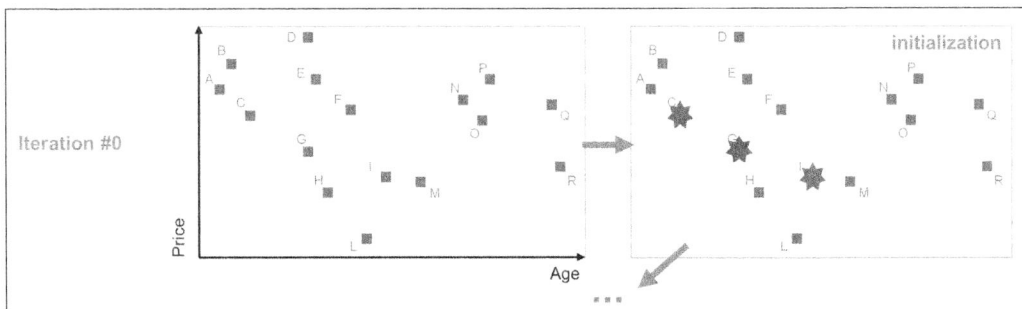

Figure 5.42: Kicking k-means off: out of the 16 properties with different prices and ages (left), three are randomly picked and elected as initial centroids (right)

The first step to run is the initialization: the algorithm will draw at random three properties, as three is the number of requested clusters (*k=3*). The algorithm has randomly extracted properties **C**, **G**, and **I**, as you can see on the right side of *Figure 5.42*. As part of the first iteration, the algorithm will proceed with the grouping step: first, it will use the Pythagorean theorem to calculate the distances between each property and each centroid and will associate every property to its closest centroid out of the three. Let's follow how k-means proceeds at each iteration with the help of the figures. As you can see in the left handside of *Figure 5.43*, the grouping step has created three first cluster compositions, each one represented by a different color. The blue-colored properties (**C**, **A**, **B**, and **D**) are the closest ones to the blue centroid that overlaps with property **C**. The ones belonging to the red cluster (**G**, **E**, **F**, and **H**) are, instead, closest to the red centroid, **G**. Finally, the green cluster is made of the points (**I**, **L**, **M**, **N**, **O**, **P**, **Q**, and **R**) whose closest centroid is **I**. The next step for the algorithm is to update the centroids: considering the points falling into each cluster, it will be enough to calculate the actual center of mass of the cluster by averaging out the prices and the ages of the properties belonging to it. For example, let's look at the green cluster: the properties forming this cluster tend to be older, leading the new centroid to be placed on the right side of the scatter plot. The centroid in the red cluster has instead moved toward the top: indeed, the properties associated with this cluster all have in common a higher price compared to point **C** (the old centroid):

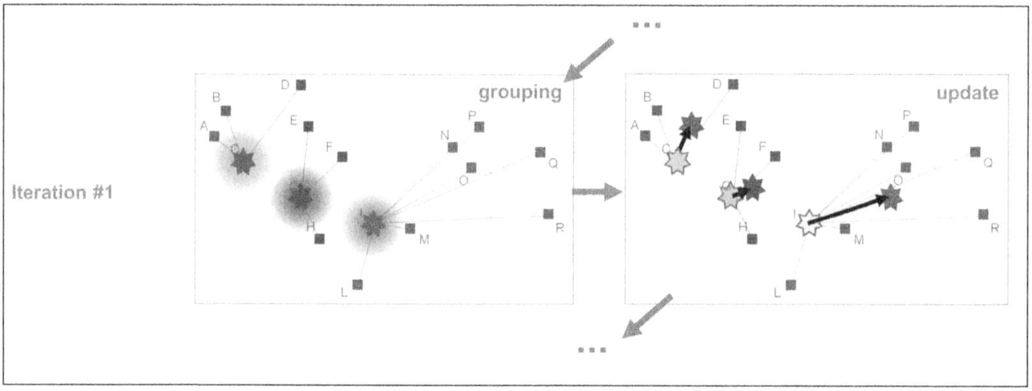

Figure 5.43: The first full iteration of k-means: with the update step, the centroids make a move

Now we can finally start the second iteration (*Figure 5.44*). Once again, we begin by grouping the points using the centroid we have just recalculated. As a consequence of this shift in the centroids, the clusters have changed, and some properties switched color: for instance, property E used to be red and is now blue as its closest centroid is now the blue one, and no longer the red one. The same applies to points I and L, which used to be green and are now red. It could appear that our algorithm has taken the right road as it is converging to a solution that makes sense: after this iteration, the clusters have changed in a way that makes their elements closer to each other. In the second step of the iteration, the algorithm will again update the centroids, taking into account the new compositions of the clusters. The most remarkable change is now in the red cluster, whose centroid has moved toward the bottom (where prices are lower), given the addition of properties I and L to the group:

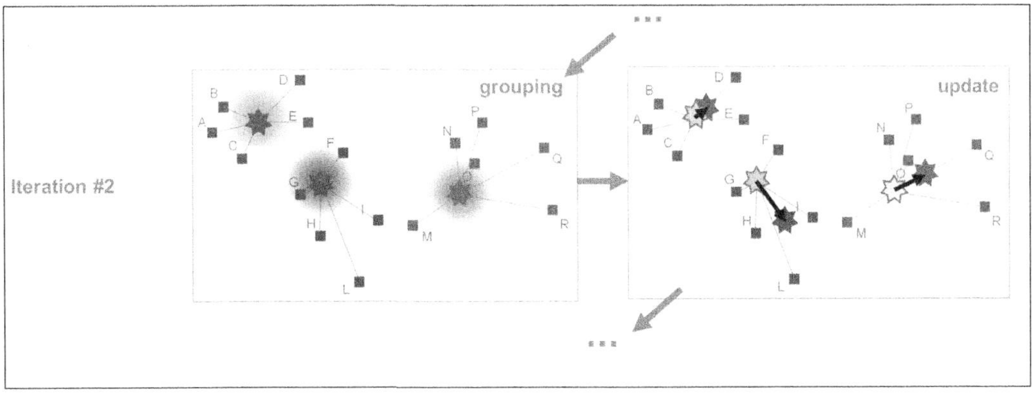

Figure 5.44: The second iteration of k-means: the groups make more and more sense

In the third iteration (*Figure 5.45*), the algorithm repeats the grouping step, and other properties change color (for instance, **M** moves from green to red, and **F** becomes blue). However, something new happens: despite having updated the centroids, the composition of the cluster does not change at all. This is the sign that our algorithm has found a stable solution and can be terminated, returning our final cluster composition:

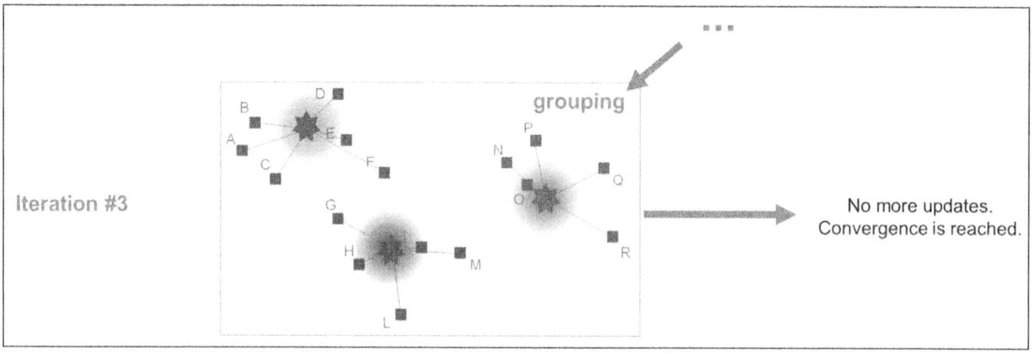

Figure 5.45: The third and last iteration of k-means: no more updates are possible and the algorithm converges

This final cluster composition seems to be making a lot of sense. By looking at the scatter plots, we can also attempt a business interpretation of each cluster:

- Blue properties (**A, B, C, D, E**, and **F**) are in the top-left corner of our diagram. They were all recently built and, as new properties, they tend to display a higher price than the rest.

- Red properties (**G, H, I, L**, and **M**) are in the bottom central part of the diagram and refer to buildings built in the seventies with lower quality materials; hence, their price is more accessible.

- Finally, the green points (**N, O, P, Q**, and **R**) are associated with older buildings, which tend to be more prestigious and come with a higher price tag.

The clusters we obtained after only a handful of iterations of the k-means algorithm can certainly help real estate agents present convincing alternatives to potential buyers. Not bad for an algorithm repeating a set of simple mathematical steps.

A natural question that comes to mind when using k-means is: what is the right value of *k* or, in other words, how many clusters should I create? Even though there are some numerical techniques (check out the **Elbow method**, for instance) to infer an optimal value for *k*, the business practice of machine learning demands taking another, less mathematically rigorous approach. When choosing the number of clusters, the advice is to take a step back and think of the actual business utilization of the cluster definitions. The right question to ask becomes: how many clusters shall I create so that the result can be used in practice in my business case? In the example of segmenting consumers for personalizing communication, is it reasonable to create — let's say — 100 clusters of consumers if I can only afford to produce three versions of a newsletter at most? We will often use the business constraints for deciding a range of reasonable values of *k* and then pick the one that looks most interpretable. The moral of this story is that data analytics is a mix of art and science, and human judgment is often needed to guide algorithms to the right path.

Before moving back to our tutorial flow, let's go through a couple of considerations regarding "what can go wrong" when using a distance-based approach like k-means and how to avoid it:

- **Outliers can spoil the game**. If some points in your dataset exhibit extreme values, they will naturally "stay apart" from the rest, making the clustering exercise less meaningful. For example, imagine that in our real estate case, we have a single property with a price ten times higher than every other property: this exceptional property will probably make a cluster by itself. Most times, we don't want this to happen, so we remove outliers upfront. The **Numeric Outliers** node will do the job for us.

- **Extreme range differences can make distance calculations unbalanced**. This one is easy to see through an example. Think again about the formula in *Figure 5.41* for calculating distances: in the real estate example, it would leverage the differences in house prices (which are in the thousands of dollars) and the age differences (which, instead, vary in the area of dozens of years). The massive gap between the two orders of magnitude becomes even wider when you square them, as the formula provides. This means that the house prices will count disproportionally more than the age, making the latter almost meaningless. To fix this numeric disadvantage, we need to normalize all the measures used in k-means and reduce their scale to a common range (generally from zero to one) while keeping the differences across data points. This is what the **Normalizer** node (and its inverse companion, the **Denormalizer** node) will do for us in KNIME.

To avoid these issues, remember this general advice: always remove outliers and normalize your data before applying k-means. With more practice and expertise, you might be able to "bend" these rules to meet your specific business needs at best, but in most cases, these two steps can only improve your clustering results, so they are no-brainers. Let's now see how to apply them in KNIME.

▶ ⚙ ▶ *Numeric Outliers*

This node (**Analytics > Statistics**) identifies outliers in a data table and manages them according to the needs. At the top of its configuration window (*Figure 5.46*), you can select which columns to consider in the outliers detection:

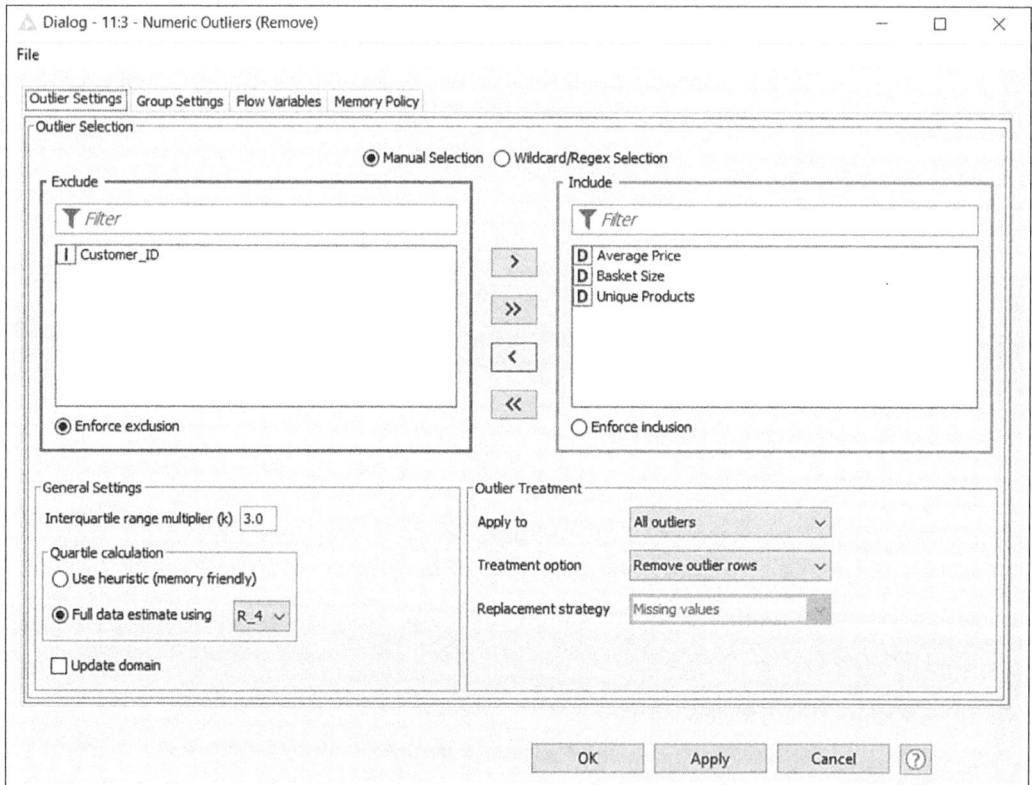

Figure 5.46: Configuration window of Numeric Outliers node:
what do you want to do with your extreme values?

In the **Outlier Treatment** panel on the bottom right, you can decide how to manage outliers once detected. In particular, the **Treatment option** drop-down menu lets you choose whether you want to **Remove outlier rows** (so as to ignore them in the rest of the workflow), **Remove non-outlier rows** (so you keep *only* the outliers and study them further), or **Replace outliers values** (by either assigning them a missing value status or substituting them with the closest value within the permitted range—you can specify your preference in the **Replacement strategy** menu).

The key parameter for setting the sensitivity to use in detecting outliers is the **Interquartile range multiplier (k)**, which you can set on the bottom-left area of the configuration window. To understand how it works, have a look at the **box plot** shown in *Figure 5.47*:

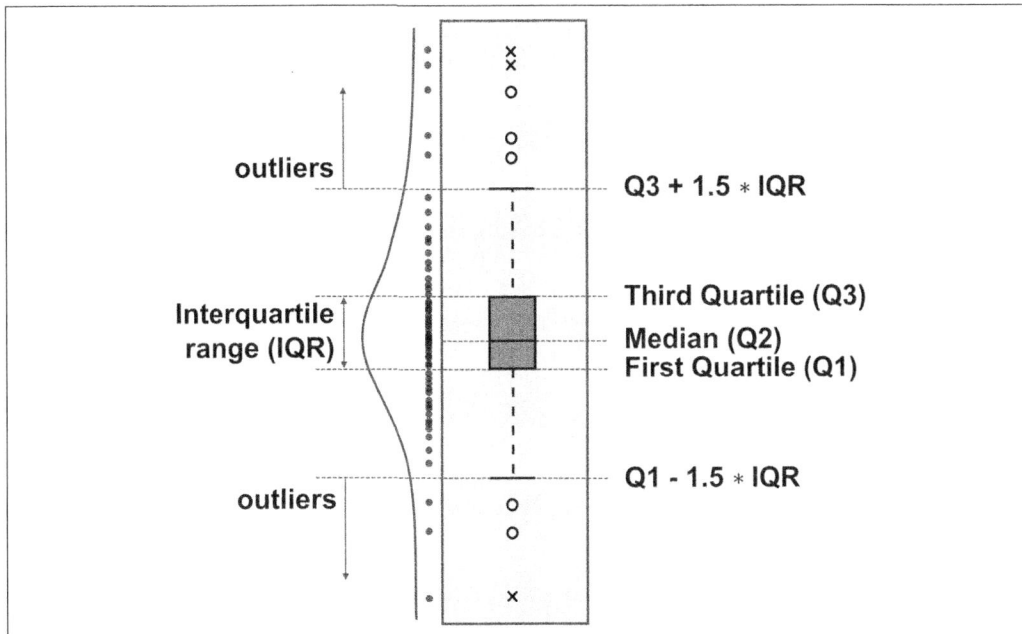

Figure 5.47: How to interpret a box-and-whisker plot: the box in the middle covers the central 50% of points in a distribution. Beyond the whiskers, you find outliers

Box plots show us at a glance the key features of a numeric distribution: quartile values (see in the picture **Q1**, **Q2**, which is the **Median**, and **Q3**) tell us where we could "cut" a population of sorted numbers so as to get 25% of the values in each slice. Now, look at the central box, whose length is called **Interquartile range (IQR)**: within this range, we will find nearly 50% of the values of the population—this is the *core* of our distribution. Keeping this in mind, outliers can be defined as the values that lie *far* from this core. Typically, the values that are further than 1.5 times the interquartile range above the third quartile or below the first quartile are considered **mild outliers**.

They are represented as circles in *Figure 5.47*, while the limit of mild outliers is represented by the dashed "whiskers" you see above and below the central box (this is why box plots are also known as box-and-whisker plots). If you increase the multiplier of the interquartile range to 3.0, you find the **extreme outliers**, which are shown as crosses in the figure. By editing the interquartile range multiplier parameter in the configuration dialog, you can tell the node how "aggressive" it should be in detecting outliers.

Let's leverage our new node straight away on the CRM dataset:

2. Implement a **Numeric Outliers** node and connect it with the output port of the CSV reader. In its configuration window, deselect the column *Customer_ID* since we don't want to use it in our clustering. Since we are after extreme outliers, set 3.0 as the **Interquartile range multiplier (k)**, and select **Remove outlier rows** as the **Treatment option**. Finally, execute the node and have a look at its output ports.

The first output (**Treated table**) is the cleaned-up version of the table, showing only 3,772 rows: this means that we removed 10% of rows as they were considered outliers according to some columns. We could have played with the IQR multiplier value and increased it to 5.0 or more, so as to focus on more extreme values and remove fewer rows, but for the sake of this exercise, we can carry on with this. The second output of the node (**Summary**, shown in *Figure 5.48*) tells us the number of rows regarded as outliers according to each individual column (*Basket Size* seems to be the one displaying more extreme values):

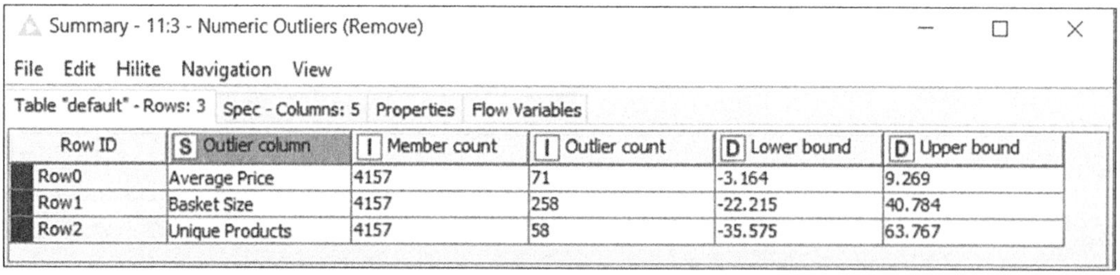

Row ID	S Outlier column	I Member count	I Outlier count	D Lower bound	D Upper bound
Row0	Average Price	4157	71	-3.164	9.269
Row1	Basket Size	4157	258	-22.215	40.784
Row2	Unique Products	4157	58	-35.575	63.767

Figure 5.48: Summary output view of the Numeric Outliers node:
which columns are causing most of the outliers?

Let's proceed with the second preparation step before applying k-means: normalize the data to a set range through the **Normalizer** node.

►⫴⁚ *Normalizer*

This node (**Manipulation > Column > Transform** in the node repository) normalizes all values in selected numerical columns of a dataset. In its configuration window (*Figure 5.49*), you first choose which columns to normalize and, then, pick a normalization method. The most useful one (especially indicated in conjunction with distance-based procedures like k-means clustering) is the **Min-Max Normalization**, which linearly projects the original range onto a predefined range (usually 0 to 1, but you can manually edit the boundaries using the text boxes provided). With this normalization approach, the original minimum value is transformed to 0, the maximum to 1, and everything in the middle is proportionally assigned to a value within the 0 to 1 range. Another popular normalization method is the **Z-Score Normalization (Gaussian)**, also known as **Standardization**. Using this method, each value is transformed into the number of standard deviations by which it is above or below the population's mean. For instance, a Z-score of –3 means that the value is three standard deviations below the population's average. This is useful when you want to assess how much your points deviate from their mean:

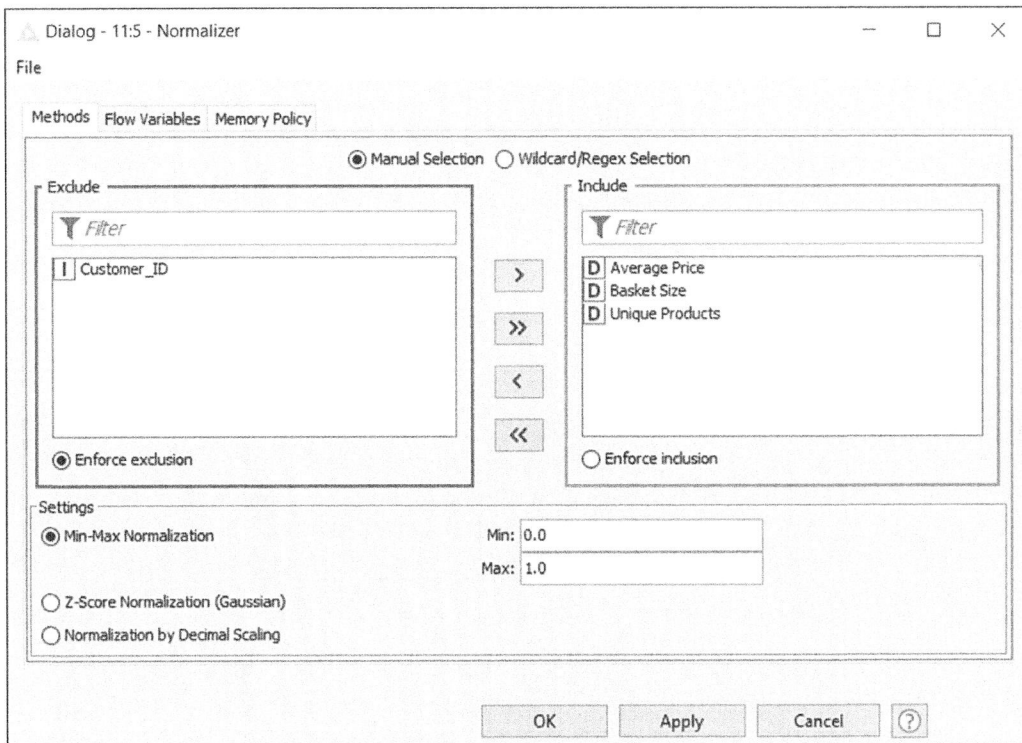

Figure 5.49: Configuration window of the Normalizer node:
select the columns to normalize and the method to apply

The node has two outputs: the upper output port returns the table with normalized values, and the bottom (the cyan square) holds the normalization model. Such a model can restate the original values using the **Denormalizer** node, which we will encounter in a few pages.

We now have all we need to proceed and normalize our outliers-less CRM data

3.   Pick the **Normalizer** node from the repository and connect its input to the first output of **Numeric Outliers**. The node configuration is straightforward: exclude the *Customer_ID* column from the normalization process by double-clicking on it and making sure it appears on the red box on the right. The default settings of the normalization method work well for us: indeed, the **Min-Max Normalization** with a range between 0 and 1 is great for calculating distances with algorithms such as k-means. Finally, click on **OK** and execute the node.

If you look at the first output of the **Normalizer** node, you will notice how the values of the affected columns are now falling in the desired range, which is exactly what we needed. Now, all columns will have the same weight in calculating distances based on the Pythagorean theorem. We can finally move on and introduce the critical node of the workflow, allowing us to cluster our customers: **k-Means**.

▶ ▒ ⊨ *k-Means*

This node (**Analytics > Mining > Clustering**) clusters the rows of the input table using the k-means algorithm. The first parameter to be set as part of its configuration (*Figure 5.50*) is the **Number of clusters**, which can be chosen by entering an integer in the textbox at the very top. You can then choose the method for the **Centroid initialization**, which, by default, happens by random draw (you can still set a static random seed to make the process repeatable), and the maximum number of iterations used to force termination (it is preset to 99, which, in most cases, is good enough since k-means would naturally converge in fewer iterations). The last configuration step is to choose which numeric columns to consider when clustering, which can be done using the **Column selection** panel at the bottom:

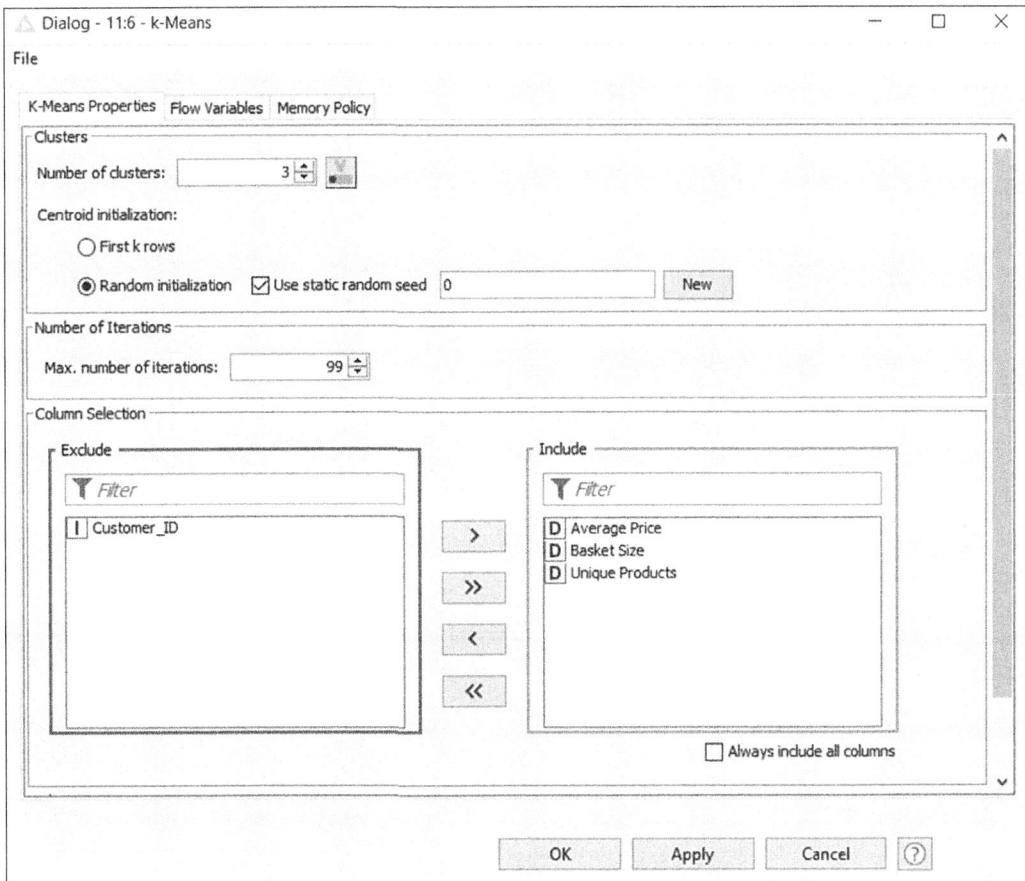

Figure 5.50: Configuration window of the k-Means node:
select the columns to normalize and the method to apply

Let's apply our new node to the normalized data and see what happens.

4. Implement the **k-Means** node and connect it downstream to the first output
    of the **Normalizer** node. We can keep its configuration simple, ensuring that
    the **Number of clusters** is set to 3 and deselecting *Customer_ID* from the list
    since we don't want to consider the column in the clustering exercise. Click
    on **OK** and then execute the node and open its main view (*Shift + F10*, or
    right-click and then select **Execute and Open Views...**).

The main view of the **k-Means** node (right-click on the node and then select **View: Cluster View** to make it appear if needed) will look similar to what you find in *Figure 5.51*:

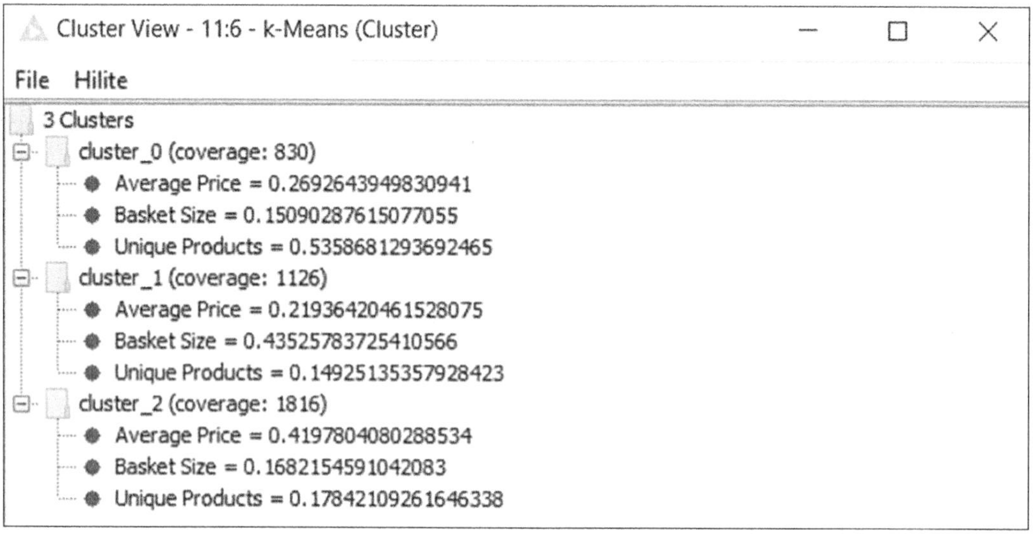

Figure 5.51: Summary view of the k-Means node: we can start seeing what the three clusters look like

This summary view is already telling us a lot: k-means segmented our customer base into three different groups of 830, 1,126, and 1,816 customers, respectively (see the **coverage** labels in the figure). If you open the different clusters (click on the **+** button on the left), you find a numeric description of the three centroids. According to what you see in *Figure 5.51*, for example, the first cluster (generically named **cluster_0** by KNIME) shows the smallest *Basket Size* of the three and the highest *Unique Products*. If you open the first output port of the node (right-click on the node and then select **Labeled input**), you will see that every row has been assigned to one of the three clusters, as indicated in the additional *Cluster* column (see *Figure 5.52*):

Row ID	[I] Customer_ID	[D] Average Price	[D] Basket Size	[D] Unique Products	[S] Cluster
Row0	12347	0.288	0.28	0.387	cluster_0
Row2	12349	0.51	0.201	0.832	cluster_0
Row3	12350	0.152	0.325	0.144	cluster_1
Row4	12352	0.412	0.118	0.13	cluster_2
Row5	12353	0.645	0.122	0.048	cluster_2
Row6	12354	0.447	0.209	0.752	cluster_0
Row7	12355	0.496	0.187	0.16	cluster_2
Row8	12356	0.606	0.436	0.261	cluster_2
Row 10	12358	0.501	0.219	0.16	cluster_2

Figure 5.52: Output of the k-Means node:
every customer — whether they like it or not — gets assigned to a cluster

As aligned with our business partner, the CRM manager, we need to go one step ahead and build a couple of visualizations to simplify the process of interpreting our clustering results.

Before doing that, we realize that our values are still normalized and forced to fall within the 0 to 1 range. To make our visuals easier to interpret, we would prefer to come back to the original scales instead. To do so, we can revert the normalization by leveraging the **Denormalizer** node.

Denormalizer

This node (**Manipulation > Column > Transform**) brings the values in a dataset back to their original range. It requires two input connections: the first one is the model generated by the previous **Normalizer** node, which carries a description of the normalization method and parameters. The second input is the normalized table to be denormalized. The node does not require any configuration.

5. Implement the **Denormalizer** node and set up the wiring. The cyan output of the **Normalizer** node should be connected to the first input of the **Denormalizer node.** The first output of the **k-Means** node should be connected, instead, to the second input port of the **Denormalizer** node. You can have a sneak view of the final workflow in *Figure 5.57* to see how to get the connections right. After executing the node, you can see how the values have been reverted to their original range.

To build the visuals, we will need three more nodes. The first one (**Color Manager**) is required for assigning colors to the various rows of the dataset (according to the cluster), while the other two (**Scatter Matrix (local)** and **Conditional Box Plot**) will generate a couple of nice charts.

◉ *Color Manager*

This node (**Views > Property**) assigns colors to each row of a dataset. Its configuration window (*Figure 5.53*) asks you to select two things. First, you specify the nominal column used to evaluate what color to assign: every possible value associated with that column will correspond to a specific color. Second, you need to select the color set to adopt. On top of the three default color sets, you can also manually define which color to assign to each possible value of the nominal column. To do so, you will have to select **Custom** in the **Palettes** tab and then use one of the tabs on the right (such as **Swatches**, **RGB**, and **CMYK**) to pick the right color for each nominal value manually:

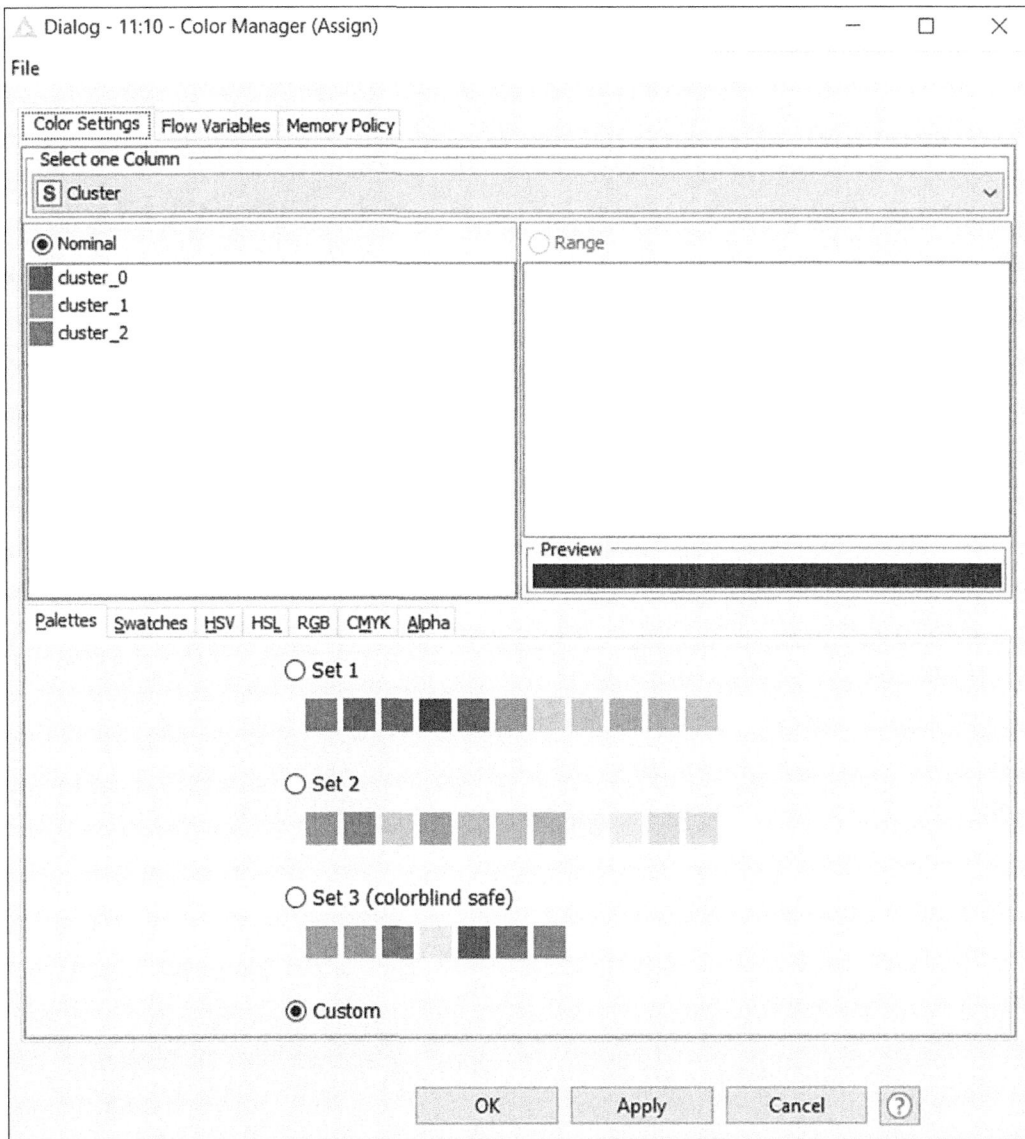

Figure 5.53: Configuration of the Color Manager node: you can pick which color to assign to which value of the nominal column of your choice

6. Add a **Color Manager** node and connect it to the output of the **Denormalizer**. Confirm the *Cluster* column in the drop-down menu at the top, and then select the color set of your choice. In the specific example of *Figure 5.53*, a custom palette has been manually created so that blue, orange, and green could be assigned to the three clusters.

Now that the colors are set, it's finally time to pull together the first chart with the help of a new node.

▸ ▦ *Scatter Matrix (local)*

This node (**Views > Local (Swing)**) generates a matrix of scatter plots, displaying multiple combinations of variables in a single view. The node does not require any configuration, but you can optionally increase the maximum number of points that will be plotted.

7. Implement the **Scatter Matrix (local)** node after **Color Manager**. Execute and open its main view (*F10* after selecting the node). From the **Column Selection** tab at the bottom, you can choose which variables to display. In our case, let's make sure we have only *Average Price*, *Basket Size*, and *Unique Products* selected on the right: you will end up with a visual similar to *Figure 5.54*:

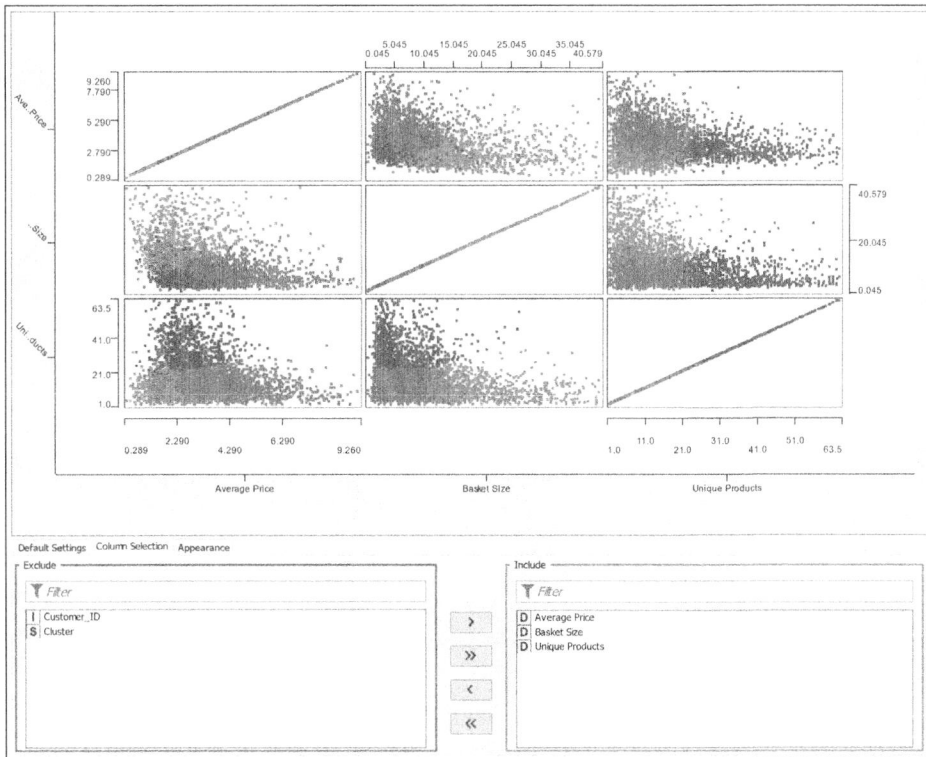

Figure 5.54: Output view of the Scatter Matrix (local) node: your customers have become colored points. By looking at how the cloud of dots is scattered, you can interpret what each cluster is all about

The scatter matrix we just obtained renders the result of the clustering in a more human-friendly way. As we look at it together with the CRM manager, we notice some initial clear patterns. For example, look at the chart at the top-right corner of *Figure 5.54*, which shows *Average Price* on the vertical axis and *Unique Products* on the horizontal axis. The blue cluster (cluster_0) clearly dominates the right-hand side of the chart, confirming that this is the segment of consumers that tend to try a more diverse set of products (high values of *Unique Products*). At the same time, the orange cluster (cluster_1) has customers that seem to go for less unique products and lower prices. Instead, the green cluster (cluster_2) includes those willing to pay more premium prices when shopping at our website. This is all starting to make sense, and the visual is already a big help in understanding how our clustering worked.

Let's add one last visual to clarify even further the composition of our segments: meet the **Conditional Box Plot** node.

▶▪▪ Conditional Box Plot

This node (**Views > JavaScript**) produces an interactive view with multiple box plots, one for each value in a given categorical column. Such a view enables the parallel comparison of distributions. Its configuration window (*Figure 5.55*) requires selecting the **Category Column** to be used for differentiating parallel box plots and the choice of the numeric columns whose distribution will be visualized:

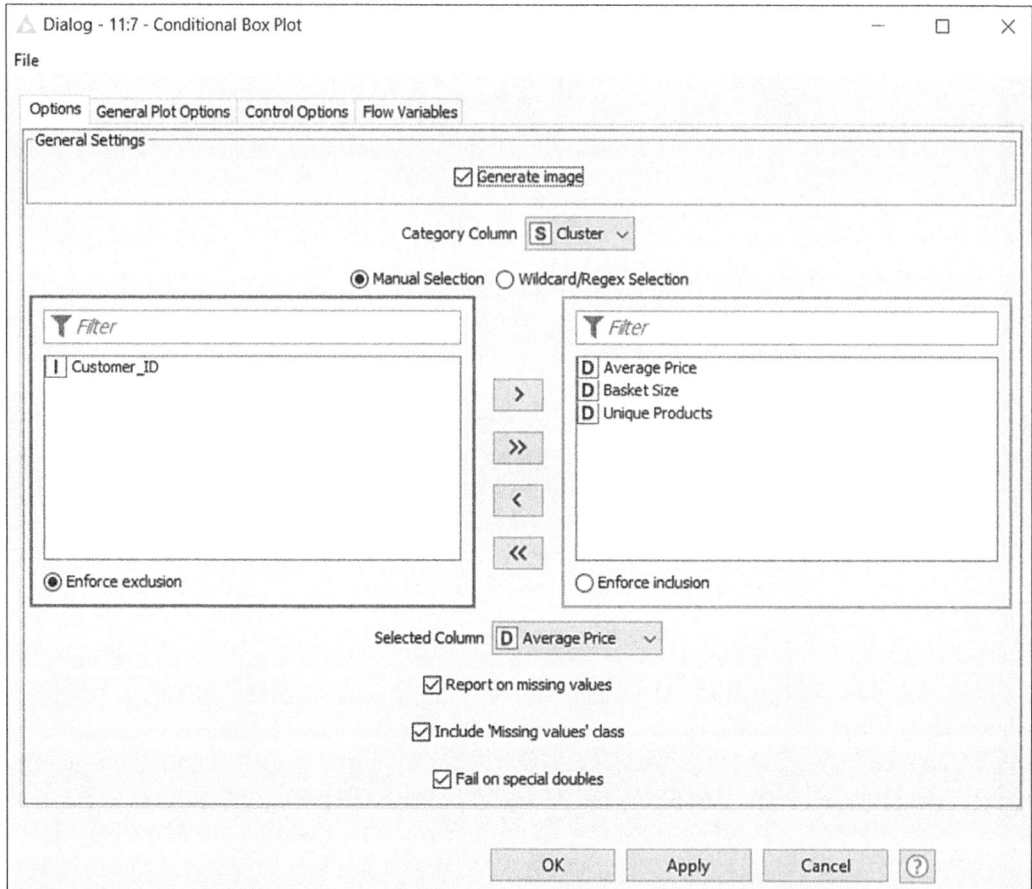

Figure 5.55: Configuration dialog of the Conditional Box Plot node: which distributions are you interested in comparing between?

8. Drag and drop the **Conditional Box Plot** node onto the workflow editor and connect it to the output port of the **Denormalizer** node. Select *Cluster* as **Category Column** and ensure that only **Average Price, Basket Size**, and **Unique Products** are on the right of the column selector placed at the center of the dialog. Click on **OK** and then press *Shift + F10* to execute it and open its main view. In the interactive window that appears, you can swap which distribution to visualize by operating on the **Selected Column** drop-down menu: you can find this selector by clicking on the icon at the far top-right of the interactive window.

The output views of the **Conditional Box Plot** node (*Figure 5.56*) clarify even better the essential features of each cluster. The k-means algorithm was able to produce three homogeneous clusters with peculiar and differentiating characteristics. The box plots are great at showing such differences. As an example, take the third plot in the figure, which refers to *Unique Products*. The blue cluster dominates when it comes to this measure: the median number of unique products purchased by customers belonging to this segment is 32, while for the others it is near 10. The lack of visual overlap in height between the blue box and the other two means this difference is meaningful. On the other hand, the orange and the green clusters seem to be quite similar in terms of unique products, as the boxes are almost coinciding:

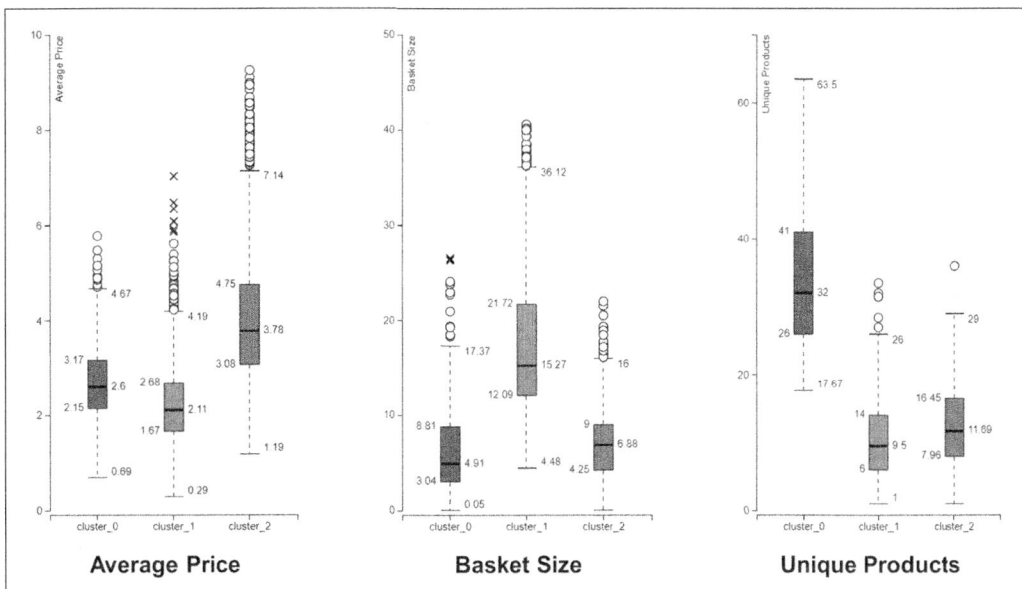

Figure 5.56: Outputs of the Conditional Box Plot node: you can readily appreciate the differences in the distributions across clusters

We can now sit together with the CRM manager and, having the scatter matrix and the conditional box plots at hand, we can finally describe each customer segment and give a business-oriented interpretation of their meaning:

- The blue cluster includes those **curious customers** who are willing to try different products. In our communication with this segment, we can give disproportionate space to the "new arrivals" and intrigue them with an ample selection of products they haven't tried yet.

- The orange cluster possibly comprises **small retailers** who buy "in bulk" from our website to resell their shops. They tend to buy relatively few products but in large quantities. We can offer them quantity discounts and regularly communicate the list of best-selling products, hopefully leading them to add our best-selling articles to their assortment for mutual business growth.

- The green cluster is made up of our **high-value customers**, who systematically put quality ahead of price in their shopping choices. Therefore, when communicating with them, we should advertise the premium end of the products portfolio and focus on topics such as the quality and the safety of our assortment, deprioritizing price-cut offers, and other types of promotional levers.

By using only 8 KNIME nodes (see the full workflow in *Figure 5.57*), we came up with a simple segmentation of customers and a first proposition of how to drive the most value when personalizing their experience. By uniting the business expertise of our partners (the CRM managers in this case) with the power of data and algorithms, such as k-means, we can make the magic happen!

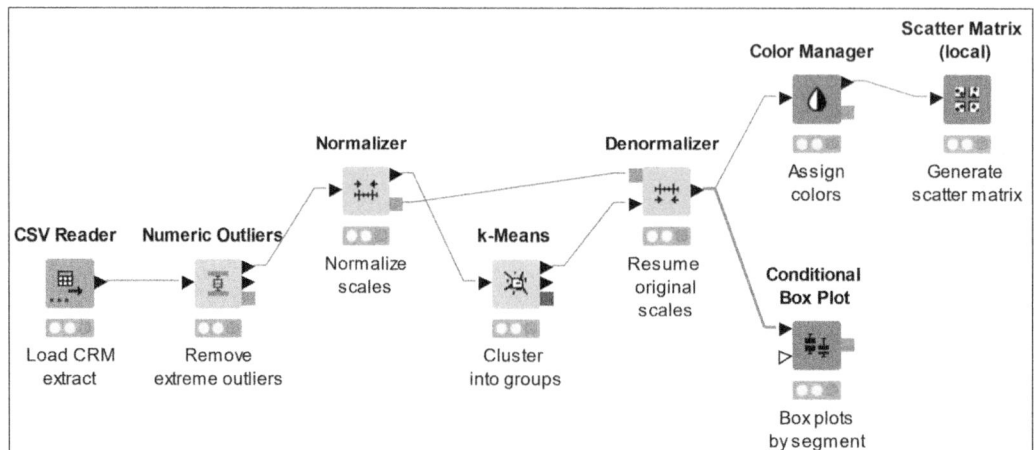

Figure 5.57: The full workflow for segmenting consumers using clustering

Summary

In this chapter, you touched on the serious potential behind data analytics and machine learning with your own hands. You have solved three real-world problems by putting data and algorithms at work.

In the first tutorial, you managed to predict with a decent level of accuracy the rental price of properties, collecting, in the process, a few interesting insights into real estate price formation. You have now acquired a proven methodology, based on the linear regression model, that you can replicate on many business cases where you have to predict numeric quantities.

In the second tutorial, you entered the fascinating world of classification and propensity modeling, experiencing firsthand the game-changing role of data analytics in marketing. You were able to put together a couple of classification models through which you met multiple business needs. First, you were able to reveal the "unwritten rules" that make a product generally attractive to customers by building and interpreting a decision tree model. Then, you built a random forest model that proved effective in anticipating the level of propensity of individual bank customers. Lastly, you managed to estimate the possible ROI of further marketing campaigns, unlocking serious value creation opportunities for a business. Also, in this case, you gained a series of general-purpose techniques that you can easily reapply in your own work every time you need to predict anything of business relevancy. By going through the tutorial, you also experienced the "back and forth" iterations needed to fine-tune machine learning models to fit your business needs.

In our third tutorial, you experienced the power of unsupervised learning. You were able to put together a meaningful and straightforward customer segmentation that can be used to design personalized communication strategies and maximize the overall customer value. With this new algorithm, k-means, in your backpack, you can potentially cluster anything: stores, products, contracts, defects, events, virtually any business entity that can benefit from the algorithmic tidying that comes with clustering. Think about the value you can create by applying this new concept to the work items you deal with on a daily basis. In the process of learning k-means, we also got acquainted with the fundamental statistical concept of outliers and saw how to spot and manage them systematically.

Let's now move on and learn how we can make our data accessible to our business partners through self-service dashboards. It's time to meet our next travel companion in the data analytics journey: Power BI.

6

Getting Started with Power BI

Visualizing data to understand "what is going on" in the business: this is the first and ever-present need that organizations have when leveraging data. Unsurprisingly, business intelligence applications are the earliest to be adopted in a company and precede by months (or even years) the arrival of their "sexier" advanced analytics counterparts. However excited and impatient we can—understandably—be about the wonders of predictive and prescriptive capabilities powered by machine learning algorithms, a simple online dashboard showing the evolution of key business metrics can easily dominate in short-term potential. Making data accessible to a broad community of employees will multiply the probability of identifying business opportunities and promoting more conscious and effective data-based decisions by business managers. This scenario is too appealing to be left by the wayside, and the time has come to equip our data analytics toolbox with a tool that can unleash the power of descriptive analytics at scale: Power BI.

This chapter will provide answers to the following questions:

- What is Power BI, and how do I get started?
- How do I load, transform, and organize data?
- How do I create data visualizations that can interact with each other?
- What does a Power BI dashboard look like, and how can I create one?

After getting acquainted with the Power BI Desktop user interface, we will build a complete dashboard step by step. The ultimate objective is to equip you with all you need to create your own dashboards as soon as you finish reading the last page. The focus of this chapter is on Power BI and on what you strictly need to start benefitting from it. We will then use the following two chapters to sharpen your data visualization and storytelling skills to make you great at building data charts that can effectively persuade others. One thing at a time: let's now meet our new hero in the quest for data analytics.

Power BI in a nutshell

Power BI is a business intelligence service offered by Microsoft that enables the creation of online data dashboards. Let's go through its most essential features:

- Power BI comes with a traditional application software called **Power BI Desktop**, which you can download and install, for free, on your computer. Power BI Desktop offers the full design functionalities of Power BI: you can use this software to create your dashboards, save them in local files (with the .pbix extension), and then share them with other users, who can, in turn, view and edit your dashboards. To complete this chapter, you will only need to use the Power BI Desktop application.

- It's important to know that Power BI is primarily offered as a cloud-based service. If you decide you want to use Power BI at scale in your company to leverage corporate data sources and make dashboards available online via browsers or mobile apps (without the need for all users to install Power BI Desktop and open files shared via email), then you can do so by acquiring Pro or Premium licenses. In this way, your dashboards will rely on the Microsoft cloud platform, called **Azure**, for hosting, processing, and making data available to end users.

> If your company uses Microsoft 365 cloud services, you might already have a Power BI Pro license: it's worth checking this out.

- Power BI leverages a user-friendly **visual interface** that lets you design dashboards without the need to write any code. Still, if you want to specify advanced queries, you can use the programming language called **DAX**, which is short for **Data Analysis eXpressions**. We will not cover DAX in this book, but it's good to know that you can extend Power BI functionalities by leveraging it if you need it.

- Power BI offers **more than plain data visualizations**. It lets you pull data from different sources, transform and harmonize tables, apply some logic and algorithms, and make data accessible through interactive charts or other non-traditional ways. For example, a remarkable functionality of Power BI is to give users the possibility to obtain data by typing questions in plain English like *what is the evolution of profit for brand X over the last two years?* In this case, your role as a designer will be to "teach" Power BI how to interpret your colleagues' questions by deciding, for instance, what words are used as synonyms to describe the same entities (for example, *articles*, *SKUs*, and *products*).

- Power BI can be **extended** with additional features and visuals. You can check the Microsoft App store called **AppSource** (appsource.microsoft.com), from where you can download additional custom visualizations for free. Another way to extend Power BI functionalities is to add Python or R code snippets as a way to implement specialized charts or add machine learning functionalities.

All in all, Power BI promises to be a powerful and well-rounded tool for democratizing data in a company through accessible dashboards: this is exactly what we need to complete our data analytics toolbox and unlock substantial value for our business. Before exploring its user interface and getting acquainted with its naming conventions, let's get Power BI Desktop up and running on your computer. You can either retrieve it from its download page (powerbi.microsoft.com/en-us/downloads) and then install it or look it up on the Microsoft Store app in Windows. Although it is not required for the sake of the chapter, you can also register for a free Power BI license. This would let you access the cloud-based services and save your reports, for your own use, on the cloud (sharing them with others would require buying a paid license).

Walking through Power BI

Building a working dashboard in Power BI requires a series of four essential steps, namely, loading your data, transforming it, defining a data model, and creating data visuals leveraging the data model. As you can see in *Figure 6.1*, the four steps alternate as a cycle—your dashboard might require a few iterations before being ready for prime time:

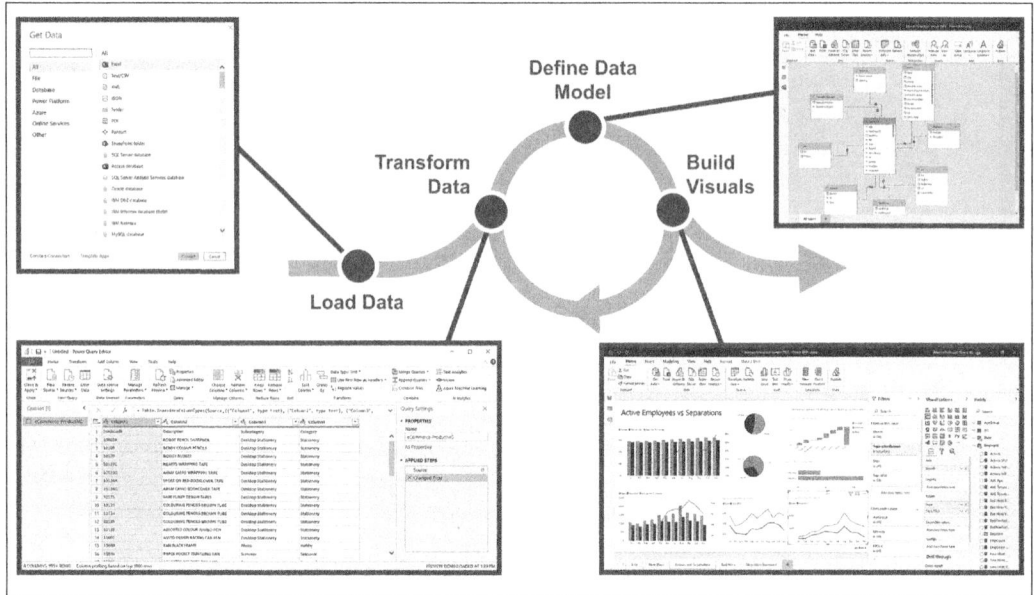

Figure 6.1: Typical Power BI design process: load the data and transform data, define a model, build visuals, and iterate

Every step of the process relies on some specific views or dialogs in the application. By using only a handful of views, you will be able to access all the functionalities you need to build a dashboard from scratch. *Figure 6.2* shows a simple "map" of where to find the most helpful Power BI views and windows so that you don't get lost along the way:

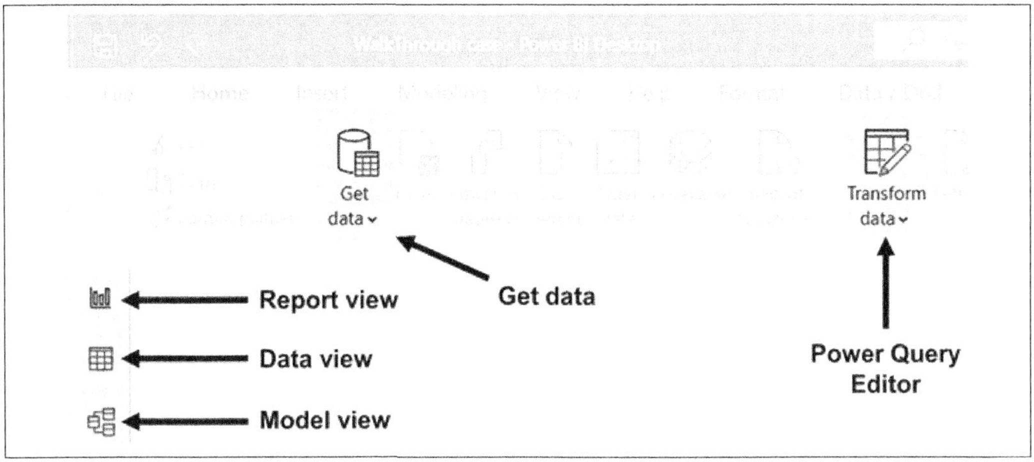

Figure 6.2: Feeling lost? This is where you find the most valuable views you will ever need in Power BI

In the following few pages, we will walk through the complete process of creating a dashboard and discover the critical Power BI functionalities that will help us along the way.

Loading data

Unsurprisingly, the very first thing you need to do in Power BI is load some data into it. If you click on **Get Data** right from the welcome screen you see as soon as you open Power BI or from the icon in the **Home** ribbon on top, you will get to the **Get Data** window, shown in *Figure 6.3*. This window boasts a wide range of possible data connectors, organized by the categories you see on the left (**File**, **Database**, **Online services**, and so on). The first and most used category is **File**: from here, you can import not only Excel or CSV single files but also entire folders, and you can extract the data stored in PDF reports. From the **Database** category, you can connect to many types of databases and specify SQL queries to retrieve the data you need. From here, you can also connect to cloud-based platforms such as Amazon Web Services (Redshift), Google Cloud Platform (BigQuery), and, of course, Microsoft Azure. The **Online Services** category lets you connect to other external services like Google Analytics, Salesforce reports, and Sharepoint lists. Have a look at the **Other** category as well: the source called **Web** will let you scrape data from web pages and download tables or other web elements of interest:

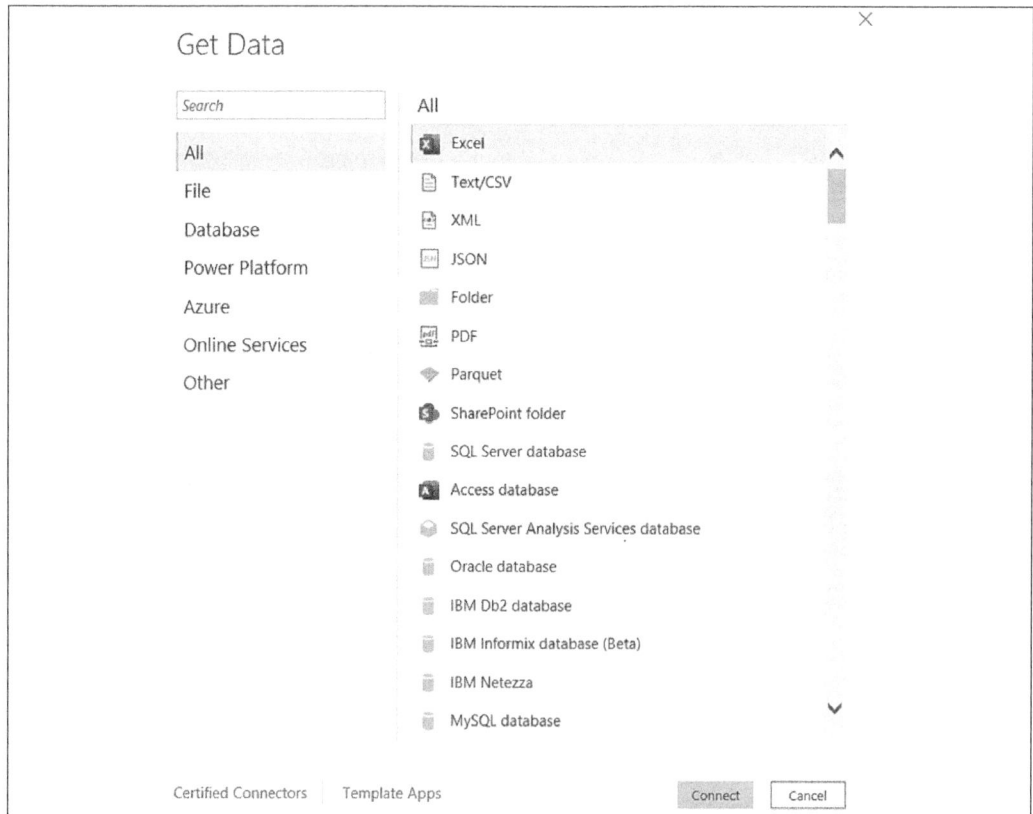

Figure 6.3: The Get Data window in Power BI: define how to retrieve the data you need

By setting up a data connector, you define the first step of a repeatable routine for retrieving and transforming your data of interest: such a routine in Power BI is called a **query**. Defining queries is a powerful way to ensure that your dashboards can be sustainably updated over time. Every time you refresh your reports, the queries will connect to the various sources and pull the most up-to-date version of the available data.

Transforming data

For every query, you can then associate a series of data transformation steps that are applied every time new data comes in. In Power BI, you can do so visually, without writing any code, by using a tool called **Power Query Editor**, which you can see in *Figure 6.4*. On the left of the query editor, you find a panel called **Queries** from which you can select the query you are setting transformation steps for: just click on the name of the query you wish to work on.

You will see an Excel-like spreadsheet view in the middle of the window, which displays a *preview* of your transformed query. The values of the cells are read-only: you cannot change them one by one, and indeed your purpose here is to define repeatable transformation steps for the whole table more than applying cell-level changes. You can use the header of the spreadsheet to apply some transformations, like filters and sorting, similar to what you would do in Excel. On the right, you find a panel called **Applied steps**, where you can find an ordered list of the transformation steps applied so far. The very first step is likely to be **Source**, as it indicates the original definition of the source of data you loaded. Some of the transformation steps will have a cog icon on the right: by clicking on it, you can edit the parameters of the transformation steps. For instance, if the query pulls data from an Excel file, you can edit the file's path to open by clicking on the cog icon beside the **Source** step.

When you select a specific step, the spreadsheet view will update accordingly, showing you a preview of the query after executing that specific step you selected: this is handy when you want to check *what is going on* in your transformation routine at every step:

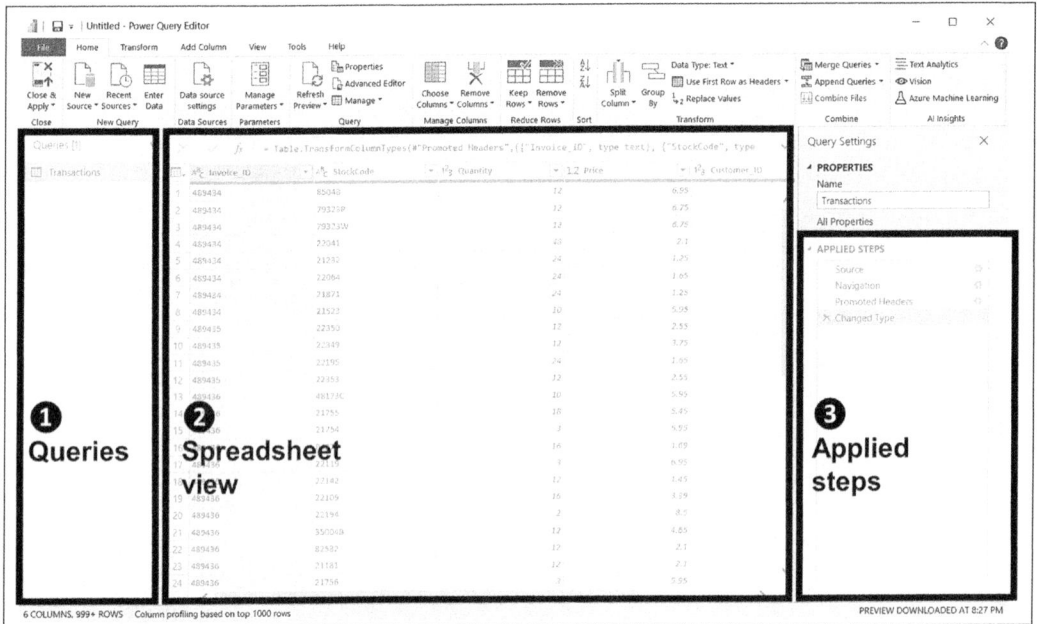

Figure 6.4: The Power Query Editor window in Power BI: design the transformation steps applied to each query

By going through the first three ribbon tabs on top of the **Power Query Editor** window, namely **Home**, **Transform**, and **Add Column**, you can find a *menu* of the many transformation steps available to you. Many of these transformation steps are the same as the ones we learned how to apply with KNIME using the nodes introduced in *chapters 2* and *3*. Let's have a look at the most popular ones in there.

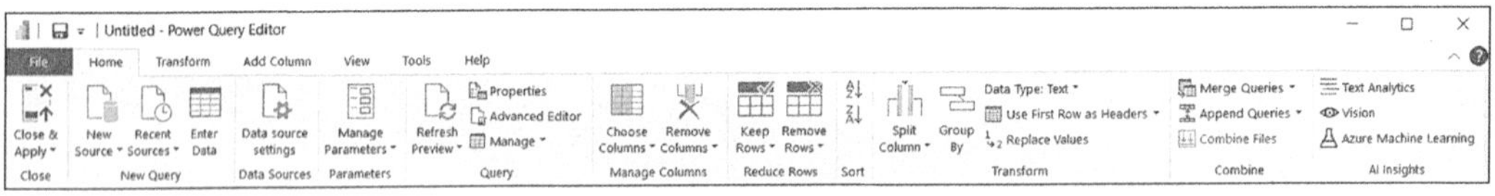

Figure 6.5: The Home ribbon tab in the Power Query Editor window

- Starting from the **Home** tab (*Figure 6.5*), you can find the **Choose Columns** and **Remove Columns** icons, which let you filter columns and keep only the ones you really need.

- Similarly, **Keep Rows** and **Remove Rows** enable you to reduce the number of rows: for instance, you can keep only the top 10 rows or remove the duplicate ones.

> Instead, if you want to filter rows depending on their values, you need to click on the arrow that appears on the right of the header of each column within the preview spreadsheet. From there, you can also sort rows using your preferred order.

- The **Split Column** icon will let you divide strings into multiple columns by either using delimiters (you can split JUN-22 into JUN and 22 by setting - as a delimiter) or counting a given number of characters.

- **Group By** will aggregate all rows according to a given group definition and a summarization logic (like sum, average, or count). If you use this transformation step, you will not be able to use the disaggregated version of the table anywhere in your dashboard, so use this function sparingly. You can always aggregate tables *on the fly* by defining the aggregation directly as you build the visuals, which we do most of the time.

- **Merge Queries** lets you combine queries by applying a one-off join operation. We will find here the same join types that we have met in *Chapter 3, Transforming Data*, such as *inner, left outer, right outer*, and *full outer*, plus some more like *left anti* (which means keeping only the rows from the left table that are not matched on the right). You can either create a new query containing the result of the join or substitute the current query with it.

  It's important to notice that the **Merge Queries function** is not the only way to *connect* two tables with matching keys in Power BI. As we will learn in the next few pages, when we build data models, we can specify relationships across tables without statically joining them once and for all. This means that you should use **Merge Queries** only if you want to run a definitive merge of two tables and accept the need to utilize some extra space required to keep the static, joined version of the table.

- With the **Append Queries** icon, you can concatenate two tables with the same columns by adding the rows of one table at the bottom of the rows of the other table.

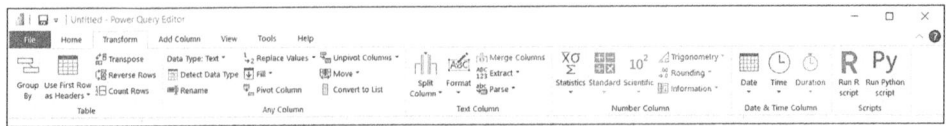

Figure 6.6: The Transform tab in the Power Query Editor window

- Moving to the **Transform** tab (*Figure 6.6*), we find the **Data Type** drop-down menu, which lets us select the type associated with a column and attempt a conversion. We can use this one, for instance, to convert a string containing a date into a Date & Time field.

- With **Replace Values**, you can substitute all cells having a certain value with a specified new value. You can use it also for applying a fixed value to all empty cells in a column. To do so, just use the `null` string to specify you want to target empty cells.

- The **Fill** icon lets you replace all empty cells with the values found above or below within the table. This is handy when you have some values sorted by time and you want to *fill the gaps* with the most recent available values.

- As the name suggests, by using **Pivot Column**, you can create pivot tables where values within a column are aggregated across as separate columns. You might also find useful its reverse functionality, **Unpivot Columns**, which makes columns of the table appear as multiple rows.

- The **Format** icon lets you manipulate the strings: you can, for instance, capitalize strings (making `tessa` become `Tessa`) or move them to an all-uppercase format (`TESSA`).

- With the **Rounding** functionality, you can specify the rounding logic for decimal numbers, fixing the decimal digits to your liking.

- Within the **Data & Time Column** section, you can extract specific Date & Time fields, such as years, months, hours, and seconds. If you want to extract more than one field, you can first duplicate the column (right-click on the column header and then **Duplicate Column**) and create as many copies as you need before replacing them with the field you need.

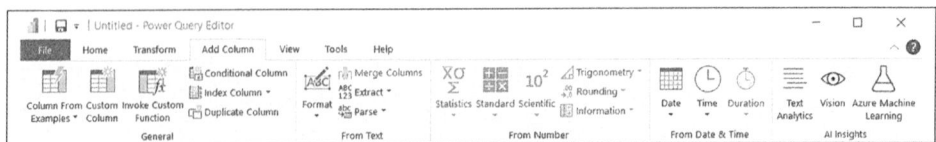

Figure 6.7: The Add Column tab in the Power Query Editor window

- Within the **Add Column** tab (*Figure 6.7*), you can create calculated columns by applying some logic. For instance, using the **Custom Column** icon, you can apply math formulas, such as [Price]*[Discount_rate], leveraging as variables the values found in other columns.

- **Conditional Column** lets you generate a new column based on evaluating some logical conditions on other columns, similar to what we did in KNIME using the **Rule Engine** node. For example, you can create a new column with the value Expensive for all rows where the *Price* column is higher than 2.5 and Cheap for all others.

As you finish applying all the required transformation steps, your queries will produce tables having precisely the shape and format you need. Once you have done so, you can save the queries (the **Close & Apply** icon in the **Home** tab) and move on to the next step of our process: the definition of the data model.

Defining the data model

At this point of the process, you need to define how the tables resulting from your queries are logically interrelated. To do so, it will be enough to declare the relationship between the **matching columns** across tables, meaning the ones that can be used for combining tables when needed. By completing this simple exercise, you will have defined a single data model that you will then be able to leverage freely in your dashboard visualizations. We do this for a straightforward and important reason: by connecting the matching keys, you can use data stored in different tables within the same visual: it's like having all tables joined and continuously available to you, which is pretty handy. A consequence of having a clear data model defined is that you can enable interactions across charts through filtering or selections. For example, let's imagine that a visual shows the total amount of sales generated by category: by clicking on a category name, you can get another visual to show the names of the most active customers within that category, an information that is stored in a different table. By knowing the matching columns between categories, sales, and customers, Power BI will be able to show the data the user is after and enable drill-downs and other forms of interaction.

It is effortless to build a data model in Power BI. Do you remember the **Entity-Relationship (ER) diagram** we introduced in *Chapter 3*, *Transforming Data* (see *Figure 3.10* to get a refresher)? Power BI lets you build a model visually by drawing ER diagrams using the available tables.

As you can see in *Figure 6.8*, the **Model** view shows tables (each resulting from the full transformation steps declared in a query) as boxes: the table name appears in bold at the top of the box while columns are listed within the box. The tables are connected through lines, which represent their relationships:

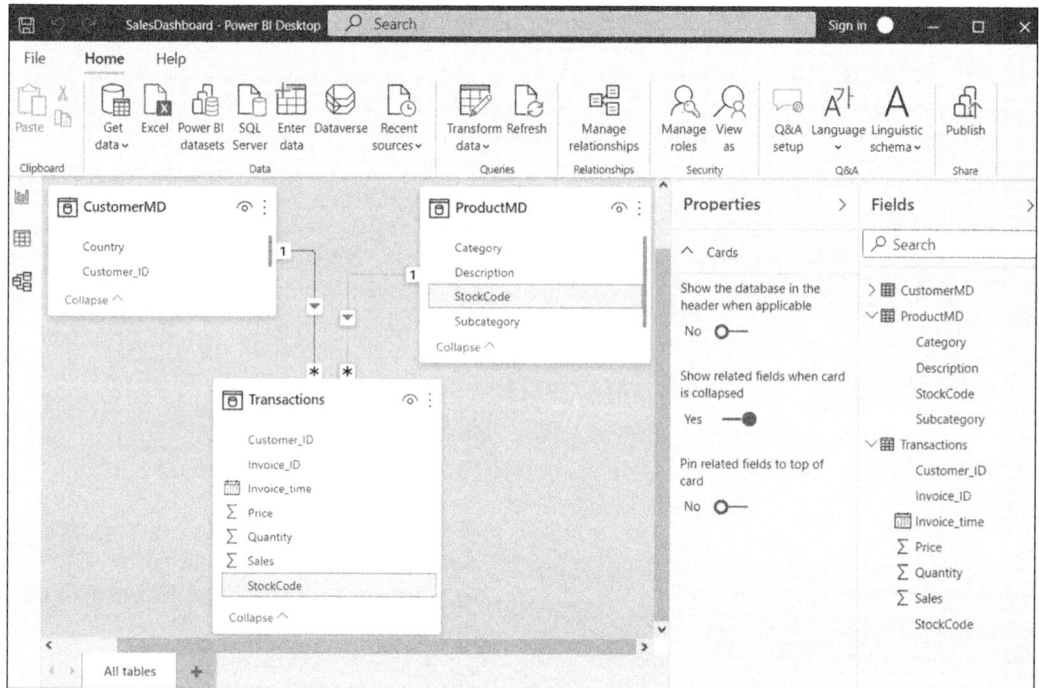

Figure 6.8: The Model view in Power BI: connect the tables and build your ER diagram

By using the **Model** view, you can easily declare relationships across matching columns. For example, to draw a relationship across matching columns in two different tables, it will be enough to *drag and drop* one column on top of its match. For instance, in *Figure 6.8*, you can see how the highlighted relationship (between the ProductMD and Transactions tables) is made using the common column, *StockCode*. The arrows appearing on the connections indicate the **cross-filter directions**: in this case, a filter applied on a ProductMD item will also filter rows in Transactions, while the opposite will not happen. The **1** and * symbols appearing at the ends of the connectors clarify the expected **cardinality** of the relationship: the ones displayed in the picture are both **one-to-many (1-to-*)** relationships, meaning that we expect one single row in ProductMD to refer to many rows in Transactions. The other possible types of relationship cardinality are **one-to-one (1-to-1)** and **many-to-many (*-to-*)**.

The role of the data model will become even more apparent when we go through the full tutorial. For now, the takeaway is that by defining relationships together with their cardinality and cross-filter directions (all visually displayed in the **Model** view), we can be sure that the behavior of Power BI is not ambiguous, even when we use multiple tables at the same time within our dashboard.

Having built the data model, we can now move to the last and most exciting part of dashboard creation: designing data visualizations.

Building visuals

Dashboards in Power BI are organized as a set of pages, each containing many interconnected visual elements such as tables, line charts, scatter plots, text labels, and buttons. As you perform this step, you will have to think like a designer by enforcing structure and visual appeal while mixing together business understanding and creativity. This activity can be as enjoyable as it is time-consuming: for sure, it can pay its dividends as you end up with a functional and valuable dashboard that people can leverage to unveil business opportunities and make superior decisions. When you open the **Report view** (shown in *Figure 6.9*), you will have at your fingertips all you need to compose the visual elements together and link them with the tables sitting in the underlying data model:

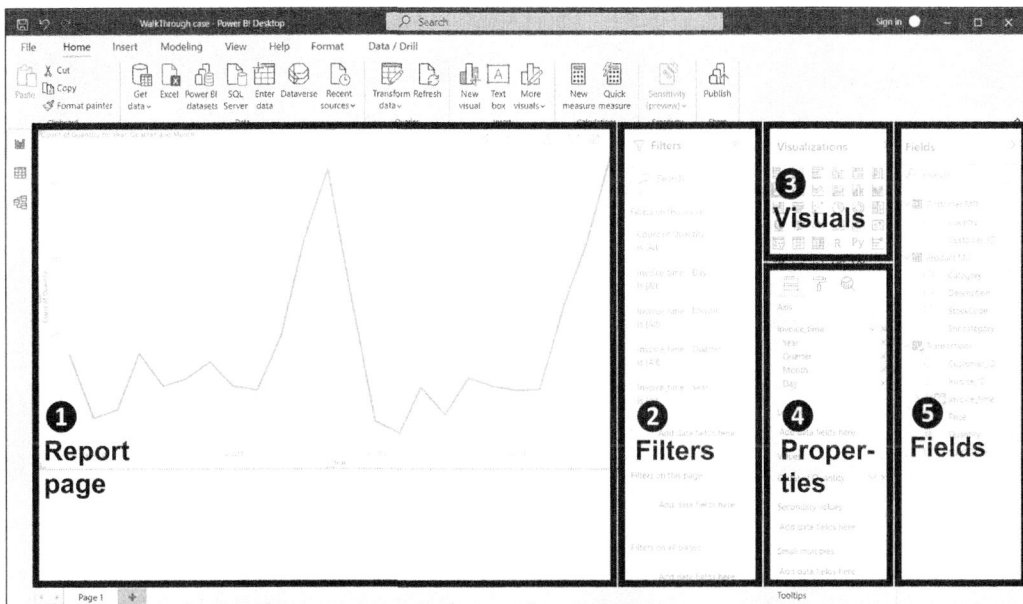

Figure 6.9: The Report view in Power BI: connect the tables and build your ER diagram

Let's go through each component of the **Report** view and learn what they are there for:

1. **Report page**: This will look at first like a blank piece of paper upon which you can draw your beautiful dashboard. By using your mouse, you can place, resize, and reposition visuals as needed. Underneath the report page, you will find a set of tabs, each referring to a separate page of your dashboard.

   > According to the official naming convention of Power BI, what we are building in this chapter is a report, not a dashboard: the latter is, instead, a one-page summary aggregation of selected visuals, a feature available in the Power BI service only. For simplicity, I will keep using the words dashboard and report to refer to our end result here: a set of connected visuals for end users to interact with.

2. **Filters**: In this section, you decide the scope of the data to be shown in each visual element by setting filters. For example, you can set up a filter on the column *Category* by dragging and dropping it from the Fields panel onto one of the boxes lying on the **Filters** panel. You can use filters to show only the portion of data you select or implement some logic, like *show only the five most selling products of the list*. The **Filters** section has three different panels, corresponding to the levels at which you want your filters to operate: some filters will limit what is shown in a specific visual only, while others will apply instead to all the visuals in a page or, even, on every visual appearing anywhere in all dashboards.

3. **Visuals**: This section is the most interesting one as it features a complete list of visualization types you can add to your dashboard. As you can see from *Figure 6.10*, more than 30 different visualization types are available for you to use as soon as you install Power BI:

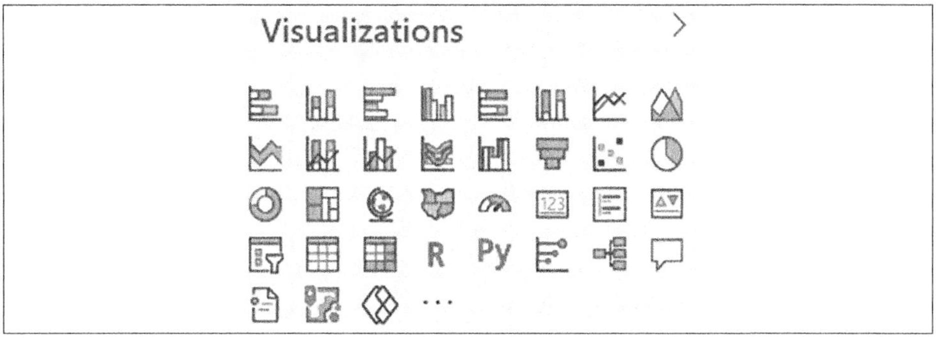

Figure 6.10: Available visualization types in Power BI: which chart makes your data speak best?

You can also add supplementary visualization types by either enabling the preview of some beta-version features (go to **File | Options and settings | Options | Preview features** to activate) or downloading them from AppSource by clicking on the last visualization **...** icon (you need to sign in to Power BI, even with a free account, to access AppSource). You can see in *Figure 6.11* a preview of the extra available visuals you can grab from there:

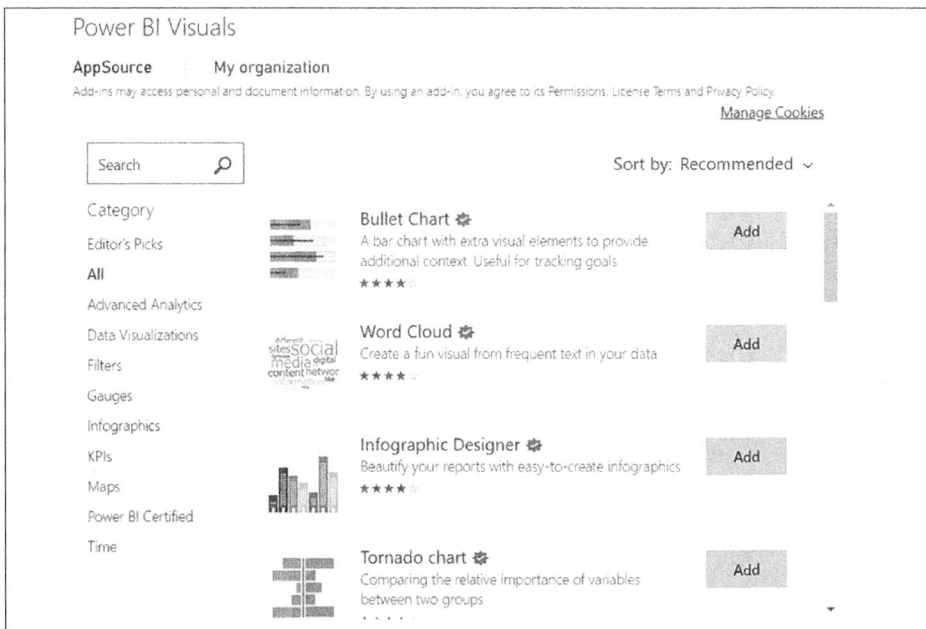

Figure 6.11: Run out of creative ideas? You can check AppSource for additional visual types and add them to your Power BI

4. **Properties**: From this section, you can configure how your visual should behave and look. As you can see in *Figure 6.12*, you have three available tabs within this section, namely **Fields**, **Format,** and **Analytics**. The **Fields** tab is the first to be looked after: by dragging and dropping the columns available in the data model into the various elements in this tab, you decide what data should be visualized. Depending on the type of visualization you are using, you will have different elements to configure. For instance, the example in *Figure 6.12* refers to a line chart where the column *Invoice_time* controls what should be in the horizontal axis, while the values visualized by the line are controlled by the column *Quantity*. In the Format tab, you have multiple selectors that let you control the "look and feel" of the visual. You can tune several visual properties, from the title to be displayed on top to the color and thickness of the line in the chart. Lastly, in the **Analytics** tab, you can activate some basic modeling features, such as trend lines (basically, the result of a simple linear regression model or a time series forecast):

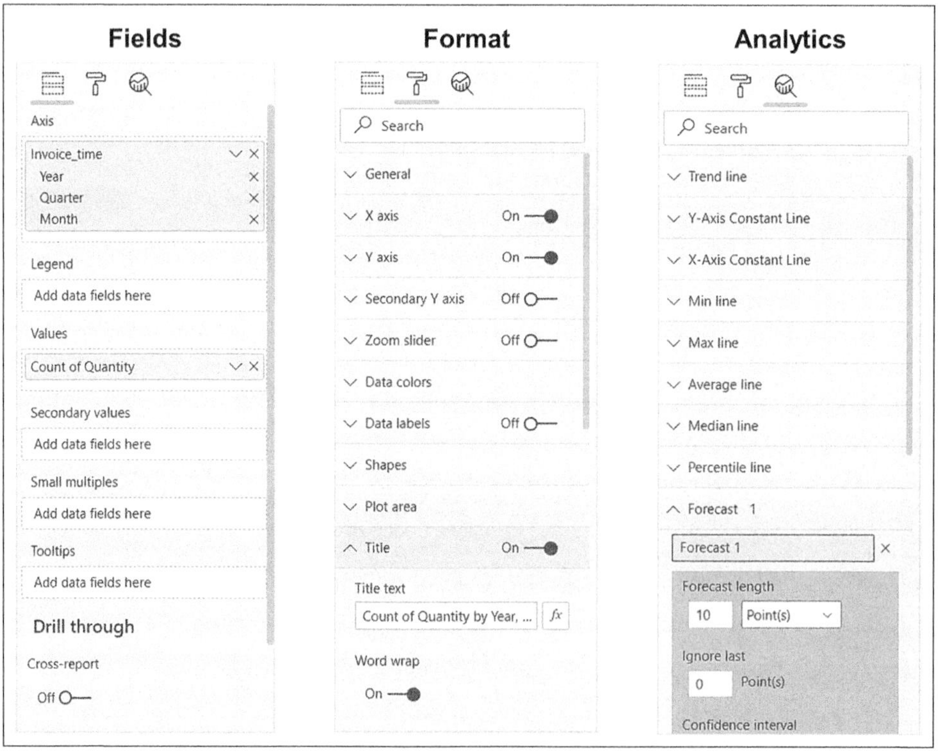

Figure 6.12: Visual properties section: connect data columns to your chart and decide how it should look

5. **Fields**: This section, which you can find on the right side of the **Report** view, does a simple but fundamental job. It carries a list of all the columns available in the different tables of the data model so that you can easily drag and drop the columns onto the filters or the properties section. When you click on any column, the **Column tools** ribbon will appear at the top of the window. You can use it to change the data type of a column or set its default aggregation method (like *Sum*, *Count*, or *Average*): this is helpful when you want to fine-tune the behavior of some columns before using them in your visuals.

We made it! We have gone through the four fundamental steps required to build a dashboard in Power BI and used this as an opportunity to have a short tour of the main functionalities of the software.

Let's summarize what we have just seen: everything started with loading some raw data into Power BI, by selecting and configuring the right connectors available in the **Get Data** window. Leveraging the rich set of functionalities of **Power Query Editor**, we took our raw data to the next level and applied an ordered series of transformation steps, which brought us to a number of tables with the right shape and format (which can be previewed at any point using the spreadsheet-like **Data view**). At this point, we used the **Model view** to connect all these tables together, defining the relationships across matching columns and building a single data model. Finally, we opened the **Report view**, where we found all the ingredients (tables and visuals) to build our dashboard. It's time to see this process in action as we build a full Power BI dashboard from scratch in the following tutorial.

Tutorial: Sales Dashboard

This tutorial will take us back to a familiar business, which we have by now grown fond of: the UK-based online retailer selling all-occasions gifts. Automating the weekly Excel reports using KNIME (something we did back in *Chapter 3, Transforming Data*) has granted us quite a reputation that is now pulling us back into the spotlight. As the business keeps growing, the hunger to make descriptive analytics available to a greater number of employees expands. Updating some Excel reports that answer a static list of given questions is not sufficient anymore. We would like to offer the opportunity to deep-dive into quarter-by-quarter and country- and product-level details so that our colleagues can "explore" data by themselves and find interesting insights.

With the help of the financial analyst (who is still full of gratitude for us) and after interviewing a few managers about their most recurrent needs, we are ready to synthesize the requirements expected by each group of users as follows:

- All managers should be able to see at a glance the relative weight of categories and subcategories out of total revenues and see the evolution of sales over time within each product group

- Marketing managers should be able to look at domestic (generated in UK) and international sales separately, having the opportunity to deep-dive by country and category and plan for country-specific digital marketing campaigns accordingly

- Category managers should be given the opportunity to deep-dive by category and spot the articles generating the most sales for each quarter and country

The data follows the same model we encountered in *Figure 3.10* and is made available to us in three separate files: SalesDashboard-CustomerMD.csv and SalesDashboard-ProductMD.csv include, respectively, the customer and the product master data tables, while SalesDashboard-Transactions.xlsx contains the latest transactions (this time, all included in one single file).

It's time to get Power BI Desktop up and running on our computer and start with the first phase of any dashboard creation: loading the required data:

1. As a first step, we load the Customer Master Data stored in a text, comma-separated value file. To do so, click on the **Get Data** icon, available on the **Home** ribbon tab, then select **Text/CSV** as a source type, and click on **Connect**. You will be prompted with a dialog from which you can choose the file to use as a source, in our case, SalesDashboard-CustomerMD.csv. At this point, you will see a preview of the table recorded in the file (*Figure 6.13*). Power BI has correctly recognized its format: there are two columns, with the header shown on top in bold. This is looking good, and there is no need to change any setting (you can see, for example, that the comma is rightly used as a column delimiter), so we can click on **Load** to complete the step:

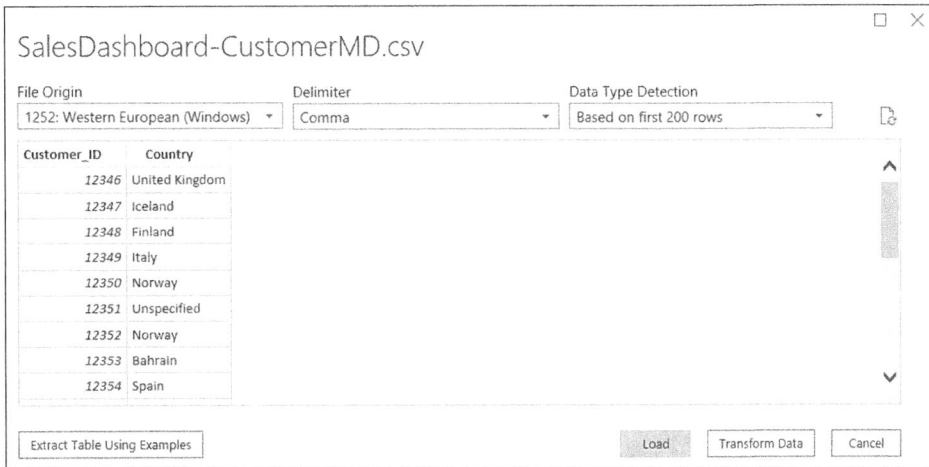

Figure 6.13: Preview of the Customer Master Data source.
You can revise the import settings from the menus in the window

2. We can repeat the same procedure (**Get Data** and then **Text/CSV**) to load the Product Master Data table. This time, the preview window (*Figure 6.14*) shows that the column names have not been recognized correctly and have been assigned instead with some default identifiers (*Column1*, *Column2*, and so on). This triggers the need for some minor transformation before using this table in our data model. Hence, this time we click on the second button at the bottom, **Transform Data**:

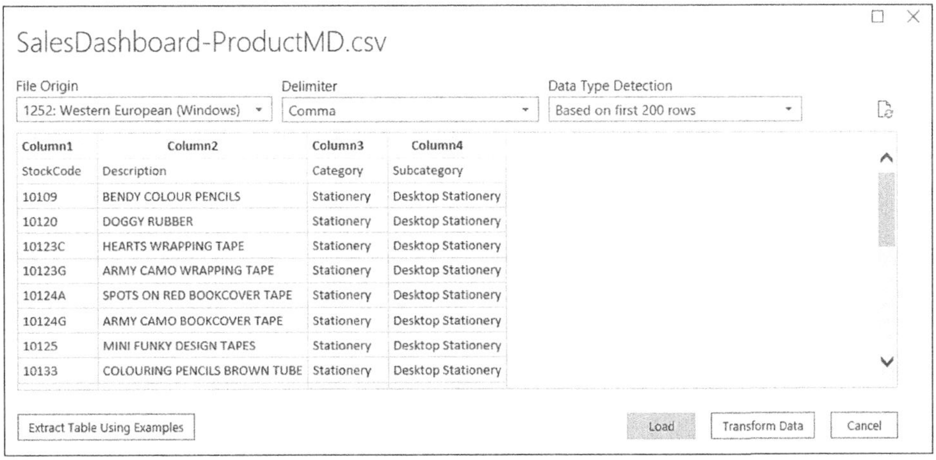

Figure 6.14: Preview of the Product Master Data table: column headers were not recognized

3. By clicking on **Transform Data**, we ask Power BI to add some transformation steps to the query that injects the Product Master Data table: this is a job for **Power Query Editor**, whose window will now appear. In this specific case, the only necessary change is to promote the first row read in the CSV file to be used as headers of the table. To do so, click on the **Use First Row as Headers** button, which you can find on the **Home** ribbon menu (see the arrow in *Figure 6.15* as a guide). Once done, the list of the **Applied Steps** on the right is enriched with a **Promoted Headers** step: this means that every time new data gets loaded, Power BI will execute this step as part of the query. We can click on the **Close & Apply** icon on the top left and move on:

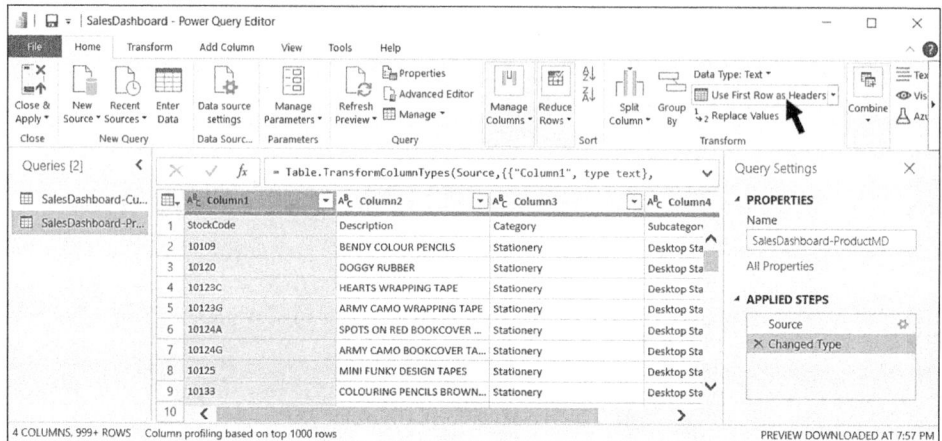

Figure 6.15: Power Query Editor for the Product Master Data table.
We need to use the first row as headers

4. The table containing the transactions is stored in an Excel file. To load it, you can either click on the usual **Get Data** and then select **Excel** or click straight away on the **Excel** icon appearing in the **Home** ribbon menu. You will be presented with a dialog that lets you preview the tables contained in the various worksheets of the Excel file (*Figure 6.16*):

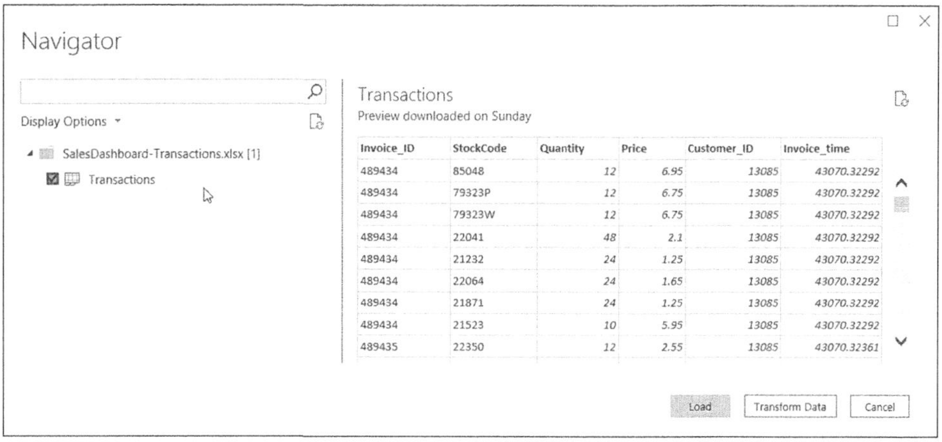

Figure 6.16: Excel preview dialog: select the tables you want to import from the Excel file

Also, in this case, we need to add some transformations to the query, so tick the Transactions box on the left and then click on **Transform Data**, which will open **Power Query Editor**.

As we look at the preview of the Transactions table, we notice that at least two transformations are required to make it usable. Firstly, the *Invoice_time* column does not look right, as it has not been recognized as a Date & Time field. Secondly, since most of our business needs require the analysis of revenues and we only have unit *Price* and *Quantity* for each transaction, we need to implement a simple mathematical formula to obtain the revenues by multiplying the two columns. Let's see how **Power Query Editor** can help us with both.

5. If you look at the headers of the spreadsheet view, you will notice that beside every column title, on the left, you can find an icon representing its data type. For example, the **ABC** icon near *StockCode* tells us that it is a text string, while the **1.2** near *Price* indicates it is a decimal number. If you click on any of these icons, you will see a pop-up menu (*Figure 6.17*) from where you can force a different data type. Power BI will attempt the conversion to the type you wish. Let's do this with the *Invoice_time* column: click on its type icon on the left and select **Date/Time** (if prompted with a window asking whether to replace the current query step or add a new one, select the first option). You will notice that the spreadsheet view now shows dates and times, which is exactly what we wanted:

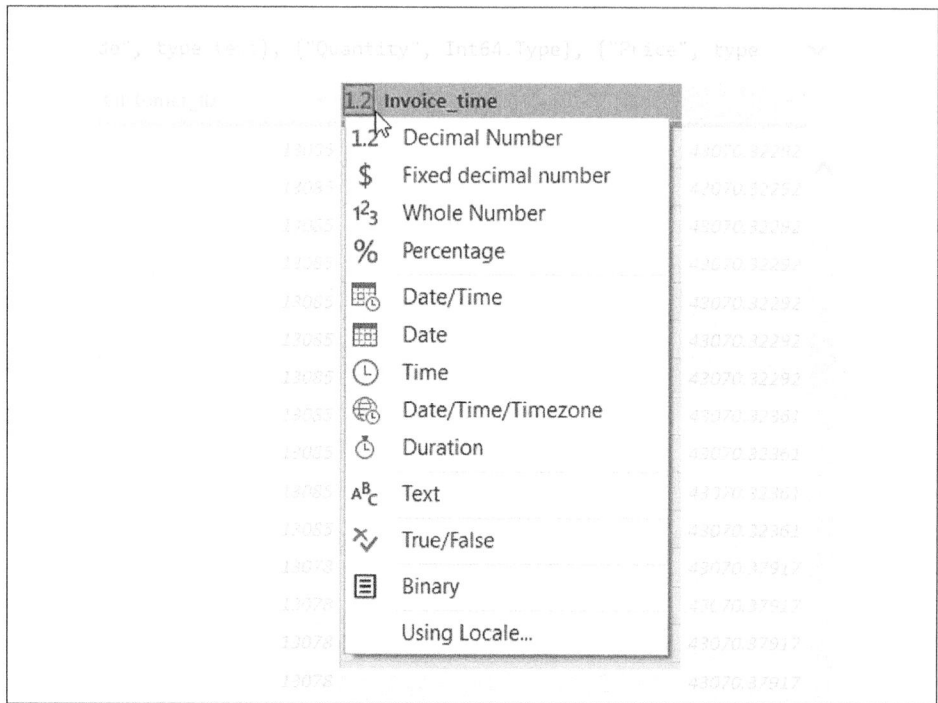

Figure 6.17: Column type selection from Power Query Editor:
convert columns by making the right selection

6. The next step is to add a new column that hosts the revenues generated by each transaction. To do so, go to the **Add Column** ribbon menu and then click on the **Custom Column** icon. You will obtain the window shown in *Figure 6.18* from where you can define your expression, similar to what we did using the **Math Formula** node in KNIME. The available columns are displayed on the right: double-click on *Quantity* to make it appear in the **Custom column formula** box, then just type * with your keyboard, and – finally – double-click on the *Price* column on the right. By doing so, you will obtain the expression [Quantity]*[Price], which is what we needed to calculate value sales. You can now specify its header by typing Sales in the **New column name** box on the top, then click on the **OK** button:

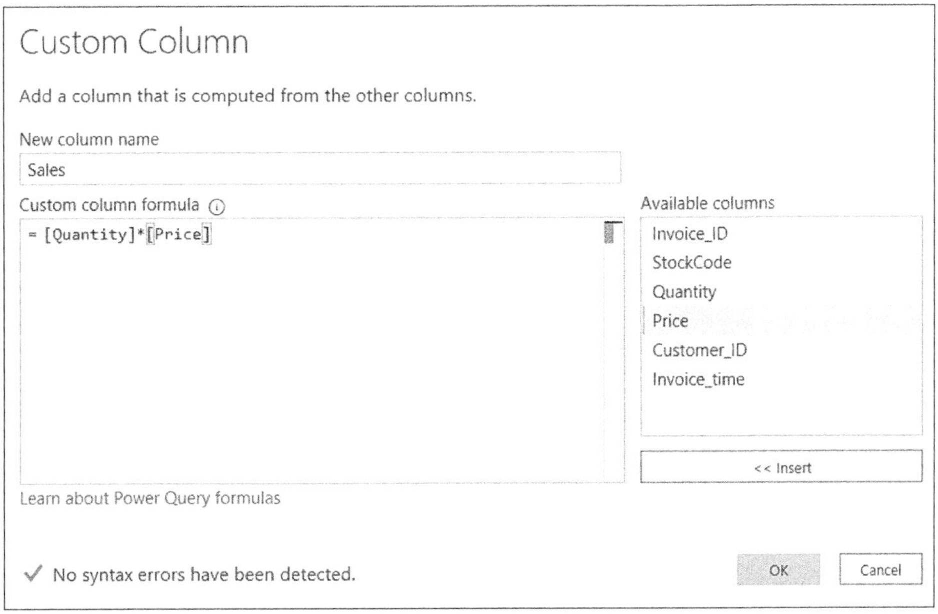

Custom Column

Add a column that is computed from the other columns.

New column name

Sales

Custom column formula ⓘ

= [Quantity]*[Price]

Available columns

Invoice_ID
StockCode
Quantity
Price
Customer_ID
Invoice_time

<< Insert

Learn about Power Query formulas

✓ No syntax errors have been detected.

OK   Cancel

Figure 6.18: Add a custom column in Power BI: define your math formula using columns as variables

You will notice with pride that the newly calculated column *Sales* appears on the right of the spreadsheet view. However, its data type is still undefined, as you will find displayed on the left of the title an ambiguous **ABC123** icon. You can quickly fix this by clicking on the icon and selecting **Decimal Number**.

> Always declare the data types of your columns. By doing so, columns can be used as optimally as possible in your dashboard visualizations, and, also, they will get appropriately aggregated. Numeric columns are, by default, aggregated in Power BI by summing values across, but you can change the aggregation function for each column at any time. To do so, go to the **Data** view (see *Figure 6.2* to find it), select a column, and use the **Summarization** drop-down menu you find in the **Column tools** ribbon menu (for numeric columns, you can go for **Sum**, **Average**, **Minimum**, **Maximum**, **Count**, and **Distinct Count**).

Once you have completed this step, you will see that with the help of Power Query Editor, you created a table with seven columns, as displayed in *Figure 6.19*. In the **Applied Steps** panel on the right, you find a sorted list of all the transformations that need to happen (like sourcing the data stored in Excel, adding columns, changing their types, and so on) to produce the table you want to use within your dashboard. You can click on each step to "*go back*" to that phase of your transformation routine. You can also remove any step (click on the **X** icon on the left that appears when you select the specific step) or edit it: for instance, you can change the definition of the custom formula we added by clicking on the cog icon on the right of the step called **Added Custom**:

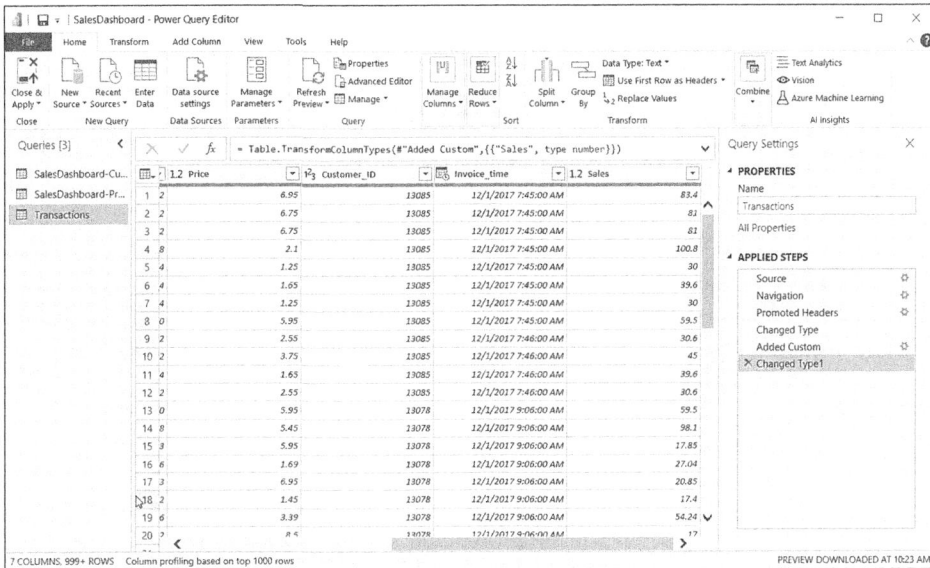

Figure 6.19: The full query definition for your Transactions table: Power Query Editor is your ally for repeatable data transformations in Power BI

Although most of the transformations are typically defined when adding new data sources, you can edit your queries later by reopening the Power Query Editor view (click on the **Transform Data** icon from the **Home** ribbon menu).

To proceed further, click on the **Close & Apply** icon in the top left, and we are ready to go to the next phase of our dashboard creation process: the definition of the data model.

7. If you go to the **Model** view (click on the third icon in the bar to the left of your Power BI main window), you will find a familiar picture: the ER model of the database made of our three tables (go back a few pages and check *Figure 6.8* to see a screenshot of the data **Model** view). Power BI has automatically recognized the relationships across the tables and built the connections without our intervention. Of course, in this case, it was rather simple since the matching columns had precisely the same name and type. In any case, we can manually declare or edit any relationship across tables by using the **Model** view. We can "drag and drop" one column in a table to another column on a different table to create a new relationship. To edit an existing connection, you can double-click on the line linking two tables. Click on the relationship between ProductMD and Transactions: you will obtain the **Edit relationship** view displayed in *Figure 6.20*. The drop-down menus let you select the two tables to be connected, while you can specify the matching columns by clicking on the preview tables displayed in the middle. In our case, we notice that the *StockCode* column is highlighted in both tables, which is what we wanted. The **Cardinality** drop-down menus at the bottom left let you select the type of relationship (**Many to one**, **One to one**, **One to many**, or **Many to many**): by doing so, you are telling Power BI how many rows in the first table should match with how many rows in the second table. In this case, we go for **Many to one** since multiple transactions (first table) can correspond to the same product, and so to one single row in the Product Master Data table (the second table). You can keep the **Cross filter direction** drop-down menu to its default value (**Single**, which is recommended, for performance reasons, in the large majority of cases). We did not have to make any changes as all the default options worked well in this case: click on **OK** and move on:

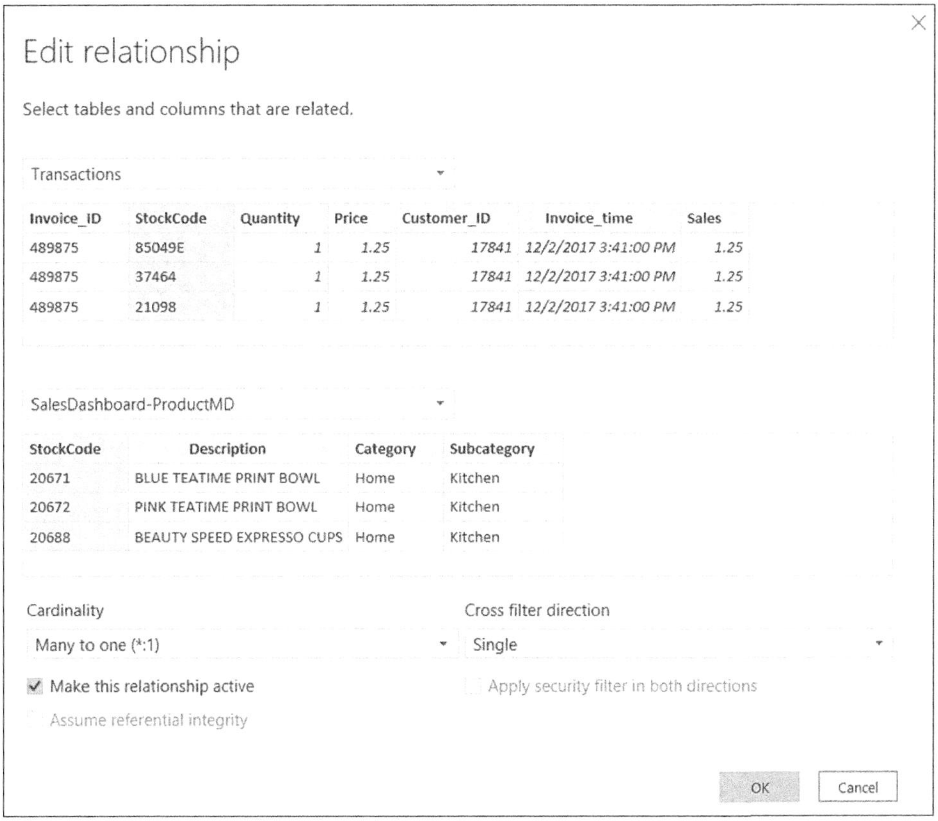

Edit relationship

Select tables and columns that are related.

Transactions ▾

Invoice_ID	StockCode	Quantity	Price	Customer_ID	Invoice_time	Sales
489875	85049E	1	1.25	17841	12/2/2017 3:41:00 PM	1.25
489875	37464	1	1.25	17841	12/2/2017 3:41:00 PM	1.25
489875	21098	1	1.25	17841	12/2/2017 3:41:00 PM	1.25

SalesDashboard-ProductMD ▾

StockCode	Description	Category	Subcategory
20671	BLUE TEATIME PRINT BOWL	Home	Kitchen
20672	PINK TEATIME PRINT BOWL	Home	Kitchen
20688	BEAUTY SPEED EXPRESSO CUPS	Home	Kitchen

Cardinality	Cross filter direction
Many to one (*:1) ▾	Single ▾

☑ Make this relationship active   ☐ Apply security filter in both directions

Assume referential integrity

OK   Cancel

Figure 6.20: Manage a relationship across tables in a data model: which columns should be matching?

In Power BI, the active relationship between two tables can only be defined through one pair of matching columns. If you want to match multiple columns across two tables, you need to go through this simple workaround: go to **Power Query Editor** (click on the usual **Transform Data** icon), select the two or multiple columns you want to use collectively as a single key, and click on **Merge Columns** from the **Transform** menu. Do this on the other table as well, and you will then be able to create a relationship across the merged columns.

8. Check the other relationship between Transactions and the Customer Master Data table by double-clicking on the line linking the two tables. Make sure that the matching columns are *Customer_ID*, that **Cardinality** is **Many to one**, and that **Cross filter direction** is **Single**. Then click on **OK,** and your data model is ready to go!

At this point, we are ready to move to the last and, for some, most exciting part: designing your dashboard by building its visuals one by one. One mistake many people tend to make the first time they create any data dashboard is to jump into crafting colorful charts without having a reasonably clear idea of what they are after. My advice is to always take some time to take a step back, think about the specific business needs you have, and put together a simple *sketch* of what the dashboard should look like. Think about your end users' questions and how to effectively guide them through the answers they are looking for. If you have the opportunity, show your sketch (or a digital *mock-up* built with any software you feel comfortable with) to some of the end users to get their first reaction. You will find that the time you invest early on in planning for your dashboard (no need for details at this stage, just a high-level view of its content will suffice) always pays its dividends as you avoid some expensive (and frustrating) rework later.

When you work on large descriptive analytics initiatives (like building from scratch the business intelligence application layer of a company), the planning phase becomes even more crucial. The advice, in this case, is to keep an *agile* mindset and work in small (but always well-planned) iterations where you add functionalities progressively at every step. In this case, the other advice is to make sure you engage your business partners (representing the end users of the dashboard) early on and *co-design* the capability together with them instead of presenting the end product when it is done.

In the case of our sales dashboard, we will need to pull together an overview page that will have to contain sales split by category and subcategory. A bar chart and a treemap can give a good indication of the relative size of each product element (don't worry about the visualization types at this point; we will learn how to pick the best ones in the next chapter). A line chart will be useful to show evolution over time, and it will be nice to visualize the distribution of sales on the world map to hint at any regional patterns. Lastly, our users will need to be able to select specific year ranges and whether to see the domestic sales only (generated in the UK), or the international ones, or both: some slicers will have to be added to give a simple way to filter the data of interest. By keeping the end users' needs in mind, we put together the sketch design that you see in *Figure 6.21*: we are, by choice, far from perfection at this stage, but at least we can confidently move on to build visuals knowing what we are aiming for:

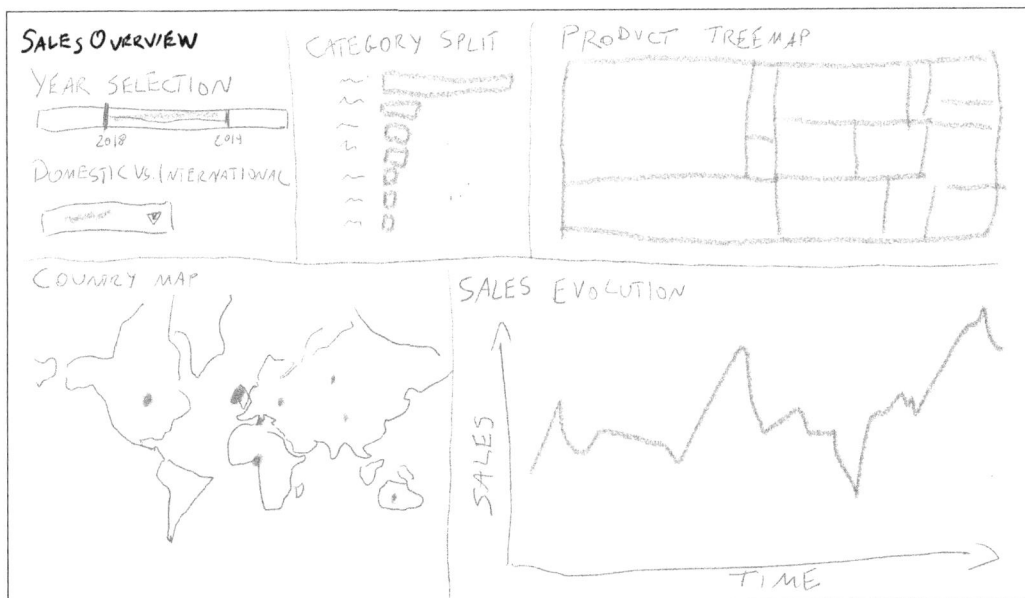

Figure 6.21: A rough sketch of the Sales Overview dashboard page: it's better to decide what data you need to visualize to meet your business needs before creating any chart

9. Go to the **Report** view (first icon on the vertical bar at the left of the main window). In the **Visualization** panel on the right (the ones with all the icons showing the different chart types), click on the icon with the horizontal bar chart (its tooltip label, obtained when you leave the mouse for a second, reads **Stacked Bar Chart**). An empty box pops us on the report page: this is a placeholder for our bar chart. We now need to tell Power BI what data we want this bar chart to show. As shown by the arrows in *Figure 6.22*, we need to drag the columns available in the data model (listed in the **Fields** panel on the right) and drop them to the properties panel of the visualization. More specifically, the column *Category* (open the Product Master Data group to find it) should end up in the **Axis** box on the properties panel, while *Sales* (in the Transactions table) should be dropped to the **Values** box. As soon as you do that, the bar will magically appear on the left, and your first Power BI visual is alive! We could change the *look and feel* of the newly created visual (changing colors, titles, fonts, labels, and so on) by using the **Format** panel (with the paint roller icon), but, for now, we focus on building the rest of the dashboard, and we move on to the following chart:

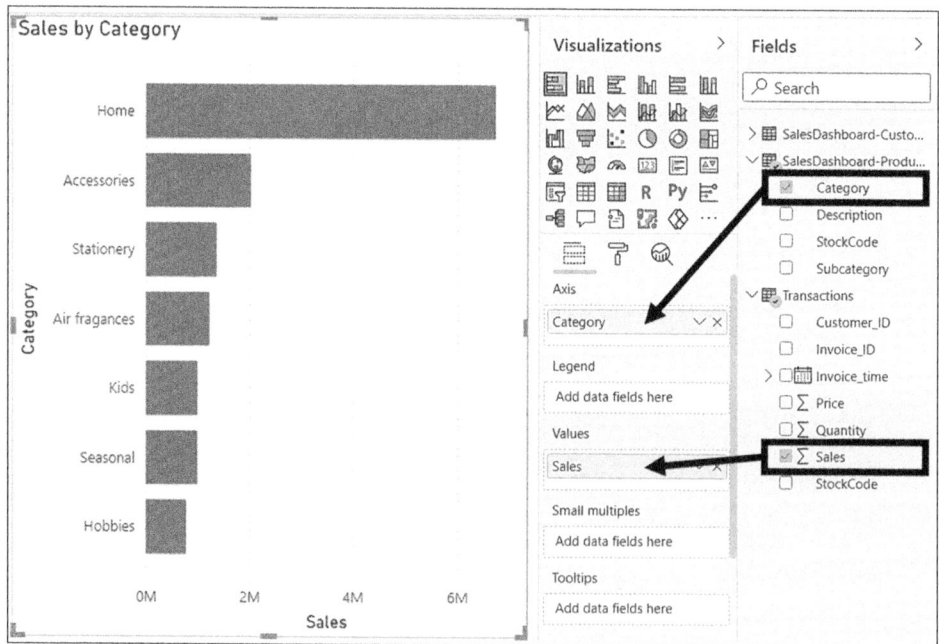

Figure 6.22: Building a bar chart in Power BI: pick the columns to be used for the axis categories and the height of the bars

10. As we follow through with our sketch, we add now a treemap: this will show the relative size of each category/subcategory combination in terms of sales. Click on an empty space in the report page and then on the **Treemap** visualization icon. To build the visual, drag and drop the fields of interest to the right property boxes (*Figure 6.23*): *Category* should go to **Group**, *Subcategory* to **Details**, and *Sales* to **Values**. By now, you should have the essence of building charts in Power BI: we decide what type of visual we need, and then we connect the data columns with the different property fields available for that type of chart:

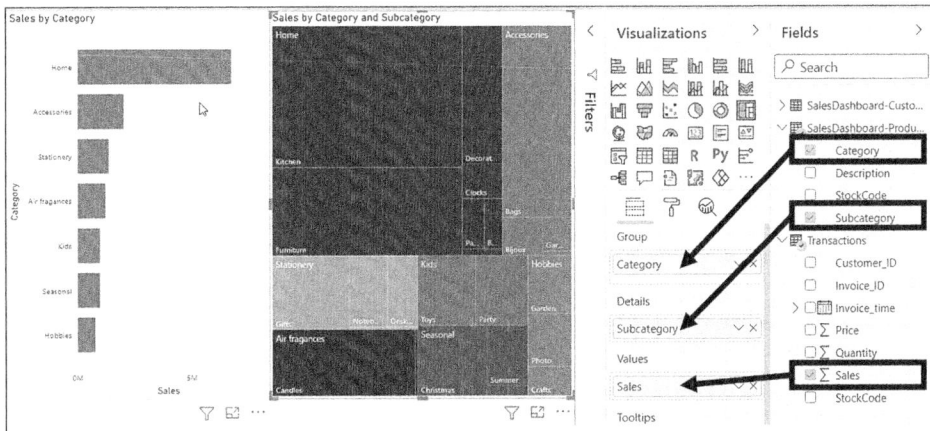

Figure 6.23: Treemap visualization: show the relative size of each group and subgroup

> You will notice that every chart has got some gray handles at its edges and corners. Use them to resize it and move the chart as needed to fit it to the position you like. Considering the sketch in mind, start putting the visuals in the place where they belong.

11. The next visual to add is a line chart that shows the sales evolution over time. Click on an empty space in the report space and then on the **Line chart** icon. You can use *Invoice_time* as the column to control the chart **Axis** while *Sales* will determine the **Values** to be visualized. Power BI uses by default only the top level of the time hierarchy: this means that, at first, the visual will show the aggregate sales by year, displaying only three values, one for each year in the 2017-2019 range. Since we would like to show the evolution by month, we need to expand to the levels below in the hierarchy by clicking on the bifurcation arrow on the top right of the visual (follow *Figure 6.24* as a guide). The next level shows the split by year/quarters, but this is not enough as we want to move to years/months, so you will need to click on the icon once again: at this point, the title of the chart will become **Sales by Year, Quarter and Month**, indicating that we obtained what we were after:

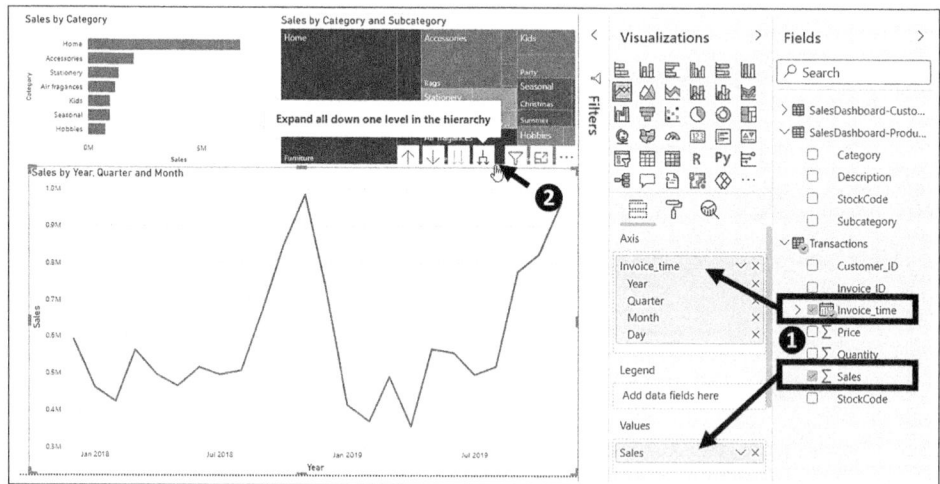

Figure 6.24: Building a line chart to show the evolution over time: you can click on the arrow icons at the top right of the chart to navigate through your year/quarter/month/day hierarchy as needed

12. The next chart in our Sales Overview page is the world map, showing sales by country. The good news is that Power BI automatically recognizes geographical names in tables, making it very simple to create map charts. Click on an empty space in the report and then on the **Map** visualization (the icon looks like a globe; don't get confused with **Filled map,** which shows a sketched map of the United States instead). As done in *Figure 6.25*, drag the column *Country* (in the Customer Master Data table) to the **Location** box and then use *Sales* to control the **Size** of the bubbles. You now have a world map showing where revenues originate from: not surprisingly, the biggest bubble is in the United Kingdom, given the prevalence of domestic customers:

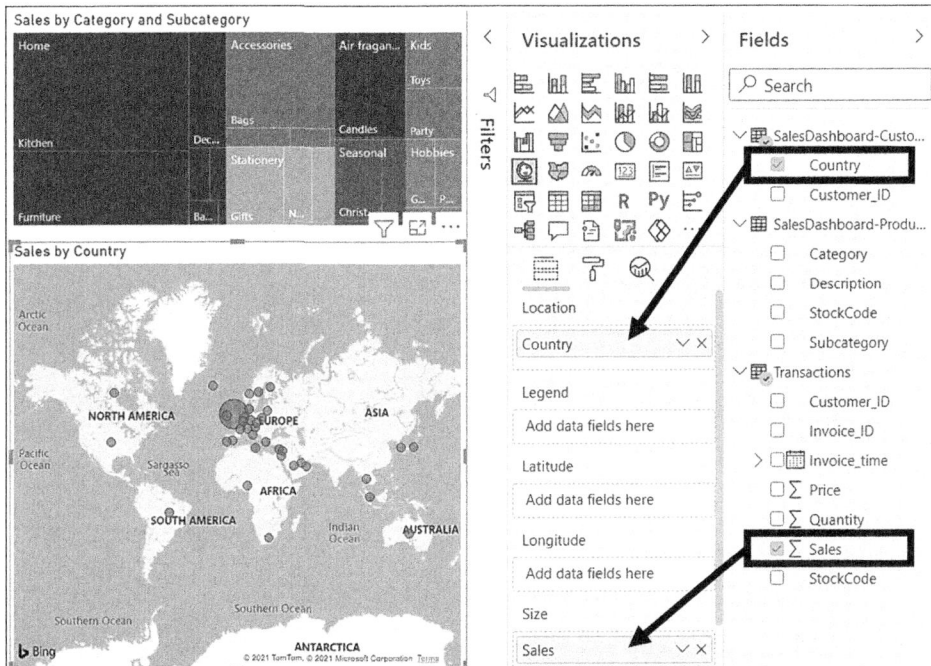

Figure 6.25: A map chart in its full glory: Power BI recognizes locations like countries, states, and city names, making it simple to build maps enriched with data

> In the map visualization (as in any other chart in Power BI), when you keep the mouse on a visual element (in this case, a bubble on the map), you get a tooltip label that gives you, by default, the precise value referring to that specific element (like the total sales originated in a particular country). Many chart types allow you to control what to show in a tooltip by adding fields to the **Tooltips** box.

13. It is time to add a couple of slicers to let the user select what to visualize on the page. The first one will control the time dimension: we want to let the users limit all the visuals on our Sales Overview page to a specific time frame so that they can assess sales by category, subcategory, or country in a given time period. To do so, it will be enough to add a **Slicer** visualization and drag the *Invoice_time* column to the **Field** box, as shown in *Figure 6.26*. Slicers are very popular in Power BI: you can add as many as you need and mix multiple fields into one single slicer to allow multi-level selection. For instance, we could combine *Category* and *Subcategory* together so that users could navigate the entire product hierarchy as they decide what to focus on:

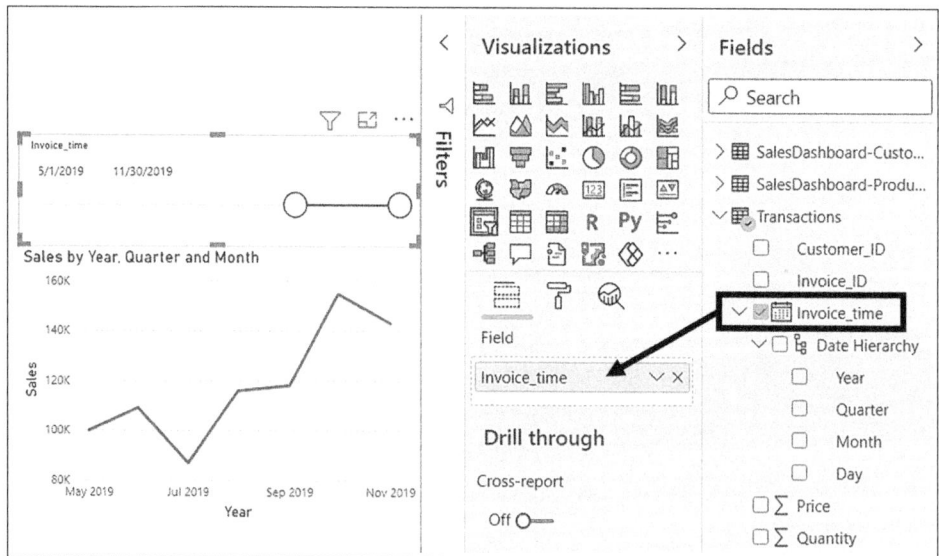

Figure 6.26: Slicers in Power BI: visually filter your data so you can focus on what matters most.

14. According to our sketch, our second slicer should discriminate between domestic and international sales. Since we do not have a column that specifies which group a customer belongs to, we need to add a new column that fulfills the need. Power BI provides for **Conditional Columns**: these are calculated columns that apply a given list of logical rules (like a set of *if-then* clauses) to determine the value for each row. You will notice that this is similar to what we used to do with the **Rule Engine** node in KNIME. To add conditional columns in Power BI, we need to go back to the Power Query Editor window by clicking on the **Transform Data** icon on the **Home** ribbon menu. After selecting the Customer Master Data query from the list on the left, we can add our column by going to the **Add Column** ribbon and clicking on **Conditional Column**. You will be prompted with a window like the one shown in *Figure 6.27*: after choosing the name of the new column using the textbox on top, you can define one or more *if-then* clauses, leveraging operators such as *equals*, *is greater than*, *includes*, and so on. You can append alternative conditions by clicking on the **Add Clause** button and also specify the default value to use if none of the conditions is met (the **Else** box, at the bottom). In our case, we just want the new column (which we can call *Type*) to show Domestic if *Country* is United Kingdom and International in any other case:

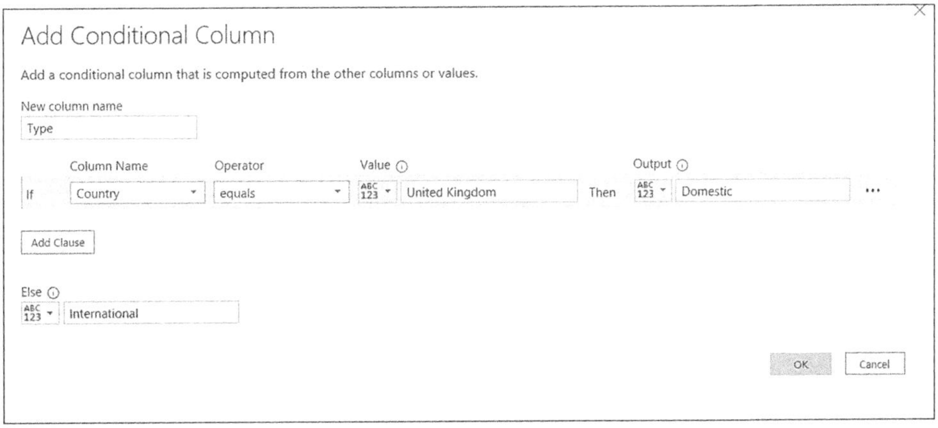

Figure 6.27: Adding a conditional column: define a set of logic clauses to control the column's values

15. Now that we have the new column *Type* available, we can add a new slicer following precisely the same procedure we saw for the time slicer and dropping the new conditional column in the **Field** box.

16. Let's equip our page with a title by going to the **Insert** ribbon menu and clicking on the **Text box** icon. We can write any text we like (in this case, we enter the page title, which is Sales Overview) and play with the font size and type to make it look good. By dragging all visuals around and rearranging them according to our original sketch, we obtain the page shown in *Figure 6.28*:

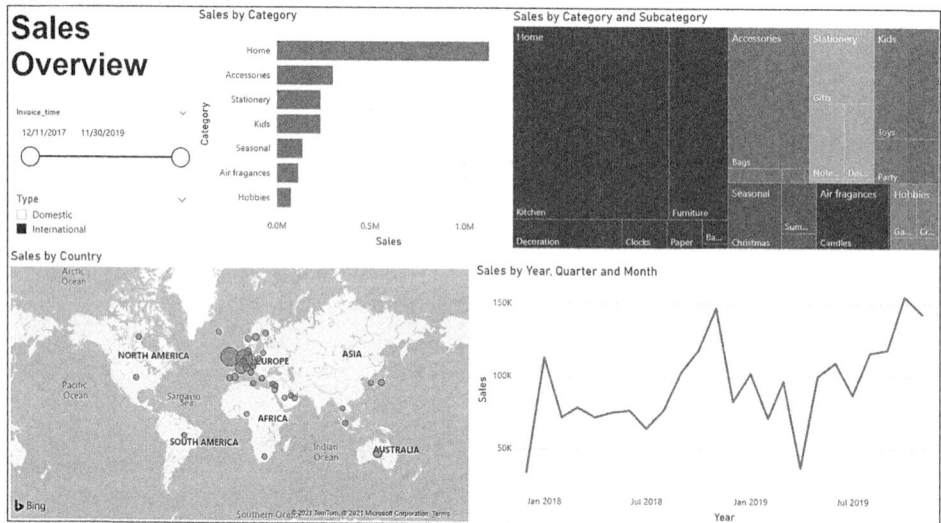

Figure 6.28: Sales Overview page: not bad at all for being our first Power BI creation!

This page is already compelling in its simplicity: it includes several visuals showing the key dimensions of interest within our online retail business. The slicers enable the users to filter their analysis within a specific time frame or country scope. Very importantly, these visuals are all connected with each other: the users can interact with a visual element, causing the other visuals to rearrange their scope. For example, try to click on any bar in the first category bar chart: the line chart will show the sales evolution for that specific category, and the world map will rearrange the size of the bubbles considering only the revenues generated within that particular country. If we select a subcategory from the treemap on the top right, the same will happen, and all other visuals will show the details for that subcategory. This is pretty powerful as we are letting the users discover the data autonomously, customize the views as they like, and, in a way, cook their own data exploration experience versus feeding them with a ready-made meal.

> In Power BI, you can select multiple elements at once by keeping the *CTRL* key pressed. Try keeping the *CTRL* key pressed and click on two different categories in the bar chart: the sales of those two categories will be aggregated together in the line chart. You can also use this feature to slice the data across visuals. For example, click on a bubble in the map chart and, while keeping the *CTRL* key pressed, click on a subcategory from the treemap: the line chart will now show the time evolution of sales for that subcategory in the specific country you selected from the world map.

Since the charts interact with each other, we might need to fine-tune and modify their dynamic behavior. For instance, if you click on any category on the bar chart, the treemap will *highlight* your selection, meaning that all other categories will have their color faded. What if, instead, we want the treemap to react differently and, instead of highlighting the category selected in the bar chart, we want it to show only that category and filter out all others? Let's take this challenge as an opportunity to see how to change the interactions behaviors across visuals in Power BI.

17. Go to the **Format** ribbon menu (it appears when you select any chart) and click on the **Edit interactions** icon on the left. Select the visual that *controls* others (we can call it **antecedent**) by clicking on it. In our case, let's click on the bar chart showing sales by category. As we do so, three icons will appear in the top right of the treemap icon (make sure you resize it accordingly to be able to see the three icons popping up). By clicking on these icons (see *Figure 6.29*), you will decide how you want the treemap to respond when a selection on its antecedent occurs: the **Filter** icon will make that visual filter out any other data and "focus" on the selection; the **Highlight** icon (which is the default behavior) will cause the visual to emphasize the selection applied on the antecedent by coloring it differently; the **None** icon will break the connection and make the treemap completely "independent" from any selection on the bar chart. In our case, we click on the **Filter** icon (this is the behavior we are after) and then click again on the **Edit interactions** icon to get back to the normal editing mode:

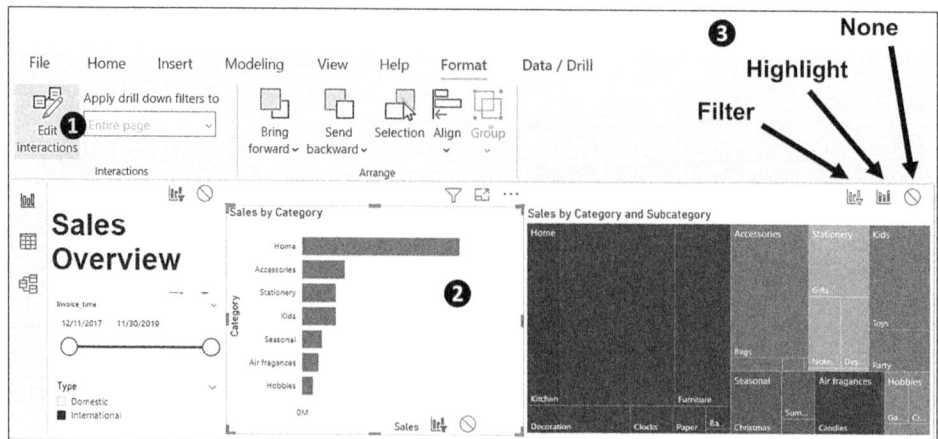

Figure 6.29: Three steps for changing the interaction behaviors across visuals: click on Edit interactions, select the antecedent visual, and then click on the resulting behavior icon (filter, highlight, or do nothing) on all subsequent visuals

> Not all visual types allow the three types of interactions we have seen in this example. For instance, line charts only allow for **Filter** and **None** interactions.

By looking at the original set of requirements, we realize that we would need a few more visuals to complete our endeavor. Both marketing and category managers need to go beyond the existing visual overview and access some more detailed tabular exhibits. We decide to complete our dashboard by adding a page, called Sales Details, equipped with a handful of tables that match our remaining needs.

18. Click on the **+** sign at the bottom of the **Report** view: this will add a blank new page to your dashboard. You can rename every page by right-clicking on its tab and selecting **Rename Page**.

19. Let's add a **Matrix** visualization to the new page (don't get confused with the **Table** visualization, which we will use later). Now, add the following fields to the various boxes: put *Category* first and then, underneath, *Subcategory* in the **Rows** box. After that, drag *Invoice_time* to the **Columns** box, and, finally, put *Sales* as **Values**.

20. At this point, the table shows only the top level of the product and the time hierarchy (like in *Figure 6.30*), as this is its default behavior. To make it useful for our business users, we need to expand those hierarchies by clicking on the bifurcation arrow at the top right of the visual (see step 2 in *Figure 6.30*). Once you have done it for rows, use the **Drill on** drop-down menus to select columns (step 3 in *Figure 6.30*) and click again on the bifurcation arrow (like we did earlier for rows). You have now obtained quite a rich table, showing quarterly sales by category and subcategory:

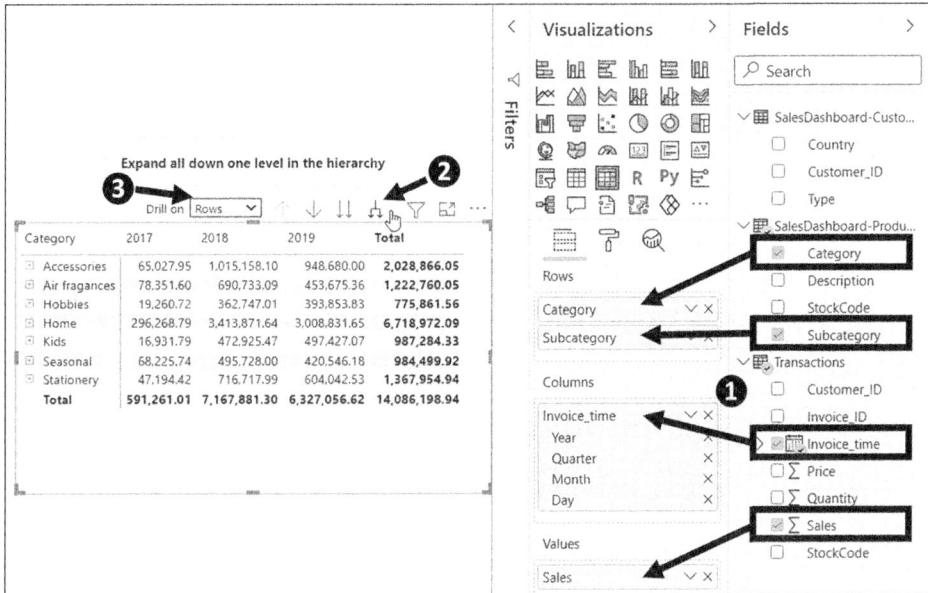

Figure 6.30: Building a matrix visualization: select the fields to use and decide the aggregation levels for both rows and columns

21. To make the matrix chart more accessible, we can fine-tune a couple of settings to remove some unneeded numbers. Go to the **Format** panel (the one having a paint roller icon), scroll down in the list of options, open the **Subtotals** view, and switch off **Column subtotals** as we don't need the yearly sums (see step 1 in *Figure 6.31*). Then scroll down and open the **Field formatting** view: from here, set **Value decimal places** to 0, so we remove all those unneeded decimal values, which only create clutter (step 2 in *Figure 6.31*):

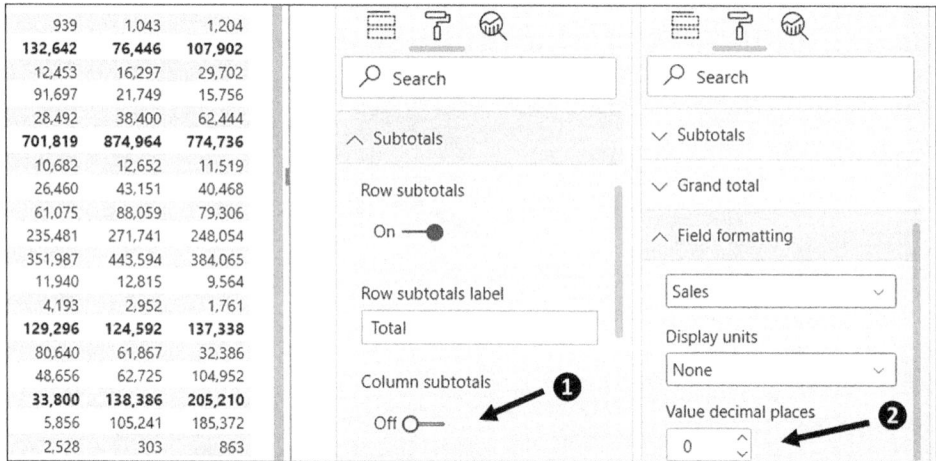

Figure 6.31: Removing the clutter from the matrix visual: deactivate columns subtotals and remove decimal digits

22. Let's add a new visual to give users the ability to focus on domestic or international sales if needs be. This time, add a **Donut chart** and set its fields as follows (we don't need to look at any screenshots as this procedure has hopefully become pretty familiar by now): let's use the column *Type* as **Legend** and *Sales* as **Values**.

23. To complete our detailed view, we shall show aggregated sales by country and by article. Let's start with the country: add a **Table** visual and drag and drop the columns **Country** and **Sales** directly into it (just make sure you follow the specified order, first **Country** and then **Sales**). By clicking on the header of *Sales* in the new table visual, the sales by country are sorted by decreasing revenues, which is what we were looking for.

24. To add the article details, let's implement another **Table** visual and then drag and drop the following columns into it, following this order: *Description*, *Quantity*, and *Sales*. Similarly, as done before, click on the *Sales* header in the table visual to put the best-selling articles at the top of the list. To avoid clutter, remove the decimal digits both here and in the previous table, using the **Field formatting | Value decimal places** selectors, as we did for the matrix view.

25. We should add a title to this page as well. Go to the **Insert** ribbon menu, click on the **Text box** icon and write `Sales Details` into it. For coherence, try to put the same font size and type you used for the first page:

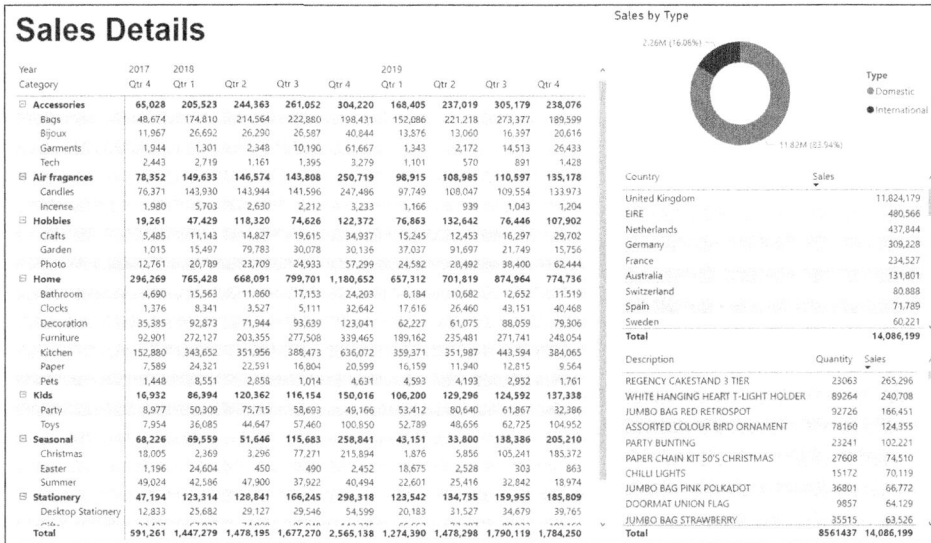

Sales Details

Year	2017	2018				2019			
Category	Qtr 4	Qtr 1	Qtr 2	Qtr 3	Qtr 4	Qtr 1	Qtr 2	Qtr 3	Qtr 4
⊟ Accessories	65,028	205,523	244,363	261,052	304,220	168,405	237,019	305,179	238,076
Bags	48,674	174,810	214,564	222,880	198,431	152,086	221,218	273,377	189,599
Bijoux	11,967	26,652	26,290	26,587	40,844	13,376	13,060	16,397	20,616
Garments	1,944	1,301	2,348	10,190	61,667	1,343	2,172	14,513	26,433
Tech	2,443	2,719	1,161	1,395	3,279	1,101	570	891	1,428
⊟ Air fragances	78,352	149,633	146,574	143,808	250,719	98,915	108,985	110,597	135,178
Candles	76,371	143,930	143,944	141,596	247,496	97,749	108,047	109,554	133,973
Incense	1,980	5,703	2,630	2,212	3,233	1,166	939	1,043	1,204
⊟ Hobbies	19,261	47,429	118,320	74,626	122,372	76,863	132,642	76,446	107,902
Crafts	5,485	11,143	14,827	19,615	34,937	15,245	12,453	16,297	29,702
Garden	1,015	15,497	79,783	30,078	30,136	37,037	91,697	21,749	15,756
Photo	12,761	20,789	23,709	24,933	57,299	24,582	28,492	38,400	62,444
⊟ Home	296,269	765,428	668,091	799,701	1,180,652	657,312	701,819	874,964	774,736
Bathroom	4,690	15,563	11,860	17,153	24,203	8,184	10,682	12,652	11,519
Clocks	1,376	8,341	3,527	5,111	32,642	17,616	26,460	43,151	40,468
Decoration	35,385	92,873	71,944	93,639	123,041	62,227	61,075	88,059	79,306
Furniture	92,901	272,127	203,355	277,508	339,465	189,162	235,481	271,741	248,054
Kitchen	152,880	343,652	351,956	388,473	636,072	359,371	351,987	443,594	384,065
Paper	7,589	24,321	22,591	16,804	20,599	16,159	11,940	12,815	9,564
Pets	1,448	8,551	2,858	1,014	4,631	4,593	4,193	2,952	1,761
⊟ Kids	16,932	86,994	120,362	116,154	150,016	106,200	129,296	124,592	137,338
Party	8,977	50,309	75,715	58,693	49,166	53,412	80,640	61,867	32,386
Toys	7,954	36,085	44,647	57,460	100,850	52,789	48,656	62,725	104,952
⊟ Seasonal	68,226	69,559	51,646	115,683	258,841	43,151	33,800	138,386	205,210
Christmas	18,005	2,369	3,296	77,271	215,894	1,876	5,856	105,241	185,372
Easter	1,196	24,604	450	490	2,452	18,675	2,528	303	863
Summer	49,024	42,586	47,900	37,922	40,494	22,601	25,416	32,842	18,974
⊟ Stationery	47,194	123,314	128,841	166,245	298,318	123,542	134,735	159,955	185,809
Desktop Stationery	12,833	25,682	29,127	29,546	54,599	20,183	31,527	34,679	39,765
Total	**591,261**	**1,447,279**	**1,478,195**	**1,677,270**	**2,565,138**	**1,274,390**	**1,478,298**	**1,790,119**	**1,784,250**

Sales by Type

2.26M (16.06%)

11.82M (83.94%)

Type
● Domestic
● International

Country	Sales
United Kingdom	11,824,179
EIRE	480,566
Netherlands	437,844
Germany	309,228
France	234,527
Australia	131,801
Switzerland	80,888
Spain	71,789
Sweden	60,221
Total	**14,086,199**

Description	Quantity	Sales
REGENCY CAKESTAND 3 TIER	23063	265,296
WHITE HANGING HEART T-LIGHT HOLDER	89264	240,708
JUMBO BAG RED RETROSPOT	92726	166,451
ASSORTED COLOUR BIRD ORNAMENT	78160	124,355
PARTY BUNTING	23241	102,221
PAPER CHAIN KIT 50'S CHRISTMAS	27608	74,510
CHILLI LIGHTS	15172	70,119
JUMBO BAG PINK POLKADOT	36801	66,772
DOORMAT UNION FLAG	9857	64,129
JUMBO BAG STRAWBERRY	35515	63,526
Total	**8561437**	**14,086,199**

Figure 6.32: Sales Details page: our Power BI dashboard is now complete with the possibility to get to the granular country and product details

We are finally done: the second page you've just pulled together (see *Figure 6.32*) has nicely provided what we were missing. Users can now dive into subcategory/quarterly/country combinations (it will be enough to click on the headers of the tables to filter down to the combination they need, keeping *CTRL* pressed) and retrieve the top-selling articles within every segmentation of the business.

When you publish your new, shiny, two-page dashboard on the Power BI service (if you have an account, even a free one, go to the **Home** ribbon menu and click on the **Publish** icon to give it a try) and share its URL with your colleagues, you will suddenly become their hero! They can now access the data they need from any browser (see *Figure 6.33*) and autonomously deep-dive to the parts of the business they are most interested in:

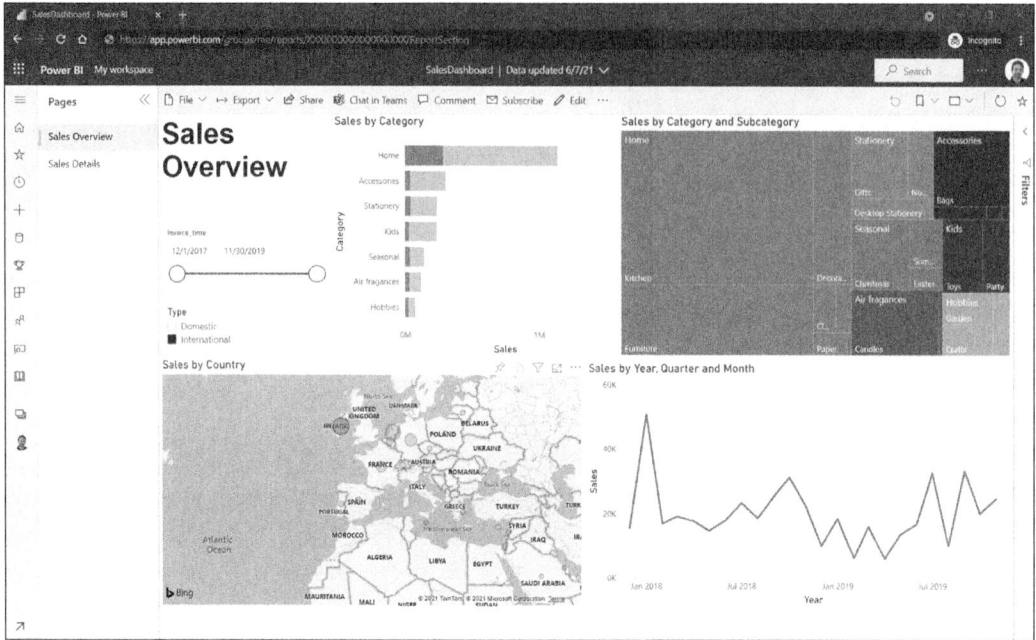

Figure 6.33: Browser view of the Sales Overview page once published on the Power BI service: our dashboard looks great from the cloud

When traveling, our colleagues can even check sales results while *on the go*: you can see in *Figure 6.34* how our dashboard looks in the Power BI app on a smartphone:

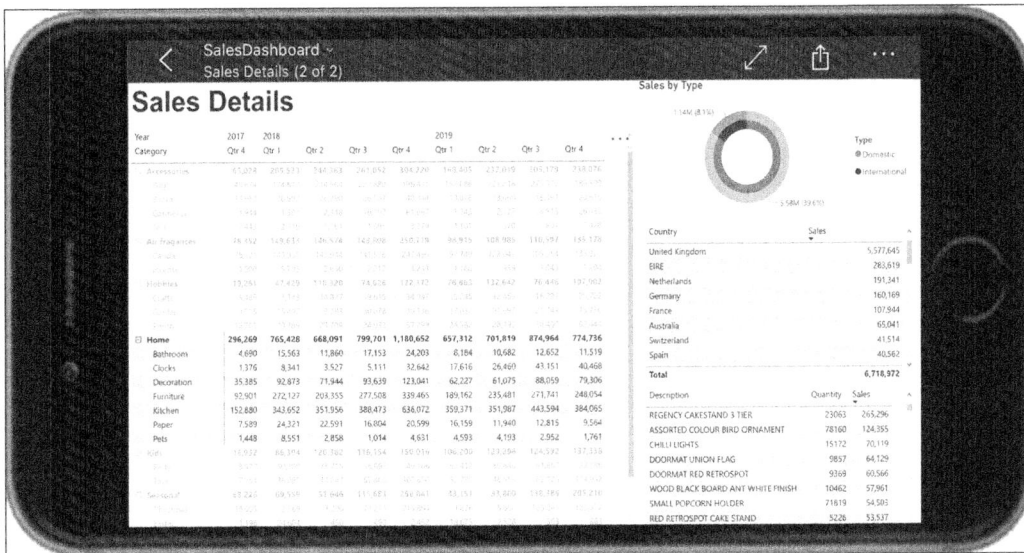

Figure 6.34: The Sales Details page accessed through the Power BI app for iPhone: you can access your data from virtually anywhere

The maintenance of the dashboard is relatively lightweight as the updating of all visuals can now happen even daily without much effort. The various queries we have defined know where to pull the data from and what transformation steps are required. When new data pops up, it will be enough to refresh the dashboard by just clicking on the **Refresh** icon on the **Home** ribbon menu, and the whole dashboard will be nicely up to date.

Not only have you finally democratized access to sales data in the company through a sustainable process that can now be repeated effortlessly, but you have also saved the financial analyst a lot of her precious time. She will not need to answer all the many "ad hoc" questions that she frequently used to receive and that forced her to set up painful manual extractions every time. As the data is now readily available, it is faster and more convenient for people to go and get what they need by themselves, giving back to our financial analyst the precious time she can use for more advanced analytics. It's a real *win-win*, and you should feel very proud of having enabled all this.

Summary

By completing this chapter, you have added another precious instrument to your data analytics practitioners' backpack: Power BI. You have learned how to load data and set up a routine of transformation steps required for cleaning that data and making it useful. You have seen how to define the relationships that connect all tables into a single and coherent data model. You have also seen what it means to build interconnected visuals that allow for human interaction. You have created a dashboard that will enable business users to explore the data they need when they need it, *fishing* for insights and unveiling business opportunities in complete autonomy.

Now, think about the amount of data that lies largely unutilized and inaccessible in company databases (or even in Excel files stored on individuals' laptops). The business opportunities that wait to be unlocked by making this data visually accessible through a simple dashboard are vast and, in many cases, reasonably at hand with tools like Power BI: what you have learned in this chapter can make you a hero to many.

In the next chapter, we will learn about some practical guidelines to sharpen our data visualization skills: the objective is to make the best out of every single chart we produce from now on.

7

Visualizing Data Effectively

A chart is worth a thousand words, goes the old adage. Visual representation is often the preferred way to communicate numbers. As you can surely validate with your own experience, data charts are ubiquitous in business memos and presentations, as well as in newspaper articles and scientific papers. However, moving from data stored in a table to its graphic representation (a process called **data visualization**) is far from being trivial and risk-free. Although many software packages (including Power BI, Excel, KNIME, and so on) provide rapid ways to build charts in a matter of seconds, making effective and professional-looking visuals is far from being easy: it requires structured planning and disciplined execution.

This chapter will give you a set of practical guidelines to ensure that your business messages are communicated clearly through an effective data visualization process. In particular, we will go through the following questions:

- What types of charts are available, and what are their peculiarities?

- Which chart should I use, considering the specific message I want to give?

- How do I ensure that visuals are immediate and less prone to misunderstandings?

- What are the common pitfalls to avoid when visualizing data?

While in the previous chapter we focused on Power BI, in this one, we will acquire techniques that work well with *any* software able to produce visuals: in fact, think of data visualization as a tool-agnostic skill that you need to have in your data analytics practitioner's backpack.

The flow of this chapter goes along the two essential phases of data visualization. The first step is to plan for our chart, considering the specific point we want to make and the chart types best serving our needs. Then, we move to build the chart, which includes finetuning the visual attributes, polishing the various graphical elements, and avoiding common mistakes: this part will be summarized into a practical list of data visualization quality rules to follow. Before getting into the planning step, let's quickly frame the ever-present need for visualizing data.

What is data visualization?

Although the general concept of data visualization is straightforward, let's take some time to set the scene properly. The essential objective of data visualization is to transfer a message made of data to another human being. Being effective at this communication process implies that the receiver comprehends the original data-based message and "makes sense" of it through cognition. *Figure 7.1* shows a graphical representation of a bad attempt of communicating data messages: presenting it all in its original format:

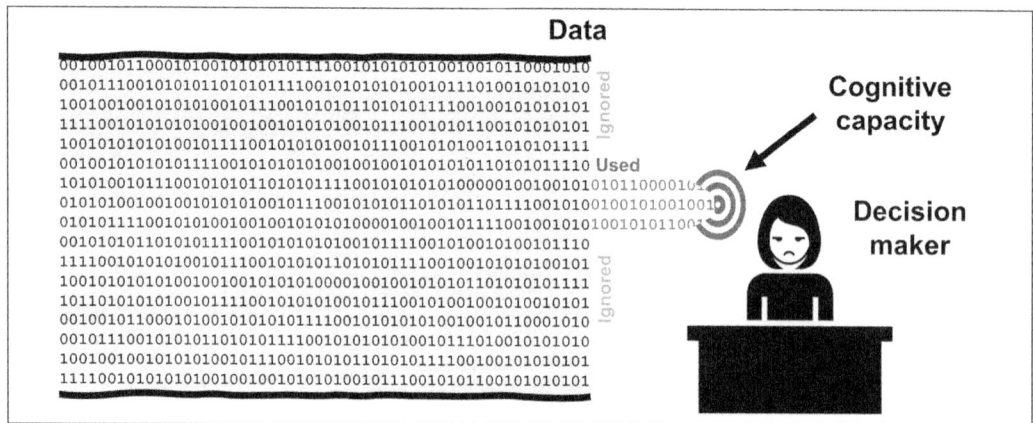

Figure 7.1: Presenting data in its original format: as you can see, the decision-maker is visibly overwhelmed, and the large majority of the data is ignored

The decision-maker here is clearly overwhelmed by such a large amount of raw data being offered. This is understandable: every human being has a limited amount of cognitive capacity, and our brains can only process a certain quantity of information at once. If we try to present too much data altogether, we will cross the cognitive limit of the receiver, who will obtain a partial or distorted version of the original message. As a result, our initial point is either missed or — even worse — misunderstood. The bad news is that whoever we have in front of us, however wise and number savvy they are, will always have a pretty limited amount of information they can make sense of: the rest will be simply ignored.

The other bad news is that if we have several people looking at the same data, their "takeaways" will diverge since their individual sensitivities will make them pay attention to different slices or aspects of the original data. The good news is that we have an established way to communicate data effectively to other human beings: transforming it into an abstract visualization that conveys the key aspects we want to transfer. This is what data visualization is all about.

> Data visualization is powerful because it leverages one of the most developed functionalities of our entire brain: vision. As part of our natural evolution, humans have relied on our eyes to perform life-critical activities such as spotting food supplies and identifying critical threats. Consequently, our brains have consistently finetuned their visual excellence. As David Williams, Professor of Medical Optics at the University of Rochester, noticed, now more than 50 percent of the cortex (the brain's surface) is involved in processing visual information: this is more than all other four senses combined! The brain can quickly interpret images by spotting some critical properties (such as size, color, curvature, position, slope, and so on) that we instinctively notice without using any conscious effort. They are called preattentive attributes, and we exploit them extensively in data visualization.

In *Figure 7.2*, you find the potential usage of data visualization: by encoding data (even a large amount of it, properly filtered and aggregated) into graphical summaries, the cognitive capacity of the decision-maker is utilized at its best, and the received message is unequivocal:

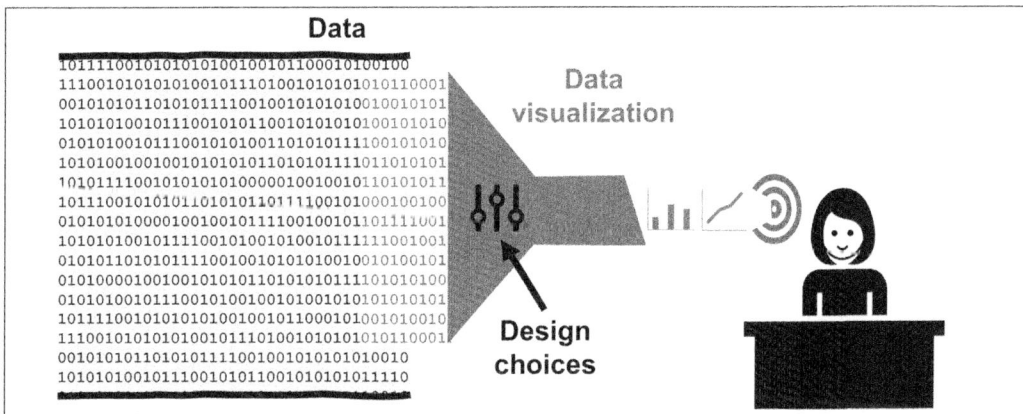

Figure 7.2: Presenting data through visualization: by applying the right design choices, the decision-maker can easily understand your message

As shown in the picture, data visualization is like a customizable funnel that requires some tuning to work properly. In fact, there is no one single way to visualize the same data: by making some design choices (the type of chart, the measures to encode graphically, the visual attributes, and so on), you can "tune" the funnel to make it best fit for reaching your precise communication objective. Your responsibility is to get this tuning right. It's important to notice that these design choices are not driven by mere aesthetic needs. Every visual pattern in a chart has a meaning and gets interpreted by our brain, which instinctively recognizes in it some visual clues (preattentive attributes). Every graphical element uses part of the cognitive capacity, so we will not use any visual clue unless it has a meaning in the context of our communication objective. As we will learn in depth later, the mantra in data visualization is *less is more*, and *minimalism* is undoubtedly the way to go.

Although the analogy with the funnel is a coarse simplification of reality (data visualization is more than just "compressing" data), it depicts well the mindset I would recommend you keep when visualizing data. Remember this: to convert data into immediate, impactful, and unambiguous visuals, you will have to make the right *design* choices. You need to act as a designer would do. In this chapter, you will impersonate the "operator" of the funnel in the picture, the visual designer who decides how to represent the data depending on the specific message to be transferred. You will learn how to make the right design choices for your charts consistently.

Now that the scene is set and your role as a visual designer is unveiled, let's move to the planning phase, during which we will make some critical design choices.

A chart type for every message

The ultimate ambition that should lie behind every chart is to carry a precise data-based message. Unsurprisingly, the very first thing we have to do when planning for a chart is to decide which specific message we want to give. You can think of this message as the answer to a certain business question, such as *is brand X growing its market share consistently?* or *how do revenues relate with the price of the service?*. Although business questions can be pretty ambiguous and multifaceted, in most cases, they fall within one of the following three types:

- **Evolution**: These questions deal with the development of quantities over time. If your business question contains words like *grow, decline, increase, decrease, accelerate, decelerate, fall behind, lag, overtake*, or *trend*, it will likely fall within the **Evolution** type. This is one of the most popular types of queries that data charts answer as the need to understand how business performance indicators are evolving is omnipresent.

- **Size**: These questions enquire on the relative proportion of components to a whole (also called **Part-to-Whole**) or the ranking across comparable quantities. The typical words you can find within this type are *drivers*, *drainers*, *high*, *low*, *top*, *bottom*, *biggest*, *smallest*, and — in general — all superlative adjectives ending in *-est*. Every time we are after a benchmark, ranking, comparison, or a drill-down into components, we ask ourselves size-related business questions.

- **Relation**: This type of question investigates mutual relationships across different measures. When we use words such as *relate* or *grow/decline together*, and, in general, when we inquire how one quantity changes *with respect to another quantity*, we fall within this bucket.

Table 7.1 provides a list of sample business questions included within each group. After going through it, think about some questions you have lately been involved with at work: chances are that you will find examples within each of the three buckets.

Type of message	Sample business question
Evolution	Are sales increasing or decreasing, and how quickly?
	Is there any acceleration or deceleration of the trend?
	Do we see any seasonality in consumption?
Size	What products are driving sales growth?
	Which brands are my biggest competitors?
	Within which product line is my competitor making the most profit?
	What are the most significant opportunities in terms of sales erosion?
Relation	How does profit distribute over increasing size of packages?
	How is the available income spread across the country?
	Is there a relationship between price and profitability across brands?

Table 7.1: A few samples of business questions organized by type of message

Identifying which type of business message you want to give is a necessary initial step for planning your data visualization design. In fact, every type of message (Evolution, Size, or Relation) corresponds to one or more matching chart types, as *Figure 7.3* shows. In the figure, every row indicates a fundamental chart type (**Bar chart**, **Line chart**, **Treemap**, and **Scatterplot**): they come with a set of alternative renderings that you might consider using depending on the specific case:

Chart type	Alternatives	Message type		
		Evolution	Size	Relation
Bar chart	Horizontal or vertical bars, Stacked, Histogram, Waterfall	★	★★	
Line chart 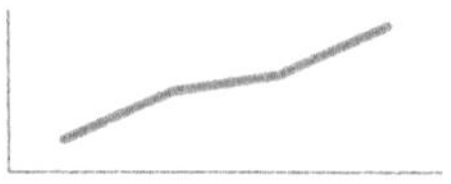	Stacked, with or without markers, Area maps	★★		★
Treemap 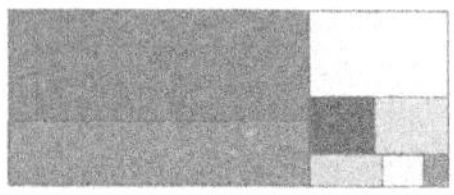	Pie charts, Donut charts		★★	
Scatterplot 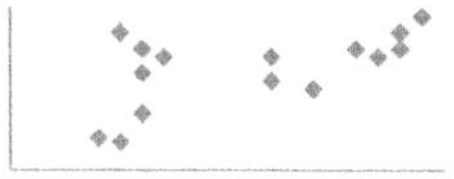	Quadrant charts, Geospatial maps		★	★★

Figure 7.3: Chart selection matrix: every message type has its preferred chart type. Two stars are no-brainer matches, but one-star combinations can work well too

I hope you find the chart selection matrix simple and easy to memorize, as it can be your best friend in deciding quickly what type of chart to use depending on the message you want to give (and, by doing so, responding to the business question you had). You should consider that there are many more chart types available out there, some of them coming with great visual appeal: however, over 90% of the time, you will be able to convey clear messages by just using this minimal list of established chart types. Another advantage of sticking to the marked path is that your business partners naturally recognize these charts and know how to interpret them, making your message—remember what the ultimate objective of data visualization is—crisper and more direct.

Having introduced the four chart types and when to choose them, let's go through each type and how it can be used optimally. For each chart type, you will find a summary description of what it is, some visual examples, and a series of rules (which you will see highlighted in bold) to keep handy when building that kind of chart.

Bar charts

Bar charts (*Figure 7.4*) are possibly the most iconic data chart type on earth. For each category represented on the horizontal axis, you have one or multiple bars whose length is proportional to the quantity you want to visualize. Length is a very immediate preattentive attribute: the brain will naturally appreciate the differences in relative size across each bar. This makes bar charts particularly well fitted to transfer messages related to different sizes across business entities (such as brands, products, or countries), allowing a quick comparison, ranking, and benchmarking (especially when bars are sorted by height, which is normally recommended). Categories can also be time periods, like months, quarters, or years: this is why bar charts are used for driving messages regarding the evolution over time, too (of course, in this case, you should never sort the bars and always keep the natural time order):

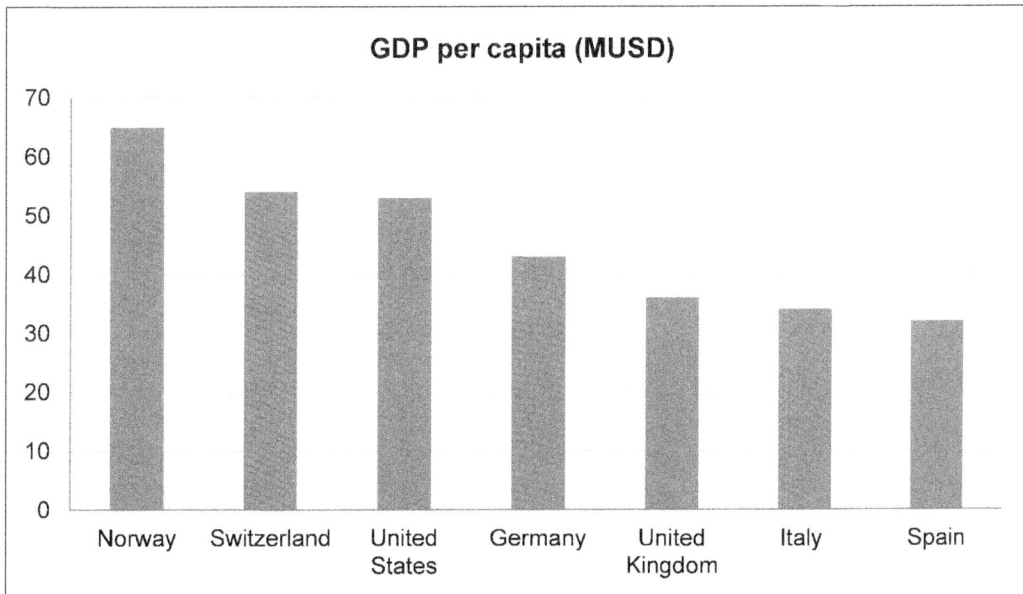

Figure 7.4: A bar chart, in all its simplicity: you can easily compare GDP levels across countries at the first glance

One simple rule to keep in mind when using bar charts is that the **scale should always start from zero**. If we do not do so, their length is not proportional to the actual value we want to display: we will be tricking the viewer's eye, misusing the preattentive attribute of length. For example, look at *Figure 7.5*: Germany's GDP per capita looks like half of Norway's, when it is actually around two-thirds of it:

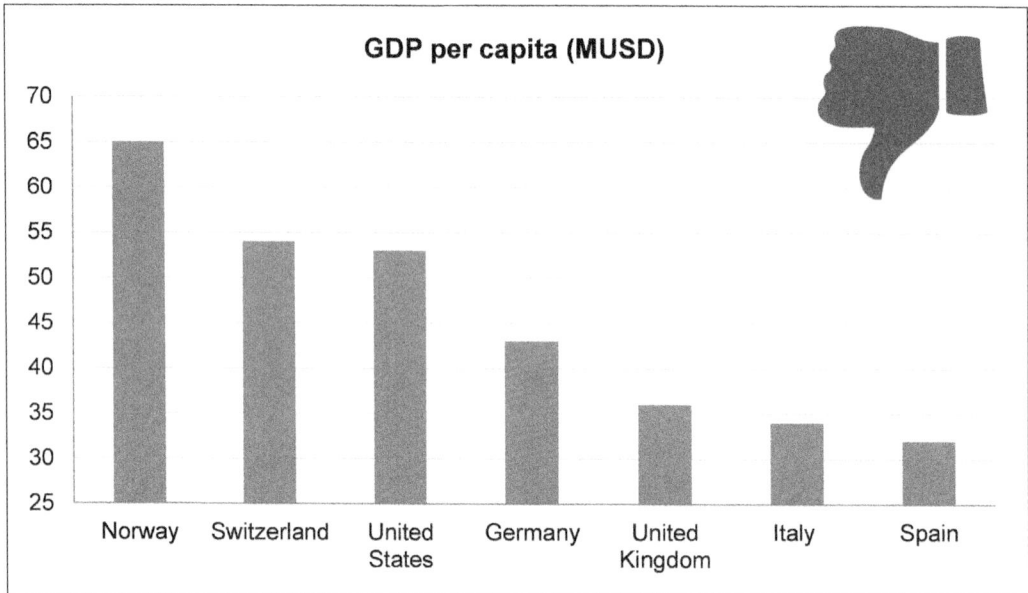

Figure 7.5: In bar charts, the bars should always start from zero (not from 25 like in this case)

One interesting variation of this type of chart is the **horizontal bar chart**: oftentimes, horizontal bars are better than vertical ones, especially when there are many categories or their labels are long. Look at the example in *Figure 7.6*: the country names do not need to be tilted (saving the reader a stiff neck), and the bars can be longer, which makes appreciating the differences across countries easier:

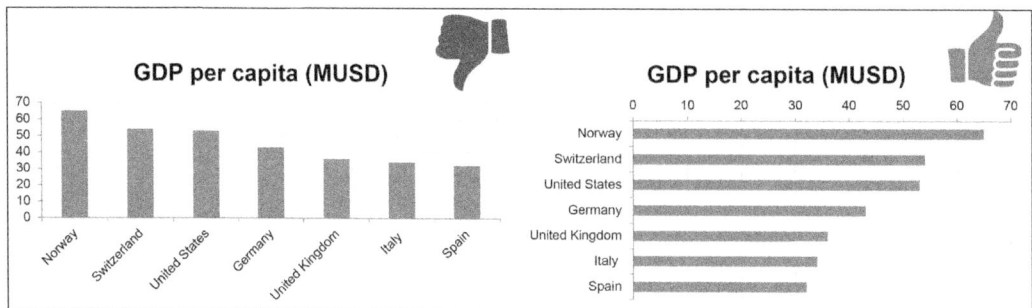

Figure 7.6: Horizontal bar charts: a simple way to better use your visual space

When you have another category variable to be encoded, you can use a **stacked bar chart**. As shown in *Figure 7.7*, every subcategory (in this case, the sector within the country) is displayed as a portion of the chart, highlighted with a different color. By doing so, you will show the size of each component relative to the whole bar, and you also enable comparisons across country/sector combinations. The advice is to use this only when there are few subcategories to be encoded (ideally no more than four); otherwise, it gets confusing for the reader to identify each bar portion:

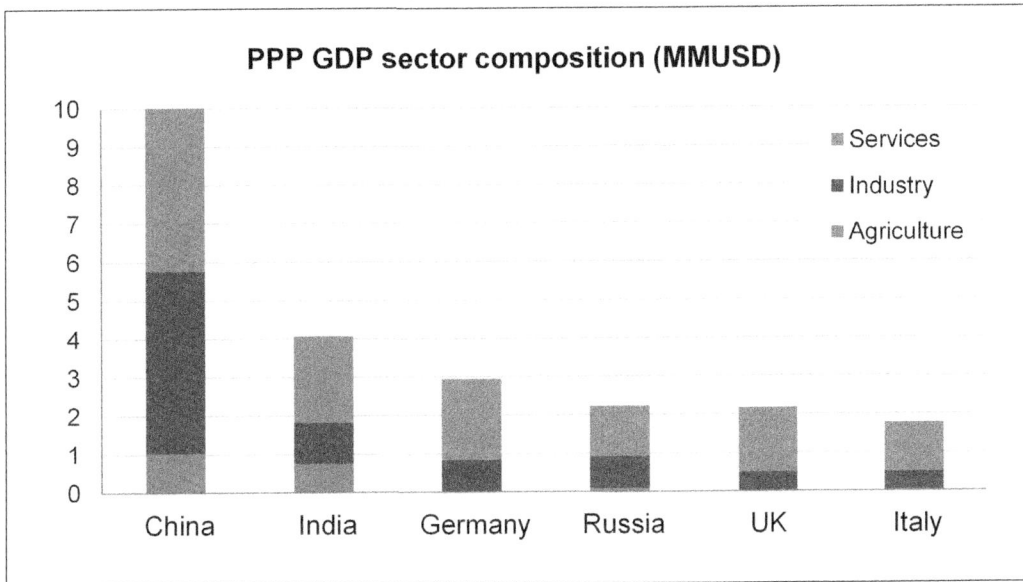

Figure 7.7: A stacked bar chart: you can distinguish subcategories through the use of color

Another extension within the bar chart family to consider is the **histogram**: this is essentially a bar chart showing the frequency distribution of a population by binned ranges. Have a look at the example in *Figure 7.8*. This chart tells us that the prices falling within the €5.8 to €5.9 bucket are the most frequent:

Distribution of prices

Figure 7.8: A histogram: you can easily see the frequency of values falling within equally-sized ranges

Lastly, another useful variation of bar charts is **waterfall charts**. These are great at unveiling the positive and negative components in a before/after comparison, like the change in GDP that you can see in *Figure 7.9*:

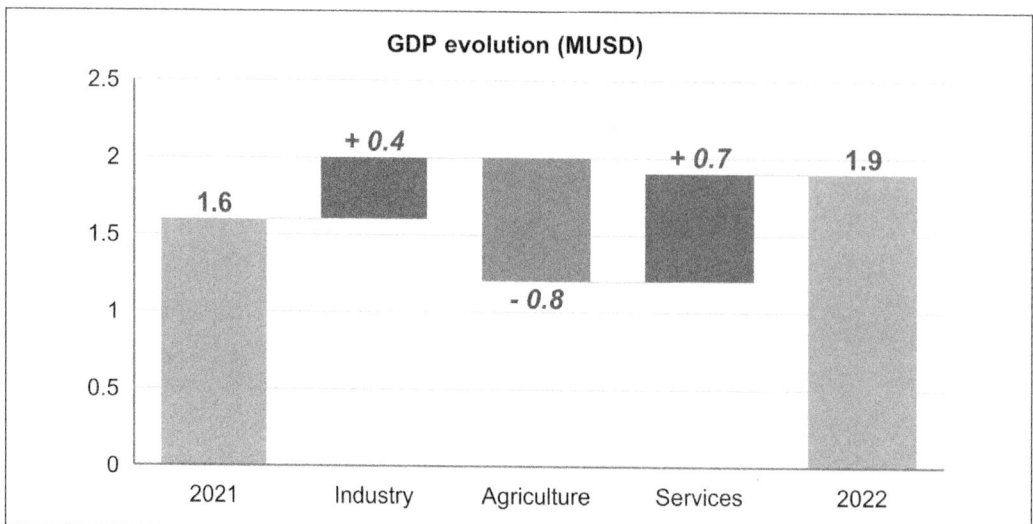

GDP evolution (MUSD)

Figure 7.9: A waterfall chart: you can unveil the drivers and the drainers of a change

Line charts

Line charts are the most natural way to show the evolution of a quantity across a continuous variable, such as time. A typical case is the one shown in *Figure 7.10*: the line is the result of "connecting the dots" among the different sales values shown on the vertical axis (which, in this case, does not need to start from zero like for bar charts) while on the horizontal axis you have the time values, organized in equally spaced intervals. The connecting lines between data points rely on the preattentive attribute of slope to carry your message of a quantity *going up or down* and at what speed:

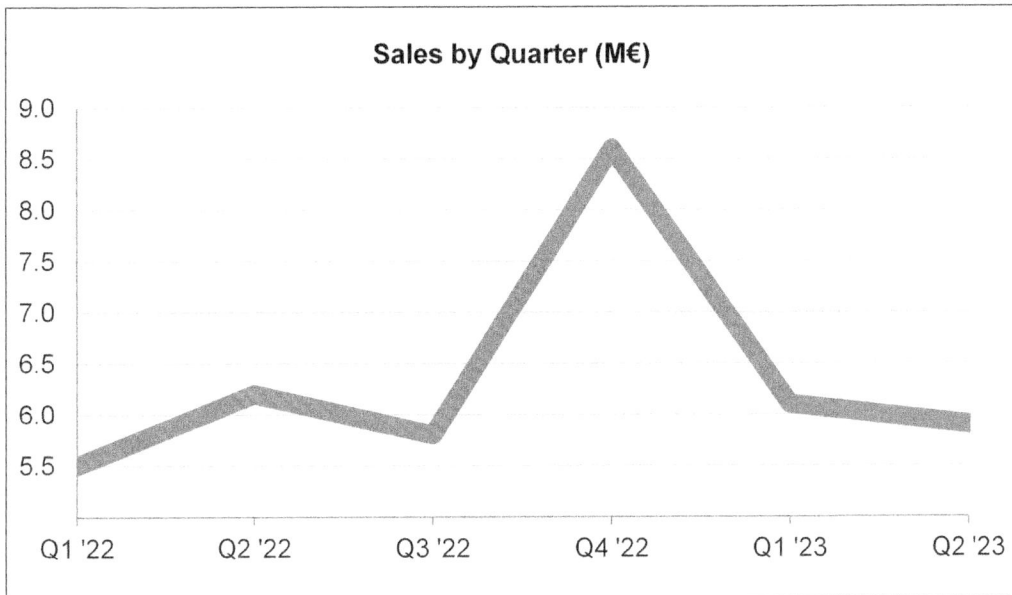

Figure 7.10: Anatomy of a line chart: the continuous variable (in most cases, time) is on the horizontal axis

Although the most common case involves evolution over time, you can use line charts to plot the trend of any continuous variable. For instance, if you want to display the number of products sold at different price points, you can set the price on the horizontal axis and see how sales degrade as price increases. In any case, **never use categorical variables in the horizontal axis of a line chart**. The reason is simple: in a line chart, the brain associates the slope of the line as the change between contiguous elements, like two subsequent points in time. Take *Figure 7.11*: there is no logical contiguity between Italy and Norway (besides alphabetical order, which is irrelevant to our message), so the steep increase we see between the two countries is both artificial and confusing:

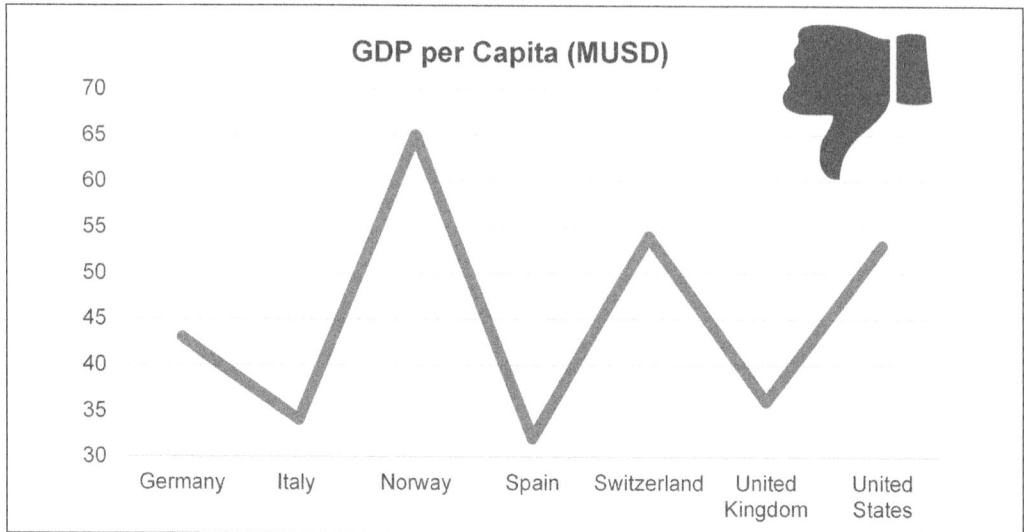

Figure 7.11: Categorical variables on the horizontal axis of a line chart: a beginner mistake to avoid

You can also use line charts to show relationships across multiple time series evolving over the same time frame, and you can use colors to differentiate between lines. However, consider using **direct labels** placed right next to each line: these are clearer and avoid the use of legends, which saves the effort of "mapping" colors to categories. Additionally, this approach allows you to use colors to visually highlight part of the data like you find in *Figure 7.12*, which will make the chart more focused on the specific message you want to convey:

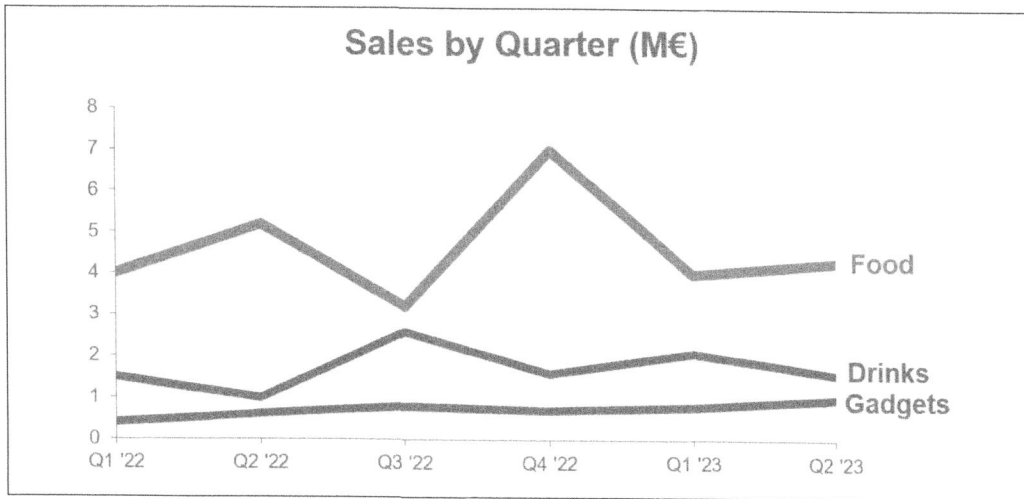

Figure 7.12: A line chart with direct labels: avoid using color legends by replacing them with direct labels whenever possible

One further piece of advice is to be very careful when adopting **dual axes**, which means allowing lines in the same chart to refer to two different references axes with different scales of measurement. One problem that can arise with dual axes is when the lines cross. Such a crossing is preemptively given attention by the brain of the reader: in other words, it *must signify something*. In reality, it might not have any meaning in relation to the message we want to give. Take the example of the left chart in *Figure 7.13*: the share and sales lines cross between Q2 and Q3, but this is solely due to the arbitrary definition of the two vertical scales:

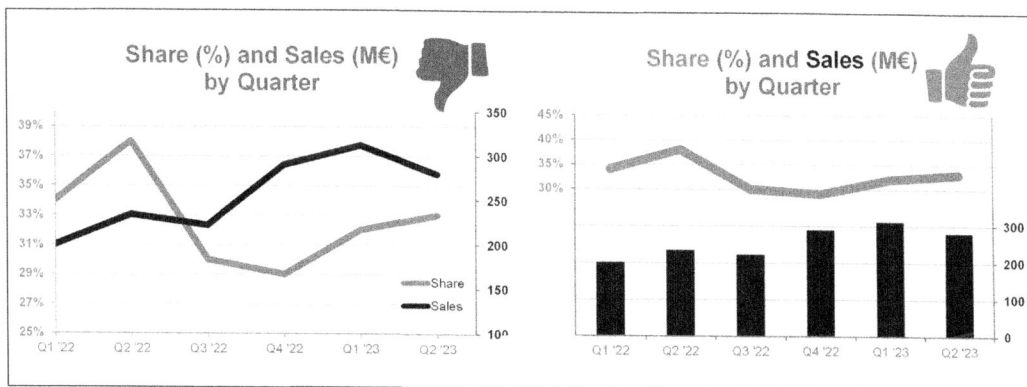

Figure 7.13: Dual axis is tricky: the left chart has an artificial crossing point and it is harder to interpret than the right one

The composition chart on the right in the figure is a more robust alternative: the bars and the line unambiguously refer to two different axes, which neither overlap nor generate any crossing. An additional reason to prefer the rendering on the right is its **simple axis increments** for shares: the choice of having increments of two subsequent odd numbers (29%, 31%, 33%, and so on) is less immediate to follow than what we find on the right (with 30%, 35%, 40%, and so on).

Another more straightforward alternative to visualize the same data is to visualize multiple lines in separate charts (generally called a trellis or panel chart), as shown in *Figure 7.14*. This approach is beneficial when trying to separate multiple overlapping data series. It is a way to **avoid spaghetti charts**, where many lines are crammed into a single chart, making them hard to follow individually and decipher:

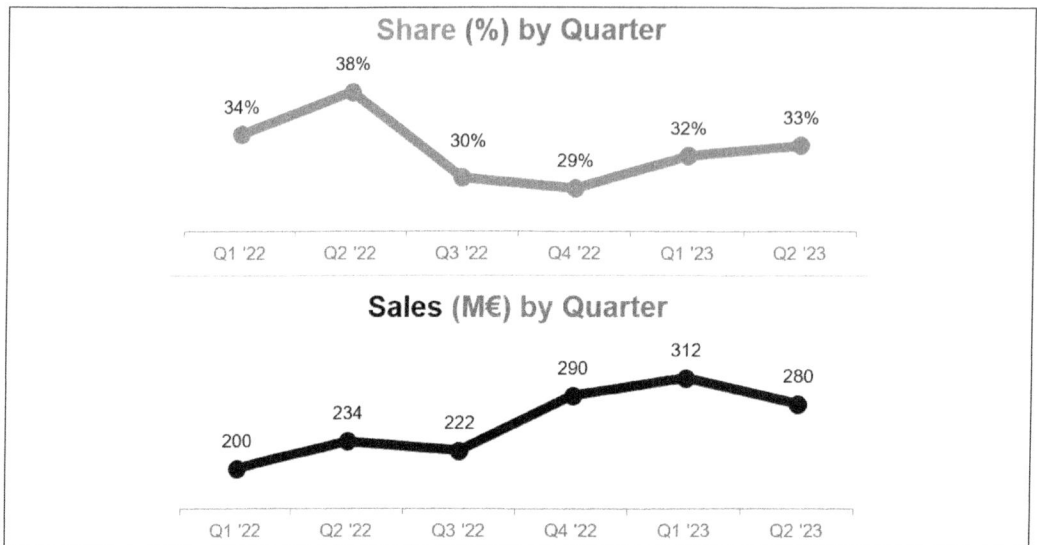

Figure 7.14: Two lines combined in a trellis chart: in this case, we avoid vertical axes by adopting data labels

In the particular case of *Figure 7.14*, you can also see that the vertical axes have been completely removed and replaced by **data labels** displaying the vertical axes values. When you prefer reporting precise values and do not have many data points to visualize, consider using data labels instead of relying on axes.

Treemaps

Treemaps are great at displaying the relative size of the various components of a whole. In a treemap, the total space is split up into multiple rectangles, each one having a size that is proportional to a numerical variable. As you can see in *Figure 7.15*, multiple levels of a hierarchy (in this case, countries and categories are the two levels used for the breakdown of sales) can be displayed at once, and the size of all elements can be compared:

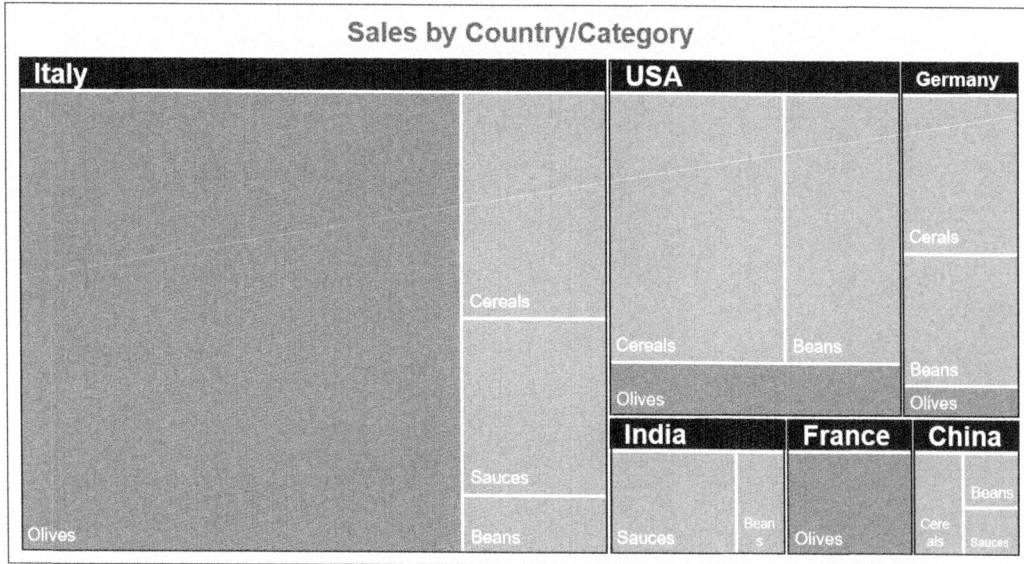

Figure 7.15: A treemap for showing relative sizes of sales by country/category combinations: colors are used to highlight the prevalence of olive sales in each country

Even when you have one single level of splits, treemaps offer a good way to convey the relative size of the parts of a whole. I bet that some of you are now thinking: *can't we use pie charts for that?* Although they are still widely used, data visualization specialists advise to **avoid pie charts**, claiming that there are more immediate and better alternatives to adopt. Information design expert Stephen Few summarizes his sentiment toward pie charts with a straight rule: *Save the pies for dessert!* It is easy to see why: *Figure 7.16* shows a pie chart and a bar chart visualizing the same data set and clearly demonstrates why pie charts are inferior. Pies use angles to encode quantitative values. Angles are a much less immediate visual attribute to perceive than length, which is used in bar charts. Our brain struggles with evaluating the amplitude of angles. Look again at the pie chart displayed in the figure: can you easily compare the size of China (first slice of the pie, starting from "midday") with the one from France (the fourth slice, moving clockwise)?

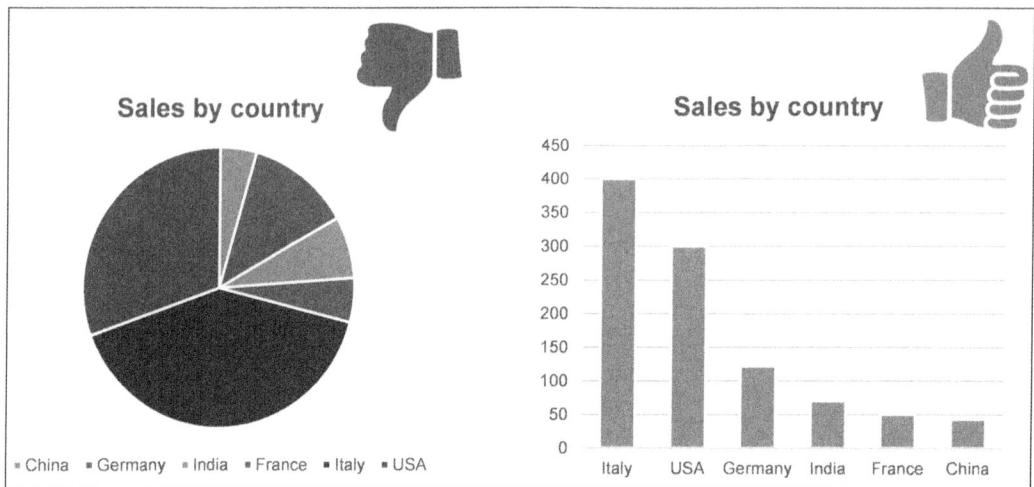

Figure 7.16: Pies are better used to accompany tea than to display data: in this case, the bar chart does a much better job

The only situation when it is acceptable to use pie charts (or their other sweet-sounding alternatives, **donut charts**) is when you have only two slices (as we did in the last chapter—see *Figure 6.32*): in this case, it is easy to see which part is bigger and it is OK to use these charts. In all other cases, you should use either bar charts or treemaps to transfer messages that deal with sizes and proportions: it's as simple as that.

Scatterplots

In scatterplots, data is displayed as a series of points on a rectangle. Two quantities are used to control the horizontal and vertical coordinates of the points appearing on the plot. In this way, you can easily show how the two quantities relate to each other. Have a look at the sample in *Figure 7.17*: the number of units sold (encoded as vertical coordinates, or *y*-axis) clearly goes down as the price per unit (used to control horizontal coordinates, or *x*-axis) increases:

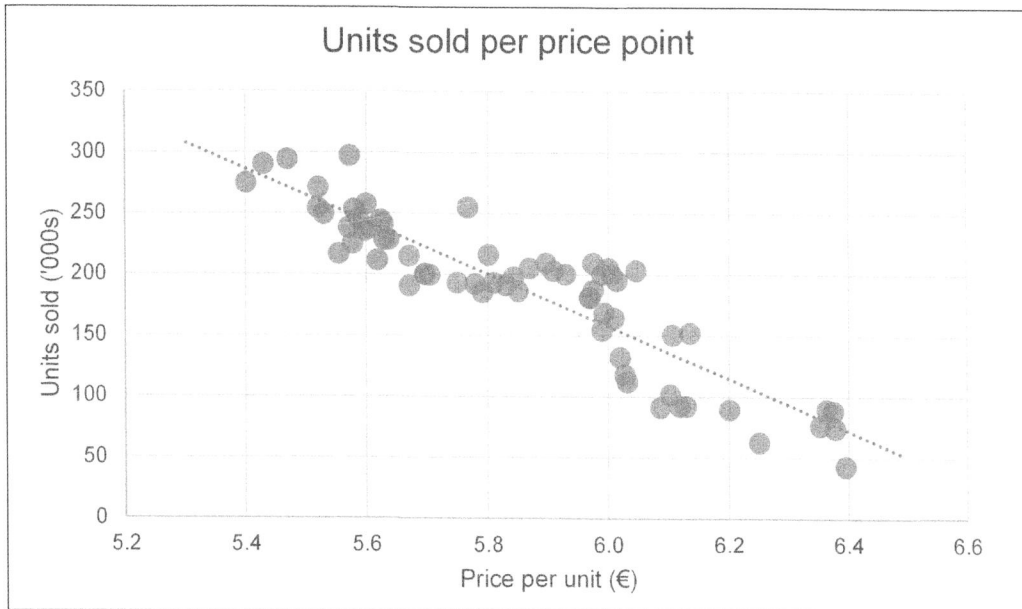

Figure 7.17: A scatterplot showing the distribution of units sold in relation to the price per unit: the higher the price, the less we sell. The dotted trendline makes the relationship evident

We can see a mutual interdependency of the two quantities (linear correlation): as price increases, we sell less. The scatterplot is giving us clear hints on non-linear phenomena as well. For example, in *Figure 7.17*, we can see that after the €6.00 threshold, there is an evident deterioration of sales. It seems that the full digit price acts as a psychological threshold: customers are attracted disproportionally more by a €5.99 price tag than by a €6.00 one. Linear and non-linear patterns like these can be easily spotted through scatterplots: this makes them a safe chart type choice when you need to convey a relationship-based business message.

> Adding a **trendline**, like the dotted one you can see in *Figure 7.17*, makes linear relationships stand out. Do you remember the linear regression algorithm we encountered in *Chapter 5, Applying Machine Learning at Work?* The trendline is just the visual rendering of the linear model that explains the quantity on the vertical axis (dependent variable) through the quantity displayed on the horizontal axis (independent variable). You can go back to *Figure 5.7* for a visual refresher on linear regression.

Quadrant charts, like the one shown in *Figure 7.18*, are interesting expansions to scatterplots. By means of two reference lines — one vertical and one horizontal — which usually are set to be in the "middle" of the range of interest, we cut the space of the plot into four quadrants. Every quadrant relates to one of the four logical combinations of "being below" and "being above" each reference threshold:

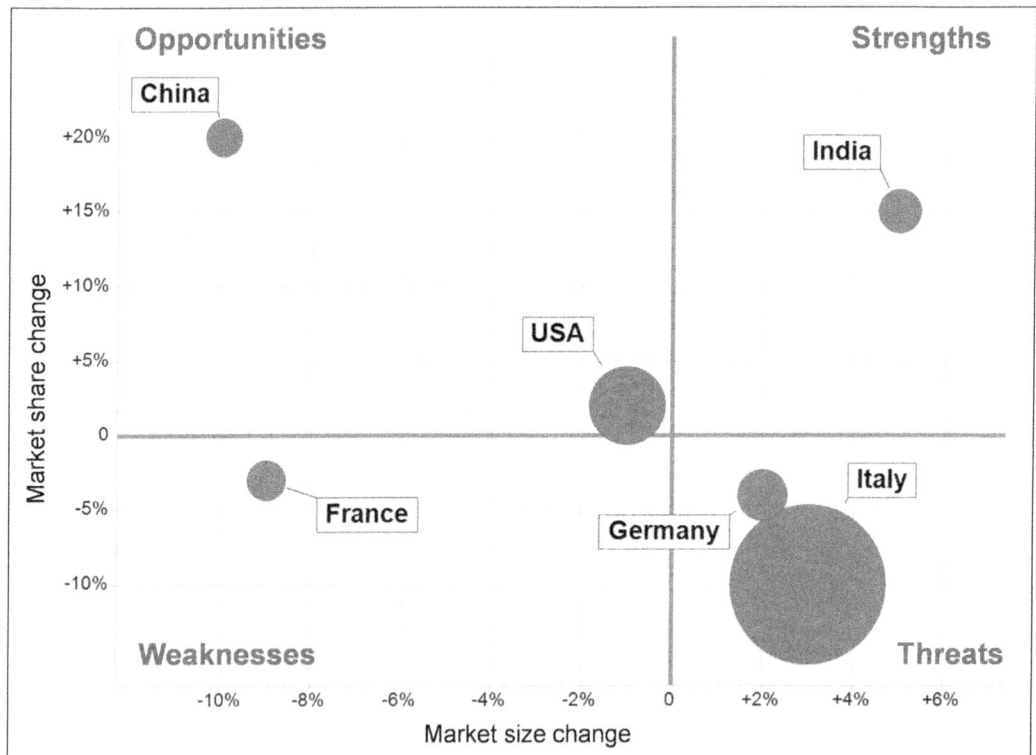

Figure 7.18: A quadrant chart showing the market size and share change (x- and y-axis) and the magnitude of the business (size of the bubble): this chart offers a framework to classify each country depending on where it lies

Such a chart becomes very powerful when you associate each quadrant with a clear business interpretation. For example, *Figure 7.18* shows the annual percentage change of a company's market share (vertical axis) and the market size where it operates (horizontal axis) by country. The countries appearing in the top-right corners (in our case, only India) are strengths: in these markets, the company is growing its share of the business, and also, the total consumption of the category is growing (maybe driven by population growth). If the trend is confirmed in the future, this market will become increasingly important to the company: combined with the growth of market share, India can be added to the list of the strategic *strengths* for the company. If you look instead at the bottom-right quadrant, we find countries where the market size is growing, but the share is declining. If we don't act, these markets will progressively hit more and more of our global share, as the country's footprint will likely increase. Thus, these are *threats* that need careful management attention. In this quadrant chart, the bubble's size is proportional to the magnitude of the current business, making it easier to see what the priorities are. This example illustrates the potential of quadrant charts to become business-sound **interpretation frameworks** for your data. Unfortunately, quadrant charts are still underutilized, and I strongly recommend thinking about possible applications in your work area, as they can make a real difference.

One last consideration on scatterplots: the scales do not need to start from zero. Consequently, you can use scatterplots in lieu of bar charts to convey size-related messages when the values you want to display are all far from "zero": this will give you a meaningful advantage in reducing the scale to a smaller range of interest, making differences more visible. For example, *Figure 7.19* is a scatterplot showing the same data as *Figure 7.4*: in the scatterplot, the gaps in GDP per capita by country are even more apparent:

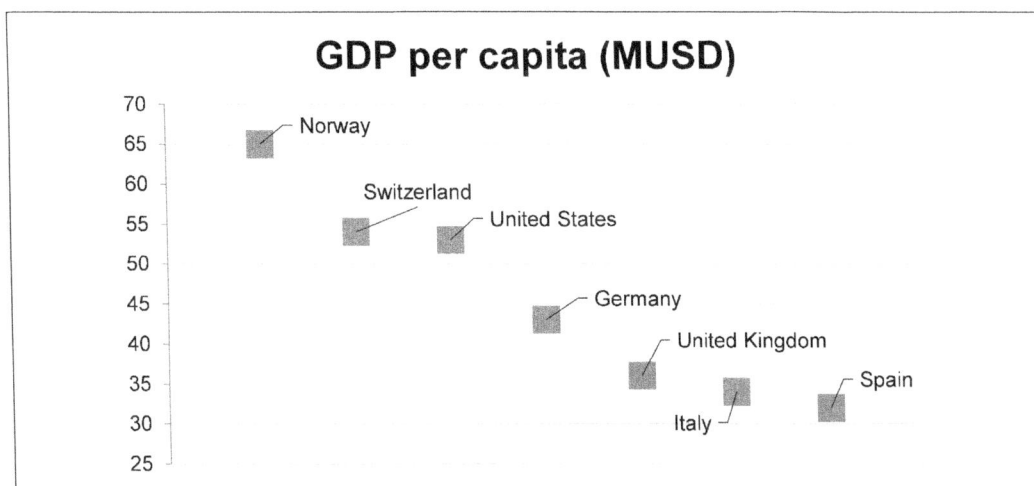

Figure 7.19: A scatterplot alternative to the bar chart in Figure 7.4: if the message is about absolute distances of GDP per capita across countries, this design can work well

We have now completed the tour through the fundamental types of charts available for your data visualization needs. Bar charts, line charts, treemaps, and scatterplots encompass the vast majority of the business messages you can convey through data. Now that we have all the ingredients ready, let's pull them all together and finalize our visual design.

Finalizing your visual

On top of the specific guidelines to follow for each type of chart, which we have encountered in the previous pages, there are some general quality design rules that apply every time. The common denominator of such rules brings us back to where we started at the beginning of the chapter: minimalism is the ultimate key to effective data visualization.

Yale University professor Edward Tufte has been a pioneer in modern data visualization. One of the key concepts he introduced is the **data-ink ratio**, which describes the prevalence of data-driven visual elements in a chart. Consider all the "ink" you use in a chart to draw the essential, non-redundant display of data information: if we erased these chart elements, we would also remove the underlying business message we wanted to convey. Now think about the total ink you would need to print the chart, which includes non-required legends, background pictures, unneeded text, and so on. Tufte found out that by removing all the clutter, we maximize the proportion of data-ink on the total ink (data-ink ratio), and, by doing so, we obtain more effective data visuals.

Let's use an example to see how bad it can get: *Figure 7.20* shows a bad bar chart that features a collection of several wrong design choices:

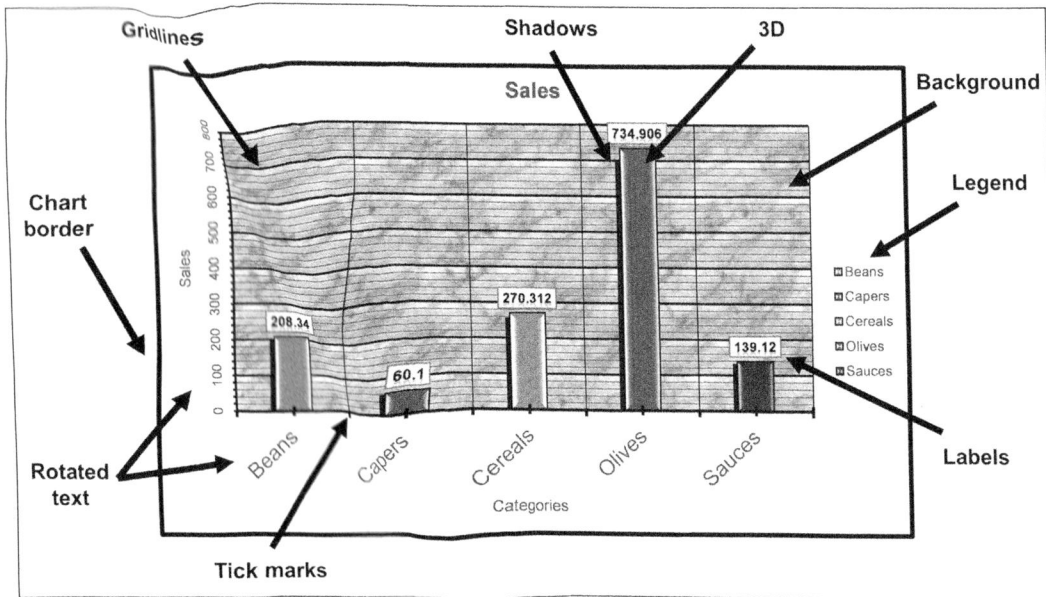

Figure 7.20: An example of what not to do when visualizing data: the data-ink ratio in this chart is at its lowest

Although it is rare to find data visuals that are as bad as this one, I am sure that many of the visuals you see at work will carry one or more of the faults you see displayed there. In the following few pages, we will go through a practical set of guidelines we can follow to avoid all these issues. We need to train our design-critical eye to spot such shortcomings so that we can build neat and professional-grade data charts all the time. Looking at *Figure 7.20*, it seems that we are spoilt for choice on where to start from:

- **Gridlines**: Gridlines can help guide the eye to connect data points with the axes, but they are not always necessary. In any case, they should always be visually muted and barely visible. Make them as thin as possible and color them with a light gray. Do not exaggerate with the number of gridlines per axis: they should not be more than 10 per dimension. If you can avoid gridlines altogether, even better: for example, if you use data labels on top of your data points, you should definitely remove gridlines and axes as they are no longer needed.

- **Tick marks:** Tick marks can help to align axis labels to data elements, like time periods, on a line chart. Similar to gridlines, tick marks should be visually muted, so keep them short and thin. Bar charts do not generally need tick marks, as it should be easy to connect every bar to a category. Like for any visual aid, if you are unsure whether to keep them or not, my advice is to remove them and then check if everything is still clear.

- **Chart border**: You can remove the external chart borders from your visuals: they consume ink but certainly do not add any information. To avoid any mix-up with the rest of the elements or text in your slide or document, leave a generous stripe of white space around the chart: it will look tidy and light, which is what you need.

- **Rotated text**: As discussed earlier, when text is vertically rotated or even tilted, it is less accessible, takes extra time to read, and should be avoided. In the case of bar charts, use horizontal bars to gain space for lengthy labels.

- **3D effects**: A data chart is an *abstract* representation of a collection of data points. When it comes to data visualization, we can surely leave *realism* out of the picture. A three-dimensional perspective in a data chart can only harm as it makes it harder to compare sizes and refer to reference lines. 3D scatterplots are sometimes used for exploring data in scientific contexts: in this case, they always allow the possibility to interact by rotating and panning the view appropriately. In business contexts, this is hardly needed. Don't use 3D.

- **Shadows**: Similar to what we said for 3D, there is no reason to add an impression of light and shadow in any data visualization. Although many software platforms allow — quite inexplicably — it, don't add shadows to your visuals.

- **Background**: The background of your chart should be neutral so that everything that lies in the foreground stays as distinguishable as possible. Sometimes, inexperienced users add color or — even worse — pictures with products and brands in the background of charts to make them "cool": they just lower their chance of success in delivering their business message as the chart is less readable. Funnily enough, Excel provides the option to add the white marble texture you see in *Figure 7.20* as a background — I haven't made it up! Don't ask me why, but Excel has also got a preloaded texture that features fish fossils. It is pretty bizarre, so check it out, but — please — never use it.

- **Labels**: Using labels to identify lines or to specify data values can be very useful. You should avoid duplications that will add non-data ink: if you have data labels on a line or bar chart, for instance, you can entirely remove axes and gridlines, as we did in *Figure 7.14*. When you use labels, make sure they don't have any border or non-neutral background. If they display data values, don't overdo it with decimal digits, like in *Figure 7.20*. In general, keep any text label as short as strictly required to deliver the message you need with clarity.

- **Legend**: Legends are used to provide the key to interpret colors or textures in a chart. The problem with using them is that they consistently require the eye and the attention of the reader to go back and forth between the data elements in the chart and the legend itself. As a general rule, we should try to avoid using them and always look for alternatives, like we did with direct labels in *Figure 7.12*. If you have to use them, try to limit the number of items by grouping elements together or filtering the unimportant ones: it is hard for the human eye to distinguish neatly between more than five colors in the same chart.

On top of the preceding elements, when refining our data chart, we should pay attention to the use of color. It is important to recognize that color is one of the most immediate preattentive attributes that our brain decodes when presented with a chart. As for the other attributes, such as length, size, and position, colors should always have a specific meaning when used in a data chart. In other words, colors are never there for decoration or to please any aesthetic need. In data visualizations, colors are there for a functional reason, such as:

- **Highlighting elements that deserve attention**, like we did when emphasizing the olives category in *Figure 7.15*. As we will see in the next chapter, colors can be very powerful when diversifying between the back- and foreground when presenting data.

- **Encoding an extra dimension**, like in the stacked bar chart shown in *Figure 7.7*, or displaying continuous variables through color gradients.

Around 5% of people are affected by **Color Vision Deficiency (CVD)**, a form of color blindness that makes some combinations of colors (like shades of green and red) indistinguishable. Therefore, try to be fully inclusive in your data visuals by adopting colorblind-friendly palettes (davidmathlogic.com/colorblind) or by using light versus dark color differences (this is also useful when your charts are printed in black and white-only ink).

In *Figure 7.21*, you find an improved version of the bad chart we saw earlier. The chart has now been treated by applying all the quality guidelines we have encountered throughout this chapter:

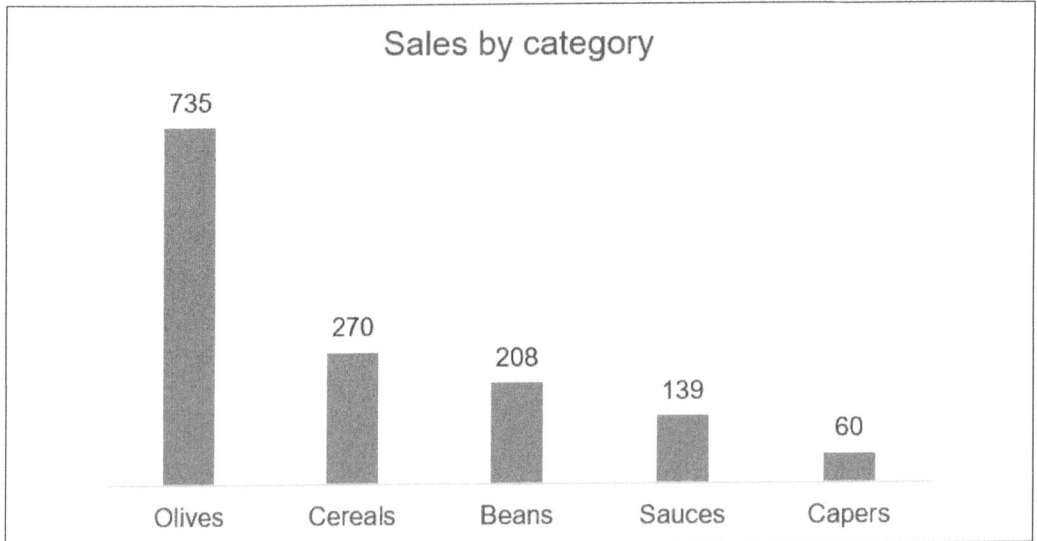

Figure 7.21: An improved version of the earlier bar chart: simplicity prevails

Judge for yourself: minimalism enhances clarity and outclasses any fancy attempt to add unnecessary graphical embellishments.

Summary

This chapter has equipped you with a set of practical tools and guidelines for designing professional-looking and effective visuals to use in your daily work. We started our journey by framing the overall objective of visualizing data: transferring data-based messages to others by leveraging human visual perception. We have seen how we need to impersonate the role of a designer, who must make choices about what and how to visualize. After selecting the specific message type to give (which can be focused on evolution over time, making sense of absolute and relative size, or relation across quantities), we learned how to pick the right chart type using the chart selection matrix. We discovered pros and cons and typical pitfalls behind the implementation of line charts, bar charts, treemaps, and scatterplots, which collectively account for the vast majority of charts we need. Lastly, we went through a set of guidelines to adopt when ensuring the quality of any data visual. We discovered that all these rules have a common goal: they all invite us to apply methodical simplification, directness, and minimalism when building charts.

All the good practices we have learned in this chapter require practice to turn into a habit. My advice is to apply all the rules we have learned here as soon as you put your hands on the next data chart you must refresh or create. Some of those rules might feel awkward at first—I know that there were some big fans of pie charts among you—but they will undoubtedly help you become more confident and successful at visualizing data.

In this chapter, we focused on transforming data into visuals and conveying a specific message. In the next chapter, we will take this a step further: we will learn how to turn data-based messages into compelling stories, which is what data storytelling is all about.

8
Telling Stories with Data

This is the chapter you didn't expect. What can be analytical, scientific, and professional in producing and delivering a work of fiction? However paradoxical it might look, storytelling is one of the most pragmatic ways to create economic value out of data. In this chapter, you will learn how this works and how you can use it to your advantage.

We will shortly answer the following questions:

- What have stories to do with business and data analytics?
- What ingredients make a story?
- How do I build one, starting from my data?
- What techniques can I use to deliver stories that drive business value?

In the first part of the chapter, you will discover what makes stories so effective at communicating with (and convincing) others. In the second part, you will learn a simple methodology and some practical tips to build powerful data stories yourself. This chapter is different from the others in the book as it aims at developing a much softer set of skills than what you have seen so far. For some of you who are more at ease with technology and science, this might feel slightly uncomfortable. In any case, I promise that it will be worth reading this chapter: you might become an unexpected data storytelling fan, like many others before you.

The art of persuading others

Being right is not enough: this is the plain and sometimes upsetting reality faced by many data practitioners who cannot have their points—however truthful and insightful—heard and accepted by those in charge. As we saw in the first chapter, there are multiple routes for leveraging data analytics to create economic value, which we called data-to-value paths. In most cases, to create value, we need data to influence others to make the right decisions or take the appropriate actions. Think about this now: all you have seen so far in the book—all the efforts to transform your data, find insights, and build robust models—will sadly remain useless if we miss the last bit of the chain, which is impacting the actions of others. It is in our best interests to protect our work from becoming irrelevant by driving it all the way through to action, without making the naïve assumption that "it is enough to do the math work." To do so, we need to communicate our points convincingly, by mastering the art and science of persuasion.

The simplest (and oldest) model that describes the dynamics of persuasion is **Rhetoric**: it summarizes the three essential features that make a speech or a written document (in our case, think about a presentation to support a management decision or a business memo) successful in convincing others. These features, also known as **Modes of Persuasion**, are:

- **Credibility**: the authority and the personal integrity of the speaker, the authors, or the supporters of an argument will make it more credible and easier to be accepted. Those who can boast a proven track record of success will have an easier job gaining approval. Also, the reliability of the sources used to support a point will undoubtedly strengthen a case.

- **Logical soundness**: a clear and solid chain of rational arguments will engage with the intellect and the sense of reason of the audience and result in higher acceptance. If you can *prove* your point using a logic that is accepted (and— notably—well understood) by others, they will ultimately buy into it. If your logic has any flaws or cannot be followed, your audience will call your entire case into question, even when you are totally right.

- **Emotional engagement**: if an audience is emotionally invested and feels personally involved in your case, it is more likely that you will get them to agree and act upon what you recommend. There are many ways to develop an emotional appeal, like using imagery that evokes feelings, choosing words with emotional emphasis, referring to first-hand experiences, drawing analogies that people can personally relate to, and creating gripping stories that keep attention high. This feature requires you to recognize emotions, discern feelings, and adjust your style and content depending on the environment, a set of abilities called **Emotional Intelligence**.

Rhetoric is an ancient discipline. It developed first in Sicily, in the Greek colonies of Syracuse and Agrigento in the 5th century BC, as a technical methodology to increase legal proceedings' chance of success. It was first described by the Greek philosopher Aristotle (384–322 BC), who came up with the 3-pillar model presented here: **Ethos** (ἦθος, which stands for credibility), **Logos** (λόγος, logic), and **Pathos** (πάθος, emotions).

Let's go back to business data and examine a few specific examples showing how we can use rhetoric to our advantage. *Table 8.1* reports only some of the techniques we can implement in data rhetoric: as you go through it, think about the situations where you have seen them already in action, and start imagining how you can leverage them in your next data presentation:

Mode	Drivers	Examples
Ethos	Credentials/Bio	I have 15 years of experience in using this methodology.
	Success stories	We've tried this approach already in France and it drove 7% of market growth.
	Authoritative sources	According to Stanford University...
	Supporters/Testimonials	This model has been vetted by our finance director.
Logos	Logical consequences	Since X is true, then Y must be true.
	Hard business facts	As the table suggests, this brand is 5 times more profitable than all others.
	Scientific validity	When tested, the model reached 92% accuracy.
Pathos	Metaphors/ Personification	Meet our typical customer, Matt: he's 35 years old and works as a...
	Emotional imagery	Looking at the trend in the survey, we are heading for a cliff edge...
	Personal references	I have recently experienced the same situation myself as a consumer...
	Pre-existing hopes and fears	Imagine the consequences of going again through the same decline we experienced last year...
	Engaging narrative and twists	And after seeing what would happen if we don't act, this is how we can win...

Table 8.1: Examples of data rhetoric in use

Depending on your background, personal inclinations, and style, you might find each of the three modes of persuasion more or less natural for you to use. In general, we can observe some patterns in these preferences.

For example, many data professionals would feel most comfortable with the logos mode: by applying scientific methodologies to the available data, they feel at ease proving their points with confidence. The world of data and logic is *their* world.

Having a preference toward the ethos mode partly depends on the history of the individual presenter and the equity she or he has in the organization. Fortunately, the element of personal credibility can be worked upon and progressively built over time.

The mode that is, for most data practitioners, the toughest to master is pathos. Emotions are harder to manage than numbers and algorithms. They fail to fall into static and pre-determined categories. A fascinating aspect of human beings is that they are all different, with each carrying distinctive levels of sensitivity. No doubt that managing the pathos mode when convincing others with data is the most arduous bit to handle, which will require extensive coverage in the remainder of this chapter.

The good news is that there is a proven way to achieve high emotional engagement when making logical arguments with data, and this is what we are going to focus on now: building great stories.

The power of telling stories

Humans are storytelling creatures. This condition is inherent to our nature. When our ancestors first gathered together around a campfire, stories started to be told, and language developed accordingly. The vital purpose of storytelling has always been to transfer knowledge so that it can *stick* in the minds of listeners and persuade them. Since the dawn of humanity, culture has been transmitted through stories: they were passed down through generations verbally, well before writing (and PowerPoint presentations) existed.

Nowadays, our daily life is utterly immersed in stories. Brands communicate through narratives: commercials will urge you to buy a product through a story instead of merely enumerating the reasons why you should do so. What do you do when you chat with a good friend or meet a colleague by the coffee machine? You will tell stories about your life rather than making a cold inventory of your past activities. And when you consume media at home, read a book, watch a play, or put your children to bed, you are taking advantage of the natural attraction to fictional stories that unite us all.

Out of the many causes that make stories so central to our life in general, there are three specific reasons why storytelling works so well when presenting data in a business context:

1. **Stories stick more than statistics**. Multiple cognitive psychology studies confirm that facts will stick in our brain much better when connected in a narrative than when they are separate. As a famous experiment by Stanford professors Gordon Bower and Michal Clark proved, people can remember a list of random words 6 to 7 times better if they are memorized by creating a fictional story that includes them. Other studies demonstrated that narrative texts could be read twice as fast and recalled twice as well compared to expository texts. By just adding a plot that "connect the dots" across facts, you are more likely to be understood and remembered: it is as simple as that.

2. **Stories encourage acceptance**. When we watch a sci-fi series, we know perfectly well that it is only a work of fiction and none of it is real. Yet we might be captivated by it and we keep watching it, moving greedily to the next episode. How is that possible? This happens because when we are in front of a story, we tacitly sign an agreement called the **Narrative Pact**. It reads something along the lines of: "I agree to momentarily suspend my disbelief as I know that something good will come out from this story, either in terms of new knowledge or experience" (such as entertainment or a momentary disconnection from reality). When somebody is telling us a story, we agree to concede the benefit of the doubt as we accept the prospect of being surprised (and even change our mind). Many business situations will require you to move your audience out of their current beliefs, so the narrative pact is exactly what you need! A large majority of decision-making is driven by gut feel and earlier personal experiences. When you begin telling a story, you get your audience to implicitly sign a narrative pact, and this is an excellent way to get open-minded listening from them.

> As fiction writers know well, the narrative pact works only if we offer coherent logic throughout our fictional world. As we will see later in the chapter, we will have to keep consistency across our data story in terms of content (underlying assumptions, use of words) and appearance (like colors and formats).

3. **Stories drive connection**. When Princeton neuroscientist Uri Hasson used fMRI scanners to study the brain activity of storytellers and their listeners, he was surprised by the results: as stories unfolded, the subjects' brains started to become aligned, showing signals with increasingly synchronized patterns. Stories have the power to create a state of emotional connection, or empathy, between the parts involved. This connection will get your audience to feel closer to you and identify with you. As a result, they will be more prone to agree with what your data suggests.

All we've seen in the last few pages leads us to a simple conclusion: stories add wheels to our data insights, making them go faster and further. Our points will be more memorable and easier to accept by equipping our data with an engaging narrative. Storytelling is an effective vehicle for taking our precious insights to where it matters: the decision makers' capacity to act, to change things, and, by doing so, to turn data into real business value. Having seen *why* storytelling is such an important skill to have, let's look at how we can put it into action with our data.

The data storytelling process

Crafting an engaging data story requires mixing the exercise of creativity with the application of a structured methodology. In the following pages, we will uncover each step of the **Data Storytelling Process**, a *recipe* you can follow when looking for the right way to influence your business partners through data and analytics. This is how it works:

1. The first step is to **Set the Objectives**, which means defining your story's expected outcome (anticipating what it will cause) and getting clarity on your audience composition, drivers, and previous knowledge.

2. Then you **Select the Scenes** your story will be made of and you draft them. We will go through five archetypal scene types you can use as an inspiration for your data to speak up.

3. Once you are clear on the scenes, you sequence them and **Apply the Structure** that will make your story flow well. We will introduce a basic 3-act structure that proves to be a good base for organizing your narrative.

4. At this point, you will **Polish the Scenes** to make their content stand out: you will be clear on what should be in the background and what deserves instead to be well lit in the foreground of each scene.

5. Your draft can go through several cycles where you progressively **Refine** it, reconsidering all scenes and their structure, to make sure you are ultimately meeting your original business objectives.

6. Your story will finally be ready for prime time, and you will feel confident to **Deliver** it in front of your audience.

Figure 8.1 shows a graphical summary of the data storytelling process: you define your objectives, then you go through an iterative process of picking, structuring, and polishing your scenes, and then you are ready to deliver:

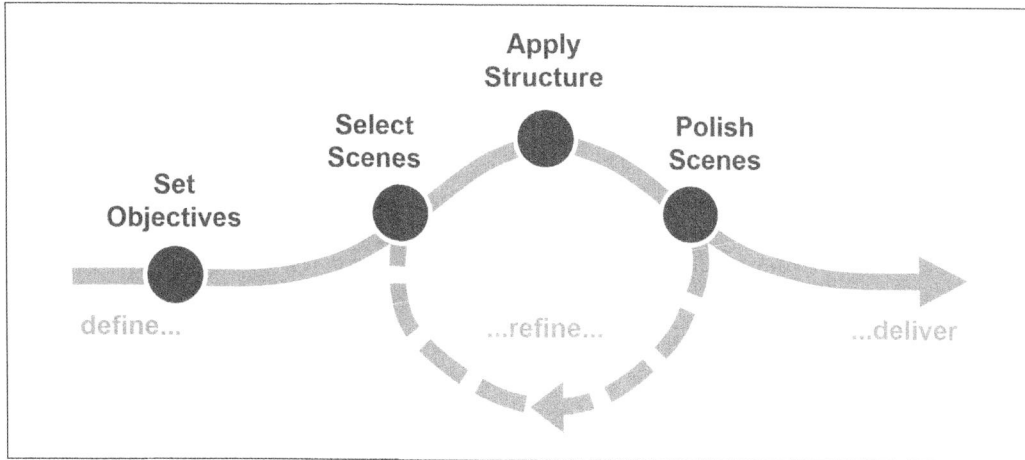

Figure 8.1: The data storytelling process: define objectives, refine your set of scenes, and deliver confidently

> Building a powerful data story and preparing for its delivery takes time! You should proactively plan for it: if possible, block some slots in your calendar and allow quality time for rehearsals before your prime time.

Let's start from the first part of the process: defining your story objectives.

Setting objectives

An essential condition to reach any goal is to be clear on what it looks like. The same applies to data storytelling: the initial step of the process is to clarify to yourself what you want to obtain and from whom you will obtain it.

Think about the precise outcome that you are after and try to see in your mind's eye a vivid picture of what it would look like to be successful:

*   Do you want to make somebody aware of some insightful data findings? By the end of your delivery, they should look convinced about your discovery and what it implicates.

- Are you trying to secure some funding for a project or extra investment for your team? The outcome you want to reach is that your decision-maker approves it right after listening to your story.

- Have you unveiled a business opportunity and want to convince a manager about the solution that you found? Your objective is to get the manager to feel uneasy about the current status quo and support your recommendation with a high sense of urgency.

These examples are a bit stereotypical and clichéd: in real business contexts, your objective will be a combination of multiple items. Still, before you start working on your story, you want to be as clear as possible on the specific scenario you want to make happen. Make a written note of it, as you will use it to check your story's validity at the end.

Storytelling always involves an audience, and its features will dictate the way you build a story and bring it to life. We cannot ignore the audience and — actually — the more we tailor our story to them, the more effective we will be in reaching our objective. In this initial phase, you want to focus your mind on two fundamental characteristics that define who you have in front of you, namely:

a. **Current knowledge and prior beliefs**: What can you reasonably assume they already know about the topic you will talk to them about? What background will they need to be able to follow you? Are they equipped to understand you when you explain the methodology you used to analyze and model your data? What are their existing beliefs on the matter of your story? Is there any convincing needed to steer them away from any pre-existing wrong assumptions? Take a few minutes to think through these points — maybe with the help of others who know them best — and take note of the no-miss items your content should include. By thinking through these points, you will also anticipate some of the questions from your audience and proactively get ready to answer them.

b. **Key business goals**: What does your audience really care the most about? What specific business measures are currently at the front of their minds? What are their strategic priorities right now? For example, is it more important to expand the business quickly in other markets or beat the competition in the current ones? Growing sales or driving productivity through savings? You want to have a clear idea of what business KPIs they care about the most so that you can share your findings and proposals in terms of those. Don't underestimate the importance of being aligned with what matters to your audience when speaking to them: many data stories go unheard because presenters are unable to appeal to their listeners. You want to talk the same language and pull the right strings.

Having a vivid picture in your mind of the desired outcome and understanding your audience's current knowledge and motives will help you stay relevant, intriguing, and focused on results: this is the best vantage point from which you can start building a great data story.

Selecting scenes

As we are talking about stories, I am sure it will not surprise you if we borrow some nomenclature typical of theater and filmmaking industries such as *scenes* and *acts*. In theater plays, scene refers to the actions that happen in a specific place at one time. In data storytelling, a scene represents a precise statement, supported by specific data findings. Scenes can be summarized in a succinct and crisp phrase, such as: *sales have been eroding as of last September by 8% every month* or *by launching this new service now, we can expect to break even within less than 2 years*. Scenes are the fundamental components of your story, the individual rings constituting the chain of your narrative: they have to be self-standing (solidly backed by data) and crisp to firmly guide the audience through the development of your logical arguments.

It is hard to pinpoint the right set of scenes to make a data story. If you have large quantities of data, you might fall into the temptation of showing more of it than necessary, including data that does not support your plot's unfolding. You might end up showing a mass download of data points without any clear findings or connections between them: by doing so, you will cause your audience to become very confused. On the other hand, if you don't have enough data evidence to support a scene, the fundamentals of your story will crumble, the narrative chain will be broken, and the logical soundness of your argument will fall apart. Moreover, a data scene must tell us something attractive, valuable, and functional to the story's development. If we show some data without clarifying why it is important, we lose the audience's engagement.

The risk of getting lost in the tricky—and many—paths data can offer is high. Fortunately, we can recognize several recurrent types of relevant data scenes: they work well as turning points in a story and can provide interesting *twists* to the narrative. Having them clear in our minds can help us define our story's scenes, which is exactly what we need to do as part of the process. The five most common **Data Scene Types** are evolution, comparison, relationship, breakdown, and distribution. We will now go through each of them, clarifying the typical data evidence you should use to support the specific point you want to make and provide examples.

Evolution

This scene is all about highlighting some sort of change over time. The typical case is to feature growing or declining KPIs (*over the past 5 years, revenues have steadily grown by 7% year on year, accelerating in the last 3 months; in December, we experienced a 13% drop in the number of users versus November*): this tells a lot about the dynamic state of a business. Analyzing the past evolution of a metric can highlight trend-breakers and relevant "exceptions" (*during the campaign, we had 2.5x more visitors on our website than in an average day*). It can also show repeating patterns and cycles, unveiling seasonal components in the way our business runs (*the consumption of hot chocolate between December and February usually accounts for two-thirds of the yearly category sales*). Using predictive models, our scene can also focus on anticipating what may occur in the future, alerting the audience about what is to come (*next year we expect a 15% drop in the number of monthly new contracts, which accounts for $2.5M*).

Comparison

You use this scene type when you take your audience through the result of a side-by-side comparison across two or more items: this is very powerful when you want to magnify significant differences (*for our dealership, selling a car of maker A is 3.4x and 3.7x more profitable than when selling a car of maker B and C, respectively*) or report differential results of what-if simulations (*option A ensures €4.5k incremental sales every week compared with option B*). This scene is ubiquitous in a data story: often, you want to use the contrast effect to enhance differences and direct your story in a specific direction.

> You will make your data story more impactful if you convey your key scenes in business-relevant terms. In comparison scenes, try to "monetize" the gap by converting it to the same unit of measure your audience is evaluated on (like dollar sales, number of new subscribers, or percentage points of cost reduction).

Relationship

By using this scene type, you show how two measures are related to each other. A common situation is when you highlight the degree to which two quantities move in relation to each other. You can summarize this relationship using a correlation coefficient (*the 85% of the variability in the sales of ice creams can be explained by weather conditions*) or the parameters of a model that fits them (*for every dollar of price increase, we expect a 12 point decrease in market share*).

> Although relationship scenes are used to suggest a cause-effect relationship across business KPIs, it will be your job to discriminate between correlation and causality links, making the difference crystal clear to your audience. Make sure to explicitly mention what the relationship you unveiled does *not* infer, ideally by proposing some counterfactuals. By doing so, you will prevent your story from being misinterpreted and damaging the business.

Another case (in partial overlap with the evolution scene type) is when you show an intersection in the progression of two metrics, flagging the point in time when one measure surpasses the other (*as of last year, manufacturer A has taken over manufacturer B and become the market leader*) or making considerations about the gap that is progressively building up across the two (*manufacturer A is now shipping twice as many bikes than manufacturer B every month*).

Breakdown

You use this scene when you break something into its components. For example, you can drill down into a more granular view to show what are the main drivers (or drainers) of a business metric (*out of the current $10.4M gap versus target, $9.2M is solely due to product X, 83% of our Europe earnings are generated in Italy while the remainder is equally split by Spain and Greece*): this is very powerful when you want to steer the attention of your audience to the (few) components that matter the most. You can also go the other way around and "zoom out" from a detailed view to an aggregated one to offer a comparison with the big picture and provide more general context to a particular matter (*our store doubled its sales in two years, but it is still the lowest-performing one in the region*).

Distribution

This scene helps you highlight interesting patterns in the way data points are distributed. For instance, you can show how similar business entities can be grouped into homogeneous clusters (*our customer base can be split into four demographic groups: A, B, C, and D*) that can be described by their typical features (*customers in group A are predominantly single and earn between 50 and 75 thousand Swiss francs per year*). Alternatively, you can shed light on the relative position of an entity in the entire group (*our company financial results are in the top quartile of the industry*) or unveil anomalies (*store X is the outlier of the region as its shelf productivity is double that of the average of all others*).

At the beginning of this section, we said a good data scene can always be summarized in a crisp, one-sentence statement: typically, this summary will leverage supporting data evidence. *Table 8.2* summarizes the five data scene types and the typical data facts you should use to make your point:

Scene type	Typical twists	Typical supporting facts
Evolution	Going up or down, accelerating or decelerating, being stable, anticipating the future, unveiling past trend breakers, seasonality	Change vs. previous period, change vs. last year in the same period, average change per period, delta vs. expected evolution, seasonal index
Comparison	Side-by-side comparison, what-if simulations, similarities and differences	Relative difference, absolute or monetized gap, difference across scenarios, and comparison of outcomes
Relationship	Correlation across different measures, the intersection of trends, gaps	Correlation coefficient, impact of one measure to another, time of inversion, extent of accumulating gap
Breakdown	Drilling down into components, building up into aggregations, zooming in to specific, zooming out to big picture	Relative contribution of parts vs. total, salience of components, difference vs. higher level, top drivers and drainers with impact
Distribution	Being an outlier, belonging to a cluster, position in ranking	Quartile, variance or standard deviation, distance vs. norm, top and bottom, ranking, number of clusters, cluster centers

Table 8.2: Data scene types with typical twists and supporting facts

As you build your narrative, you can use this table as a reference and decide the specific twist you want to add to your data story and — importantly — which measure you will use to support it.

Applying structure

Having selected your data scenes, it is time to pull them together in a coherent and engaging structure. Simplicity and directness always pay when communicating data insights, especially in a business environment. Hence, we are going to adopt a straightforward 3-act model for arranging our data story: it is based on the evergreen narrative structure of **Beginning**, **Middle**, and **End**. This has been the backbone underlying the works of fiction from the Greek tragedy to the latest TV series on Netflix. Think about one of your favorite books or movies: it probably starts with an introduction to the main characters and a description of their normal life (the beginning), with maybe some hints of suspenseful anticipation of what is about to happen.

Then (in the middle), a series of exciting events starts to occur: they take the characters through some significant changes with complications and obstacles on the way. These make the tension fluctuate and ultimately lead to a major crisis, or climax. Finally (in the end), tension falls, leaving the characters in a state of "new normality," which is usually different (and better, in the case of a happy ending) than the one depicted in the beginning.

This structure works! In its simplicity, it can keep the tension moving in a way that makes the audience keep turning pages or staring at the screen. Let's go through each of the three acts and see how we can apply this structure (depicted in *Figure 8.2*) to build a compelling data story:

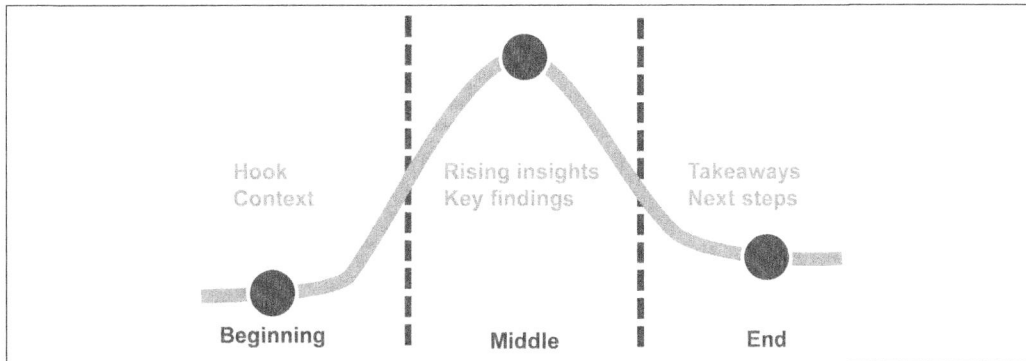

Figure 8.2: The 3-act model of data stories. The ageless split of beginnings, middles, and ends still works

Beginning

As you start your data story, you want to quickly grasp the attention of your audience by employing the so-called **Hook**: this is a short statement (might not need any specific visual or supporting detail) that makes the audience eager to hear the rest of the story and willing to invest their mental energy in following you and your tale for a few minutes. Hooks that work well in a data story can be:

- A partial preview of your key finding (*we are going to see what led to the 10% drop in customers satisfaction we experienced last month*).

- A statement supporting the urgency of the topic you are going to talk about (*data suggests that we have only 20 days to reinforce our production line without impacting the fulfillment of open orders*).

- The anticipation of the possible consequences if your recommendation gets acted upon (*we will learn how to increment sales in the coming summer by $2.1M versus last year*).

The other thing you need to do at the beginning of a data story is to provide some general **Context** that puts everyone on the same page concerning the matter you are going to discuss. Think about the data scenes you want to stage later in the story: what background would the audience need to comprehend them fully? What is the current status of the business? Also, if some previous efforts have already been made on this subject (like earlier attempts to solve the same issue), it will be helpful to remind the audience right at the beginning what they were and why they were yet not entirely satisfying.

Sometimes, data presentations start with a full description of the data sources, their scope and freshness, and detailed disclaimers related to its limitations. This is a double-edged sword, as it can stop the talk before it even starts: it can certainly lower the attention of the audience members who are less interested in those details. The advice is to keep this technical content to a minimum, mentioning only the highlights and keeping some backup material ready for you to go into more details only if it pops up as an issue.

Another pitfall many presenters fall into is to share too much detail about their personal background relating to a project. This is another way to lose your audience's interest quickly. Only talk about yourself if it is useful to bolster your authority on the topic, and—even then—do that sparingly: talking too much about yourself will make your story go in the background. Being humble pays.

By dropping an attractive hook and laying down the necessary context, you have completed the beginning of your story and are ready to move to its central part.

Middle

The middle of your story: this is where most of the action happens. In this part, you want to lay down the chain of scenes that gradually builds the logic supporting your case. As pointed out by data storytelling expert Brent Dykes, the first thing you want to do is to identify the **Aha Moment**: this is the climax of your data story—think of it as the play's focal scene. Once you are clear on the aha moment, you plan backward all previous scenes so that the audience is guided through a supporting flow of rising insights, which will ultimately lead them to the peak.

Pixar's film director Andrew Stanton noticed that an audience always likes to *work for their meal*. Given our human tendency to deduce and deduct, he suggests that the build-up in the middle of a story should leave an opportunity for the audience to put things together by themselves, taking an active part in the process, without being handed every single step on a silver platter. *Don't give them four*, Stanton advises—*but give them two plus two*. When decision-makers feel they are part of the thinking process (instead of being spectators), they will be more likely to buy into your proposal.

It's like a "connect the dots" puzzle game: the numbered dots tell you precisely what to do, but you still find some inner satisfaction in drawing the lines yourself and — maybe — unveiling something unexpected. One practical way to implement this trick of the trade is to present only part of the available data in a scene and ask the audience to think through what the rest would be. For example, you can leverage animations to visually enforce the gradual unveiling or stop and use a flipchart to gather ideas from the audience (and get them thinking) before resuming the flow and sharing your views. By asking them to participate in the thinking, you'll draw them into the process, which will connect them more closely to you. As they take a position on the matter, they will also directly confront their previous beliefs and maybe prove themselves wrong.

> Allowing audience participation can backfire: for example, some participants may intervene to distract attention to their specific objectives, jeopardizing your narrative. A trick to avoid this is to clearly state what you want your audience to do when requesting their participation: instead of just stopping and asking for general comments, pose a specific question and be clear on what particular action you expect in return.

When you are clear on how the rising insights lead to the aha moment scene, you can get to the next and final part of the story structure.

End

So what? This is the most dreaded response an audience can have to a data story. You want to stay away from it at all costs. Remember: working on storytelling is not a way of *dressing up* data so it looks aesthetically pleasant or making its delivery more engaging just for the sake of it. A data story is instead a practical vehicle for facilitating a very practical goal: driving business action! The end of the story has the vital role of making the audience move forward from theory to practice, from a good idea to an actual change, from a solid insight to an impactful decision. Many data stories — however logically sound and emotionally engaging — fail in the last leg of their journey and do not bring any significant consequence. To avoid this, you need to have two crucial elements in the concluding part of a story.

The first one is a list of the key **Takeaways**: these are the three to five messages that, no matter what, you want your audience to remember. Takeaways will undoubtedly include the summary of the aha moment scene and every recommendation you are leaving your audience with. Pick your takeaways carefully: they should be selected not depending on how proud you feel about having found them, but instead on how value-accretive for the business they would be for people to keep in mind (and act upon).

The second element of a data story end is the list of proposed **Next Steps**: this can be as simple as a bullet-point list or a table with the *What, Who,* and *By when* elements of every meaningful action you expect to happen after the session. It's essential not just to put the easy part (the description of what needs to happen) but also the name of the owner and the deadline for getting it completed to prevent your propositions from falling through the cracks of an ambiguous sense of accountability. Some of the next steps might be prepopulated in your delivery material as you anticipate them being needed, given what you plan to present. Some others might be decided on the spot when the audience finally gets a say on your story. In any case, you want to make sure you capture them in writing and validate the alignment of the various owners.

Depending on the context in which your story is delivered (a short call with a few decision-makers, a large team meeting, or a townhall presentation, to name a few cases), you need to appropriately fine-tune the format of the end act of your story. You might need to add a short or long Q&A and discussion part, so as to call the audience to actively participate and contribute to the decision or to define the required next steps.

There is no one-size-fits-all format for it: just think through what your specific audience will likely prefer to do in the end part of your story and plan accordingly. Once you have prepared a sharp list of takeaways and some pragmatic next steps, you have all you need to end your story confidently, and you are ready to move to the next step of the data storytelling process: refining your scenes to make them great.

Polishing scenes

Sometimes, inexperienced data storytellers make the naïve assumption that it is enough to "let the data speak": their story ends up being an **Infodump**, a conglomerate of charts copy-pasted in a long series of PowerPoint slides. The result? Making the audience confused, disengaged, and driving them further away from the original objective. By selecting the right (few) scenes and putting them in a solid 3-act structure, you have already taken some effective steps to avoid falling into the infodump trap. However, this is not sufficient, and before closing your story, you need to invest some time into polishing your scenes to make them **Focused** and **Accessible**.

Focusing attention

In data storytelling, as in many other things in life, *less is more*. Your audience's attention is a scarce and fragile resource, and you need to protect it at all costs. If you are telling your data story using only your voice, without any visual aids, then you want to keep your speech minimal: make your sentences short and crisp; refrain from adding unnecessary details unless your narrative requires them. If, as in most cases, you are putting together some supporting visual material (like slides with charts), you need to pass them through the *x-rays* of a rigorous necessity check. Every visual element in a slide will utilize part of the cognitive bandwidth of the viewer. You cannot afford to waste this resource — always in such a short supply — with embellishments, clutter, and nice-to-have additions.

An effective way to systematically preserve the focus in your data scenes is to follow this simple 2-step methodology:

1. Recognize what needs to be in the **Foreground** and what will remain in the **Background**. Think about the key message you want to pass in the scene: all facts that directly support your point deserve to stay well lit in the foreground. On the other hand, all other data points providing contextual support to your message should be removed or visually muted. Differentiating between fore- and background elements is not hard work. If the message is *brand X is disproportionally growing versus the competition*, the line showing the growth of brand X is in the foreground, while competitors' brands are in the background. If, instead, you want to say *patients displaying these 2 symptoms (out of the 10 possible ones) are disproportionally more likely to be positive*, the 2 key symptoms should be in the front, leaving all others in the back to serve as context.

   > Non-data elements like graphical aids (gridlines, axes, and legends, to name a few), repeated text, and logos should always go in the background and should be visually muted (or, when not necessary, removed).

2. Once you are clear about what should be in the two layers of your scene, you need to leverage your graphical settings to "minimize" the prominence of the background elements in favor of those in the foreground. In many cases, data stories fail in differentiating these layers: all chart settings are just maintained in their "default" mode, forcing every graphical element (lines, bars, cells of tables) to be treated equally and none of them to stand out. You want exactly the opposite to happen: the attention should naturally flow to a subset of the few items that should emerge from the mass. It's better to **Carve Out** the nonessential instead of strengthening the crucial: by doing so, you avoid adding yet more visual elements, which might further distract your audience.

Here are the most frequently used ways you can direct the audience's attention to what matters the most:

- **Color**: Give background elements a low-saturation color, preferably gray, and assign a high-saturation one to foreground elements. Most of the time, it will be enough for you to use a single, high-saturation color (like blue, orange, or even black) consistently in the foregrounds of all your scenes and just shades of gray for everything else. If only a specific part of a chart deserves to go in the foreground (like a portion of a line or a particular bar in a bar chart), apply your color to that part only: this will clearly highlight its unique role in the story.

> Careful with colors! Avoid the unconsidered use of many different colors in your story as they can seriously distract. The fewer colors appear in a data scene, the better: as a rule of thumb, never use more than five different colors in a single view.

- **Size**: Use thinner lines and smaller fonts for what should stay in the background. Thicker elements and bold typeface work very well to clearly distinguish what goes in front.

- **Grouping**: An effective way to give focus to the foreground is to group together the background elements that do not need to stay separate. The typical cases are when you have many overlapping lines in the same chart (making them indistinguishable), or several (small) sub-bars stacked together that are hard to discern: you can fix them by aggregating the background smaller elements into a single item, which you may call *all others*.

The first part of your polishing is done: you have recognized what deserves to be in the foreground and have made it stick out from everything else.

Making scenes accessible

Clarity in data storytelling is a must, yet is quite tough to achieve. Your audience might be very diverse in terms of background, seniority, prior knowledge on the matter, and attention span. Because of this diversity, presenting clearly to every single member of the audience requires some extra effort. If you want to be inclusive, your data scenes should be easily accessible by everyone and, as much as possible, self-explanatory. You might be an expert on what you are presenting: yet— remember—it shouldn't take your expertise to follow your story in full.

As you build the visual support of your data story, you can make use of some proven methods to make your slides straightforward and accessible to everyone:

- **Action titles**: Make sure that the title of every slide directly conveys the point you want to make with it. A bad title is *Sales evolution forecast (in US$), next three years*, while a good title is *We expect sales to grow by 50% in 2.5 years from now*. Use the title to tell your audience what you want them to know rather than just providing contextual information on what they are seeing. You can use other features (like axis titles) to explain the metrics you display. Do you remember when we said that scenes could be summarized by using a succinct and crisp sentence? Make that sentence the title of your slide.

- **Guiding labels**: Add textboxes that signal and explain the interesting part of the data you are showing. The typical case is when you circle some data points or a portion of a line and add some text nearby to explain *what's going on* there. If needs be, feel free to use lines or arrows to connect the data you want to specify with the text annotation it refers to. By just looking at the guiding labels, the audience should automatically understand most of the action in your scene, without any need to explain.

> Use colors to link text and visual elements referring to the same entity. For example, if a blue line refers to a specific brand, use precisely the same blue when mentioning that brand in the title or a label. This is a very effective way to make your material self-explanatory and unambiguously guide your audience through it. Remember to stay consistent in color choices across the whole story.

- **Build-up animations**: Consider structuring your visual material in a way that builds up progressively in a few steps. This is a powerful way to convey more complex thinking, which lets you guide your audience progressively, showing more and more labels and chunks of the data as they enter one scene after another. Animations are also suitable for reinforcing the emotional load of some scene types like evolution (*this is the profit we made in the last year, and...* (animation proceeds adding forecasted development)... *this is where it can go next year if the product launch is successful*) and breakdown (*out of all the new users who subscribed in Spain...* (animation proceeds showing a drilldown)... *more than 80% were solely due to the acquisition*). Moreover, animations prevent the audience from reading ahead on your material: their curiosity can distract them from the points you want to make and derail their attention away from the flow you prepared so carefully for them.

- **Readability**: A too-busy slide is likely to cause your audience to stop focusing on your narrative while trying to decode what they see. Avoid the visual infodump: if it's too much content, you should ask yourself what can be removed or kept as a backup material. If it is all needed, you can use multiple charts for it. Be miserly in the number of words you write: the fewer, the better. By keeping the word count at a minimum, you also protect yourself from the unfortunate choice of "reading your slides" instead of making their content shine through your delivery. You should also check the readability of the fonts you use: take two steps back from your computer screen and check if you can read with ease all the numbers and text in there.

Using titles, labels, and animations wisely, you can make the visual material supporting your data scenes self-explanatory and easily understandable by everyone in your audience. Once you have polished all the parts of your story, you are finally able to move further.

Finalizing your story

The data storytelling process is iterative. Now that you have the full picture of what your data story looks like as a whole, you can go through it and critically assess whether you have opportunities to improve it further. The following **Checklist** includes a set of valid (and sometimes harsh) questions you should ask yourself at this stage:

- Does the story meet its original objective? Picture in your mind the desired outcome (a decision, a change, an approval): how likely is it to become reality thanks to this story's delivery?

- Is the current script in line with the logistic constraints you have? Is it reasonable to think that you will have enough time to deliver it fully? Are you giving enough time for Q&A and discussions?

- Is this going to be compelling for the audience and, in particular, for the key decision-makers? Put yourself in their shoes, one by one: how will they react? Is this resonating with what's hot in their mind now? Is this what you want them to be thinking? Is this really what they care about? What questions will they ask?

- Do you have a strong and clear initial hook? Is it compelling for the key decision-makers?

- Are you providing enough initial context? Are you making the objective clear for the audience at the beginning?

- Have you got a clear list of data scenes you will stage? Out of these scenes, is there one prominent versus the other? Is this one really going to drive an "Aha!" reaction?

- Are the rising insights building up in a way that the audience can easily follow? Are you clear on the one single message you want to leave in each scene?

- Are you using the right supporting facts for each scene, according to type (see *Table 8.2*)?

- In the visual materials you use to support the data scenes, are there clear action titles? Is the data in the foreground standing out from everything else? Are you highlighting the crucial elements with crisp guiding labels? Are colors used consistently? Are the fonts too small?

- Are you wrapping up your key takeaways in the end? Are the takeaways no more than 5?

- Do you have a list of proposed next steps with a clear owner, a description, and a deadline for each?

- Are you leveraging rhetorical modes to be persuasive (see *Table 8.1*)? Are you and your story looking credible? Is there anything you can add, like sources, a bio, and testimonials to enhance credibility?

- Rethink carefully the logical thinking you are offering and ask someone to be critical and play the role of the devil's advocate. Is it sound? Will it be understood and followed by all of your audience? Is there a weak link in the logical chain?

- Are you creating an emotional connection with the audience by using imagery, metaphors, and personal experiences? Will your result be agreeable and humble or unpleasant and arrogant?

As you get ready for your story delivery, make sure you allow for some quality time for some good rounds of **Rehearsals**. Some of the weaknesses of your story will only become apparent when you are actually going through it. There is no better way to refine your story and acquire self-assurance for the delivery than rehearsing a couple of times. I strongly recommend preparing a **Script** of what you want to say. Depending on your confidence level in speaking, you can jot down just a summary or a bullet-point list of the key messages to give or write a full word-by-word script. Even if you don't have the opportunity to read through the script when delivering the story live, you will highly benefit from having prepared the script: trust me, it works!

> If you decide to put together a full script of your story, make sure your delivery does not come across as robotic or mechanical. Rehearse the script a few times so you don't have to read it through.

The data storytelling canvas

The many concepts, models, and tips we encountered in this chapter's content-rich pages will certainly need some practice to become habits. To keep them all at hand, you can use the **Data Storytelling Canvas**, which you find in *Figure 8.3* (you can also download a printable version from the book site if you wish):

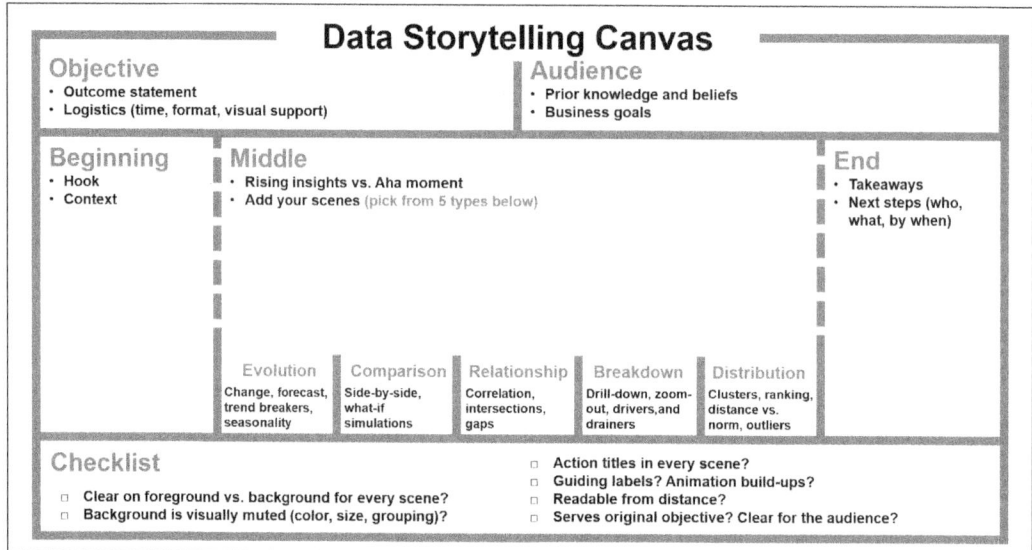

Data Storytelling Canvas

Objective
- Outcome statement
- Logistics (time, format, visual support)

Audience
- Prior knowledge and beliefs
- Business goals

Beginning
- Hook
- Context

Middle
- Rising insights vs. Aha moment
- Add your scenes (pick from 5 types below)

End
- Takeaways
- Next steps (who, what, by when)

Evolution	Comparison	Relationship	Breakdown	Distribution
Change, forecast, trend breakers, seasonality	Side-by-side, what-if simulations	Correlation, intersections, gaps	Drill-down, zoom-out, drivers, and drainers	Clusters, ranking, distance vs. norm, outliers

Checklist
- ☐ Clear on foreground vs. background for every scene?
- ☐ Background is visually muted (color, size, grouping)?
- ☐ Action titles in every scene?
- ☐ Guiding labels? Animation build-ups?
- ☐ Readable from distance?
- ☐ Serves original objective? Clear for the audience?

Figure 8.3: The data storytelling canvas. Follow the structure to build your next story

The structure of the canvas serves as the scaffolding to build a data story effectively. The boxes of the canvas will:

- Force you to think through some preliminary aspects such as the objectives and the audience (first things first!).

- Guide you through the unmissable parts of a data story (beginning, middle, and end), giving you space to add placeholders for your scenes as you build the narrative.

- Provide a quick reference (like the list of data types and a short version of the checklist) that is useful to keep handy during the preparation process.

You can use the canvas in solo mode to guide your individual thinking. If you have the opportunity to build a story as a team effort, you can reuse the structure of the canvas to support a cooperative design session. In this case, all inputs and ideas can be added as post-it notes in the various boxes or as text annotations on a virtual whiteboard when meeting virtually. Give it a try next time: it is an efficient way to brainstorm and gather collective ideas, ultimately leading to great stories.

Summary

I hope you enjoyed as much as I did the intense journey in the vast and fascinating world of data storytelling that this chapter took us through. We can be great data analysts or respected business domain experts. However, in a business organization, we will often lack the full authority required to make decisions freely and make things happen, even if data certifies the validity of our points. Storytelling extends the potential of data analytics as it lets us transform data into value-creating actions.

We started by applying the ageless enablers of persuasion (being credible, offering logical reasoning, and driving emotional engagement) to business data, and we explored the many reasons stories can make a difference in advocating our data-based recommendations. Then, we went through a systematic process for building data stories that stick, leveraging the (simple but effective) 3-act story structure and the five archetypal data scene types. Afterward, we acquired a set of practical tips for polishing our story and finetuning it to make its delivery most likely to secure our desired outcome. We concluded by exploring a practical tool (the data storytelling canvas) that we can leverage at the time of need.

One last consideration before closing and moving on: strangely enough, in this data storytelling chapter, you didn't find any data charts. You should now be clear on the difference between storytelling and data visualization, which are sometimes mixed together confusingly. Charts do not "convince" anyone by themselves, while stories do. It's much easier to craft a nice-looking visual than to actually build an engaging story based on a solid narrative. I hope you are convinced about the need to be good at both, and that you now see the utmost centrality that storytelling has in data analytics.

I told you so: this was the chapter you didn't expect!

9

Extending Your Toolbox

Getting up to speed with the latest tools and novel techniques in data analytics is surely a never-ending process. In this field, you need to be ready to update and expand your knowledge continuously. So far in this book, we have acquired a number of vital, application-agnostic data techniques such as data cleaning and modeling, machine learning, data visualization, and storytelling. We have also learned how to apply them through a solid application toolbox made of KNIME and Power BI. As we approach the end of our journey, we should see what else is available and how to integrate all the applications together to make the best out of all of them.

In particular, we will cover the following questions:

- What is Tableau, and how can I use it for visualization and storytelling?
- What is Python, and how do I get started with it?
- How can I boost my workflows by integrating Python or any other code?
- How can I use KNIME extension packages to add functionalities?
- What is automated machine learning, and what should I expect from its future business applications?

This chapter is not meant to make you an autonomous user of Python, Tableau, and other tools. There is no need for it at this stage. Your initial toolbox (KNIME and Power BI) covers your essential analytical needs well. The point of this chapter is to show you what *else* is available and make you curious and excited about the many directions you can take to expand your abilities in data analytics from now on.

We will first look at Tableau, another data visualization tool: by means of a simple example, we will see how what we learned for Power BI can be easily applied in Tableau as well. Then, we will learn about Python and get a friendly introduction to how it is used in analytics. We will see how to integrate Python code into KNIME through extension packages. Lastly, we will learn about automated machine learning and see the concept in action with the help of the H2O.ai platform. All the tools in this chapter are either open source or provide free trial options so that you have the opportunity to put your hands on them and evaluate by yourself how they can help you and your business.

Getting started with Tableau

Founded as a Stanford University spin-off, Tableau has pioneered in the data visualization arena for nearly two decades and is now regarded as one of the leading business intelligence platforms. Its straightforward drag-and-drop user interface, the integration with many data platforms, and its highly customizable, high-quality chart types have made Tableau very popular among business professionals, analysts, and data journalists.

Similar to Power BI, Tableau comes in different versions. In this chapter, we will use **Tableau Public**: this is a free desktop application (you can download it from `public.tableau.com`) that has nearly all the functionalities included in the full version (called **Desktop Professional**) but also a couple of important limitations. First, it relies on local data, so you cannot connect to remote data sources. Additionally, the public version lets you save your result solely on the public Tableau server, which is open to everyone: this means you cannot save your work on your computer. Given its lack of privacy protection, Tableau Public is not viable for day-to-day business needs, but we can still use it for exploring Tableau functionalities and comparing them with Power BI's.

> You can publish dashboards online using the cloud-based service called **Tableau Server**. You can also design dashboards just using your browser and avoid the installation of new software. To do so, you will need to register with the Tableau Public website mentioned above, go to your profile, and click on **Create a Viz**. The user interface on the web app is very similar to the one you could find in the desktop application, which we will use in this chapter.

Following the spirit we kept throughout the book, let's explore Tableau through practice by getting our hands on it. In this short tutorial, we will create a couple of visualizations based on the sales database we leveraged in *Chapter 6, Getting Started with Power BI*: a treemap to display the relative weight of categories and a line chart that shows the evolution of sales over time. This time, the three tables (Transactions, ProductMD, and CustomerMD) are saved as separate sheets in one single Excel file (SalesDashboardTableau.xlsx):

1. Open Tableau Public. In the first screen (which looks similar to what you see in *Figure 9.1*), click on **Microsoft Excel** on the left and open the file containing our data:

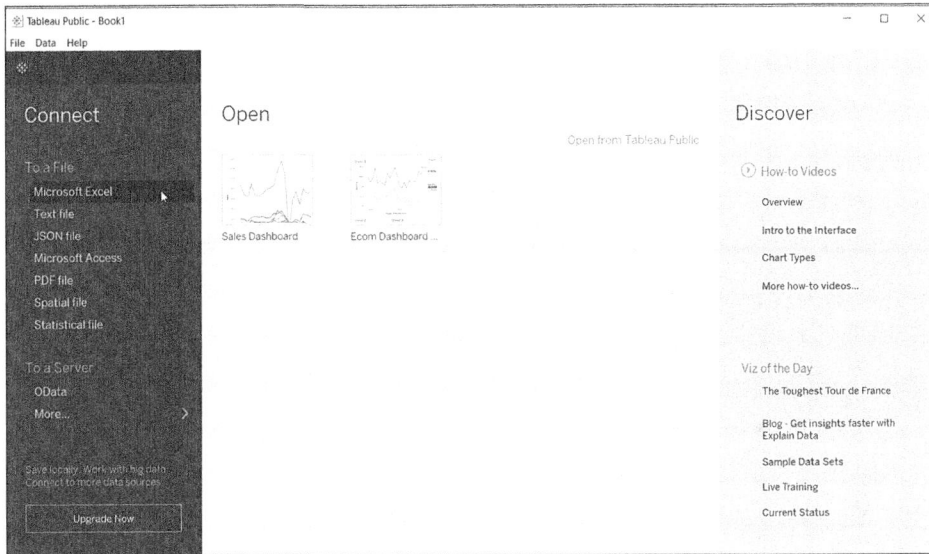

Figure 9.1: The initial screen of Tableau Public: select the type of files you want to use on the left

2. In the next window, called the **Data Source** screen (*Figure 9.2*), you will find on the left the three sheets included in the Excel file we just opened. By dragging them on the blank area on the top left, you can build an entity-relationship diagram that defines the dashboard's underlying data model:

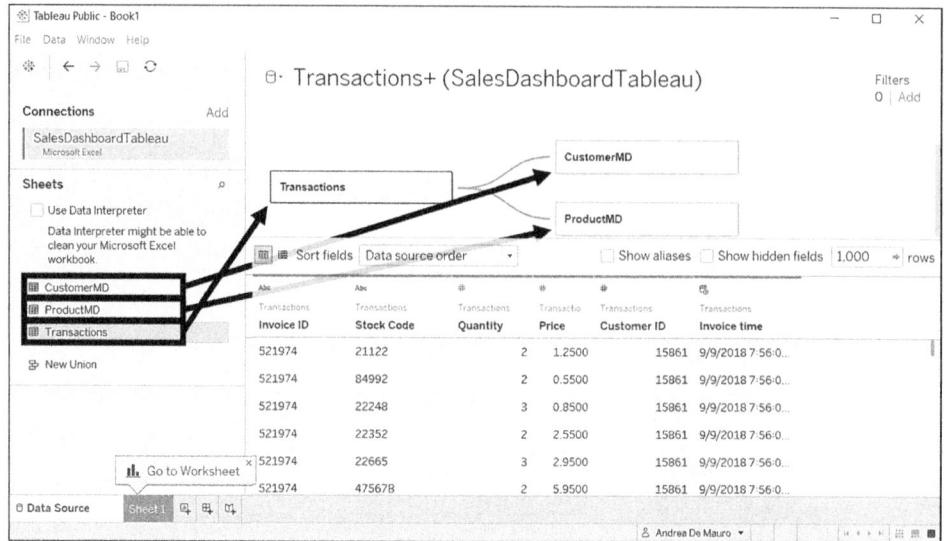

Figure 9.2: The Data Source screen in Tableau: drag and drop your source tables and build the data model

To do so, we need to follow the right order. First, drag the **Transactions** table and wait a few seconds for the data to load and the preview to appear on the bottom. Then, drag the Customer Master Data (**CustomerMD**) table and drop it on the right of the **Transactions** box: the line between the two indicates that Tableau will join the two tables. As you release the mouse button, the **Edit Relationship** window will appear (*Figure 9.3*): Tableau has successfully identified *Customer ID* as the column to be used for matching rows. We can confirm the relationship by closing the window, without making any changes to the default settings. Once this is done, it's time to drag also the Product Master Data (**ProductMD**) table to the right of **Transactions**, making sure that the resulting connections look similar to what you had in *Figure 9.2*. Finally, confirm *StockCode* as the matching column by closing the window that pops up: your data model is good to go:

Edit Relationship   ✕

How do relationships differ from joins? **Learn more**

Transactions   CustomerMD

  # Customer ID   =   # Customer ID (CustomerMD)

  ⊕ Add more fields

  〉 Performance Options

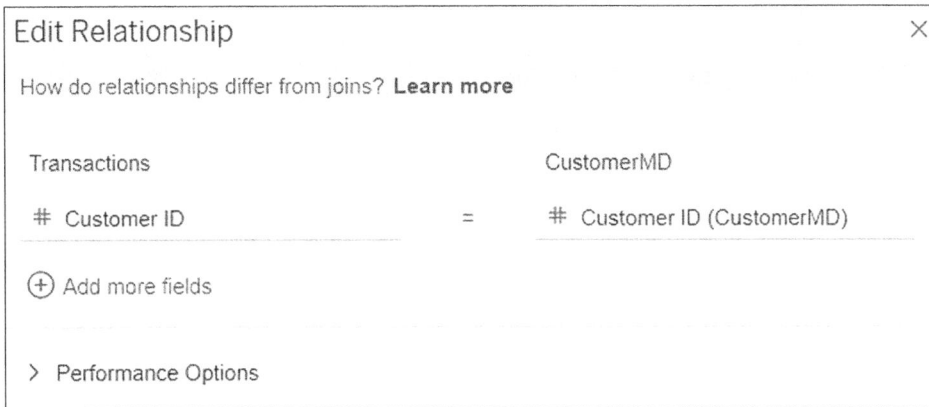

Figure 9.3: Edit Relationship window: select one or more matching conditions for your joins

To proceed further, click on the **Sheet 1** tab on the bottom left: you will land in the main interface of Tableau, called **Workspace** (*Figure 9.4*). Let's explore the four fundamental sections in the workspace:

A. The **Data Panel** is where you find all your data columns, organized by table. From here, you will drag the quantities you wish to use in a visualization or create calculated fields. This is similar to the **Fields** section in Power BI.

B. The **Visualization View** is where you can build your visuals. From here, you can connect the fields available in the data panel with the visual attributes in a visual, which in Tableau are called **Shelves**. For example, the height of bars, the position of points, their color, size, and the text appearing on the labels are all controlled through the **Rows**, **Columns** and **Marks** shelves that you find in the visualization view (their usage will become clearer as we go through the tutorial). From the same view, you can also implement pagination and split one visual into multiple pages, each one showing different values for a given column (that you have to drop in the **Pages** shelf). Additionally, from the visualization view, you can decide which fields to use for limiting the data to be visualized (**Filters** shelf).

C. The **Show Me Panel** is where you can select the type of chart to use, such as line charts, treemaps, histograms, or geographic maps.

D. The bar at the bottom lets you add **Sheet tabs** and navigate through them. In Tableau, every sheet can be one among three different types: a Worksheet (a single chart), a Dashboard (a composition of multiple charts), or a Story (a controlled sequence of worksheets or dashboards that progress to convey a data story, as you learned to do in *Chapter 8, Telling Stories with Data*):

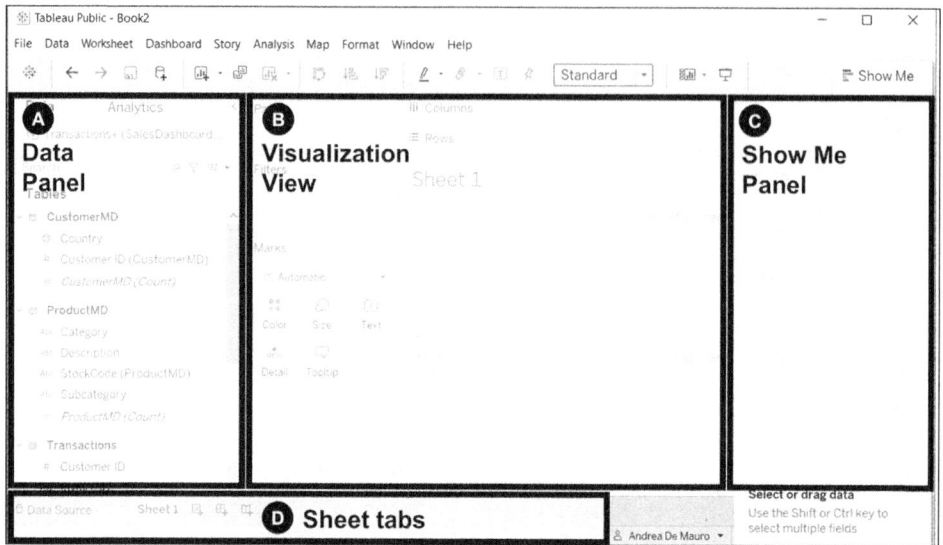

Figure 9.4: The Workspace screen in Tableau: drag and drop columns to the visualization features, pick chart types, and move across visuals, dashboards, and stories

Now that we are acquainted with the workspace interface, we can build our first chart to show the relative size of each category and subcategory in terms of sales. However, we do not yet have a column carrying the revenues generated by each transaction and, so, we need to first add a calculated field that does the math for us.

3. Right click on the *Price* column available in the **Data Panel** and then select **Create | Calculated Field…** as shown in *Figure 9.5*:

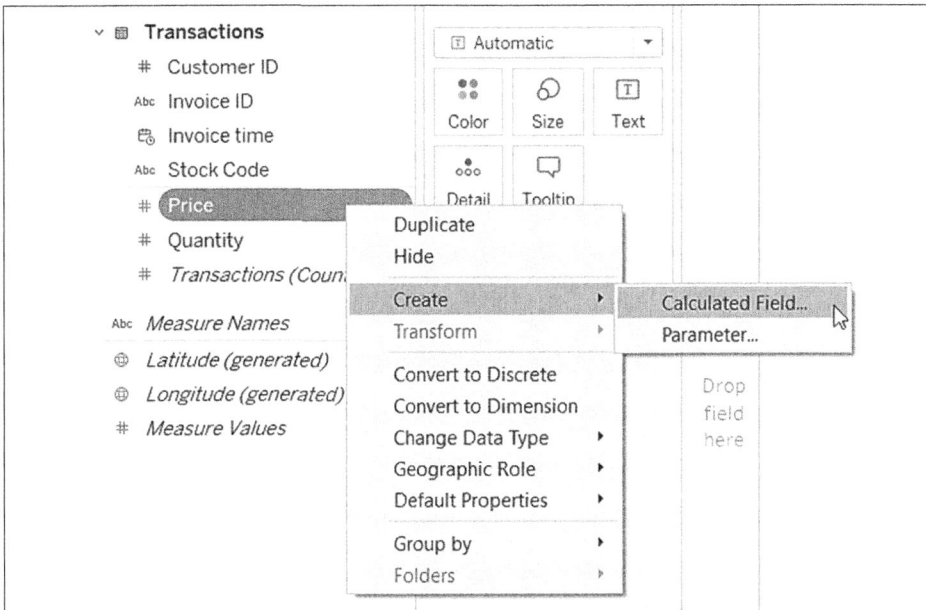

Figure 9.5: Creating a calculated field in Tableau: we can add math formulas and generate new quantities to be visualized

You will be prompted with a dialog (*Figure 9.6*) that lets you enter the name of the new column (in the text box on the top left—we are going for Sales in this case) and the mathematical expression to be used, where fields are indicated through square brackets. Click on the little arrow showing on the far right of the window. You will open an extra panel that, similarly to what we had in the **Math Formula** node in KNIME, provides many logical and mathematical functions to be used, together with a textual description on the right. In our case, the expression [Price]*[Quantity] will do: write it in the box on the left (Tableau will help by attempting to autocomplete the names of the columns as you type them) and then click on **OK** to move on. The new calculated field will appear in the **Data Panel** and can now be used as we wish:

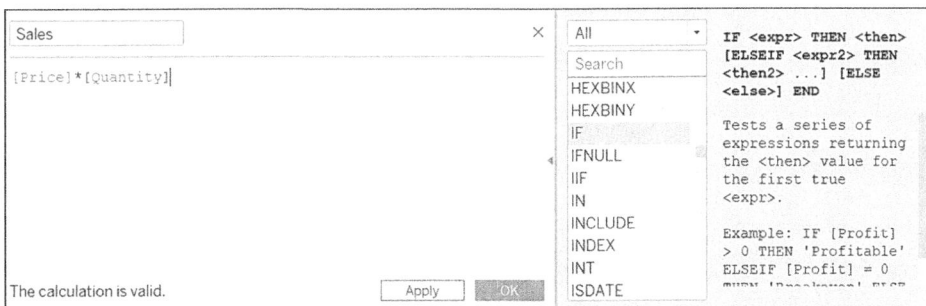

Figure 9.6: Defining a calculated field: add the math expression that combines columns as you need

4. We now have all the ingredients to bake our first visual: having learned in *Chapter 7, Visualizing Data Effectively BI*, how to resist the sweet temptation of using pie charts, we want to build a nice treemap that shows the relative magnitude of sales by category and subcategory. Building a visual in Tableau requires dragging the data fields of interest (the columns listed in the data panel on the left) and dropping them to some visual attributes (the shelves appearing in the visualization view). In the case of the treemap, you can follow the arrows in *Figure 9.7* as a guide. Start by dropping *Category* (first) and *Subcategory* (second) in the box called **Text** (it will be automatically renamed to **Label** later, when the chart type is established). Then, take the newly created *Sales* field and drop it in the **Size** box. Lastly, get the *Category* field to also control the color of the areas by dropping it to the **Color** box:

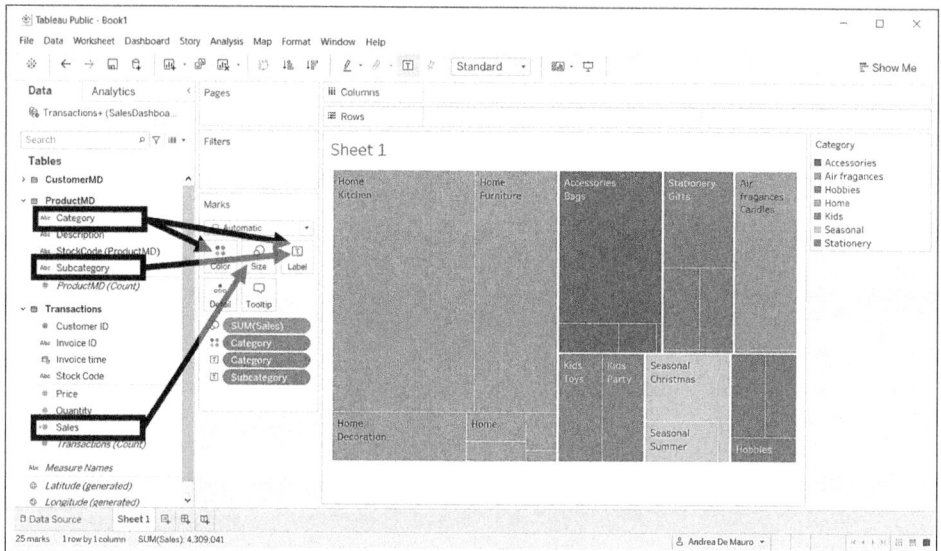

Figure 9.7: Building a treemap in Tableau: take the fields on the left and drop them to the right box in the Marks shelf

After you build a visual in Tableau, you can easily explore alternative versions where different chart types are applied to the same data. To try this, click on the various boxes you find in the **Show Me** panel on the right. The chart types that cannot be rendered given the current data are grayed out, and you cannot select them. Tableau might also recommend one specific chart type and highlight its border in orange. I recommend you choose the chart type by always keeping the business question in mind, as you learned in *Chapter 7, Visualizing Data Effectively*.

Well done! With just four drag and drops, you have built your first visual in Tableau. We can easily see how the "Home" *Category* (and—within it—the "Kitchen" *Subcategory*) generates the biggest revenue bucket in our business.

Let's move to the second business question: this time, we want to focus our message on the trend of *Sales* by *Category*. We decide to put together a line chart as it is our natural chart type for communicating insights related to the evolution of quantities over time.

5.   To create a new visual, click on the first small **+** icon on the right of the **Sheet 1** tab at the bottom (alternatively, you can click on **Worksheet | New Worksheet** from the top menu, or just press *CTRL + M*). By doing this, a blank **Sheet 2** appears: this is the space to draw our line chart on.

6.   The first field to drag is *Invoice time*: drop it to the **Columns** shelf. Given its type (carrying the date and time of each transaction), we need to tell Tableau at which level of granularity (years, quarters, months, weeks, and so on) we want to aggregate. In this case, we want to visualize one data point for every month of transactions: right-click on the field as it appears on the shelf, and then select the second **Month** entry in the pop-up menu (use *Figure 9.8* as a guide):

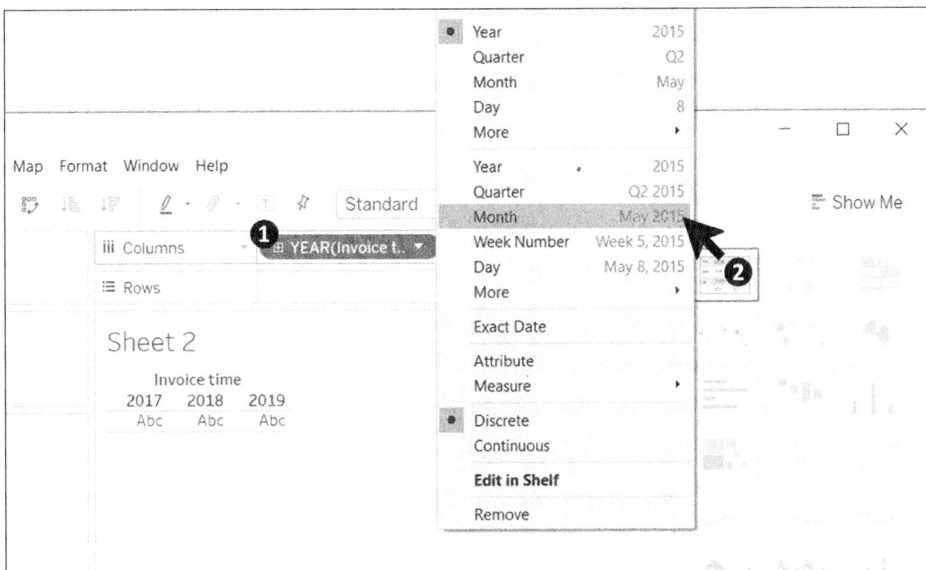

Figure 9.8: Using a date field for a line chart: right-click on the field and select the time granularity you need. In this case, we go for months

7. Let's move on to implementing the other fields we want to use, following the drag and drops you see in *Figure 9.9*. Drop *Sales* to the **Rows** shelf (by default, the aggregation by sum is applied, but you can change it easily by right-clicking on the field and picking the proper function in the **Measure** submenu). The following field to move is *Category*. Drop it twice: first to the **Color** box (so we differentiate lines by *Category*) and then to the **Label** box (so we show a direct label for each line):

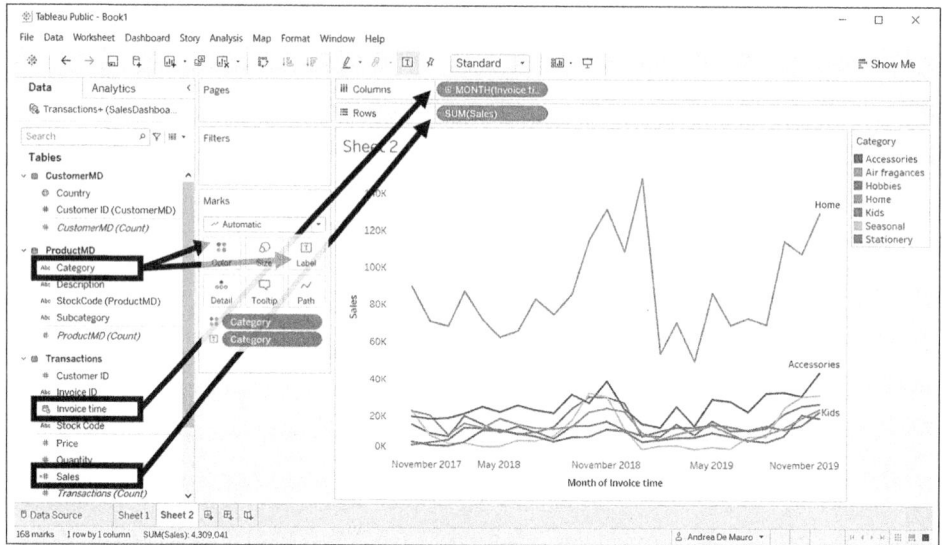

Figure 9.9: Building a line chart in Tableau:
the columns and rows shelves control the x- and the y-axis, respectively

8. Before composing our dashboard, we can edit the sheet names at the bottom by right-clicking on each tab and selecting **Rename**. We can go for something more meaningful like Business by category and Sales trend for the first and the second visualizations, respectively.

9. It's time to build the dashboard by combining the two visuals. Click on the second **+** icon in the **Sheets** tab at the bottom or select **Dashboard | New Dashboard** from the top menu.

10. On the left of the new dashboard view, you will find a list of the two worksheets we built, one for each chart we created. To create a dashboard, you will just need to drag and drop the worksheets in the blank area on the right, as you can see in *Figure 9.10*:

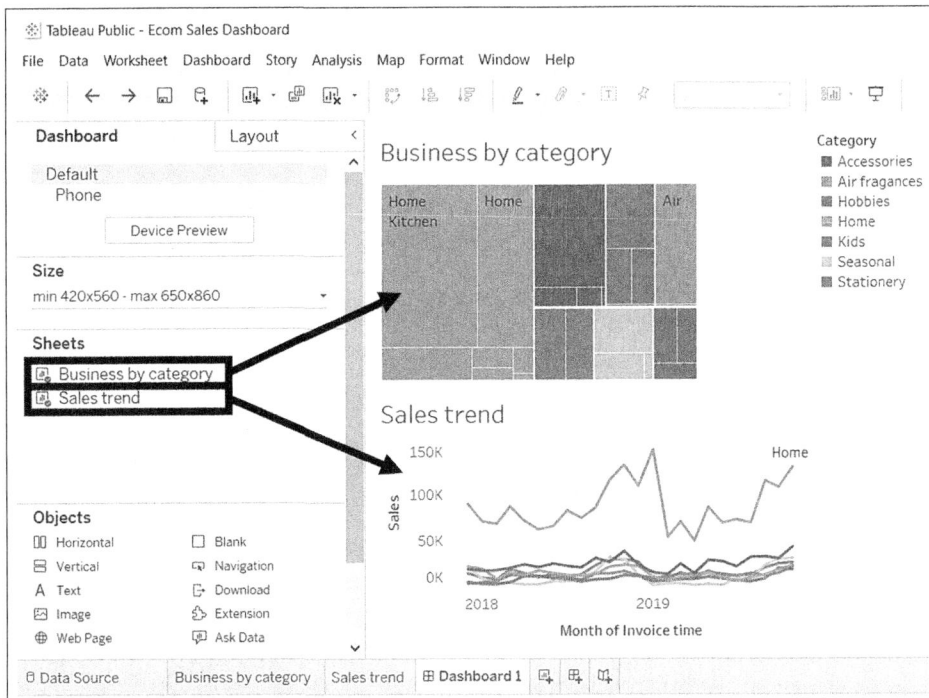

Figure 9.10: Building a dashboard in Tableau: drag and drop the visualizations to their positions

> On the bottom left of the dashboard view, you find several icons that you can drag and drop to your dashboard to add additional objects, such as text labels, images, web pages, or extensions. Check it out.

11. Before publishing the dashboard, let's configure the interactions across visuals. If you click on any empty space of the first visual, you will select it, and its borders get highlighted (letting you adjust its shape, if you wish). Also, a few icons will appear on the top right of the selected visual, as you can see in *Figure 9.11*. If you click on the filter icon, as the arrow in the picture indicates, you will set that visual as a filter for every other visual in the dashboard. You can quickly test that this works properly: if you click on any subcategory in the treemap (you can select more than one at once by keeping the *CTRL* key pressed), you will notice that the line chart updates accordingly, showing only the trend of the selection portion of business. This is exactly what we were after:

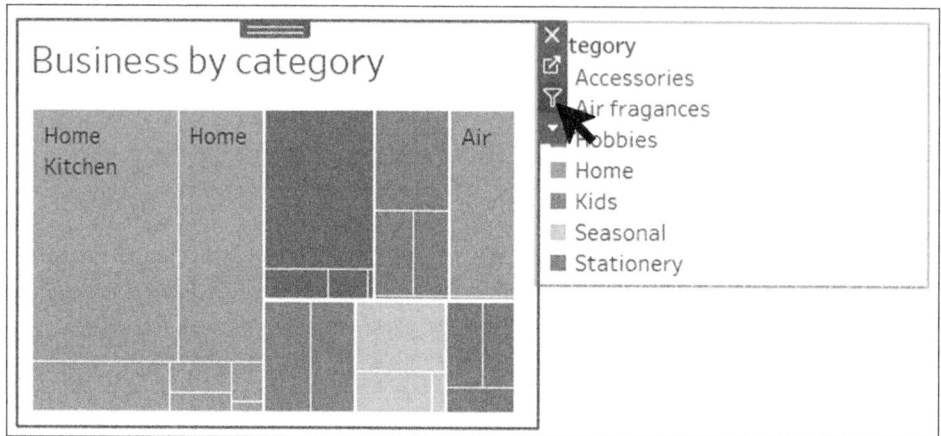

Figure 9.11: Use a visual for filtering subsequent charts in a Tableau dashboard.
Click on the filter icon in the top right

12. We can now publish our work on the server: just open the **File** menu at the top and then click on **Save to Tableau Public...**. Next, pick a name (I went for Ecom Sales Dashboard), click on **OK**, and wait for a few seconds for the data to upload. Your browser will open up and show your published dashboard in all its grace (you can check my version out at tiny.cc/ecomdashboard and in *Figure 9.12*):

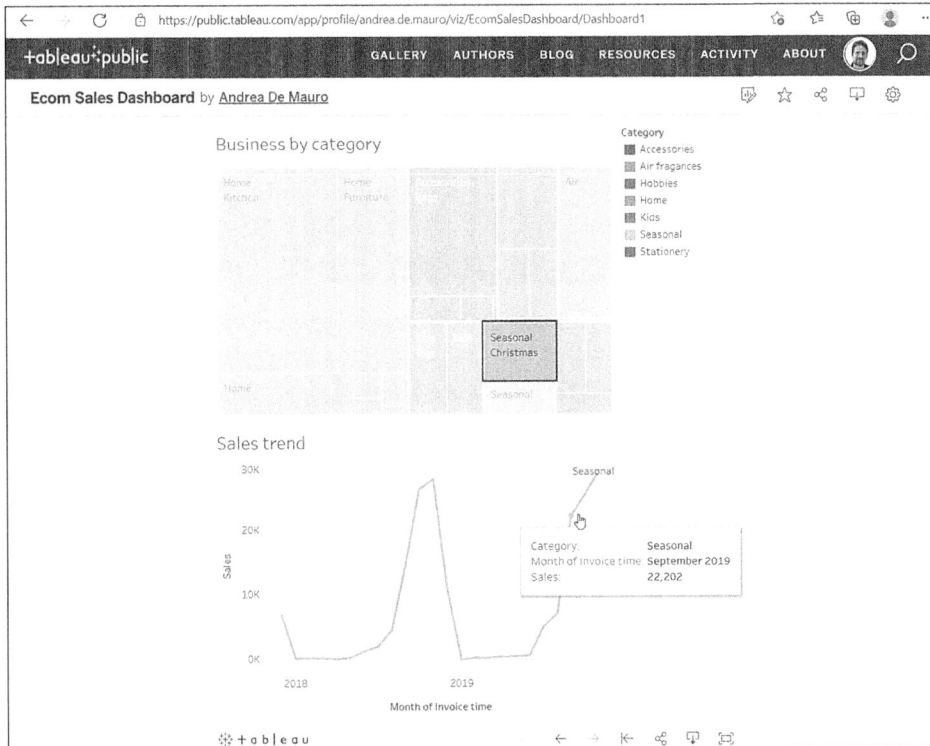

Figure 9.12: The dashboard published on the Tableau Public server: let others access your work and interact with it

In the last few pages, we ran through the fundamental functionalities of Tableau: we have learned how to load data, combine it in a simple data model, created calculated fields, and built visuals and combined them in an interactive dashboard. I am sure you noticed the extensive similarities between Tableau and what we have learned on Power BI. We could carry on in the exploration of other business intelligence platforms such as Qlik, MicroStrategy, and TIBCO Spotfire, to mention a few. The (exciting) reality is that the *bulk* of how they work is very similar, and the last few chapters have equipped you with all you need to get started and create value for your business, irrespective of the tool you used.

Let's now move to the next "expansion" phase of our data analytics toolbox with Python.

Python for data analytics

Python is an increasingly popular high-level programming language that is particularly well suited for data analytics and machine learning applications. The ample availability of analytics-related libraries and its easy-to-learn syntax make it the preferred choice for many data science practitioners.

> The story behind Python's name has nothing to do with snakes. Its creator, Dutch programmer Guido van Rossum, was a big fan of the 1970s BBC comedy series "Monty Python's Flying Circus." So he picked Python as the name of the project to honor the irreverent genius of the British comedy troupe running that show.

As this book focuses on visual programming, we will not go through any thorough explanation of coding principles. Instead, the purpose of this section is to let you see Python in action on a familiar problem and get some perspective on how it can be used in our everyday work. We will first go through a script that repeats the exact same regression tutorial we saw in *Chapter 5, Applying Machine Learning at Work*. Then, we will see how Python can smoothly integrate with KNIME to make the best out of the two complementary approaches to programming for analytics.

A gentle introduction to the Python language

To use Python, you can either install a development platform like Anaconda (we will do this later) or leverage a web-based interface such as Colab. Google Colab (short for Colaboratory) is a free cloud service that lets you write and run Python code without any setup being needed: you can access it at colab.research.google.com.

As you can see in *Figure 9.13*, the user interface of Colab is an interactive web page where you can add text and code and then run it, line by line:

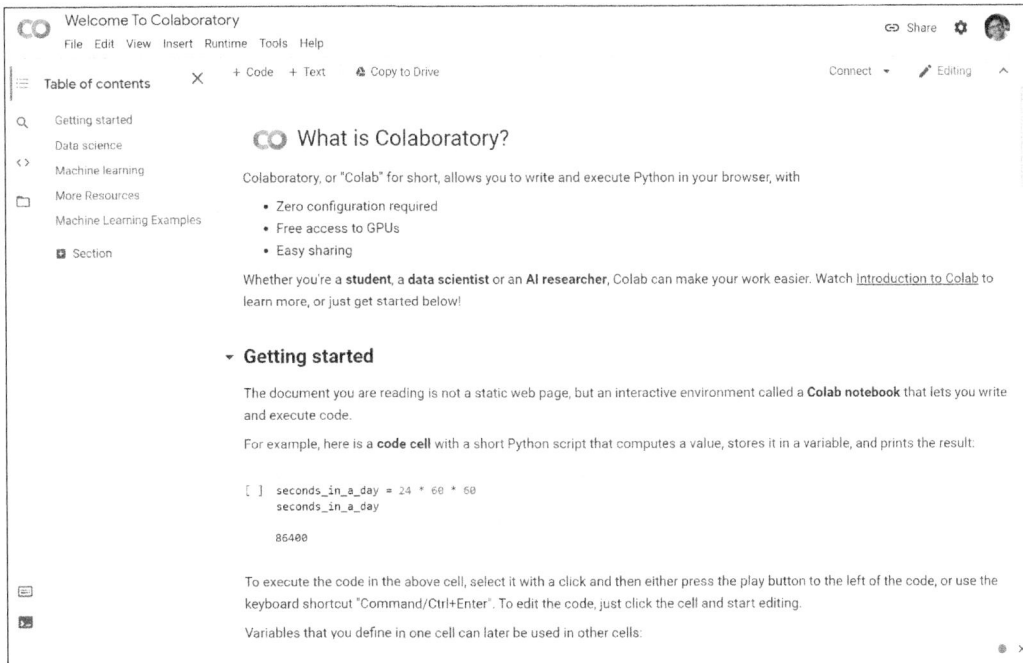

Figure 9.13: The welcome screen of Google Colab: get some Python going without installing any software

To simplify the comparison with KNIME, let's use Colab on the same Rome housing business case we encountered in *Chapter 5, Applying Machine Learning at Work*. As a reminder, the objective is to predict rental prices by applying the linear regression learning algorithm to the database of historical rental agreements. You can follow step by step the full Colab script by connecting to `tiny.cc/romecolab`.

Let's go through the code and, for each portion, understand what is going on:

```
import pandas as pd
import numpy as np
import statsmodels.formula.api as smf
from sklearn.model_selection import train_test_split
from sklearn.metrics import r2_score, mean_squared_error
```

The first step is to import some useful libraries into the Python environment. This will make a few extra functionalities (like loading Excel files and calculating a linear regression) available for us to leverage in our code. In particular, in the preceding code, we use a few import statements to include some of the most popular Python libraries used for data analytics, namely: **Pandas** for data manipulation, **NumPy** for numerical routines and array calculations, **Statsmodels** for hardcore statistics, and **Scikit-learn** (`sklearn` in the code) for machine learning:

```
full_data = pd.read_excel("RomeHousing-History.xlsx")
full_data.head()
```

As a next step, we read the data stored in an Excel file by using the `pd.read_excel()` function and assign its content to the `full_data` variable. We can then check the imported data by visualizing its top five rows, using the function `head()`, producing the output shown in *Figure 9.14*:

	House_ID	Neighborhood	Property_type	Rooms	Surface	Elevator	Floor_type	Floor_number	Rent
0	103501	Cassia	Flat	2	65	0	Upper	2.0	900
1	105122	Collatino	Flat	2	30	1	Ground floor	0.0	500
2	104125	Collatino	Flat	3	80	1	Upper	4.0	950
3	104675	Infernetto	Flat	3	75	0	Upper	2.0	800
4	102481	Ostia	Flat	3	70	1	Ground floor	0.0	800

Figure 9.14: The output of the head() function as displayed in Colab:
a useful peek into the top five rows in our dataset

The data we obtain is exactly what we encountered at the beginning of the first tutorial in *Chapter 5, Applying Machine Learning at Work* (see the first rows in *Figure 5.2*). We can move on and proceed with the first step of every supervised machine learning procedure, that is partitioning:

```
train_set, test_set = train_test_split(full_data,test_size=0.3)
```

With the help of the `train_test_split()` function, we apply a random sampling to our full data and obtain the training and the test set (which we set to be 30% of the total), which are stored in the `train_set` and `test_set` variables. This line of Python code implements what the **Partitioning** node did for us in KNIME. We now have all we need to learn the model using the training set:

```
model = smf.ols(formula='Rent ~ Rooms + Surface + \
                         Elevator + Floor_number + \
                         C(Neighborhood) + C(Property_type) + \
                         C(Floor_type)',data=train_set).fit()
print(model.summary())
```

Leveraging the function `smf.ols()`, this code portion trains an Ordinary Least Square regression model (OLS, which we encountered in *Chapter 5, Applying Machine Learning at Work*) using the `train_set` variable as an input. The output model is stored in an object called `model`. As we train the model, we can edit the formula string you see in the code (`Rent ~ Rooms + Surface + ...`) to select which column is the target (in our case `Rent`, which appears before the ~ sign) and which other columns should be used as predictors (the ones that go after the ~ symbol, separated by a + sign) in the linear regression. Categorical columns need to be encapsulated by the `C()` function (like in `C(Neighborhood)`): by doing so, Python converts them into multiple numerical columns (dummy variables) that are compatible with a linear regression model. The definition of the linear regression formula and the conversion of the nominal variable were done "under the hood" by the **Linear Regression Learner** node in KNIME, while in Python, they need to be specified in the code. Finally, the `summary()` function summarizes the regression results, including coefficients and p-values for each feature. If you compare the output obtained in Python (*Figure 9.15*) with the one obtained as an output of the **Linear Regression Learner** node in KNIME (*Figure 5.9*), you will find different numbers (of course, the random sampling will always produce slightly different results), but they are consistent. For instance, we notice that Piazza Navona is a pricey neighborhood (since its coefficient, displayed in the `coef` column, is higher than all others) and that the presence of elevators can be ignored (high p-value, as you can see in the `P>|t|` column):

```
                      OLS Regression Results
=========================================================================
Dep. Variable:               Rent   R-squared:                     0.931
Model:                        OLS   Adj. R-squared:                0.930
Method:             Least Squares   F-statistic:                   1286.
Date:            Sun, 25 Jul 2021   Prob (F-statistic):             0.00
Time:                    12:57:03   Log-Likelihood:               -17138.
No. Observations:            2800   AIC:                        3.434e+04
Df Residuals:                2770   BIC:                        3.451e+04
Df Model:                      29
Covariance Type:          nonrobust
=========================================================================
                                     coef   std err      t    P>|t|     [0.025     0.975]
-------------------------------------------------------------------------
Intercept                         567.0761   22.490   25.215  0.000    522.978    611.174
C(Neighborhood)[T.Cassia]        -359.4917   22.668  -15.859  0.000   -403.940   -315.043
C(Neighborhood)[T.Castelli Romani] -696.5811 21.992  -31.675  0.000   -739.703   -653.460
C(Neighborhood)[T.Cinecittà]     -567.9157   22.201  -25.581  0.000   -611.448   -524.383
C(Neighborhood)[T.Collatino]     -552.7227   22.428  -24.644  0.000   -596.701   -508.745
C(Neighborhood)[T.EUR]           -402.7789   26.779  -15.041  0.000   -455.288   -350.270
C(Neighborhood)[T.Infernetto]    -601.9284   23.029  -26.138  0.000   -647.083   -556.773
C(Neighborhood)[T.Magliana]      -599.2370   33.000  -18.159  0.000   -663.945   -534.529
C(Neighborhood)[T.Marconi]       -488.1459   24.694  -19.768  0.000   -536.567   -439.725
C(Neighborhood)[T.Montagnola]    -467.0944   25.219  -18.521  0.000   -516.545   -417.644
C(Neighborhood)[T.Monte sacro]   -512.8984   22.442  -22.855  0.000   -556.903   -468.894
C(Neighborhood)[T.Monti]         -102.8431   23.122   -4.448  0.000   -148.182    -57.505
C(Neighborhood)[T.Ostia]         -555.5006   26.525  -20.943  0.000   -607.510   -503.491
C(Neighborhood)[T.Parioli]       -195.7433   21.870   -8.950  0.000   -238.627   -152.860
C(Neighborhood)[T.Piazza Navona]  234.1949   22.231   10.535  0.000    190.604    277.786
C(Neighborhood)[T.Portuense]     -507.3857   30.926  -16.407  0.000   -568.025   -446.746
C(Neighborhood)[T.Prati]         -167.4902   22.204   -7.543  0.000   -211.028   -123.952
C(Neighborhood)[T.Termini]       -251.8464   23.943  -10.519  0.000   -298.794   -204.899
C(Neighborhood)[T.Testaccio]     -189.1236   29.240   -6.468  0.000   -246.457   -131.790
C(Neighborhood)[T.Trastevere]     -67.1782   23.748   -2.829  0.005   -113.744    -20.613
C(Neighborhood)[T.Trigoria]      -507.1393   27.838  -18.218  0.000   -561.724   -452.554
C(Property_type)[T.House]          -0.6905   32.334   -0.021  0.983    -64.091     62.710
C(Property_type)[T.Penthouse]      14.5069   11.546    1.256  0.209     -8.133     37.147
C(Property_type)[T.Villa]         -20.4411   55.676   -0.367  0.714   -129.612     88.730
C(Floor_type)[T.Mezzanine]         30.1353   11.618    2.594  0.010      7.355     52.916
C(Floor_type)[T.Upper]             24.1025    7.157    3.368  0.001     10.069     38.136
Rooms                              20.0038    3.964    5.046  0.000     12.231     27.777
Surface                             9.7001    0.133   72.751  0.000      9.439      9.962
Elevator                           -2.5663    4.598   -0.558  0.577    -11.583      6.450
Floor_number                        4.8361    1.468    3.295  0.001      1.958      7.714
```

Figure 9.15: The summary output of the OLS regression in Colab: you will get different numbers as the randomized portioning makes each specific model unique

We can now move the final bit of our machine learning procedures: predicting on the test set and scoring the results:

```
predictions = model.predict(test_set)
print('R2 score is',r2_score(test_set.Rent,predictions))
print('Root Mean Squared Error is', \
        np.sqrt(mean_squared_error(test_set.Rent,predictions)))
```

Similar to what we would do with the **Regression Predictor** node in KNIME, we need to apply the regression model to `test_set` and obtain some `predictions`: as you can see in the first line of the code, we use the function `predict()` to do exactly that. Afterward, we need to calculate two metrics for scoring our regression by comparing the real rent values in the test set (`test_set.Rent`) with our predictions, similar to what we did with the **Numeric Scorer** node KNIME tutorial. Specifically, we calculate the two main summary metrics for assessing regression accuracy, which we introduced in *Chapter 4, What is Machine Learning?*:

- The **Coefficient of Determination**, R^2, using the function `r2_score()`, which takes as parameters the two columns to compare.

- The **Root Mean Squared Error** (**RMSE**), which gives us an idea of the level of error to expect in the predictions. To calculate this metric, we need to combine the functions `mean_squared_error()` to get the average of the squared residuals and `np.sqrt()` to obtain its square root.

When we run this last portion of code, the output we obtain confirms that we have built quite a robust model as R^2 nears 0.91 and the RMSE is around €118 (of course, you will obtain slightly different values):

```
R2 score is 0.9144775136955545
Root Mean Squared Error is 117.92107041510327
```

New tools, same story: by writing around a dozen lines of Python code, we replicated the bulk of what we did in KNIME. Have a look at *Figure 9.16*: the gray boxes contain the key Python functions that do the same job as the KNIME nodes we met earlier in our journey:

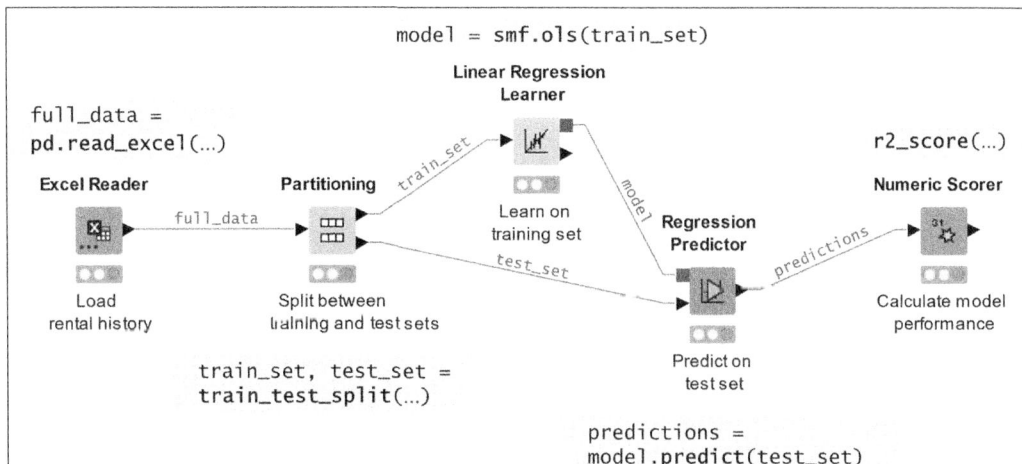

Figure 9.16: A comparison view showing Python's key functions together with the corresponding KNIME nodes required for linear regression: the fundamental steps are exactly the same

This exercise has clarified the differences between visual programming (what you can do in KNIME) and traditional programming by coding (which you can do using Python or any other language). There are pros and cons to each approach, and it is natural to have personal preferences toward any of the two routes. The good news is…you don't have to make a definitive choice among the alternatives. In fact, visual programming and coding can also be mixed together, making a powerful potion for your data analytics magic to shine. In the following few pages, you will learn how to embed pieces of Python code into a KNIME workflow. This is a valuable trick to know, as it allows you to "make the best" out of the joint power of KNIME accessibility and "Python's" breadth of functionalities. Even if you are not interested at this stage in the integration of KNIME and Python, I would suggest you go through the next few pages anyway. They will give you the opportunity to acquaint yourself with two powerful features you should know: KNIME extensions and KNIME Hub.

Integrating Python with KNIME

First, you need to make sure you have a local installation of Python up and running on your computer. The easiest way to procure one is to install **Anaconda Individual Edition,** one of the most popular Python distribution platforms for data analytics. Download and install the latest version of the software, available for free at anaconda.com/download. Anaconda comes packed with several applications for coding both in Python and in R. An example is **Jupyter Notebook,** which lets you create Python scripts using a web browser—similarly to what we did in Colab but without any restrictions. From the welcome page of **Anaconda Navigator** (*Figure 9.17*), you can launch Jupyter Notebook or install additional applications, like RStudio for developing in R:

Figure 9.17: The welcome screen of Anaconda Navigator: from here, you can launch Jupyter notebooks for coding in Python or install additional free packages

As anticipated in *Chapter 2*, *Getting Started with KINME*, you can expand KNIME functionalities by installing additional extensions. To embed Python in our workflows, we need to install the **KNIME Python Integration** extension. To do so, open KNIME, go to **File | Install KNIME Extensions...** in the top bar and search for the right extension by typing python in the text box at the top (*Figure 9.18*). Check the box for the **KNIME Python integration** option, click on **Next**, and follow the installation process:

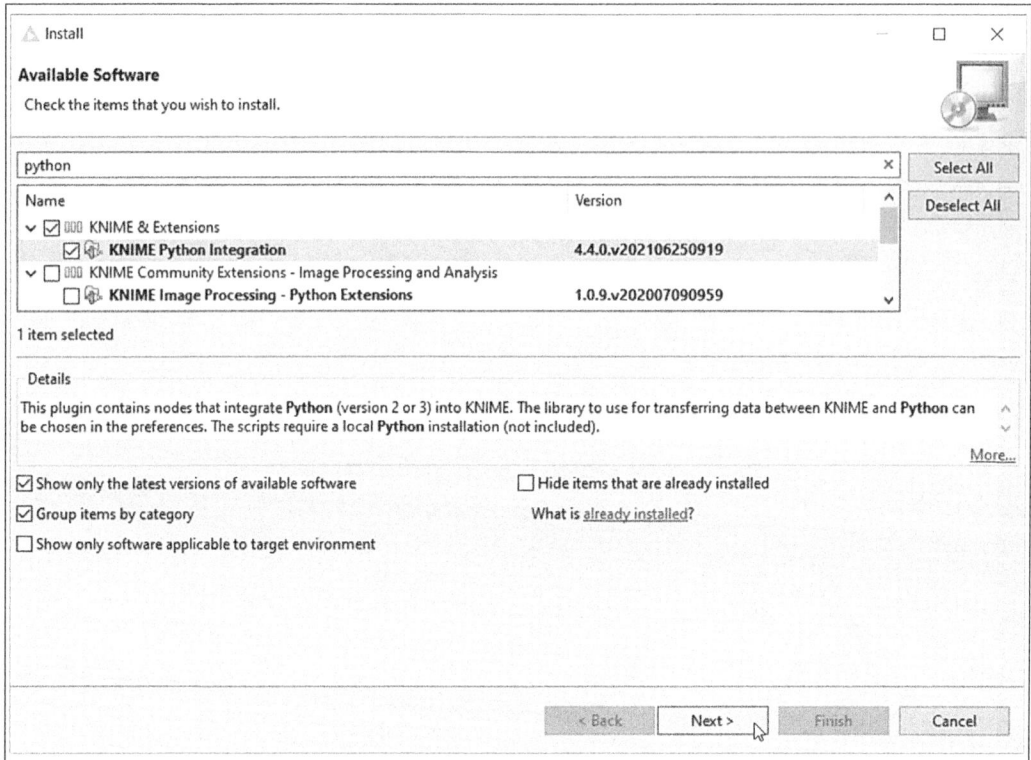

Figure 9.18: The dialog for installing extensions in KNIME. Look at the list of available packages: you can easily extend your analytical toolkit with thousands of new KNIME nodes

Once finished, you will be prompted with a message asking to restart KNIME to apply the software update. After the restart, go to the node repository and open the **Scripting > Python** folder. As you can see in *Figure 9.19*, you have gained several new nodes to be used in your workflows by installing the extension:

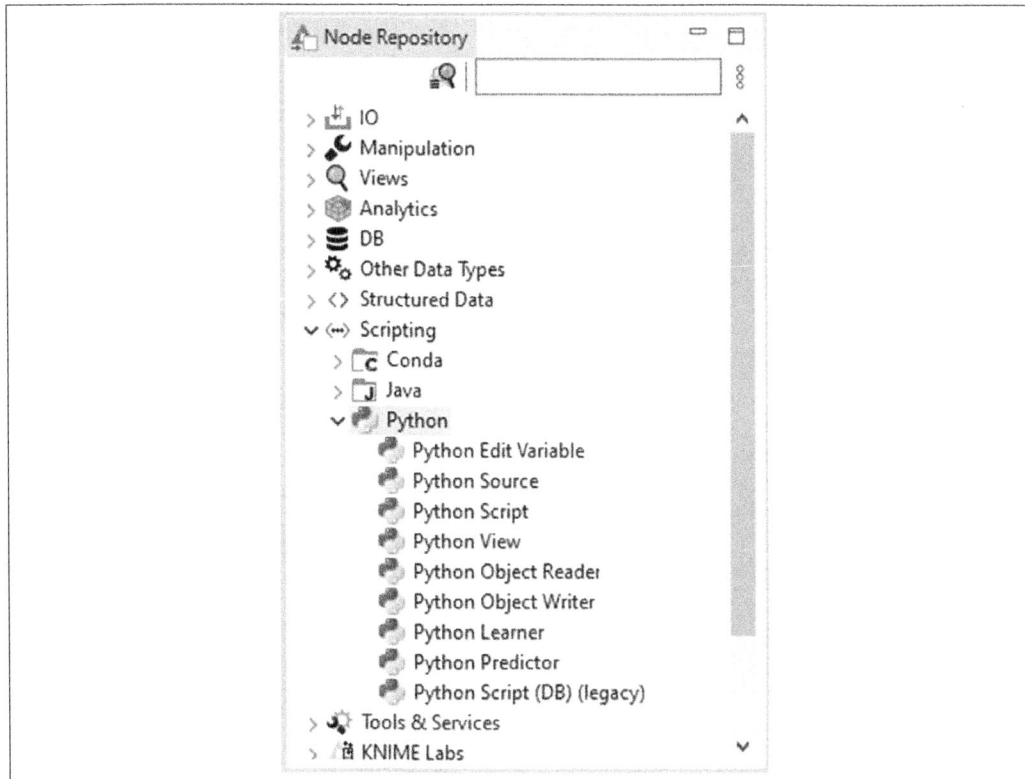

Figure 9.19: The Node Repository after installing the KNIME Python Integration extension: several new nodes have materialized

Before getting there, let's perform the last step needed to set KNIME up so it can connect with the Python environment that came with Anaconda. To do so, go to **File | Preferences** in KNIME. Then, in the menu appearing on the left, go to **KNIME > Python** or use the text box on the left to look up the Python preferences window, which you can see in *Figure 9.20*. You should find the path to your Anaconda installation directory prepopulated (if that's not the case, you will have to set it up by clicking on the **Browse...** button). Once done, click on the second **New environment...** button in the **Python 3 (Default)** section, as you can see in the following figure: this will create a new Python environment with all the packages needed for integration with KNIME:

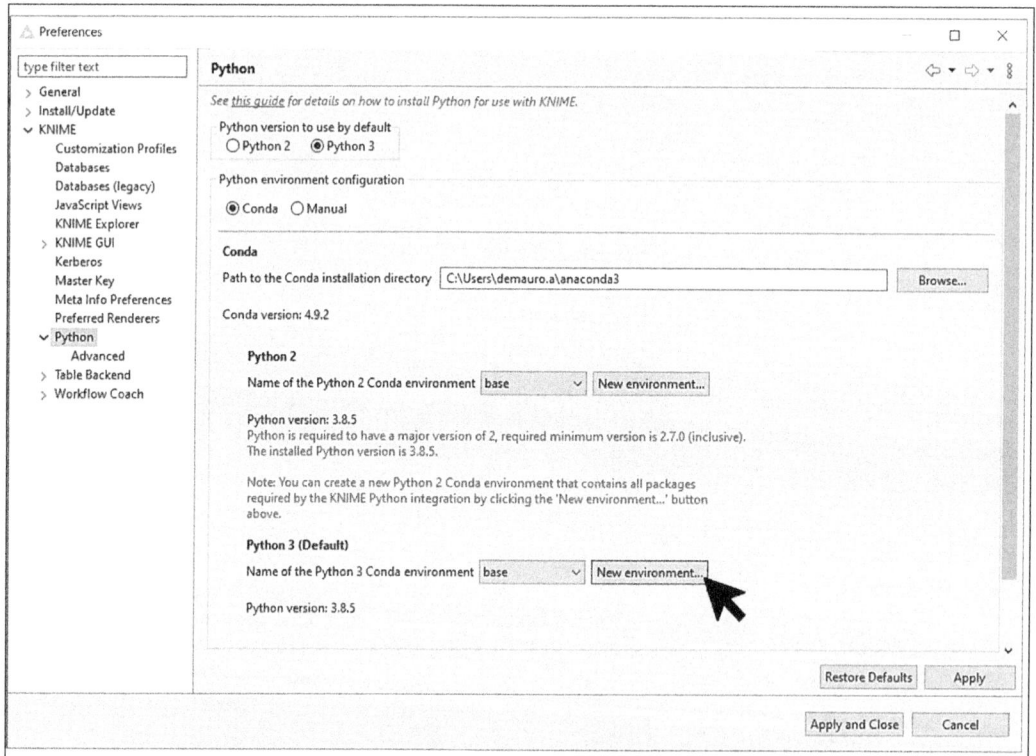

Figure 9.20: The Python window within the KNIME preferences: you need to tell KNIME where the local Python environment lies

In the next window (*Figure 9.21*), click on **Create new environment** and wait patiently for the environment to be generated. After this, you are done and all set up for enriching your KNIME workflows with all the Python you need:

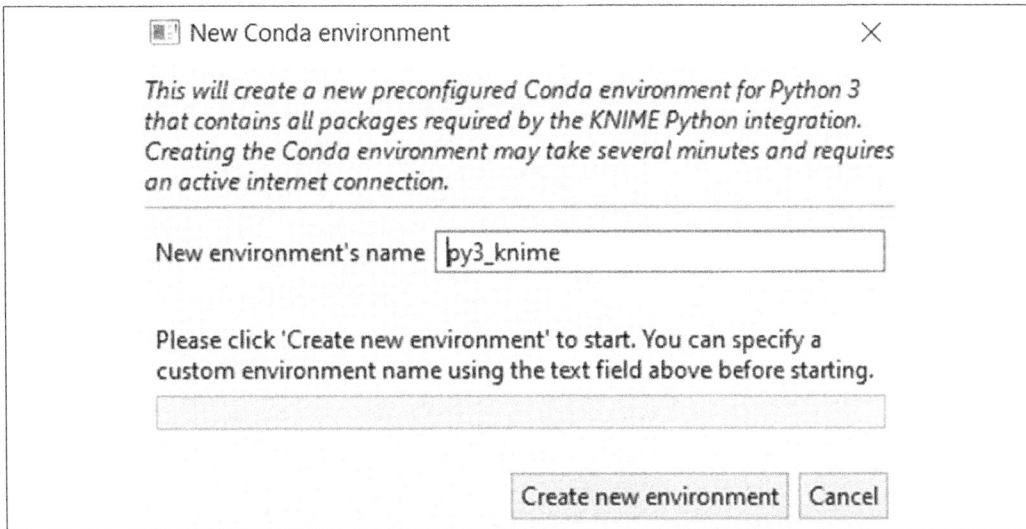

Figure 9.21: New environment dialog: the final step for getting up and running with Python in KNIME

> If, instead of Python, you want to use R in your KNIME workflows, you will have to install the **KNIME Interactive R Statistics Integration** and set up the R environment from the preferences menu, similar to what we did for Python. KNIME also allows you to run some Java code for every row of a table: check the **Java Snippet** node to find out more.

Among the new nodes you acquired by installing the Python extension (*Figure 9.19*), **Python Script** is certainly the most versatile one: the node lets you embed a sequence of Python code that gets applied to the data stored in the input table (generically called input_table_1) to generate one or more output tables (called output_table_1). You can refer to these tables in your script and freely utilize them as you would do with any data frame in Python. For instance, if you wanted to apply a simple multiplication across two columns (*Quantity* and *Price*) and output an additional column (*Sales*) with the result, the Python script to be used with this node will be:

```
output_table_1 = input_table_1
output_table_1['Sales'] = output_table_1['Quantity'] * output_
table_1['Price']
```

The first line of code is just copying the input table to the output one, leaving it unchanged. The second line is applying the multiplication across the two columns—that's it. We could have imported any library (provided that they are installed in the Python environment within Anaconda) and leveraged it to perform any operation we need.

Let's look at a simple workflow that illustrates the power of integrating Python in our analytical workflows. Instead of building this workflow from scratch, we can find it already available in **KNIME Hub**, the online repository of workflows, extensions, components, and nodes. As depicted in *Figure 9.22*, open the **KNIME Hub** panel (you'll find it beside the **Node Description** tab in the top right) and type Python Gaussian Fit in the search box. Among the many alternatives, you should find a workflow with my name and picture on it: this is the workflow I have prepared for you. To import it into your KNIME installation, you can just drag the box (highlighted in the figure) and drop it onto your workflow editor. An alternative approach would be to import the KNIME workflow (**File | Import KNIME Workflow...**) that you will find in the GitHub repository:

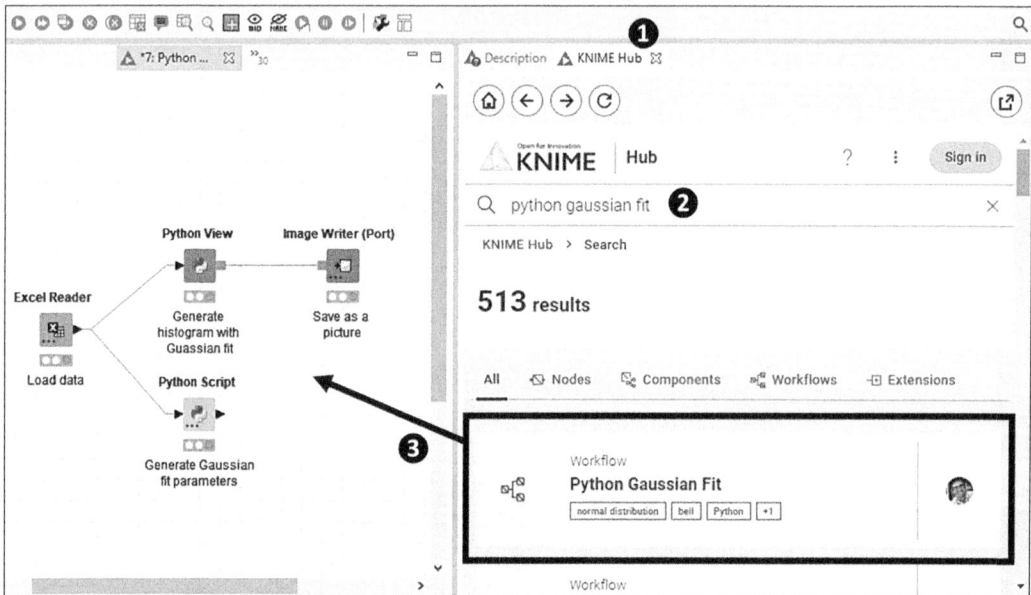

Figure 9.22: The KNIME Hub panel: search for the workflows, nodes, or components you need and drop them onto your workspace

If you open the configuration dialog of the **Python View** node, you will find the code window shown in *Figure 9.23*. The large text box in the middle is where you can write your Python code. On the left, you have the list of columns available in the input table: by double-clicking on them, the corresponding Python data frames are added to the code. You can also test your code by clicking on the **Execute Script** or **Execute selected lines** buttons and checking whether it works fine. If you receive any warnings or errors during the execution of the script, they will be conveniently displayed in the console box at the bottom of the window:

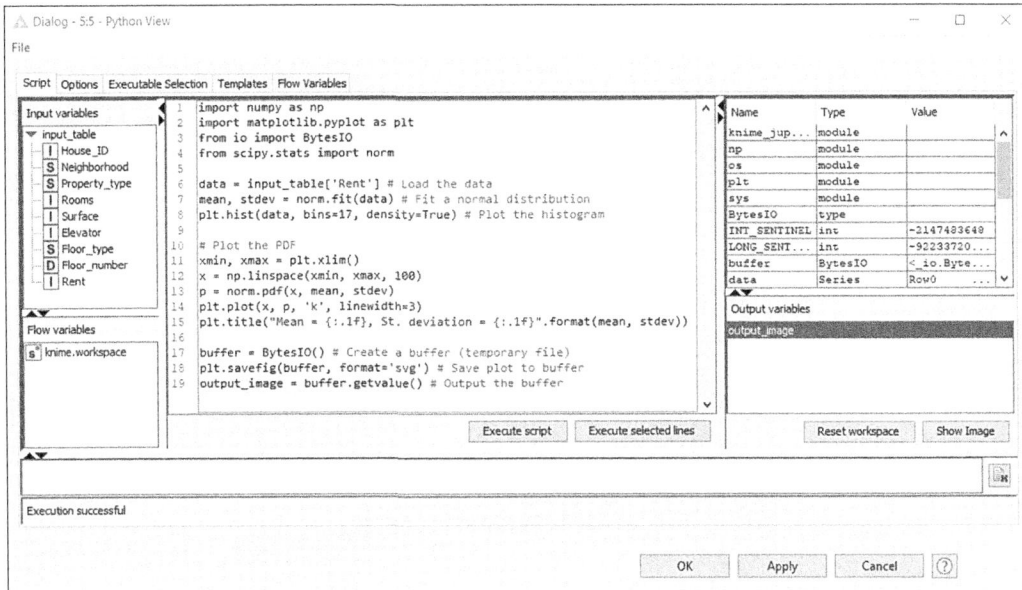

Figure 9.23: Configuration window of the Python View node: use Python graphic libraries to generate any chart you like

In this specific case, we leverage the **Python View** node to fit a Gaussian function (the famous bell curve) to the distribution of Rome rental prices and return the histogram with the fitting curve. Going through the details of the code is not needed at this stage. However, you will notice that the *Rent* column has been referred to in the code with the name input_table['Rent'] while the generated chart has been saved to the variable called output_image: you find the final result in *Figure 9.24*:

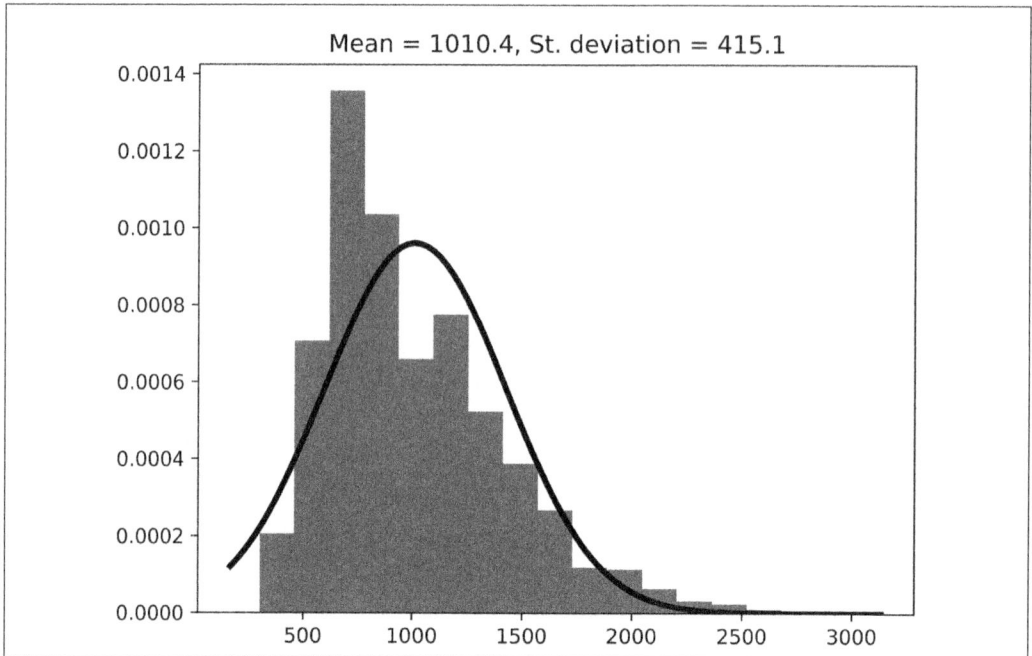

Figure 9.24: The output of the Python View node: rent prices in Rome are centered around €1,000

This gives you an illustration of how Python nodes work: the data at the input port is translated into input variables, and, at the end of the script, whatever is assigned to the output variables gets returned at the output port of the node. In the same workflow you downloaded from KNIME Hub, you will also see an example of a **Python Script** node: essentially, both nodes run Python code on the input data, but the **Python View** node is "specialized" in outputting images.

Interlacing code within a workflow has massive potential. If you want to apply some complex logic or reuse specialized code that has been developed outside of KNIME for solving your specific business need, you can now seamlessly integrate it all and significantly expand the power of your toolbox.

After seeing Python in action, let's go back to the world of codeless analytics and meet one of the promising directions of advanced analytics: automated machine learning.

Automated machine learning

"Brute-force patterns finding": this is how we can briefly (and colorfully) summarize what **Automated Machine Learning** or, for short, **AutoML**, is all about. As you saw in *Chapters 4* and 5, building a machine learning model is far from being a linear, single-attempt endeavor. The usual procedure for obtaining high-performing supervised models is to go through a series of "back and forth" attempts: each time, we apply some "tuning" to the model or its features and check whether the predictive performance increases or not. We have seen already some of these mechanisms in action:

- **Hyperparameters optimization**: this is when you apply changes to the way the learning algorithm operates, like when we activated pruning in decision trees or changed the degree of a polynomial regression. In more complex models (like in the case of deep neural networks), changing parameters (for instance, the number of neurons in the network) can make a significant difference to performance.

- **Feature selection**: by selecting a subset of features (and removing the redundant ones), you make your model learning focus on what matters most, increasing its ability to predict. We did this when we decided to remove some high p-value features from regression models. Additionally, making a model run on fewer features means saving time and computing resources.

- **Feature engineering**: you can generate new features by combining or transforming the original ones to make them more informative for the model. For instance, this is what we did when we created dummy variables in regression.

- **Stacking**: we said that sometimes we could combine different algorithms together in a single learning procedure. Think of predicting rental prices using five different intermediate regression models and then adopting the average of the five intermediate predictions as the overall prediction: by collating alternative models together, you might obtain a more robust one.

Instead of manually checking the effect of each tuning step one by one, we can build a procedure that leverages all the available computing power to find the way to the best possible model. This is what the AutoML approach promises to do: automating the "trial and error" process of identifying parameters, features, and model combinations that maximize the overall performance (and — hopefully — the business impact) of our machine learning procedure.

AutoML is currently a trending topic in business-applied AI, and there is a growing number of products and open-source libraries available out there for applying AutoML to real-world tasks, including H2O.ai, DataRobot, auto-sklearn, Google Cloud AutoML, IBM AutoAI, Amazon AutoGluon, and Azure AutomatedML. As we explore ways to expand our analytics toolbox, let's see one of these products in action: this will give you an idea of what is already available and what's to come from our companies in the next few years.

We will explore **H2O Driverless AI**, a cloud-based service that lets you use a web interface to upload data, run AutoML to make predictions, and interpret results. If you want to test it yourself, go to h2o.ai/products/h2o-driverless-ai, register for a free account, and create an instance of Driverless AI.

AutoML in action: an example with H2O.ai

In this example, we will reuse the Rome housing business case once again: this time, we will upload the Excel dataset and create a new experiment. *Figure 9.25* shows what the interface looks like: you can select the **Target Column** (*Rent*, in our case), pick a metric for the **Scorer** (in the figure, you can see we picked RMSE), and then turn the three knobs at the bottom to set the expected level of prediction **Accuracy**, the **Time** required for training the model, and the level of human **Interpretability**. This bit is fascinating: as you operate the knobs, the system updates its "trial and error" strategy (you can see a dynamic summary on the left) to be performed during the AutoML search routine. If you go for high accuracy and low interpretability, you will end up with high-performing black-box models, while if you set interpretability to a high level, you will obtain simpler models with fewer features so that you can explain to your business partners how it works:

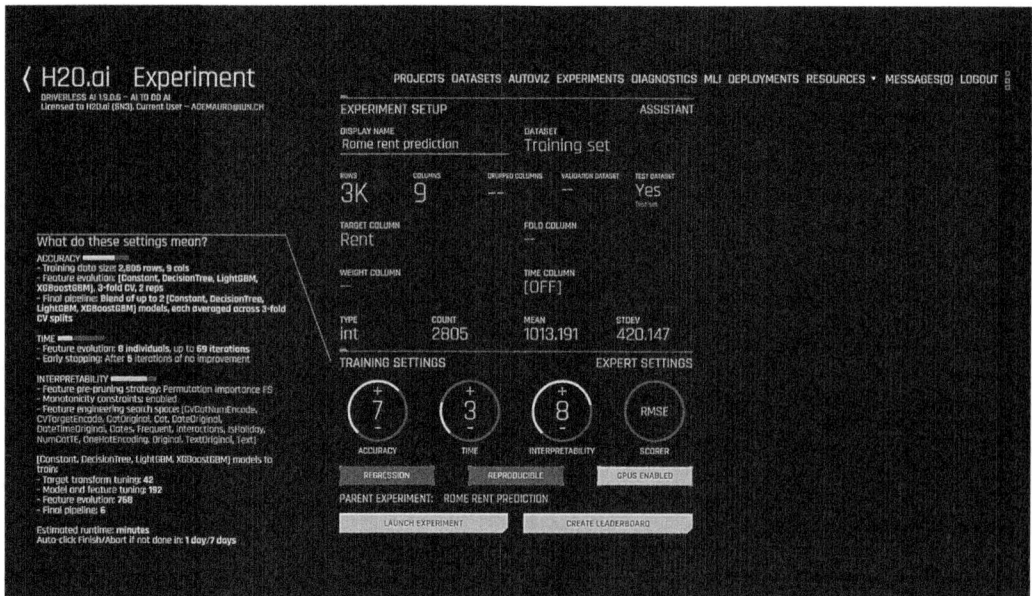

Figure 9.25: The experiment setup page in H2O Driverless AI:
play with the knobs to determine how you would like your generated model to be cooked

After clicking on **Launch Experiment**, the remote computing power will do the hard work for you while you grab something to drink. The following view shows you the live evolution of the score metrics as more and more models are iteratively tried and, when completed, will display the best results (*Figure 9.26*):

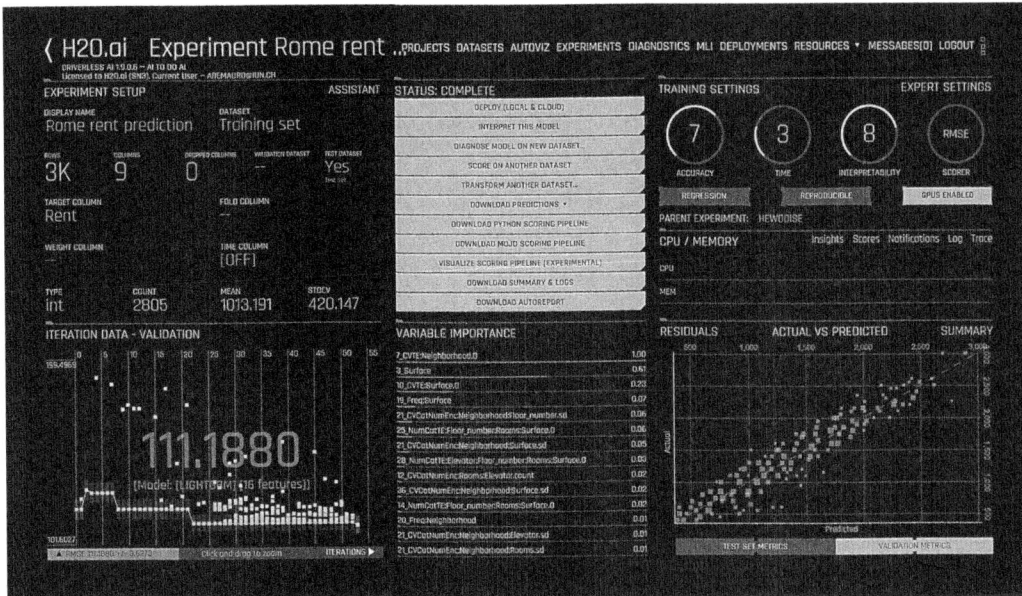

Figure 9.26: The results of an AutoML routine:
at the bottom left, you can see how the scoring metric changes as the search iteration progresses

As part of the AuotML procedure, we also get some useful views that equip us for understanding how the model works. Have a look at the interpretation dashboard generated for our rental price predictions (*Figure 9.27*):

- At the top right, we see a bar chart displaying **Features importance**: unsurprisingly, *Neighborhood* is the single most useful column when predicting the rent, followed by the *Surface* of the property.

- At the bottom left, we have a tree-based **Surrogate model**: this is the "minimalist" version of the actual, full-on prediction model generated by the AutoML routine. By looking at the first three levels of this tree, we get a high-level, easy-to-explain view of the patterns that link the most important features to the rental price.

- At the bottom right, we find the **Partial dependence** plot: this shows us the marginal effect of a specific feature (*Surface*, in the case of *Figure 9.27*) on the predicted outcome (*Rent*). This chart provides us with an additional interpretation key, revealing "how" the rent increases as the surface grows:

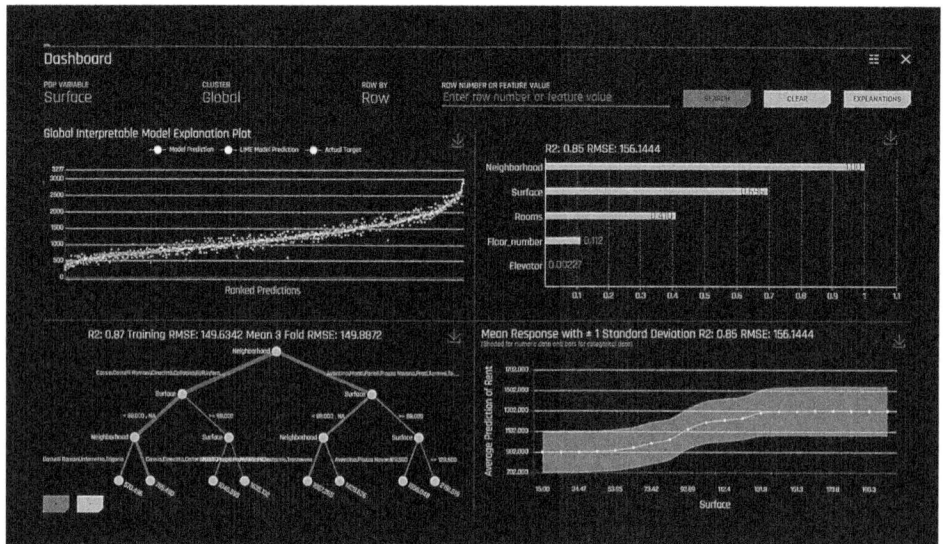

Figure 9.27: The model interpretation dashboard: get some hints on how the prediction model works

With this example, we have admired the AutoML approach in all its potential. With only a few clicks, we obtained a robust predictive model (that can be exported and deployed for further use) and a simple framework for explaining its results. It's important to make a further consideration: although it looks like the "holy grail" of machine learning, leveraging AutoML in a business context will still require its users to always "know what they are doing." This means that building machine learning expertise and, in general, data analytics fluency (like you did in this book) is and still will be crucial for making the best of this technology, however automated and easy to use it looks.

AutoML can be another valuable tool to keep in our data analytics kit. The good news is that you find this approach nicely implemented in KNIME as well, so you can connect it with everything else you have learned in the book. If you open the example workflow called H2O AutoML for Regression (you will find it in the Examples server in **KNIME Explorer** or by searching in **KNIME Hub**), you will be asked to install a new extension: **KNIME H2O Machine Learning Integration**. By installing this extension, you make many of the AutoML functionalities we have seen in H2O Driverless AI available to you in KNIME. Look at the sample workflow mentioned earlier (*Figure 9.28*): by employing a few H2O nodes — organized as per the usual supervised machine learning structure with partitioning, learner, predictor, and scorer — you get the full power of AutoML directly in KNIME:

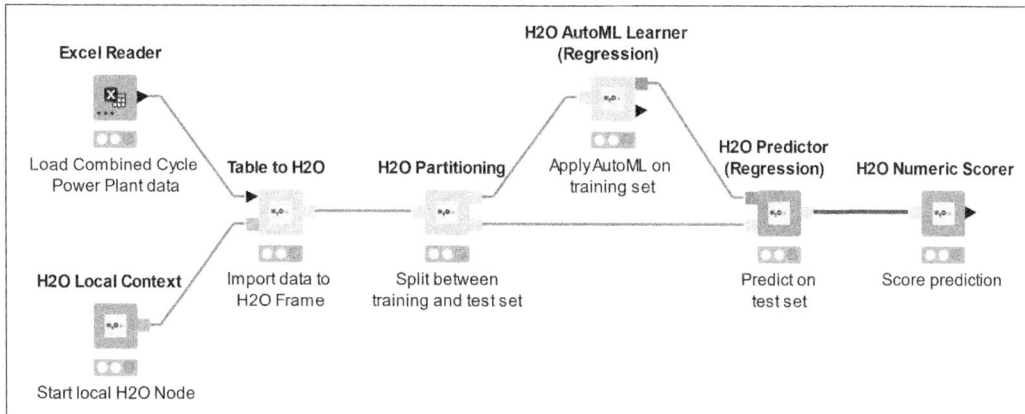

Figure 9.28: The H2O AutoML for Regression KNIME workflow: use AutoML to find the best model for you

Summary

I hope this final chapter got you excited about all the directions you can take to further expand your data analytics toolbox. We took our first steps in Tableau and realized how similar it is, in its fundamental features, to Power BI. We have also gone through a friendly introduction to Python, the ubiquitous programming language in data science. As we integrated Python in KNIME, we have seen how to take the best from both the visual and coding programming worlds. As we did so, we took the opportunity to learn how to expand KNIME further by using its vast extensions base and leveraging the public KNIME Hub environment. Lastly, we got a quick tour through the attractive land of AutoML, being exposed to its promising ability to simplify the process of building high-performing machine learning models considerably.

In this chapter, we extended our toolbox by exploring new tools and approaches to run better data analytics in our everyday work. My advice is to make this a habit. One limitation I have seen in many data practitioners is to think that the few tools they feel comfortable with will *always* be the best for them, falling in the limiting bias of self-sufficiency. So instead, don't feel satisfied with the toolbox we have just built—be ready to explore continuously: stay curious, as the expanding world of data analytics will have a lot to offer!

And now?

It was a long ride, but you made it: what a terrific journey you have just completed!

In the nine chapters, we have harnessed, with our own hands, the potential value of data analytics, recognizing several practical ways to unlock it. We have built a toolbox of ready-to-use data applications (with KNIME and Power BI at the core), which you can now utilize when needed. Most importantly, you have acquired a broad set of tool-agnostic data competencies that you can leverage with *any* application. Organizing, cleaning, and transforming any data; building, validating, and interpreting models based on machine learning algorithms; designing, preparing, and delivering data stories based on effective visualizations...this wide spectrum of fundamental knowledge and data abilities will empower you, no matter the specific software you happen to use today or will use tomorrow. The tutorials you completed gave you some real-world experience on relevant business needs, such as automating data pipelines, predicting consumer behavior, anticipating prices, creating meaningful customer segments, and building interactive dashboards. Congratulations on getting all of this done—you have a lot to be proud of!

If you enjoyed this journey, you might be asking "...and what now"? As we conclude the ride, let me share two pieces of advice I received earlier in my journey, which I have found tremendously helpful in my personal and professional life.

The first one is to **stay curious** and never stop learning. That is easier said than done. Personal development will not happen by itself and needs proper planning. Book some time in your weekly schedule (why not a couple of hours every Friday?) to read more books on the aspects of data analytics that intrigue you the most. Follow blog posts (*Towards Data Science*, *Data Science Central*, *Low Code for Advanced Data Science*, and *Storytelling with Data* are some of my favorites), and take online or traditional courses (*Coursera* and *edX* platforms are packed with free, high-quality university courses—a "classic" one that meant a lot to me was *Machine Learning* by Andrew Ng). You want to stay constantly aware of what's being done and what's coming. Data analytics is a multidisciplinary, fluid field, and you need to embrace a true growth mindset to navigate it fully. Transform every situation in which you don't know how to do something into an opportunity to learn. Stay curious!

The second one is to intentionally scout for opportunities to **apply what you learned to your daily work**. I suggest you plan what to do with your new skills down the line. Since you have everything fresh in your mind, do it now: take a blank piece of paper and draft the two or three experiments you can put into practice right away. How about putting together a simple dashboard with the data your team uses the most? Or, creating a compelling story with the hottest business challenge? Try automating a tedious data cleaning process, or use one of the machine learning algorithms you have learned to improve the way decisions are made today. You don't need to aim for anything sophisticated and glamorous. I have seen many great data analytics initiatives start with only two basic ingredients: the excitement of a small group of people who enthusiastically believe they have a great idea and a quick and dirty prototype that proves the value of the idea and gets more people on board. My advice is to do this systematically: force yourself to select a few ideas to test. Start now.

If you are out of ideas or you don't have enough data, consider joining kaggle.com and participating in some of its analytics contests: you will receive juicy datasets, some real briefs, and the opportunity to compete with other professional or amateur data practitioners. Alternatively, ask a local charity whether they need any help tidying their data or creating value for their cause. There are plenty of opportunities around you to leverage data analytics today: go find them.

I wrote this book to empower you and to get you excited about data analytics. I hope it did the trick. In any case, I would be delighted to connect with you: do get in touch with me (you will find my contact details below; the easiest way is to add me on LinkedIn and send me a message). Every bit of feedback, every opinion, or—even better—the story of a data analytics success you drove will be highly appreciated, and I promise to respond in any way I can.

I wish you all the best in your continuous development, and I hope that data analytics will benefit you on your path!

Andrea De Mauro

Contact details:

- Book satisfaction survey: tiny.cc/dataanalyticssurvey
- LinkedIn: linkedin.com/in/andread
- ResearchGate: researchgate.net/profile/Andrea_De_Mauro
- Twitter: @about_big_data
- Web: www.aboutbigdata.net

Useful Resources

Chapter 1

- For a comprehensive review of data analytics job families and related skills, you can check out some of my research papers on the topic, in particular: De Mauro, A., Greco, M., Grimaldi, M., Ritala, P. "Human resources for Big Data professions: A systematic classification of job roles and required skill sets." *Information Processing & Management* 54.5 (2018): 807-817, `https://doi.org/10.1016/j.ipm.2017.05.004`.

- To get a visual summary of the plethora of tools available in the broader area of data analytics, you can review the Data & AI Data Landscape, which is updated every year, by Matt Turck: `http://tiny.cc/datalandscape`.

- To learn more about the ongoing convergence of operational research and machine learning into prescriptive analytics, you can read Lepenioti, K., Bousdekis, A., Apostolou, D., & Mentzas, G. "Prescriptive analytics: Literature review and research challenges." *International Journal of Information Management* 50 (2020): 57-70, `https://doi.org/10.1016/j.ijinfomgt.2019.04.003`.

Chapter 2

- I recommend having a look at the KNIME cheatsheets: they are 1-pager visual summaries of all the "nodes that matter" within a specific topic. Check them out at `https://www.knime.com/cheat-sheets`.

- Regular expressions can extend your pattern matching dramatically. They are very useful when you need to clean data and check for adherence to complex formatting rules. Get a crash course on RegEx from `https://regexone.com/` or use `https://regexr.com/` to test your expressions directly on the web.

- KNIME channel on YouTube is full of short videos to explore nodes and techniques. Have a look at it: `https://www.youtube.com/user/KNIMETV`.

Chapter 3

- To learn more about how to build a data inventory, have a look at the IBM guide available at `https://www.ibm.com/cloud/learn/data-catalog`.

- For a short introduction on loops in KNIME, check out the self-paced module available at `https://www.knime.com/self-paced-course/l2-dw-knime-analytics-platform-for-data-wranglers-advanced/lesson4`.

- To learn more about variables in KNIME, you can go through this additional KNIME learning module: `https://www.knime.com/self-paced-course/l2-ds-knime-analytics-platform-for-data-scientists-advanced/lesson2`.

- If you need to add some visual formatting (like font types and colors) when exporting data from KNIME to Excel, I recommend the Continental community extension at `https://www.knime.com/community/continental-nodes-for-knime-xls-formatter`.

Chapter 4

- For a general introduction on topic modeling, see `https://monkeylearn.com/blog/introduction-to-topic-modeling`. In particular, LDA is implemented in KNIME within the **Topic Extractor** (Parallel LDA) node, which is part of the KNIME Textprocessing extension.

- The following paper reveals the challenges related to the implementation of reinforcement learning in real-world problems: Dulac-Arnold, G., Mankowitz, D., & Hester, T. "Challenges of real-world reinforcement learning." *arXiv preprint arXiv:1904.12901* (2019), `https://arxiv.org/pdf/1904.12901.pdf`.

- One of the most promising types of machine learning algorithms is neural networks. They make a machine learning subdiscipline by itself, called Deep Learning. To get started with deep learning in KNIME, I recommend reading Melcher, K., Silipo, R., *Codeless Deep Learning with KNIME: Build, train, and deploy various deep neural network architectures using KNIME Analytics Platform.* Packt Publishing Ltd, 2020.

- To learn about the differences between weak and strong AI and the reasons that make the latter nearly unreachable, you can read Fjelland, R. "Why general artificial intelligence will not be realized." *Humanities and Social Sciences Communications* 7.1 (2020): 1-9, `https://doi.org/10.1057/s41599-020-0494-4`.

- For an interesting (but demanding) read on the various scenarios related to the arrival of machine superintelligence, read Bostrom, M. *Superintelligence: paths, dangers, strategies.* Oxford Press, 2014.

- Accuracy, Precision, and Sensitivity are not the only summary metrics used to assess classifications. Have a look at this presentation by Maarit Widman to learn more about the other measures you can calculate in KNIME: `https://www.slideshare.net/KNIMESlides/scoring-metrics-for-classification-models` or the ebook: Widmann, M., Roccato, A., "From Modeling to Model Evaluation", KNIME Press, 2021, `https://www.knime.com/sites/default/files/2021-05/Book-From-Modeling-Model-Evaluation-KNIME-05052021.pdf`.

Chapter 5

- To learn how to run time-series analytics using KNIME components, check out the following: Tonini, D. Weisinger, C., Widmann, M. "Time Series Analysis with Components", Low Code for Advanced Data Science (2021), `http://tiny.cc/KNIMEtimeseries`.

- To get a step-by-step demo of how the k-means algorithm works, check out this simulator by Naftali Harris: `https://www.naftaliharris.com/blog/visualizing-k-means-clustering`.

- Read the following to learn about more ways to detect outliers using KNIME: Widmann, M., Heine, M., Four Techniques for Outlier Detection, Low Code for Advanced Data Science (2021), `http://tiny.cc/outlierdetection`.

Chapter 6

- There is plenty of sample Power BI dashboards available for you to become more familiar with its features. To learn how to access them, read `https://docs.microsoft.com/en-us/power-bi/create-reports/sample-datasets`.

- To extend your Power BI skills after finishing this book, check out this book: Powell, B., *Mastering Microsoft Power BI: Expert techniques for effective data analytics and business intelligence*. Packt Publishing Ltd, 2018.

Chapter 7

- On the superiority of vision on the other senses or, like John Medina puts it, on the fact that "vision trumps all other senses", see: Medina, J. J., *12 Principles for Surviving and Thriving at Work, Home and School*. Pear Press, 2009.

- On the importance of vision in human cognition, which includes Prof. David William's claim on the portion of cortex dedicated to vision, visit `https://www.rochester.edu/pr/Review/V74N4/0402_brainscience.html`.

- To learn more about preattentive attributes, you can read the book Few, S. "Show me the numbers." *Analytics Pres* (2004) or read Few's article, "The visual perception of variation", at https://www.perceptualedge.com/articles/visual_business_intelligence/the_visual_perception_of_variation.pdf.

- An earlier version of preattentive attributes was published in 1984 by Cleveland and McGill from Bell Labs. The paper exhibits a number of vintage charts from the 80s, and it is worth a read: Cleveland, W. S., McGill, R. "Graphical perception: Theory, experimentation, and application to the development of graphical methods." *Journal of the American statistical association* 79.387 (1984): 531-554.

- For a broader selection of charts, I recommend the Graph Selection Matrix published by Stephen Few on the Perceptual Edge website: https://www.perceptualedge.com/articles/misc/Graph_Selection_Matrix.pdf.

- To read more about Stephen Few's sentiments towards pie charts and the many reasons for not using them, you can read his article "Save the Pies for Dessert", available at https://www.perceptualedge.com/articles/visual_business_intelligence/save_the_pies_for_dessert.pdf.

- To learn more about the effect of rotated text on readability, check out Wigdor, D., & Balakrishnan, R. "Empirical investigation into the effect of orientation on text readability in tabletop displays." *ECSCW 2005*. Springer, Dordrecht, 2005.

- To read more about how color blindness can affect data visualization and how to make our charts accessible, read the article at https://www.tableau.com/about/blog/examining-data-viz-rules-dont-use-red-green-together.

Chapter 8

- If you want to learn more about the cognitive psychology studies confirming the importance of narratives in storytelling, have a look at https://www.storypack.co/post/stanfordstorytelling-why-retention-is-higher-through-stories.

- Swedish professor Hans Rosling has been a giant among data storytellers. Check one of his inspiring videos, like the TED Talk "The best stats you've ever seen", available at http://tiny.cc/beststats, and the BBC documentary "200 Countries, 200 Years, 4 Minutes", http://tiny.cc/200countries.

- Two books I've found particularly useful on data storytelling are Dykes, Brent. *Effective data storytelling: how to drive change with data, narrative and visuals.* John Wiley & Sons, 2019 and, more focused on data visualization: Knaflic, C. N. *Storytelling with data: A data visualization guide for business professionals.* John Wiley & Sons, 2015.

Chapter 9

- To learn more about Tableau, I recommend Meier, M., Baldwin, D. *Mastering Tableau 2021: Implement advanced business intelligence techniques and analytics with Tableau.* Packt Publishing Ltd, 2021 and Loth, A. *Visual Analytics with Tableau.* John Wiley & Sons, 2019.

- To begin your first steps in Python, check out: Matthes, E. *Python crash course: A hands-on, project-based introduction to programming,* No Starch Press, 2019, and then to deep dive on machine learning applications: Raschka, S., Mirjalili, V. *Python machine learning: Machine Learning and Deep Learning with Python, scikit-learn, and TensorFlow 2.* Packt Publishing Ltd, 2019.

- A good example of integrating KNIME, Python, and Tableau is Ganzaroli, D., "Data Science With KNIME, Jupyter, and Tableau Using COVID-19 Projections as an Example", Low Code for Advanced Data Science (2021), `http://tiny.cc/knimefusion`.

- To learn more about integrating H2O Driverless AI with KNIME, you can refer to this guide: `https://docs.knime.com/2020-07/h2o_driverless_ai_guide/h2o_driverless_ai_guide.pdf`.

Packt>

Other Books You May Enjoy

If you enjoyed this book, you may be interested in these other books by Packt:

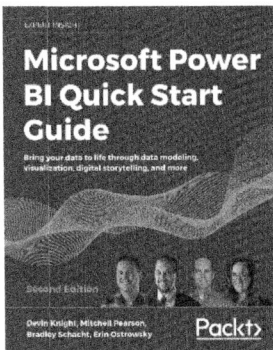

Microsoft Power BI Quick Start Guide – Second Edition
Devin Knight
Mitchell Pearson
Bradley Schacht
Erin Ostrowsky

ISBN: 978-1-80056-157-1

- Connect to data sources using import and DirectQuery options
- Use Query Editor for data transformation and data cleansing processes, including writing M and R scripts and dataflows to do the same in the cloud
- Design optimized data models by designing relationships and DAX calculations
- Design effective reports with built-in and custom visuals
- Adopt Power BI Desktop and Service to implement row-level security
- Administer a Power BI cloud tenant for your organization
- Use built-in AI capabilities to enhance Power BI data transformation techniques
- Deploy your Power BI desktop files into the Power BI Report Server

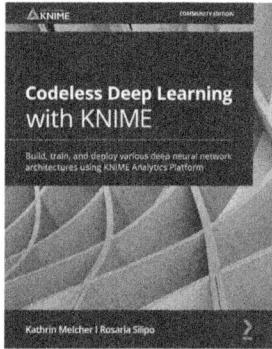

Codeless Deep Learning with KNIME

Kathrin Melcher

Rosaria Silipo

ISBN: 978-1-80056-661-3

- Use various common nodes to transform your data into the right structure suitable for training a neural network
- Understand neural network techniques such as loss functions, backpropagation, and hyperparameters
- Prepare and encode data appropriately to feed it into the network
- Build and train a classic feedforward network
- Develop and optimize an autoencoder network for outlier detection
- Implement deep learning networks such as CNNs, RNNs, and LSTM with the help of practical examples
- Deploy a trained deep learning network on real-world data

Share your thoughts

Now you've finished *Data Analytics Made Easy*, we'd love to hear your thoughts! Scan the QR code below to go straight to the Amazon review page for this book and share your feedback or leave a review on the site that you purchased it from.

https://packt.link/r/1-801-07415-1

Your review is important to us and the tech community and will help us make sure we're delivering excellent quality content.

Index

U

underfitted models 142
underfitting 138
Unpivoting 81
unsupervised learning 126, 127

V

values
aggregating 76, 77
aggregating, with GroupBy 77-79
aggregating, with Pivoting 80, 81
Variance Inflation Filter (VIF) 169
visual design
finalizing 296, 297
Visualization View 331

W

waterfall charts 286
weak AI 118
well-fitted models 142
workflow 24
Workflow Groups
creating 31, 32
Worksheet 332
Workspace 331

Printed in Great Britain
by Amazon